TOWARD
A DEFINITION
OF
ANTISEMITISM

▲

GAVIN I.
LANGMUIR

University of California Press
Berkeley   Los Angeles   London

TOWARD
A DEFINITION
OF
ANTISEMITISM

Published with the cooperation of the

CENTER FOR MEDIEVAL AND RENAISSANCE STUDIES

University of California, Los Angeles

University of California Press
Berkeley and Los Angeles, California

University of California Press, Ltd.
London, England

Copyright © 1990 by The Regents of the University of California

First Paperback Printing 1996

Library of Congress Cataloging-in-Publication Data

Langmuir, Gavin I.
    Toward a definition of antisemitism / Gavin I. Langmuir.
        p.   cm.
    Includes bibliographical references and index.
    ISBN 0-520-06143-8 (pbk.: alk. paper)
    1. Antisemitism.   2. Christianity and antisemitism.   3. Jews –
Legal status, laws, etc. – France.   4. Blood accusation.   5. France –
Ethnic relations.   I. Title.
DS145.L32   1990
305.8′924 – dc20   90-41686
                                                                    CIP

Printed in the United States of America

1   2   3   4   5   6   7   8   9

*IN MEMORY OF
SERGEANT LEO R. LALONDE
ROYAL HIGHLAND REGIMENT OF CANADA
KILLED IN ACTION 26 FEBRUARY 1945*

Contents

Preface

Eleven of the following essays have been published previously; three, chapters 5, 8, and 11, are new. Since some of the republished essays were written many years ago, I had to decide whether to revise them in the light of later work in the field. I decided not to because it would have distorted their historiographical context. Although much remains to be done, historical scholarship on Jews and on attitudes toward them has changed rapidly in recent years. Since the essays republished here were written while that advance was occurring and may have contributed to it, it would have falsified their historiographical significance to change them. I have taken the opportunity to improve some of the phrasing and, very rarely, to add a new citation, and I have omitted some passages that would have been repetitious, but the republished essays appear here almost unchanged and reflect the state of scholarship at the time they were written.

This book is neither a history of antisemitism nor a flowing intepretation of the development of antisemitism throughout the centuries. Indeed, the historical essays are only concerned with the period up to the end of the Middle Ages. And rather than forming a connected narrative, they are separate studies of particular problems that had to be resolved before I could arrive at the historical interpretation of antisemitism I have presented in *History, Religion, and Antisemitism*. Yet if the essays jump from topic to topic, I think the sequence in which they are presented provides a fairly clear idea of the main stages in the development of hostility to Jews in the Middle Ages, the period in which, I maintain, antisemitism narrowly defined first appeared. They also provide the empirical ground for my effort in the last chapter to develop a more precise definition of antisemitism that might enable us to distinguish antisemitism in any period from other forms of hostility.

I have incurred many debts over the years while working in this field. I will always be grateful for the support of Bernhard Blumenkranz, even though his recent death makes it impossible to thank him again. My debt to Léon Poliakov is incalculable. I would also like to thank David Jacoby and Jacob Neusner for encouraging me to republish some of my articles as a book. And once again I would like to express my warm thanks to Stanley Holwitz, Shirley Warren, and Nicholas Goodhue of the University of California Press for their patient and invaluable help.

Introduction

These essays were written at different times, for various reasons, and differ widely in subject matter and approach. Some are very general, some highly specific; some were to be heard, some to be read. Nevertheless, as my title indicates, they are part of a single quest. With one exception, they are efforts from different angles to answer the same basic question: What is antisemitism, when did it start, and why? Like many quests, however, my search took me along unfamiliar paths, sometimes to dead ends, and brought me to unexpected turnings. Since the essays are places where I stopped rather than the end of the journey, an explanation of the path I took and the obstacles I encountered may make the connections between them clearer.

I was launched on my quest by a seeming accident, the article republished here as chapter 6, the only one not inspired by my question about antisemitism. Like all my work up to that time and much of my work thereafter, it dealt with French medieval legal and institutional history—in this case with a debate as to which of several royal ordinances was the first legislation by a Capetian king intended to apply to the whole kingdom. Though the subject matter of the ordinances in question was the treatment of Jews, that fact had attracted little attention from earlier institutional historians. They had focused on the development of legal or constitutional principle, and disregarded the immediate purpose of the ordinances as irrelevant to the broader constitutional issue.

Times had changed, however. Writing after 1945, I was much more

1

sensitive to evidence about how non-Jews had treated Jews. I wondered whether some knowledge about what kings and barons were doing with Jews might clarify which of those ordinances was intended to apply to the whole kingdom. Was it something about the status of Jews and attitudes toward them that had enabled the king to use them as the occasion for a major institutional advance in royal power? I found there was an obvious connection, and my discussion of the constitutional issue therefore dealt incidentally with the treatment of Jews.

All unwitting, I had started on a long journey. The article apparently suggested I was more familiar with Jewish history than I was. To my surprise, I was asked to review books dealing with Jewish history written by far more knowledgeable scholars such as Jacob Katz. And when I rashly agreed to write an extensive review essay around a book about the treatment of Jews in Angevin England, I had to learn a lot more about medieval Jewish history and about how non-Jews had treated Jews. Since I had gone to France to spend a year working on Capetian legislative history, I had time to devote to the assignment, which proved a turning point in my work.[1]

The more I read about Jewish history and how Jews had been treated by non-Jews, the more my interest grew. And as I read, I could not help noticing how diversely scholars dated the appearance of antisemitism and explained its causes. From religious motives, some depicted antisemitism as a millennial reaction to the unique values of Judaism. Others, concerned to assess the responsibility of Christianity for what Hitler had done, located its emergence in the first centuries of Christianity. Others, less concerned with religion or determined to absolve Christianity more completely, held that antisemitism was a secular phenomenon that only appeared in the nineteenth century.

One explanation of the disagreement was obvious; different scholars had examined hostility to Jews in different periods and called what they found "antisemitism." Hence, not surprisingly, they gave different meanings to the term, different dates for its emergence, and different explanations of why it had appeared. They could do so because, even though Hitler had made the need to understand the nature and causes of antisemitism imperative, there was no definition of antisemitism sufficiently precise to enable historians to agree when it started and why. The need for a sharper definition or conception of antisemitism thus seemed clear. But since the issue was remote from my work, I would not have pursued it further had I not had an idea I thought might resolve it—or at least be an interesting way to raise and clarify it.

Starting about 1938, sociologists and psychologists had developed a new concept, that of ethnic prejudice, but most scholars who had written on the history of antisemitism were not familiar with it. I was because, as a North American product of my times, I had read Gordon Allport's magisterial work, *The Nature of Prejudice*.[2] Since it emphasized the role of irrationality in prejudice, and since one of the distinguishing characteristics of the "Final Solution" was its monumental irrationality, I thought that, if I used Auschwitz as a touchstone and employed Allport's concept of prejudice to define antisemitism, I as a historian could then locate when antisemitism so defined first appeared and suggest why it had appeared then and there. I anticipated a short and rapidly completed work that would do no more than use the new ideas about ethnic prejudice to reinterpret the detailed knowledge already provided by historians of Jews and non-Jews. *Sancta simplicitas* or rash presumption.

Part 1 deals with the first problem I encountered. I rapidly discovered that much of the historiography by both Jewish and non-Jewish historians on postbiblical Jewish history and on the attitudes of non-Jews toward Jews and their treatment of them was remarkably parochial or seriously biased. And not only was it unreliable; on many matters it was simply lacking. I criticized that state of historiography in the two essays of 1966 and 1968 that constitute Part 1 of this book. Interestingly enough, they are the only articles I ever had rejected. The essay criticizing the treatment of Jews in histories and textbooks by non-Jews was rejected by the *American Historical Review*; the essay criticizing historiography by Jews was rejected by *Conservative Judaism*. Fortunately for my self-esteem, the former was printed by the *Journal of the History of Ideas* and the latter, thanks to Jacob Neusner, by *Jewish Social Studies*. Since then, with the great increase in more objective scholarship by both non-Jewish and Jewish historians, the situation has changed greatly, making those essays period pieces. But precisely for that reason, they may still be of interest to students of antisemitism—and of historiography.

In 1964, however, my expectation that I could rely heavily on existing historiography was disappointed. Consequently, when I began to work on the formation of antisemitism, I had to cover a wide range of history and spent much time trying to get a grip on many matters that were poorly treated or overlooked in the existing historiography. In one sense, that was effort wasted. In the following years, a number of books by specialized historians appeared that covered many of those gaps much better and more thoroughly than I ever could have. But if their detailed descriptions of events provided factual information I badly needed, most of these scholars still used "antisemitism" loosely and therefore disagreed about when it appeared and why. I still did not have an answer to my fundamental questions about antisemitism.

Part 2 deals with another major problem I soon encountered, a question that any effort to define and date antisemitism immediately raises. What, if anything, preceded it? Is antisemitism as old as Jews or did it only emerge later? Was there anti-Judaism before there was antisemitism, and if so, what is anti-Judaism?

As soon as I began to read about the history of antisemitism, I inevitably encountered the pioneering works of James Parkes and Jules Isaac and other works in the same vein that relied explicitly or implicitly on a distinction between anti-Judaism and antisemitism to determine when antisemitism started. But although these scholars were very interested in drawing a distinction and determining when antisemitism appeared and why, their perspective was very different from mine. Focusing almost exclusively on the painful question of the extent of Christian responsibility through the centuries for the twentieth-century tragedy, they typically used their faith to distinguish when Christians had strayed from the message of Jesus and become antisemitic, which led them to date the appearance of antisemitism early. Most located the origins of antisemitism in the first centuries of the Christian era, if not earlier among non-Christians.

Central to their arguments was the distinction between anti-Judaism and antisemitism, but their distinction rested on premises of faith. To put it loosely, they used "anti-Judaism" to refer to the kind of negative attitude that adherents of one religion have often manifested toward religions they do not accept. Christian anti-Judaism thus referred to the attitudes of rejection, whether mild or intense, that those who believed in the divinity of Jesus of Nazareth displayed toward Jews and Judaism because Jews refused to believe in that divinity. By contrast, they used "antisemitism" to refer to any hostility of Christians toward Jews that was not necessitated by faith in the divinity of Jesus or that ran counter to that faith.

Many Christians who have discussed the subject have used the distinction to absolve what they believed to be the genuine Christian message from any responsibility for the twentieth-century tragedy. Though most of them emphasized and deeply regretted that many Christians became antisemitic as well as anti-Judaic during the first centuries of Christianity, they were equally or even more concerned to deny any connection between proper Christian faith and antisemitism. But their use of "antisemitism" for any hostility that went beyond what their faith necessitated could not be justified empirically and had suspicious implications. It implied that, however great the difference in historical specifics, there was no difference in kind between Hitler's hostility and that of many early Christians; like Hitler, though in differing degree, many bishops, church fathers, and other Christians of the first centuries were antisemites.

That indistinctness reinforced my conviction that a more precise definition of antisemitism was badly needed. In any case, since I was not using theological premises, I disagreed with their explanation and dating of the origins of antisemitism. I was looking backward from Hitler rather than forward from Jesus of Nazareth. My conception of antisemitism depended, not on the beliefs of any religion, but on the empirical studies of various examples of prejudice by sociologists and psychologists, and on the facts of the "Final Solution." And as far as I could see, socially significant antisemitism so conceived could not be found in the first Christian centuries. But what, then, was anti-Judaism, and how did it differ from antisemitism?

Both "anti-Judaism" and "antisemitism" refer to hostility directed at those identified as Jews. Whether or not one thinks the terms denote markedly different kinds of hostility depends largely on whether one thinks that Jews were primarily responsible for the hostility or that non-Jews were. If—despite all the changes over millennia of history and all the obvious differences in culture of non-Jews—one focuses on Jews and maintains that real millennial Jewish characteristics (whether judged good or bad) have always inspired the same kind of hostility in non-Jews of very different kinds, then, as Bernard Lazare maintained a century ago, hostility to Jews has varied only in intensity and historical specifics, not in kind or cause. And for those who take this position, there will be little difference between antisemitism and anti-Judaism. If, however, one examines the characteristics of non-Jews and thinks that major differences, not simply in the intensity of the hostility but also in its basic nature, can be detected, and if the irrational hostility of Hitler (whose knowledge of real Jewish characteristics was minimal) is considered the most undeniable example of antisemitism, then antisemitism cannot be explained primarily as a reaction to some real millennial characteristics of Jews, and antisemitism can be distinguished from anti-Judaism.

Perhaps because I was not a Jew and was writing after Hitler, I found the latter position far more convincing and accepted its consequences. It followed that if antisemitism was not coeval with Jews, it must have appeared at some time between the beginning of Jews and Hitler, and that its emergence had to be explicable by historical changes in the characteristics of Jews and non-Jews, but primarily of non-Jews. But when? If antisemitism was defined as irrational prejudice against Jews, with Hitler's irrationality as the clearest example, I thought I could trace it back to northern Europe in the twelfth and thirteenth centuries, but no further. I also thought that it emerged then primarily because of a major change in the mentality of medieval Christians.

To think that socially significant antisemitism emerged then and there does not imply that there was no earlier hostility to Jews or no earlier changes in the character of hostility to Jews. Once one abandons the conviction that millennial Jewish characteristics have always caused the same kind of hostility, one would expect different kinds of non-Jews in different contexts to have been hostile in different ways and different degrees. Even though I thought that a deadly change in the basic nature of hostility to Jews had occurred in medieval Europe, I still had to acknowledge that a different and very important change had occurred much earlier with the emergence of Christianity.

Hostility to Jews had, of course, appeared before the triumph of Christianity—as had also hostility between Greeks and Romans and between Romans and Germans. That hostility to Jews is typically exemplified by the story of Haman, the riots in Alexandria in 38 of the Common Era, or the writings of Tacitus. Some Persians, Greeks, and Romans, who had their own social and cultural identity, hated the Jews in their midst because of a real Jewish characteristic, their insistence on maintaining their Judaic identity as a separate people. It is important to note, however, that the cultures that gave those Persians, Greeks, and Romans their sense of cosmic and social identity had developed independently of Judaism and had no Jewish components. Consequently, those who identified with those cultures could hate or ridicule Jews without feeling any threat, other than the fact of difference, to the foundations of their own sense of identity. Though they hated Jews for what Jews were really doing—or not doing—they had no need to examine seriously the beliefs of Judaism and try to demonstrate their errors. Their anti-Judaic hostility thus differed little from many other instances of ethnocentric hostility throughout history.

How different the situation of Christians. Christianity had started as a Jewish sect, and even when Christians separated from Judaism and created their own Christian religions, their reliance on Jewish beliefs and practices remained enormous, nowhere more obviously than in their Old Testament. Indeed, in recent discussions, Christians have often spoken of Jews as "separated brothers," a term with peculiar biological and gender overtones that underlines both the separation and the deep dependence of Christian identity on Judaic beliefs. And because of that patriarchal connection, Christians from the beginning reacted to Judaism and Jews very differently than had the non-Christian Persians, Greeks, and Romans.

Like many non-Christians before them, Christians were anti-Judaic, that is, they were reacting to real characteristics of Jews and Judaism. But Christian anti-Judaism differed markedly from that of non-Christians because the Christians' sense of identity forced them to come to grips with Judaism. Since their sense of identity had so many Jewish components, Christians could not simply dismiss Judaism as wrong and irrelevant. To assert the distinctiveness and superiority of their own identity, Christians had to think about Judaism and argue amongst themselves and with Jews that Christians were right and Jews wrong. Thus, for Christians, the ability of Jews to maintain their own identity was not only annoying or hateful in the way ethnic differences so often are; it was an intimate and enduring threat to their sense of identity, a challenge built into their own religion.

The challenge was difficult, and Christian leaders, starting with Paul, devoted much energy to meeting it. Their labors produced something new: the first systematically elaborated rationalization that justified hostility to Jews. By the beginning of the fifth century, the Christian anti-Judaic doctrine that depicted Jews as reprehensible, wrong even in their own terms, indeed eternally damned, was firmly established. It would be preached ever more widely and endure with little change for centuries.

Christian anti-Judaism thus seemed an important precondition for European antisemitism, a halfway station between a very common kind of ethnocentric hostility and the peculiarly irrational hostility of Hitler. And if, like many Christian scholars but for my own reasons, I wanted to distinguish it from antisemitism, I had to clarify my thinking about its nature and consequences. Chapters 3 and 4 are early efforts to do so. Chapter 3 is a brief effort to distinguish Christian anti-Judaism from other forms of anti-Judaism, to indicate its different forms of expression, to sketch some of its effects, and to indicate how it differed from Christian antisemitism. Chapter 4 is an analysis of what anti-Judaism meant in practice and how it changed as it was transmitted to different peoples from about 400 to 1096, that is, from the time when the Christian doctrine about Jews had been firmly established to the date of the first major massacre of Jews in Europe. It suggests an explanation for the changes and argues that the massacres of 1096 were an expression of anti-Judaism, not antisemitism. But here my path led me onto very perilous ground.

Chapter 4 was my first involvement in something I had hoped to skirt. Because I was relying on a loose sociopsychological definition of antisemitism that denoted empirical phenomena, stressed irrationality, and did not refer to religion in general or any religion in particular, and since I did not think that belief in a religion was necessarily irrational, I thought, simplemindedly, that I could avoid the whole religious debate. I thought I could determine when indisputably irrational attitudes to Jews emerged without making any assertions about the nature or origin of religious beliefs. But how could I explain the changes in anti-Judaism without giving some explanation of the manifest changes in Christian beliefs that lay behind the changes in anti-Judaism?

It was certain that different groups of Christians had reacted to Jews differently in the course of the first ten centuries of the Common Era, that Christian anti-Judaism had varied both in intensity and character. But why? The obvious answer was that the mentality of Christians had changed and, consequently, the meanings they gave to formulations of Christian beliefs, including anti-Judaic beliefs. But I could not explain the changes in anti-Judaism simply by describing the changes in Christian beliefs. For if I used their beliefs as a *sufficient* explanation for the changes in anti-Judaism, I would be accepting their religious beliefs as premises of my own explanation; and that would have embroiled me, at least tacitly, in the theological debate I was trying to avoid. As a historian, I needed to have my own explanation of why those changes in Christianity had occurred, and I needed to make it explicit. The result was a theoretical section about religion in the original version of chapter 4 that must have seemed unusual, to put it kindly, when I delivered it at Spoleto.

Willy-nilly, the problem of Christian anti-Judaism—and the fact of Judaism—made the issue of religious belief increasingly unavoidable, and so did another feature of religious thought. When, for a different purpose, I examined developments in Christianity that had no direct connection with Jews, I was struck by the importance of doubts for the development of Christianity. And when I then examined anti-Judaic and antisemitic attitudes more closely, I became convinced that they were in large measure a reaction to those doubts. That conviction is expressed in chapter 5, which deals directly, if all too superficially, with Christian doubts and their impact on attitudes to Jews. I argue there that the nature of Christian doubts changed from the first century to the twelfth as the mentality of Christians changed, and that the striking change in mentality apparent in the eleventh century—a new emphasis on empirical knowledge as well as on logic—brought a new kind of doubt. That new kind of doubt made Jewish disbelief more menacing and, for the first time, drove some Christians to the verge of irrationality when they thought about Jews.

The more I became convinced of the importance of religious doubts for the emergence of antisemitism, however, the more I was forced to face the basic historiographical problem I had unrealistically tried to circumvent, the problem of the relation between religion and antisemitism. The question that bothered me increasingly was how, and how far, historians of any period and subject could discuss religious phenomena objectively. So unavoidable did that problem come to seem for any fundamental rethinking of the problem of antisemitism that it finally compelled me to devote a book to it and its implications for an explanation of antisemitism.[3]

Yet if religious attitudes were crucial for attitudes to Jews, religion was not the whole story. If it seemed undeniable that Christians had exploited Jews ideologically to satisfy their religious needs, I knew that exploitation had not stopped there. The dispersion of Jews as a controlled minority among Christians made it possible for Christians to extend their exploitation from the ideological to the practical realm.

Part 3 deals with a major example of the economic and political exploitation that ensued. I had always taken that kind of exploitation for granted, for the article that launched me on my unexpected pilgrimage (chapter 6) dealt with the secular exploitation of Jews and the conflict that conduct caused between the French kings and their barons on the one hand and the papacy and churchmen on the other. It was clear that, although the inferior religious status attributed to Jews was a precondition for what the kings and barons did with them, those authorities were primarily moved by political, economic, and legal considerations that owed little to religious beliefs, indeed often ran counter to them, and that their nonreligious actions also affected attitudes to Jews.

Before the twelfth century, Jews were neither unusually prominent in moneylending nor stereotyped as moneylenders. By 1150, however, Jews in northern Europe were becoming disproportionately involved in moneylending, and the new stereotype of the Jews as usurers began to appear in northern Europe.[4] What made Jewish moneylending possible was not religious attitudes; it was the economic advance that started in the late tenth century, the new demand for credit it stimulated, which was satisfied by monasteries, urban Christian lenders, and Jews, the efforts of secular rulers to profit from it, and the effect of their efforts on Jews.

Since Jews were already damned, secular authorities were, for purely material reasons, quite willing to support Jewish moneylending energetically so long as they could exploit it without political repercussions. Thanks above all to that support and deprived of other opportunities, Jews engaged more and more in moneylending. They did so even though many debtors disliked or hated their creditors, and even though Christian ecclesiastical authorities were condemning ever more stridently the kind of credit transactions in which Jews typically engaged. Credit was so needed that even though Christians were the major source of credit, Jewish moneylenders could also profit—so long as they were supported and not overly exploited by the secular authorities. But the ultimate price was high. Since Christians did not want to acknowledge their own involvement in moneylending openly, it served many interests to emphasize the role of Jews and stereotype Jews as the archetypal usurer. That intersection of religious and material interests made Jews seem even more evil; their fundamentally evil nature found expression not only in their killing of Christ but also in their addiction to usury.

Chapter 6 discusses those developments, but it is now outdated. Since it appeared, other scholars have examined royal treatment of Jews more thoroughly and corrected my errors.[5] I have included it nonetheless, for it was the beginning of my quest and may still have some significance for French institutional history. A further reason is that it illustrates all too clearly an error I corrected myself. When I wrote it, I took for granted a long-established view about the nature of Jewish legal status in the twelfth and thirteenth centuries, to wit, that Jews were legally considered serfs of the king. But when I examined their status in different kingdoms more closely, I concluded that the traditional description not only was wrong but also concealed a major change that was very important for the way people thought about Jews.

As I argue in chapter 7, Jews were not fitted into the legal category of serfs, a category that also applied to many Christians; Jews were legally categorized separately as Jews. They were assigned a distinctive legal status that set them apart as different from and inferior to all others, a status that enabled secular authorities to exploit Jews and their moneylending as they could not exploit any Christians. And because Jews were being differentiated ever more completely from Christians, the way was opened for some Christians to exploit Jews in yet another and peculiarly deadly way.

Part 4 is devoted to that new kind of exploitation, which might be termed psychological or irrational exploitation. These chapters describe how Christians came to believe that Jews committed ritual murder. They are the empirical core of my argument about the emergence of antisemitism. They examine the new irrational exploitation of the existence of Jews that was expressed by a new kind of belief about them and a new kind of hostility toward them. To repress their own doubts, some Christians now imagined that contemporary Jews engaged in evil conduct that could not be seen.

The old anti-Judaic accusations against Jews had always had an obvious kernel of truth, however exaggerated. Though Jews placed a different value on the conduct, it was true that Jews did not understand their scripture as Christians understood their Old Testament, did not believe in the divinity of Jesus and approved of his execution, displayed their contempt for Christianity and its sacred symbols openly whenever it was safe, and were disproportionately engaged in moneylending in northern Europe by the latter twelfth century. But about 1150, just when a new kind of Christian doubt had appeared, when Jews were becoming disproportionately involved in moneylending, and when they were being assigned a legal status that set them apart as inferior to all Christians, beliefs appeared that lacked any kernel of truth but served to buttress Christian beliefs against the menace of new doubts. Antisemitism by my definition was emerging.

To protect their threatened beliefs, some troubled Christians created irrational fantasies: that Jews ritually crucified young children, engaged in ritual cannibalism, tried to torture Christ by attacking the consecrated host of the Eucharist, and attempted to destroy Christendom by poisoning wells and causing the Black Death. The fantasies appealed to other Christians who came to believe them in such numbers that they became part of European culture.

The falsity of those accusations seems glaringly obvious now, but that was not the case before Hitler. Of course, historians had long known that those accusations were made and that thousands of Jews were killed because of them. But not until the late nineteenth and the first half of the twentieth century was there a serious attempt by some Jewish and non-Jewish historians to disprove them. They had a hard time convincing others, however, because of the way they went about it. Strangely enough, or perhaps all too understandably before Hitler and Freud, they did not focus on the accusations themselves; they focused on the Jews and tried to prove that Jews had never done such things.

That defensive posture considered Jews guilty until proven innocent, and it set the historians an almost impossible task, for it was and is impossible to prove conclusively that no Jews ever engaged in such physically possible conduct in secret. In a period of widespread hostility to Jews, however, the approach had the advantage for Jewish historians that they could try to exculpate Jews without criticizing Christianity directly—a feature that made the approach attractive to Christian historians as well. Its weakness was that it ignored the obvious. If the evidence to support the truth of the accusations was highly suspect, as it was, it was nonetheless certain that people had made those accusations and used them to justify the killing of thousands of Jews. The first question for objective historians should therefore have been, not whether Jews could have done something like that, but what had Christians in fact done? How did those accusations arise? Who made them and why? How did they "know" that Jews had done such things?

The essays in Part 4 are the result of that simple change in optic. They show how the fantastic accusations arose and demonstrate their irrationality. Chapter 8 is a prelude that picks up the subject of Christian doubts discussed in chapter 5 and examines the reactions to doubt of one individual about 1150, in greater detail. It demonstrates that the combination of Christian anti-Judaism and a new kind of Christian doubt could drive Peter the Venerable, a highly educated man, to make accusations against Jews that bordered on irrationality.

Other Christians, however, went well beyond. Chapters 9 and 10 describe how the fantasy that Jews ritually crucified young children was created and became embedded in England. Chapter 11 explains how the fantasy of Jewish ritual cannibalism appeared a century later. For although Jewish historians have usually referred to the earlier crucifixion accusations in England and France as instances of the "blood libel," chapter 11 argues that a fantasy that can legitimately be called the blood libel only emerged a century after the crucifixion libel, in Germany in 1235.

Chapters 9–11 are detailed studies of crucial events in the creation and spread of the fantasy of ritual murder. They are not, of course, a history of all the irrational accusations of ritual murder from the twelfth to the twentieth century. Before that history can be written, there will have to be many more studies of all the other instances of such accusations in different areas by historians more familiar with the local context and the specific actors than I can ever hope to be. Nor do I examine here the other, equally fantastic, accusations of host profanation and well-poisoning. Nevertheless, a close analysis of the origin and impact of the crucifixion and cannibalism accusations suffices to reveal a characteristic common to all the accusations, their irrationality. The people who created them, and those who used them to incite massacres of Jews, never said that they themselves had actually observed Jews doing any of those things. And not surprisingly, since what the fantasies alleged was unobservable, we find that many people at the time had not believed them any more than we do.

The primary explanation of this new irrational hatred of Jews seems to be that many Christians were now plagued by a new kind of doubt, by conflicts between what they could or would know if they used their ability to think rationally and empirically and what they wanted to believe—for example, that Christ was really physically present in the Eucharist. Of course, many people were able to face their religious doubts more or less directly or set them unthinkingly aside, and many were not fearful of the presence of Jews. But many others could not or would not confront their doubts. Instead of examining what was really bothering them, they defended their beliefs by imagining that contemporary Jews were acting in ways that demonstrated empirically the truth of Christian beliefs. To repress their doubts, they suppressed their capacity to think rationally and empirically and instead imagined "Jews" according to their threatened beliefs. But doubts still plagued them, whether consciously or subconsciously. Their projections could not remove the real source of their anxiety, for it was buried deep within them, and their projections only drove the real problem farther underground. And since they could not recognize what was disturbing them, that only heightened their sense of a menace and their hatred of it and drove them to seek an outlet for their emotions. Revealingly, the surrogate on which they vented their hate was "the Jews," the supreme symbol of disbelief.

It should be emphasized, however, that unlike the well-poisoning accusation at the time of the Black Death, the accusations of ritual murder and host profanation were not scapegoating in the normal sense. If the Christians involved felt guilty about their own doubts, they did not displace or project the blame for their doubts on the Jews. They did not accuse and punish Jews for not believing in Christ and the Eucharist. Just the reverse. In a contorted way, their fantasies made Jews believers in Christ! The fantasy that Jews were still trying to harm and torture Christ made it seem that even Jews believed, however antagonistically, in Christ's continuing supernatural existence and presence in the Eucharist.

However irrational those accusations seem to us now, and seemed to some people at the time, their psychological appeal is all too obvious. Not only did they inspire many massacres in the Middle Ages, they became embedded in European culture, disseminated and made plausible by its art, literature, and historiography. For centuries, many people believed them, even some well-educated people in the twentieth century. Chapter 12 describes one aspect of that long life, the contribution of non-Jewish historians and pseudohistorians, from the twelfth century to the twentieth, to the spread and preservation of the myth that Jews conspired to crucify Christian children.

The irrationality of these chimerical fantasies is central for my conception and dating of antisemitism. Their rationalization of hostility to Jews differed radically from the justifications of anti-Judaic doctrine; no mere exaggeration of what some or many real Jews had done, they attributed to all Jews characteristics no one had ever observed. And whatever precise psychological explanation be given, they expressed and engendered a new and peculiarly violent hatred. More and more non-Jews came to hate those they thought of as "Jews" because of something that existed only in the hater's head: the chimerical fantasy of the mysterious Jew who was dangerously different from what he or she seemed to be and who secretly conspired to do immense evil to Christians. To me at least, it seems clear that, already by the end of the thirteenth century, many Christians in northern Europe were manifesting the same kind of completely irrational hostility toward Jews that Hitler would express much more devastatingly six centuries later. Part 5 summarizes my thesis. Chapter 13 does so historically. It is a brief narrative that puts the developments discussed in the previous chapters together chronologically. Chapter 14 is a very different kind of summary; it is an attempt to place what I had learned about hostility to Jews in a broader context and to resolve a theoretical problem.

What had started me on my quest was the concept of ethnic prejudice developed by psychologists and sociologists. It was an important advance in the study of intergroup conflict, but here again I ran into problems. When I examined the theories of prejudice more closely, I found they did not enable me to distinguish clearly between an unusual kind of hostility to Jews and more normal forms of intergroup hostility. There were two main problems. In the first place, the theories of prejudice were based almost entirely on synchronic studies of prejudiced attitudes in the present; they did not answer the historical question of how those attitudes had come into existence. In the second place, although the studies focused primarily on the apparently unusual kind of hostility directed against African Americans, Jews, and some other groups, their definitions of prejudice were so broad as to be applicable to almost any form of strong intergroup hostility.

I could have avoided the problem raised by those considerations had I contented myself with using the new insights about prejudice heuristically to sharpen my eye as a historian without becoming embroiled in questions of theory myself—which is more or less what I have done briefly in chapter 13. To leave matters there, however, would have left my original question of what antisemitism was unanswered. And without an answer to that question, there could be no clear answer to the question of whether there was a fundamental similarity between what had happened in the Middle Ages and what Hitler did.

Another set of basic questions would also have remained unanswered. Have Jews had to face a unique kind of hostility that no other group in history has confronted? Or is there an unusual kind of hostility that has only been directed against a few groups and is called "antisemitism" when directed against Jews? Or is antisemitism no different from the kind of hostility that all major groups have experienced, even though it has been directed with unusual intensity against Jews because of their long and dispersed existence?

To argue with sociological and psychological theories so remote from my training seemed unnecessary. Though I thought what I had uncovered historically suggested a way of modifying them, I might never have tried to deal with them in any depth had I not been invited to criticize the way the term *racisme* was used in France, where it was the preferred term for what North Americans think of as "prejudice" and was often used very loosely. The invitation forced me to formulate my ideas explicitly.

Chapter 14 is the result. It is concerned with theory rather than historical facts, with present intepretation rather than past events, with intergroup hostility in general rather than antisemitism in particular. As originally published, it was an effort to criticize prevailing ideas about prejudice and racism and to present my own theory of chimerical hostility. Though it indicated a definition of antisemitism, it did so only implicitly. Indeed, the term hardly appeared, for I was concerned to identify what was unusual about the hostility toward a number of groups, not just toward Jews. In the revised form in which it is published here, however, the theory developed is applied directly to the problem of defining antisemitism.

What is antisemitism? However we answer that question, our words or definitions cannot change what has happened. No one now can change Hitler's obsession to eliminate the human beings he thought of as "Jews" from the face of the earth or alter its effects. A definition of an observable phenomenon does not change the reality of the phenomenon, nor does it describe all the observable characteristics and occurrences of the phenomenon. My effort at definition seeks only to sharpen our focus on what non-Jews have done to Jews. The need for a more precise empirical definition of antisemitism is, I think, obvious, and I suggest that we use "antisemitism" only for a kind of hostility directed at Jews which has an observable characteristic that clearly distinguishes it from other forms of hostility to Jews.

The word "antisemitism" has been given many meanings. Since there is in fact no such thing as "semitism," save when referring to a language, the term is literally meaningless when applied to Jews, which is why I refuse to hyphenate "antisemitism." Moreover, since the word has been used to denote such a remarkably diverse variety of phenomena over millennia of history, it is semiotically ambiguous. That meaninglessness or ambiguity has made it a very unreliable and often misleading tool for the analysis of historical or contemporary events. Yet its continuing use is testimony to the conviction that there has indeed been something either unique or highly unusual about hostility to Jews.

And that, whether we use "antisemitism" or some other term to denote it, is the fundamental issue. Has there or has there not been an unusual kind of hostility to Jews? The issue is important both for our descriptions and explanations of historical events and for our understanding of contemporary and future events.

In these essays, I have attempted to demonstrate historically that Jews did indeed become the target of an unusual kind of hostility in northern Europe in the twelfth and thirteenth centuries, and that that hostility was the same in kind as Hitler's hostility.[6] What was unusual about it was its chimerical character. Though I think that chimerical hostility has also been directed at some other groups and their members, I am convinced that Jews in Europe have suffered in ways beyond description because of the completely irrational way in which many non-Jews—whether Christians, Nazis, or others—tried to defend themselves from doubts about themselves by attributing unreal characteristics to "Jews." And if this theory makes it any easier to detect such madness in the present and prevent it in the future, I will think my quest well worth the effort.

Part 1

Historiography

1.
Majority History and Postbiblical Jews

That history is a seamless web, that any scheme of periodization is an arbitrary convenience to suit a point of view—these are well-known propositions. Yet the most influential of all periodizations, that which divides history before the Incarnation from history after, is as unmodifiable as our sense of historic time itself. It orders the passing years for agnostics and Communists as for Christians. For the Jews the standard is dual, yet the Christian scheme is by far the more influential. If for some members of the majority the Christian ordering is a reflection of God's providence, while for others it is a mere convenience, for many in both camps the Incarnation (note the capitalization) still corresponds to one real division in history, whether that caesura be seen providentially or secularly. Before the first century A.D. the Hebrews were of great historical importance; thereafter the Jews are of little significance. The reign of a new truth had begun.

So deep are the roots of identity that historians whose religion, if any, is well concealed have remained faithful to this element of Christian historiography even when they have abandoned the Christian account of Christianity, the criterion of success having replaced the sanctification of election. After the emergence of Christianity, a reprobation falls on the Jews, and a dark night of ignorance conceals their activities from the historical consciousness of most of Western society until Dreyfus, the Balfour Declaration, or Hitler once more draws historical attention to the Jews.

It may be felt that to put the matter this way is to exaggerate either the importance of Jews to anyone save Jews or the silence of non-Jewish historians about Jews. The first problem may be left until later; the latter may easily be assessed by an honest answer to some simple questions. What understanding of the history of the Jews and of the majority's relation to the Jews will a student graduating from a liberal arts college have to give him or her intellectual and civic guidance? Will the student who has majored in history differ in this respect from other graduating seniors? Indeed, what of the student who has gained his or her doctorate in history? The answer in all three cases is, I believe, self-evident, but it would be well to document it and to give some explanation of why the situation is as it is.

Assume a student who, for some peculiar reason, became interested in the postbiblical history of the Jews. Since Gooch's history of historical writing is in paperback and happens to be on his bookshelf, our neophyte opens it to discover what the more important studies of the topic are. He turns to the chapter on "The Jews and the Christian Church" only to discover that the thirteen pages on the Jews are entirely devoted to the biblical period. With a sense of disillusionment, tempered by youthful optimism, he looks at the relevant paragraph in the introduction devoted to "Recent Historical Studies," and discovers that, up to 1951, there had apparently been no historical work of any importance on the Jews in the postbiblical period.[1] Finally in desperation, since he had seen the works of Graetz and Dubnow in the stacks, he checks the index only to discover that his somewhat exiguous knowledge is already superior to that of Gooch.

At this point, our discouraged student decides that he should look at Thompson's older but larger work. Had not Gooch called it the "most comprehensive survey of historical scholarship through the ages ever attempted"?[2] Admittedly Thompson only discussed historians who had written up to 1914 and were no longer alive, but his footnotes referred to more recent literature. To our student's happy surprise, not only does he find a chapter with the somewhat suspicious title of "Biblical and Jewish History" but also numerous references in the index. He encounters discussions of the Old Testament, of Josephus, of Agobard's polemics, of Thietmar of Merseberg's passing reference to Jewish merchants. Encouraged by this attention to Jews in the ancient and medieval worlds, he perseveres into the second volume in search of modern scholarship. He reads of Eduard Meyer and Renan's work on the biblical period, and notes with foreboding that the reference to Milman's *History of the Jews* only pays attention to Milman's treatment of the Old Testament period.[3] He is barely surprised when he reaches the chapter on biblical and Jewish history and discovers that whereas Thompson seems fascinated by Jewish history before Christ, he is little more concerned with the postbiblical period than Gooch. But wait. There is mention of Graetz.[4]

> The story of the race since then has naturally been most cultivated by its own members. Perhaps the broadest sweep, from the beginning to the third quarter of the nineteenth century, has been attempted by Heinrich Graetz (1817–91). But his History of the Jews is full of prejudice, and glaring inaccuracies of scholarship. He was ignorant of the immense progress made in biblical studies of either the Old or the New Testament. What can be thought of a writer with any pretensions to history who began his work with the words: "It was on a sunny spring day that some pastoral tribes passed across the Jordan"? Or a writer on ancient Jewish history who omits any mention of the works of Jost, Bleek, Graf, Nöldeke, Schrader, Reusch, Delitzsch, Keunen, Welhausen, and Stade? Graetz's wise and good men in history are almost constantly Jews, his weak and foolish men as constantly Christian. St. Louis of France is said to have "acquired his reputation for piety from the simplicity of his heart and the narrowness of his head"; St. Ambrose of Milan is described as "a violent official, ignorant of all theology, whom a reputation for violence in the church had raised to the rank of bishop."

Our student is shocked at the retrograde state of Jewish scholarship but sufficiently independent to wonder which side was fuller of prejudice, for Thompson's comment referred primarily to the biblical period and said almost nothing about the bulk of Graetz's work. Since Thompson had indicated in a footnote that the best one-volume history in any language was that by Margolis and Marx, the student looks for their evaluation of Graetz and discovers that, although Margolis and Marx recognize Graetz's unmistakable romanticism and obvious prejudices and shortcomings, they nonetheless say, "His 'History,' completed in 1870, was distinguished by vast erudition, a critical handling of the sources, and especially the happy instinct for discovering in the most unpromising material a mine of information."[5]

Moved by a malign spirit, our student looks to see how Thompson deals with E. A. Freeman, another example of wide knowledge and one-sided views: "Yet Freeman was not only an honest and forthright man, he was also one of England's greatest scholars."[6] Our student cannot help wondering whether Graetz and Freeman had been measured with the same yardstick. Once he encounters specialized bibliographies such as the bibliographies of Cecil Roth and Guido Kisch,[7] he may wonder even more why Thompson and Gooch had overlooked so much readily available historiography. He would wonder particularly how Thompson, a historian of medieval Germany, had remained ignorant of the works of Otto Stobbe, J. E. Scherer, Georg Caro, Cecil Roth, James Parkes, Salo Baron, and Guido Kisch, to mention a few authors of invaluable studies. He would gradually realize that there was a very substantial, if uneven and frequently parochial, body of historiography on the Jews in the postbiblical period. Reluctantly he might conclude that Gooch and Thompson knew not whereof they spoke, but also that Thompson covered his ignorance with his preconceptions.

Were our student to pursue his weary and largely profitless path through the histories of historical writing, he would have discovered that Eduard Fueter in 1911 and his editors in 1936 were unaware of postbiblical Jews, but that the collaborative study put out by the *Revue historique* in 1928 had a special section on "Judaisme post-biblique," which owed its excellence to its author, Maurice Liber, who was a historian of the Jews.[8] Surprisingly, in 1937, that ardent revisionist, Harry Elmer Barnes, at least had a section on Jewish national history which specifically mentioned Jost, Graetz, Dunow, Aronius, and the *Jewish Encyclopedia*, and referred generally to the "many histories dealing in a comprehensive way with the history of the Jews in the several European states."[9] In 1938, however, Allan Nevins referred the reader only to the *Jewish Encyclopedia*, the *Jüdisches Lexicon*, Dubnow, and the journal *Kiryat Sepher*.[10] Von Srbik in 1950, moreover, was still unaware of any relation between historiography on Jews and the history of Germany other than the references to Jews in the racist ideology of Treitschke, Lagarde, Gobineau, and Chamberlain.[11]

In contrast with the histories of historical writing, bibliographies pay more attention to the history of the Jews, for canons of thoroughness here oppose the direction of social attitudes. This can be seen from bibliographies for the history of the Middle Ages, a period of crucial importance in Jewish history and a period in which there was much official and unofficial action by the majority concerning the Jews. If Molinier's sources relevant to the history of the Jews are somewhat scanty and peculiarly selected, Charles Gross, who had written on the Exchequer of the Jews, included some thirty-seven sources and secondary works on the Jews in medieval England. Dahlmann-Waitz had a very extensive bibliography for the Jews in Germany during the Middle Ages. Paetow's reference to some forty-seven publications for the whole Middle Ages is respectable but falls far short of Roth's bibliography of eleven pages published in the next year.[12]

If bibliographies are more reliable than histories of historical writing, they too cannot be counted on, as Calmette's analysis and bibliography of medieval studies in 1951 shows. His text includes a dubious section on lending at interest and the Jews, but the bibliography for the section includes no work on the Jews, not even Caro's excellent economic history. In the whole book there seem to be only three references to works or documents relating to the Jews. Although these concern Spain, Baer's work is not mentioned![13]

Why the history of the Jews in the postbiblical period has received such scanty and erratic attention from all but Jewish historians is a complex question and one that raises questions about historians and historical method. Yet although there have been studies of the treatment of Jews in literature, there have been none, so far as I know, of their treatment at the hands of historians of the majority. The exiguous and highly eclectic sketch of historiography that follows makes no pretension to fill that gap. Since it is mainly intended to help explain the treatment of Jews in textbooks that may confront the American student, it stresses historiography in English. Moreover, since in the national histories of the nineteenth and even of the twentieth century the Jews are usually introduced and their character most fully discussed in connection with the Middle Ages, the emphasis will be on references to medieval Jews.

The roots of the distortion of the history of the Jews at the hands of the majority go back to the Christian appropriation and reinterpretation of Hebrew scripture in the first century. That misinterpretation of Jewish history was further developed by the church fathers and medieval theologians.[14] In the Middle Ages, nature was made to imitate art by medieval anti-Judaism and antisemitism which segregated and degraded the Jews, thereby giving further plausibility to the theory of divine retribution upon those who had obstinately refused to enter the way of truth. After the Reformation, although Protestant concentration upon the Old Testament and early Christianity placed Jews in a more favorable light, it did not remove the basic stain. Melanchthon's reworking of John Carion's *Chronicle* reveals "what sort of madness with fatal punishments is forced on the impious who are rejected by God."[15] When the myth of Reason shook the myth of

Revelation, the Christian view of history was widely criticized, and toleration became a virtue for some. Yet the Enlightenment intolerance of religion did not immediately profit the Jews, for were they not fanatically religious, incredibly superstitious, and unamenable to Reason? Voltaire's hostility to Jews was little weaker than his hatred of priests. The Enlightenment did, however, provide a neutral ground on which Jew and non-Jew, a Moses Mendelssohn and a Lessing, could meet,[16] although that neutralization had less effect on historiography than might have been predicted.

David Hume, whose *History of England* appeared from 1754 to 1762, paid considerable attention to the treatment of Jews in the Middle Ages and condemned their persecutors.

> On the approach of Easter, the zeal of superstition, the appetite for plunder, or, what is often as prevalent with the population as either of these motives, the pleasure of committing havoc and destruction, prompted them to attack the unhappy Jews, who were first pillaged without resistance, then massacred to the number of five hundred persons.[17]

He suspected that Christian moneylending, because concealed, was more unfair than Jewish, yet he believed that Jews carried usury "to the utmost extremity" in recompense for their perils.[18]

> The prejudices of the age had made the lending of money on interest pass by the invidious name of usury; yet the necessity of the practice had continued it, and the greater part of that kind of dealing fell everywhere into the hands of the Jews, who, being already infamous on account of their religion, had no honor to lose, and were apt to exercise a profession odious in itself, by every kind of vigor, and even sometimes by rapine and extortion. The industry and frugality of this people had put them in possession of all the ready money, which the idleness and profusion common to the English, with other European nations, enabled them to lend at exorbitant and unequal interest.[19]

Despite the air of impartiality, Hume's tone is hardly welcoming. When the *Decline and Fall of the Roman Empire* appeared between 1776 and 1778, it demonstrated no improvement over previous Christian historiography—or Voltaire—on this topic. If, for Gibbon, Christianity bore much responsibility for the end of the golden age, the Jews were enemies "who boldly professed, or who faintly disguised, their implacable hatred to the rest of human kind."[20]

> Humanity is shocked at the recital of the horrid cruelties which they committed in the cities of Egypt, of Cyprus, and of Cyrene, where they

dwelt in treacherous friendship with the unsuspecting natives; and we are tempted to applaud the severe retaliation which was exercised by the arms of the legions against a race of fanatics, whose dire and credulous superstition seemed to render them the implacable enemies not only of the Roman government, but of human kind.[21]

The romantic movement renewed interest in medieval history, but its empathy rarely extended to Jews. Michelet's *Histoire de France,* whose medieval volumes appeared between 1833 and 1843, suggests that a romantic love of humanity and liberty, combined with a developing anticlericalism, could produce a picture of Jews that differed little from that of Gibbon.

> To remain tied to one's origins, to preserve one's self from external influences, and to reject the ideas of others is to remain incomplete and weak. This it is that has constituted both the greatness and the feebleness of the Jewish people. It has had only one idea, has given it to the nations, but has received practically nothing from them. It has always remained itself, strong and limited, indestructible and humiliated, the enemy of humankind and its eternal slave.[22]

Another fierce opponent of religious bigotry had turned his attention to the end of the Middle Ages. Prescott's study of Ferdinand and Isabella appeared first in 1837 and then in a considerably strengthened edition in 1841. But we cannot call in the New World to redress the Old, nor a Protestant background to offset a Catholic. Prescott's hatred of the Inquisition prompted no reexamination of the fate of the Jews.

> But all this royal patronage proved incompetent to protect the Jews when their flourishing fortunes had risen to a sufficient height to excite popular envy, augmented as it was by that profuse ostentation of equipage and apparel for which this singular people, notwithstanding their avarice, have usually shown a predilection.[23]

In England between 1819 and 1831, a Catholic historian, Lingard, published his *History of England.* Despite its intentional moderation and temperance on religious issues, the Jews do not come off too well. Lingard paid considerable attention to the Jews, devoting three pages to the massacres of 1189/90. Like Hume, Lingard condemned the massacres, taking more care, however, to exculpate the role of religious considerations, which were but a "cloak."[24] As in Hume, the tone is neutral but mildly—when we remember the prevailing ignorance—derogatory. Extortion is the Jewish vice.

The Jews of this period were, in every *Christian country*, the sole or the principal bankers. As no law existed to regulate the interest of money, their profits were enormous; and at a time of military expedition, and *especially of a crusade*, their demands always rose in proportion to the number and wants of the borrowers. Hence, sensible that they had *earned* the hatred of the people, they were careful to deserve by the value of their *offerings* the friendship of the prince.[25]

In 1830, the year that Macaulay made his maiden speech in favor of the removal of Jewish disabilities, a liberal cleric of the Church of England brought out a *History of the Jews*. Milman's study was re-issued in a revised version in 1863, fourteen years after he had been made dean of St. Paul's. Its 1,468 pages rest upon very considerable, though considerably unreliable, research. Although Milman's basic assumption was that Jews would reach the spiritual and creative level of Christians only when they accepted Christianity and became fully assimilated,[26] he broke sharply with the picture of the eternal unchanging Jew so characteristic of much previous historiography. The great turning point after the Incarnation was the Middle Ages, when the Jews were confronted with the avarice of monarchs, the bellicosity of the feudality, and the bigotry of the clergy.

Each of the great changes which were gradually taking place in the state of the world seemed to darken the condition of this unhappy people, till the outward degradation worked inward upon their minds. Confined to base and sordid occupations, they contracted their thoughts and feelings to their station. Individual and national character must be endowed with more than ordinary greatness if it can long maintain self-estimation after it has totally lost the esteem of mankind; the despised will usually become despicable.[27]

This startling anticipation of the "self-fulfilling prophecy" is carried much too far, however, for Milman sees the Jews in the Middle Ages primarily as a collectivity with common—and unpleasant—characteristics, and there is little or no discussion of the internal life of the Jewish communities. The essence of the Jew was avarice.

In the nation and in the individual, the pursuit of gain as the sole object of life, must give a mean and sordid cast to character. To acquire largely, whether fairly or not, was the highest ambition of the Jew, who rarely dared or wished to spend liberally.[28]

Milman's work is fascinating testimony to the extraordinary combination of understanding and prejudice even of a man who was extremely tolerant for the period and had read widely in the history of the Jews.[29] But the *obiter dicta* that reveal his mind and that were so characteristic of historiography up to the middle of the nineteenth century were to fall into disrepute as the influence of Ranke and the scientific conception of history gained ground. It becomes difficult to find flagrantly prejudiced passages. References to Jews become more factual, and there is a limited gain in accuracy, but at the same time they become briefer, less informative. As factual precision came to predominate over religious and philosophical theorization, historical mention of Jews could no longer be a vehicle for emotional expression, and the interest in postbiblical Jews seems to wane.[30]

The apparent impartiality of the new "scientific" history probably contributed little to the various changes in attitudes toward the Jews in the latter nineteenth century. The new techniques could only have made a serious difference if the historians of the majority had applied them to the postbiblical history of the Jews. They did not, but left the task to Jewish historians, whose works they largely neglected. Moreover, it is now a commonplace that the apparent objectivity of the new history was quite compatible with the maintenance of strong biases, perhaps all the more influential because better concealed. How historians of the new school would treat Jews depended less upon their methods than upon their personal outlook, although it is probably true that the greater the historian the less likely he was to be prejudiced. Characteristic of the school in general, however, was the paucity of attention paid to the Jews and the consequent failure to "explain" them.

Giesebrecht, one of Ranke's leading disciples, is a good illustration of the effect of the Rankian conception of history. When we first meet the Jews, it is from a void to learn that the Rhine trade was in large measure in their hands. Thereafter he refers briefly to Jewish medical knowledge and mentions the high points of the relations between Germans and Jews up to the time of Frederick Barbarossa. He views the plight of Jews sympathetically, condemns the massacres, but maintains that religion was only a cover for the massacres of 1096. It is left to the reader to surround these brief references with his own conception of Jews and his own explanation of their plight.[31]

The *Deutsche Verfassungsgeschichte* of Georg Waitz, possibly the greatest of Ranke's disciples, was published between 1844 and 1878. In view of the specialized nature of the work, the five pages devoted to the Jews are more than might have been expected, and the tone is all that could be desired. Unlike J. W. Thompson, Waitz discusses Stobbe's work, and his impartiality has sympathetic overtones.

For centuries they seem to have lived under the Germans peacefully and without particular opposition. At the end of the eleventh century, however, as the lower classes were set in motion by the preaching of the crusade, and disordered bands moved on through the region of the Rhine, the Main, and the Danube, they then inflicted a bloody persecution because of religious fanaticism and also certainly because of their irritation at the riches which were to be found in the hands of the Jews. He who wished to save his life had to allow himself to be baptized.[32]

The problem here, as with Giesebrecht, is that the Jews appear on the historical stage from nowhere without further explanation as rich merchants persecuted for religious and economic reasons. Although the facts given are, on the whole, accurate and relevant, there is little with which a fervent antisemite might wish to disagree, save for the implied condemnation of the persecutions and the lack of explicit condemnation of the Jews. The discussion is insufficient to explain the position of the Jews, particularly since prejudice against them was rising in Germany in the later years of the nineteenth century at the same time that the works of Ranke and his school were being republished in various editions.

No discussion of the rise of scientific history in Germany could omit Mommsen, a slightly younger contemporary of Ranke but not one of his disciples. Mommsen did not follow Gibbon on the Jews and explicitly opposed Treitschke's antisemitism. His treatment of the Jews received universal praise.[33] Nonetheless there are traces of erroneous and derogatory stereotyping.

We speak of the Jews. This remarkable people, yielding and yet tenacious, was in the ancient as in the modern world everywhere and nowhere powerful. . . . Even at this time the predominant business of the Jews was trade; the Jewish trader moved everywhere with the conquering Roman merchant then, in the same way as he afterwards accompanied the Genoese and the Venetian, and capital flowed on all hands to the Jewish, by the side of the Roman, merchants. At this period too we encounter the peculiar antipathy of the Occidentals toward this so thoroughly Oriental race and their foreign opinions and customs.[34]

Liberal though he was in politics and unusually impartial on the question of the Jews, Mommsen nevertheless accepted the assumption that the Jews were the same in modern as in Roman times. He pictured a Jewish personality that was the fruit of the ghetto rather than of antiquity and gave his imprimatur to the fallacious view that Jews had always been equally concerned with commerce. Although his language about Jews was far from that of Gibbon, his description was hardly sufficient to change the basic view that Jews had given what they had of value in biblical times and had since remained unchanging, without leaven, and peculiarly addicted to the role of middleman. Indeed, what is striking in the adherents of the more scientific history is their relinquishment of the religious charge against the Jews and their maintenance of the economic. Does the change reflect the changing importance of religion and commerce in the nineteenth century?

The exaggeration of the economic role of Jews is particularly clear in a work that helped fashion the minds of Englishmen in the late nineteenth and early twentieth centuries. J. R. Green could describe the expulsion of Jews by Edward I as the great blot upon his reign and speak of the fanaticism of Edward's subjects which brought persecution,[35] but it was the role of Jews as capitalists which fascinated him and which he exaggerated out of all measure.

> That the presence of the Jew was, at least in the earlier years of his settlement, beneficial to the kingdom at large there can be little doubt. His arrival was the arrival of a capitalist and heavy as was the usury he necessarily exacted in the general insecurity of the time, his loans gave an impulse to industry such as England had never felt before. The century which followed the Conquest witnessed an outburst of architectural energy which covered the land with castles and cathedrals; but castle and cathedral alike owed their existence to the loans of the Jews. . . . But to the kings the Jew was simply an engine of finance. The wealth which his industry accumulated was wrung from him whenever the Crown had need, and torture and imprisonment were resorted to if milder entreaties failed. It was the gold of the Jew that filled the royal exchequer at the outbreak of war or of revolt. It was in the Hebrew coffers that the Norman kings found strength to hold their baronage at bay.[36]

After 1926 the work of that great exponent of history as literature, G. M. Trevelyan, replaced Green's *Short History*. Here there is the usual liberal condemnation of persecution, a brief reference to Jewish immigration in the eighteenth century, and one page of rhetorical description of the role of the Jews in the Middle Ages, which represents no gain in accuracy, but whose emotive language places these "foreigners" in a clearly unfavorable light in the English saga.

> The Jews throve on money-lending for interest, a practice forbidden by the Church, which Christian traders, having no gold to lend, were fain to abandon with a curse to the infidels who had it. The Jews were the King's sponges. They sucked up his subjects' money by putting their own out on usury and were protected from the rage of their debtors solely by the strong arm of the king, who in his turn drew what he wanted from their ever-

accumulating wealth. . . . They were utterly at his mercy, for he was their only friend in a hostile land.[37]

Both Green's and Trevelyan's histories illustrate a characteristic of majority national history. The Jews are introduced into the epic as part of medieval history, and the principal, albeit scanty, description of them occurs in the period of their greatest debasement. Thereafter we hear of persecution and changes of legal status, but not of change in occupation and outlook. An excellent American textbook, whose first edition appeared in 1928 and whose fourth in 1957, is an extreme example of this procedure. W. E. Lunt was a medievalist, and the earlier parts of his book are admittedly better than the later. Nonetheless it is striking that, while we hear of the Jewish moneylenders of medieval England, we are never told of the readmission of Jews under Cromwell, nor do we learn that Jewish as well as Catholic disabilities were removed in the nineteenth century. What is said of the Jews, and that in the two editions that appeared *after* World War II, is neither accurate nor calculated to broaden the students' understanding. We learn that Jews were rightless aliens, that kings profited from them, and "Christians would have no social intercourse with them."

> Practically the only pursuit they followed was that of lending money. Medieval men, regarding capital as unproductive, thought it was wrong to lend money at interest. The practice was forbidden to Christians by both ecclesiastical and secular laws. The Jews, who were not bound by this Christian teaching, reaped a rich harvest wherever rulers allowed them to operate. Money was exceedingly scarce, and those who wanted to borrow were hard pressed to meet immediate engagements. The Jews consequently could command a rate of interest that varied from forty to eighty percent. . . . Among medieval Christians the Jews were intensely unpopular. Their disbelief in Christianity, their social seclusion, and their extortionate practices aroused popular animosity.[38]

Lunt does speak of the Lombards as important after 1290 in England, but the language used to describe their activities not only contradicts what was said of the Jews but also places their lending in a much more favorable and less "extortionate" light. Hall and Albion are little improvement. The Jews are introduced as persecuted moneylenders, their expulsion is seen as a loss to royal revenue, and although their readmission is never mentioned, their entry into Palestine is recorded. The remaining references deal with Palestine and Israel, and after the description of the end of the British mandate, one is not surprised to find that Roth's *History of the Jews in England* does not seem to figure in the bibliography.[39]

Admittedly these textbooks could get little sane counsel from the man who more than any other had dominated the history of medieval England. The judicious language of Bishop Stubbs barely covers a derogatory judgment.

> The enormous sums of money raised by way of fine and amercement show how largely they must have engrossed the available capital of the country. As the profits of the Jewish money trade came out of the pockets of the king's *native* subjects, and as their hazardous position made them somewhat *audacious speculators* and at the same time *ready tools* of oppression, the *better sense* of the country coincided with the religious prejudice in urging their banishment.[40]

It is a pleasure, as ever, to turn to Maitland, whose attitude to Jews contrasts sharply with that of Stubbs. He recognized that "for about a century and a half they were an important element in English history,"[41] and devoted eight pages to them in a history of law.

> The system could not work well; it oppressed both Jews and Englishmen. Despised and disliked the once chosen people would always have been in a society of medieval Christians; perhaps they would have been accused of crucifying children and occasionally massacred; but they would not have been so persistently hated as they were, had they not been made the engines of royal indigence.[42]

Maitland's acute magnanimity had little influence on the authors of the relevant volumes of *The Oxford History of England*. While A. L. Poole describes Jewish lending and royal taxation of the Jews with some care, and recognizes that they were not the only moneylenders of the twelfth century, his principal description of the Jews represents no advance on Green and Trevelyan. Since this passage has already drawn a merited reprobation from H. G. Richardson, I shall forbear to quote it.[43] Powicke, so sensitive to some religious nuances, avoids such condemnation, but, despite his excellent bibliography on the subject, he is hardly informative. Scattered widely through the book, in text and notes, are some twelve sentences devoted to the Jews. Half of one sentence in the text and a reminder in a footnote are devoted to the expulsion that was to last for three and a half centuries![44] But then G. O. Sayles devotes only one sentence to the Jews, despite Maitland's dictum on their importance.[45] Only Lady Stenton has included a respectable section on the Jews as part of a survey of England in the

twelfth and thirteenth centuries, although G. G. Coulton's highly col-
ored account should be mentioned also.[46]

The Jews have been little better served in recent general histories of
the Middle Ages, as a few examples from the work of prominent historians may suggest. Pirenne refers to Jews only four times and that
briefly in his *History of Europe*.[47] In the *Economic and Social History*,
in which he is concerned only with Jewish economic activities, he neglects their involvement in agriculture, mentions their early commercial
activity, and stresses that their later role as suppliers of credit has been
much exaggerated and that the ecclesiastical establishments were the
first real suppliers. Yet he feels it necessary to assert that Jews un-
doubtedly abused their freedom from the prohibition of usury: "For no
one came to their doors save in case of need and necessity enabled
them to exploit their clients as much as they liked."[48]

The third edition of Halphen's survey of Europe from the eleventh
to the thirteenth century appeared after World War II. In it he discusses Maimonides and the Jewish contribution to philosophic advance, mentions that Henry III of England confiscated Jewish goods,
and observes that the role of Jews as moneylenders has been
exaggerated.[49] But he does not mention the persecutions accompanying the First or Second Crusade, nor the demand for distinctive clothing of the Fourth Lateran Council. It would be impossible for anyone
to gain any idea of who the Jews were or what happened to them in
this crucial period from his treatment. But it is still preferable to that
of Christopher Dawson, who can discuss the role of religion in the
formation of medieval culture without any reference to the presence of
Jews or Judaism![50] That silence is, however, less misleading than the
erroneous and stereotypic account in a recent history of the crusades.[51]

The medieval volume of a recent collective survey of world history
is a good illustration of the erratic treatment of the Jews. Arno Borst,
in a chapter on the religious and intellectual movements of the High
Middle Ages, notes the apocalyptic trends and the association of Jews
with the Devil connected with the massacres of 1096 and 1251; this is
the first indication that I have noticed that the work of Trachtenberg
and Norman Cohn has affected the discussion of Jews in medieval
surveys.[52] But in the same volume, Ganshof discusses the High Middle
Ages up to nearly 1300 with only a single reference to Jews, a passing
reference to the massacres of 1146 stopped by St. Bernard.[53] A. R.
Myers's mention of the massacres attendant on the Black Death and of

the movement of Jews to Poland represents a more typical middle ground.[54]

Christopher Brooke's very recent survey of the two centuries from 962 to 1154 is an outstanding example of such idiosyncratic treatment of Jews. He manages to omit all mention of the massacres of 1096 and 1146. We hear nothing of Anselm, Gilbert Crispin, Abelard, Peter the Venerable, and St. Bernard on the Jews, nothing needless to say of Rashi. We meet Jews only as moneylenders. Paying no attention to monastic credit, Brooke still believes that the Christian doctrine against usury was so efficient a barrier to the development of credit that "... it was singularly fortunate for the Europe of the eleventh and twelfth centuries that there was a substantial group of active and intelligent people to whom usury was not forbidden."[55] This example of erroneous and stereotypic thinking in 1964 in a work aimed at the advanced student is a suitable prelude to the peculiarities of textbook treatments.

The treatment of the Jews in ten of the better and more recent surveys of the Middle Ages varies enormously. If we exclude the references to relations between Judaism and Rome and early Christianity, there are few events of Jewish history whose mention may be reasonably anticipated. Only Jewish involvement in moneylending is almost certain to be noticed: nine of these ten books refer to it, and some spend one or two paragraphs on it. Stephenson and Lyon refer to Jews in connection with the Roman Empire and Islam, but, with the exception of one passing reference to the Jews in Sicily, they devote only one paragraph to the Jews within medieval Europe, beginning: "Among the moneylenders of Europe there were many Jews...."[56] Everything of importance said about the Jews in this period is arranged under this heading, and there is no mention of Maimonides, and no mention of any specific persecution, save a brief reference to the expulsions by Edward I and Philip IV. The paragraph follows Pirenne in recognizing that the role of the Jews in the financial history of Europe has been exaggerated, but discusses only their trade and lending.

At least Stephenson and Lyon, like Strayer and Munro,[57] are abreast of current historiography on the importance of Jewish lending. The earlier text of Thompson and Johnson leaves the Jews in lonely glory as the pioneers of moneylending.[58] Similarly, Sidney Painter states that "in the eleventh, twelfth, and thirteenth centuries the moneylending business was in the hands of the Jews, who were not bound by Chris-

tian law."[59] In a textbook published in 1964 Dahmus refers to the
Jews only in connection with moneylending and explains that the Jews
were the only people with enough money to lend in the early Middle
Ages, although he says that Christians later entered moneylending
"with enthusiasm."[60] La Monte, Previté-Orton, Davis, and Scott seem
to assume by their brief references that Jews were always and everywhere moneylenders.[61] Of these authors, only Hoyt, in a total of some
eight widely scattered sentences about Jews, makes no mention of the
Jews as moneylenders.[62] Whether such neglect is more salutary than
uninformed attention is a moot point.

No other subject is mentioned in connection with the Jews with
anything like the frequency of moneylending. Their expulsion by Philip
IV is alluded to in six books, that by Edward I in only four. Six
mention the massacres of 1096, which are often seen as the great
turning point in the medieval history of the Jews.[63] Only one mentions
the massacres of 1146, which were stopped by St. Bernard; only three
mention the massacres of 1189/90 in England. Only four mention the
massacres accompanying the Black Death, and what is more striking,
only four mention the expulsion from Spain in 1492. The canon of the
Fourth Lateran Council prescribing distinctive clothing is mentioned in
only three, although Hoyt's vague statement that in the council "the
status of Jews in Christian society was defined" might be considered to
bring the total up to four.

Scattered references to Jews in connection with Moslems, whether
in the eastern Mediterranean area, in Moslem Spain, or in Sicily and
at the court of Frederick II are unpredictable but fairly frequent. What
is astounding is that Maimonides is mentioned only by La Monte and
Scott, despite his importance in the controversy over Aristotle. Rashi,
the greatest Talmudic scholar in Christian Europe, whose commentary
still bears authority and whose biblical commentary is still used, is
unknown to any of these books. There may be occasional passing
references to the role of Jews in the transmission of Greek and Arabic
knowledge and a couple of references to Jewish medical knowledge,
but the only specific reference to Jewish scholarship within Europe is
R. H. C. Davis's mention of the consultation of Jews by Stephen Harding to establish the Cistercian Bible. Obviously moneylending, not
scholarship, was the Jewish métier.

Only La Monte mentions the conversion of the Khazars to Judaism,
and only La Monte and Previté-Orton indicate that by the late Middle
Ages the majority of northern Jews were living in Poland! Of the five

of these books that mention the Jews in the Roman Empire, only the *Shorter Cambridge Medieval History* mentions the persecution of Jews by Christians. There is no mention of the anti-Judaic doctrine of the Catholic church and no description of papal policy toward the Jews save the passing references to the Fourth Lateran Council, when these occur. Not a single author reminds us that members of the majority used accusations of ritual murder to torture and kill Jews, despite papal prohibitions.

There is little need to carry this analysis further. Although by utilizing all the ten books examined it is possible to accumulate brief references to many of the chief events of Jewish history in the Middle Ages, in not one of them is there anything approaching a respectable treatment of the minority within Europe that was, at least initially, on the same cultural level as the majority. In some cases, such as that of Davis, the treatment is so idiosyncratic as to approach irresponsibility. In most cases, the treatment not only is unpredictable and brief but, by emphasis, omission, and error, reinforces dubious stereotypes. The only one of these books in which there seems to be a conscious effort to avoid reinforcing stereotypes, Strayer and Munro, is also the one that is most conscious of the development of antisemitism in the Middle Ages.

Three recent books stand apart. Robert S. Lopez refers frequently to Jews and devotes a small section of his survey to "Non-conformists: Heretics and Jews." A Jewish source is there quoted, and the tone is noticeably different.[64] Friedrich Heer, possibly because he is arguing a thesis that criticizes the developments of the thirteenth and fourteenth centuries, notes that little attention has been paid to the Jews in many of the surveys of the Middle Ages, devotes half a chapter to them, and, at a total expense of nine pages, gives far more information and understanding than all the ten books discussed above taken together.[65] Finally, the recent textbook by Norman F. Cantor has treated the Jews fairly satisfactorily. If there is no mention of the Khazars, of the massacres of 1146, 1190, and those accompanying the Black Death, and no mention of the expulsions from England, France, and Spain, or of the migrations of Jews to eastern Europe, Avicebrol, Rashi, Judah Halevi, Maimonides, and Jewish scholarship in general are not only mentioned but discussed at some length. The Jewish participation in and exclusion from agriculture is recognized in the best discussion of the economic role of the Jews in any of these books.[66]

Not until the 1960s was there any survey designed to introduce the

student to the Middle Ages which presented a discussion of the Jews
that in any way adequately explained why the Jews entered the modern
period as an oppressed and degraded group. And textbooks such as
those of Dahmus and Scott, together with more intensive surveys such
as that of Christopher Brooke, appearing in 1964, indicate that such
a presentation has by no means become habitual.

There is no space here to discuss the way Jews are treated in mon-
ographic work or in textbooks on modern Europe. To a large extent
such an analysis would repeat what has already been said. But it would
probably be discovered that there is more, and more informed discussion of Jews, and that frequently more sympathetic in tone.[67] The
availability of evidence and the proximity in time make it harder to
view Spinoza, Moses Mendelssohn, Disraeli, Dreyfus, the Rothschilds,
the Vienna circle, and many others simply as bearers of the abstract
qualities attributed to a group. Even the victims of Pobiedonostsev and
Bratianu are likely to impinge on historical consciousness somewhat
more as suffering individuals and less as a faceless collectivity. Nonetheless, there is generally the same failure to explain how Jews had
come to be what they were and to be treated as they were, and the
same inability to recognize the "inside," in Collingwood's sense, of
Jewish history. To an amazing extent the word "Jew" is supposed to
be self-explanatory in a way that, paradoxically enough, "Christian,"
"French," and "socialist," for example, are not.

The distilled essence of the attitude of majority history toward the
Jews can be found in the many one- and two-volume histories of Western civilization, or of civilization at large, for the numerous introduc-
tory survey courses usually required of undergraduates. I shall not
report on the results of pursuing "Hebrews," "Jews," "Judaism," and
"antisemitism" through the indexes and texts. The result is predictable, an exiguous and more erratic version of the presentation already
analyzed above. One extreme example may suffice. In a collaborative
work in which the *Diary of Anne Frank* is quoted in a section on the
horrors of World War II, the index lists no reference for the Jews in
the Middle Ages (or for the modern period), and the only reference in
the text on the Middle Ages is to the fact that Jews dominated pawnbroking but not banking in the Middle Ages.[68] There are no references
to any of the persecutions attendant on the crusades, or to any legislation against Jews, or to any of the expulsions of Jews. From the birth
of Christianity and of Islam to Dreyfus and Hitler, the only appearance
of the Jews is as petty pawnbrokers! Extreme as this case is, it dem-

onstrates the basic pattern of majority historiography: an emphasis on biblical Judaism in antiquity, on Jewish moneylending in the Middle Ages, and on antisemitism and Zionism in the nineteenth and twentieth centuries, accompanied by a thoroughly inadequate explanation of the characteristics of and forces acting upon the Jews in any period after the biblical.

In general, majority historiography as it relates to Jews has been marked by lack of interest and by ignorance, when it has not also been marked by derogatory attitudes. Most majority historians may not have been notably prejudiced personally, but they have been influenced by the prevailing attitudes of their society. Inheriting a historiographic tradition hostile toward or ignorant of Jews, or both, and writing for a society little interested in Jewish history or more or less hostile to Jews, historians of the majority have been little attracted to Jewish history, little inspired even to read the work of Jewish historians, let alone study the matter for themselves.[69]

In the nineteenth and early twentieth centuries, history was largely the history of a given people, the Romans, the French, the Germans, the English, and so on. From this viewpoint, the postbiblical Jews always appeared in the story as aliens who had not properly participated in the achievements of *the* people. In the twentieth century, history has gradually become less national and more comparative and specialized, but to a remarkable extent it has remained the history of the majority, and the Jews have continued to be viewed as an alien element of little importance. In consequence there has been little increase in historical knowledge about Jews. The void left by the negligence of scholarship and education has been filled by the half-truths and myths of what may fairly be called the folk-memory of each region and class, supplemented by the simplicities of early religious education, the resonances of literature, and individual contacts with Jews. And actual contact has been less educative than it might have been against a background of ignorance that makes it difficult to distinguish projection from reality and cause from consequence in the condition of the Jews.

Not only has this historiographic mold not contributed to a reduction of false beliefs about Jews, but the silence of the official guardians of social memory has given tacit authorization to the perpetuation of those beliefs. If history ought not to be a tool subservient to particular social policies, historians nonetheless bear the responsibility for ensuring, so far as possible, that people will not fashion their future on false

beliefs about the past. The failure of majority historiography, for whatever reasons, to deal responsibly with the history of the Jews is certainly one, if only one, of the factors contributing to the perpetuation
of antisemitism.

In the last analysis, the argument—or exhortation—of this article
must rest upon that most difficult of judgments, an assertion of the
relative importance of a particular subject of study. We might claim
that the contribution of the Jews to Western civilization has been out
of all proportion to their numbers. But that claim is valid only for
certain periods, and its terms are difficult to define; it is, moreover, an
argument proper to the "history of the people" type of historiography,
to that Whig history which, however diluted, expresses pride in af-
filiation with the achievements of a given group. A clue to a more
profound argument may lie in the increased attention that some majority historians have been paying to the Jews since confrontation with
the Hitlerian horrors.

Hitlerian propaganda and action demonstrated something that historians had too easily forgotten: from the Middle Ages to the present
there have been few words more certain to elicit some emotional response from most Westerners at most levels of society than the word
"Jew." The existence of Jews and the majority's reaction to them have
been an enduring element in Western consciousness, an element whose
precise nature has varied with social change, but an element that has
nonetheless maintained a striking continuity. Even when Jews were
least important or were physically absent, they have been part of the
mythology of the West: *The Jew of Malta* and *The Merchant of Venice*
were written in and for a society in which the residence of Jews had
been illegal for three hundred years.[70]

If we are as concerned with the enduring characteristics of groups
and individuals as with their achievements, with their failures as with
their successes, then the history of the postbiblical Jews assumes an
obvious importance. The significance of postbiblical Jews for the history of the West lies not so much in the realm of religion, of econom-
ics, or of science, although there can be little doubt of the importance
of Jews in all those realms; it lies in the intangibles of social psychology. Not only is the treatment of Jews in any period or by any class
a valuable indicator of other aspects of people's attitudes, not only are
the attitudes and actions of Jews in important measure a product of
their experience in Western society, but the Jews have been the oldest

and most universal focus of a social and psychological phenomenon that has been characteristic of the rapidly evolving society of the West, prejudice. That so little attention has been paid to the Jews may be, in part, a reflection of the tendency of historians, until recently, to stress actions more than attitudes, to divide ideas under convenient categories rather than to search for their underlying basis, to avoid the shadowy area of social psychology. It seems safe to predict that more attention will be paid to the history of the Jews as the influence of social sciences on history increases. But there are other reasons why this ought to be so.

2.
Tradition, History, and Prejudice

Tradition, it may be suggested, tends overwhelmingly to be ethnocentric and to emphasize continuity rather than change. Like prejudice, it is a handing down, a carrying over, and a reception of bits of information and misinformation, of attitudes and values, all without critical examination. Developed by a group to buttress its identity, it serves to separate the group from other groups, almost inevitably drawing invidious distinctions in the process. And like prejudice, it tends to subordinate individuals to the group and its identity. That there may be good traditions, that tradition may have good effects, I would not wish to deny, but what I would like to stress here is that tradition not only has affinities with prejudice and the psychology of prejudice but also is an excellent perpetuator of prejudice—all the better because it makes the failings of outgroups an essential counterpart of the virtues of the ingroup.

If there is an affinity between traditional beliefs—or belief in tradition—and prejudice, there is an even more obvious relationship between tradition and history. If tradition and prejudice are both marked by motivated credulity, tradition and history are obviously linked by their common concern with the past. Both seek to make the past meaningful to the present, but history is distinguished from tradition by the historian's critical attitude toward information about the past and by his or her consciousness of change and discontinuity. Although history is concerned with continuities, it is suspicious of allegedly unchanging attitudes and identities. The present may have developed out of the past, but it is something different from the past.

Historical writing at its best tends to be a solvent of tradition. Yet in modern society, history is frequently called upon to fulfill the needs formerly satisfied by tradition; it preserves and reveals the past of various groups; and people look to history, under compulsion of the classroom or from interest, to understand where they have come from and who they are. Historians are thereby confronted with conflicting demands that account, in part, for the charge of subjectivity so often levied against them. On the one hand, historians must be ruled by purely intellectual concerns, by the methods and the data available to them, without favoritism to any group or cause; on the other hand, their interests inspire their questions, and both their interests and their knowledge of their audience influence their presentations. If the dangers of subjectivity are limited in the scholarly article and the carefully circumscribed monograph, works of synthesis are something else. The textbooks, the surveys, the historical best-sellers are written with a particular, nonscholarly audience in mind and are intended to make sense, from a particular perspective, of a wide sweep of human experience. Here the perils of subjectivity are more apparent, and history may betray its ancestry in tradition and its susceptibility to prejudice.

The influence of tradition on historical writing is likely to be strongest whenever present values are perceived as peculiarly historical products, as in the case of nationalisms, Western civilization, and the historical religions. It takes little examination of the required curricula in schools, colleges, and seminaries in the United States to realize the extent to which history is called upon, if not to indoctrinate, at least to inform with a sense of the group's historical identity. In the historical education of Americans, the national majority usually appears as a primary reference group, with Western civilization as a weak secondary group, and with certain groups within Western civilization and non-Western groups coming in a very weak third. Moreover, the evolution of the home-group tends to be the standard by which the experiences of other groups are evaluated.

To use the area with which I as a medievalist am most familiar, medieval textbooks in English focus overwhelmingly on events in France and England, since these were most influential for the formation of English-speaking culture. Attention is inevitably paid to the Catholic church, but because of the implicit sense of reference groups,

the papacy frequently emerges not simply as one of the major protagonists but rather as an external and somewhat threatening power.
Mediterranean and eastern Europe receive far less attention than
northern Europe. In college course offerings, if there is a course on a
specific area in addition to a general medieval survey, the probability
that it will be a course on English medieval history is very high. The
curriculum in modern history, which cannot cover everything, will
show a heavy bias in favor of American history and will deal most
selectively with European history, not to speak of Asian history.

At the level of secondary education, the concentration upon primary
reference groups and the neglect of secondary is usually much more
marked and the historical vision more emphatically ethnocentric. In
the case of denominational schools, colleges, and seminaries, religious
reference groups supply another strand of ethnocentric perspective.
These varying forms of implicit ethnocentrism in formal education
reinforce—and are reinforced by—the more explicit ethnocentrism of
the traditions (in the normal sense) within the country, save for those
groups whose traditions are not recognized or are contradicted by the
perspective of the educational system.

Obviously, there are good reasons why this should be so, arguments
as to why those areas and periods must be presented when all cannot
be. If selectivity in historical emphasis is inescapable, is it not essential,
for both civic and psychological reasons, that students should be instructed about themselves and their society, and that in some depth,
instead of a vain attempt at an impartial and necessarily superficial
coverage of the known historical canvas? Could anyone seriously argue for an educational system that left students knowing as much or
rather as little about their own as about Chinese, or French, or African
society? The argument seems irrefutable, yet we should recognize that
it derives its strength from an appeal to the sense of separate identity and the consciousness of particular interests of a national—or
religious—group. If history from a cosmopolitan point of view may be
approximated by scholars speaking to scholars, historical education is
almost inevitably ethnocentric, particularly since education proceeds
from the known to the unknown and students know much more about
their own group and its values than about any other.

What has been said so far is not intended to allege that historians
are particularly ethnocentric or prejudiced. It is intended to suggest,
however, that historians, when writing for a general audience, are
likely to pay more attention to some groups than to others, and may

neglect or misinform about groups that are not recognized as significant by the audience. Thereby ethnocentrism and a sense of social distance are perpetuated and stereotypic conceptions of distant groups remain unaltered, if not enhanced.

A further reason why general historical works and historical education may perpetuate rather than combat prejudice is that historians tend to view intergroup conflicts in a rationalistic way as competition rationally springing from a clash of interests. Since historians are concerned with the conflicts of particular groups, their attention has not been drawn to the general characteristics of group conflict as such, but to the particular values, goals, and policies involved in very specific conflicts. Hence they have tended to overlook the irrational components of prejudice which sociologists and psychologists have emphasized. In the case of the oldest prejudice in Western civilization, antisemitism, historians, at least until very recently, have usually written off the wilder aberrations as examples of superstition and general human folly.

In fact, the study of group conflict, of ethnic prejudice, and of antisemitism in particular is relatively recent and owes little to historians. Particularly since the 1930s, a large number of sociological and psychological studies have dramatically increased our understanding of prejudice. But their concern has been with contemporary prejudice, and their historical basis has been very shallow for reasons of both methodology and interest. They have little to say about the historical development of antisemitism, and what they do say is highly unreliable.

A particular aspect of prejudice that has received too little attention from sociologists, psychologists, and historians is the way in which a society can retain the basic beliefs of a prejudice, little affected even by the disappearance of the object of prejudice and of any element of realistic competition that might have been involved. The endurance of antisemitism in England from the fourteenth to the seventeenth century despite the absence of Jews would be a striking case in point, as would the endurance of medieval stereotypes about Jews into the modern period despite drastic changes in the culture both of the majority and the minority. Such maintenance of prejudiced stereotypes is less a function of the sociological and psychological conditions and stresses of a society than it is a function of the society's memory. However such beliefs may have been engendered initially, they have become an accepted part of a society's traditions, and they will tend to endure so long as those responsible for preserving and communicating the society's official conception of the past refuse to criticize or reformulate them. In our society, that is the function of historians and the relevant authorities of the historical religions.

Most of what people know is guaranteed by what might be termed social epistemology, that is, much knowledge is accepted on the basis of social rather than intellectual validation. Social epistemology assesses ideas on the basis of which and how many people have originated or accepted them. At its best, this means no more than the inevitable reliance on respectable authorities, duly warranted by academic titles, by religious position, by governmental support, or, as in the case of science, by certain obviously impressive results. But at its worst, it may mean reliance upon traditional ideas that have long been generally current in the society because it was in no one's interest to criticize them energetically.

What needs to be stressed here is that from the point of view of the generality of the population, social epistemology provides approximately the same warranty for a generally accepted miscomprehension as it does for generally accepted ideas derived from the most reputable investigations, for the ultimate guarantee is the same, trust in the operation of the society that provides its members with their identity and security. For centuries, the majority in Western civilization has believed that Jews have a peculiar innate ability in financial matters, and the wide acceptance of this idea has given it the same authentication as, for example, the popular reception of Newtonian ideas.

That the genesis and perpetuation of this idea about Jews is related to prejudice cannot be denied, but the point to be noted is that, once the idea had been originated, had been given a measure of reality by social arrangements, and had attained general acceptance, its acceptance thereafter by any particular individual could be independent of most of the mechanisms of prejudice described by the sociologists and psychologists. Lacking direct evidence and unable to examine the foundations of all the vast knowledge handed to him or her by the society, the average individual could accept this idea, along with other elements of the cognitive map provided by the society, without reflection and without any strong personal motives. What would be surprising would be not the acceptance of this element in an individual's mental horizon but its rejection in the face of an overwhelming social consensus.

Thinking in terms of simple, naive, but firmly held generalizations about little-known people, things, and events is very normal, as all studies of categorization suggest; what is rare is the conscious acknowledgment of ignorance and the suspension of judgment about little-known matters. The desire of the individual for certainty combines with the need for social consensus to fill mental horizons and conceal the immense variation in validity of the ideas by which people live. People who would not act in the area of their own competence without adequate investigation and critical examination act and react in other areas of life with almost equal assurance on a minimum of information and critical reflection. The confidence which personal expertise cannot provide is here supplied by trust in the ideas and convictions of the group to which a person belongs. And since the areas in which people are competent are highly specialized and heterogeneous, the ideas they share, which bind them as a group, are likely to be those on which they are least capable of reaching an independent judgment and which they are most likely to accept on the basis of social authority, both good and bad, which brings us back to tradition and historical education.

The way in which Jews have been discussed in histories of the majority in Western civilization is a classic example of both the ethnocentrism and the reliance on social epistemology that I have been discussing.[1] The great development of scholarship on postbiblical Jews since Graetz has had little influence on majority scholarship; traditional perspectives on Jews still dominate the selection and presentation of information on that subject. If majority historiography has become decreasingly national and increasingly comparative and objective, it has maintained a broader ethnocentrism based on the majority culture of modern European civilization and its offshoots. After Christ, Jews figure as aliens who are not part of *the* people whose development is being recounted.

Let us now turn to the other side of the coin. Very understandably, since the history of postbiblical Jews has been written primarily by Jews for a Jewish audience and against a background of antisemitism, ethnocentrism has marked historiography on the Jews even more than majority historiography. As Albert Lewkowitz noted, the *Wissenschaft des Judentums* and the Breslau Seminary sought to offset the tendency to assimilation and dissolution after the Emancipation: "It was the idea of Krochmal, Zunz, Frankel and Graetz to conceive of the individuality of the Jewish people in its historical development. With this ideal in mind they tried to find a way towards a Jewish future."[2]

On the centenary of the appearance of the first volume of Graetz,

Moritz Güdemann asked rhetorically what the Jews owed to Graetz. "The answer is simply: Graetz restored to the Jews their lost consciousness."[3] Or as Solomon Grayzel put it, "Graetz, in addition to writing a history book, had thus written a justification of Jewish life and, in a sense, given a pledge of Jewish continuity."[4] However great Graetz's contribution to historical knowledge, his ethnocentrism is obvious, and it has long been known that it extended to biased stereotypy of the majority. And although his depiction of the continuity of Jewish life, scholarship, and suffering would be criticized by Dubnow, it was to remain the dominant influence on Jewish historiography through the first quarter of the twentieth century, if not longer.[5]

In 1928, Cecil Roth mounted an attack upon the school of historiography that had developed around the Breslau Seminary, an attack whose virulence testified to the hegemony of the school attacked:

> Jewish history is written and taught today by persons whose education may qualify them to deal with rabbinical texts, but who have not mastered even the elements of the historian's craft. In some cases the least inkling of modern historical method or of the treatment of historical material is absent. Without special study, they know nothing of the background of the events about which they presume to write. In teaching, they give the impression that Jewish history took place in a vacuum, because they are ignorant of the very atmosphere of the external world in which it was enacted.[6]

Yet it should be noted that the title of Roth's article was "Jewish History for Our Own Needs." Roth sought to raise the standards of Jewish historiography but not change its underlying purpose.

In 1928 also, Salo W. Baron attacked "the lachrymose theory" of Jewish history up to the French Revolution and called for greater attention to the history of the majority.[7] Yet in 1939, while again criticizing the lachrymose theory, he drew attention to the difficulty of "indoctrinating Jewish youth in a convincing, because uniform, view of the Jewish past" until a new philosophy of Jewish history and some new comprehensive explanation of Jewish history had been developed.[8] Again in 1951 he affirmed that the lachrymose conception of Jewish history was not "of service to our generation."[9] A Social and Religious History of the Jews, with its more sociological approach and greater emphasis on the surrounding environment, was his reaction to the need that he perceived.

In the second edition in 1952, he regretted that no comprehensive studies of "the philosophy of Jewish history" had appeared since the first edition in 1937 and stated his own position that "the unity of Jews and Judaism thus has a deep meaning, and the interrelation between the two, the interplay of social and religious forces throughout the entire course of Jewish history, appears to be of controlling significance."[10]

It is perhaps not surprising that, despite Baron's effort to transcend the old interpretation which he and Roth had criticized, Irving A. Agus criticized his great achievement on the ground that it gave a false impression by its overemphasis on the unity of Jewish history, and that it frequently reverted to a nineteenth-century conception of the actions of the majority and their influence on Jews.[11] Perhaps such emphases are inevitable in something as nineteenth-century as a history of *the* people—covering millennia.

In 1963, Baron expressed his gratification at the extent to which scholars had come to recognize the dependence of Jewish history on external developments, which he considered a gain for historiography in general: "An incidental gain of this new approach will be the light which the specific Jewish evolution is able to shed on general history as well, if viewed not from the traditional angle of the majority peoples, but rather from the vantage point of a permanent minority."[12] That gain, however, was incidental; the major advantage was that the newer history was more suited to the needs of the present generation of Jews. The ideal of pure historical research from a cosmopolitan perspective is recognized, but it is still seen as a history of peoples rather than a study of problems, and the primary task of the historian of Jews is still seen as service to the present generation of Jews.

By the mid-twentieth century, Jewish historiography had acknowledged the methodology and the ideal of objectivity which majority historiography had at least avowed a century earlier.[13] But just as acceptance of that ideal did not by any means signify the end of ethnocentrism and prejudice in majority historiography, so it will be some time before Jewish historiography ceases to be history written in the interests of a particular community and becomes history written simply for the sake of historical knowledge. And that will be particularly true in the case of broad surveys of Jewish history and the teaching of Jewish history.

Two factors, one immediate and one more essential, make objectivity unusually difficult in Jewish history. In the first place, the Hitlerian horrors interrupted the change in historiographic orientation announced in 1928 and made history written without loyalty to the

Jewish community seem cowardice and treason. Hence, while as a historian one is shocked by the following statement by Yitzhak Baer, as a human one can only be sympathetic:

> Jewish history, from its earliest beginnings to our own day, constitutes an organic unity. Each successive stage in its development reveals more fully the nature of the unique force guiding it, a force whose initial vitality is universally recognized and whose future course arouses wide interest. Let this observation be the key to our study.[14]

Grayzel, writing during the disaster, stated his desire to be objective but recognized that his objectivity was conditioned by his belief in Judaism and his faith in the Jewish people, and he acknowledged that his historical work had the same purpose as tradition: "One of my reasons for writing *A History of the Jews* has been my desire to fortify the spirit and strengthen the determination of my fellow Jews to persevere in the paths of our ancestors, and patiently and hopefully to labor for the welfare of mankind."[15]

In 1952, Baron sounded a similar note: "The preponderant instinct among the majority [of Jews], in any case, still perceptibly tells them that the Jewish religion, buttressed by Jewish nationality, supernationally rooted in the Jewish religion, will weather the forthcoming storms too, and that together they will continue their historic march into the unfathomable future."[16]

Cecil Roth has sounded the same note much more strongly in a passage that deserves quotation as the most explicit example of these dangers to historical objectivity.

> Today, the Jewish people has in it still those elements of strength and of endurance which enabled it to surmount all the crises of its past, surviving thus the most powerful empires of antiquity. Throughout our history there have been weaker elements who have shirked the sacrifices which Judaism entailed. They have been swallowed up, long since, in the great majority; only the more stalwart have carried on the tradition of their ancestors, and can now look back with pride upon their superb heritage. Are we to be numbered with the weak majority, or with the stalwart minority? It is for ourselves to decide. But from a reading of Jewish history, one factor emerges which may perhaps help us in our decision. The preservation of the Jew was certainly not casual. He has endured through the power of a certain ideal, based upon the recognition of the influence of a higher power in human affairs. Time after time in his history, moreover, he has been saved from disaster in a manner which cannot be described excepting as "providential." The author has deliberately attempted to write this work in a secular spirit; he does not think that his readers can fail to see in it, on every page, a higher immanence.[17]

The implication that Jewish history can be properly understood only from a particular religious perspective brings us to the more basic factor that has made objectivity, as historians use that term, difficult in Jewish historiography. Since Judaism has always been the most essential distinguishing element in Jewish identity, there is an enduring tendency to confuse theological history, the history of a religion, Judaism, and the purely historical investigation of all the activities of those who have been associated with Judaism. The confusion of these three different kinds of inquiry has been aggravated by the extent to which Jewish history has been written by the rabbinate, but it has been aided by the religious commitment of many other Jewish historians.

It is difficult enough for any scholar to surmount the biases of his society with its traditions, but it is much more difficult to maintain a religious commitment and to write the history of that religion and its adherents without implying that they possessed a superiority which cannot be evaluated by normal historical techniques yet which accounts for the basic structure of their history. My objection is not to any of these three kinds of inquiry when pursued separately, but to the ethnocentrism that appears when the three are confused.

In *The Meaning of Jewish History*, Jacob B. Agus claims that his "is not a metaphysical or meta-historical undertaking, but a purely analytic and empirical task."[18] Yet the title itself contradicts his claim, and Toynbee comes irresistibly to mind as selected events of Jewish history are arranged around the central theme of oscillations in the interpretations of Judaism. Even were we to understand "Jewish history" as meaning "the history of Judaism," the problem would remain. It comes as no surprise when the work ends not only with an appeal that religious subjectivism and ritualism may not be permitted to submerge the vision of a worldwide fellowship but also with an appeal for loyalty to the common tradition that will preserve the family of Jewish communities.[19] The empiricism claimed turns out to be a tool subservient to a particular tradition and to the desire to preserve a particular community. Normal history will not yield as much. Historical analysis can indeed render meaningful—or more comprehensible—many sections or aspects of Jewish history, but historical techniques by themselves cannot uncover one overall meaning.

Only some transcendent belief can order the almost infinite events of the millennia of Jewish history into a single controlling pattern, a pattern that is persuasive only for believers. A significant distinction that denotes what is to be discussed (those people who have believed in or been associated with Judaism through its historical changes) is transmuted into the most important factor in all aspects of the lives of these people. What distinguishes Jews, whether devout or nominal, from other people is assumed from the outset always to have been more important than any other factors, and more important than anything that Jews may have shared with other people. Instead of the meaning of Jewish history, we are confronted with the meaning of Judaism, which is not quite the same thing.

This strong ethnocentrism, enhanced by external pressure and frequently combined with a religious sense of uniqueness, can easily lead to the appearance of prejudice in historical work. That in many histories of the Jews the majority is discussed primarily as it impinges unfavorably on the Jews is understandable, if as regrettable as the parallel treatment of Jews in majority historiography. But there is frequently something stronger. The elements of stereotypy in Graetz, which influenced many of his followers, are now recognized and might be written off as comprehensible results of the youth of modern Jewish historiography and its context. But what are we to make of Roth's references to the "weak majority" in 1954? And how shall we interpret the following statement by Howard M. Sachar in 1958? "Certainly if the Church had had its way, the 'infidels' would not have been permitted to 'contaminate' Christian communities. In fact, the Catholic hierarchy, and later the Protestant clergy, continually besought the sovereigns of Europe to exile their Jewish populations altogether."[20] A reader might have difficulty perceiving that, as Grayzel had pointed out in 1933, papal protection was largely responsible for the survival of Jews in medieval Europe.[21] As Agus put it more recently, "The 'final solution of the Jewish problem,' to use a Nazi phrase, was disfavored by the Church. This is the basic reason for Jewish survival in Christian Europe."[22] In the case of Protestantism, it is evident in Dutch and English history that Calvinism brought with it a revived interest in Judaism and frequently a somewhat more tolerant attitude toward Jews.

Yet even Agus, who stresses the dependence of a dynamic Judaism upon its European context and can say some kind words about crusaders, falls into a sweeping and derogatory picture of the majority when he gives a capsule categorization of the Middle Ages: "Throughout that cruel era, when private wars were virtually a way of life and religious fanaticism fixed the coordinates of all thought and feeling, the Jews did not sink to the lowest levels of society."[23] So much for a period that produced Anselm, Abelard, Bernard, Francis of Assisi, Romanesque and Gothic architecture, the universities of Bologna and Paris, and the economic and political structures that were the base for the phenomenal expansion of Europe in the modern period. The explanation of this depiction of "the dark night of the Medieval era," as Agus also terms it, would not be far to seek. The counterpart to the majority stereotype of the medieval Jew as unbelieving usurer is the minority stereotype of the medieval gentile as a violent Christian fanatic. Since Agus is eminently fair-minded, such stereotypic thought comes not from personal bias but from the bias enshrined in Jewish tradition and historiography.[24] Graetz would have found the outlook familiar.

The main point that emerges from an examination of the way that Jews and the majority are treated in majority and Jewish historiography is that the more historical scholarship appeals to a particular group and fulfills the function of tradition or is dominated by a particular religious vision, the more it tends to ethnocentrism and prejudice. In discussions of general historical methodology, the point is a truism; what is not so clearly recognized is the extent of the bias on both sides in this particular instance. The prevalence and the depth of the bias should not be exaggerated. It rarely appears in works written by historians for historians. But if we view the role of historical writing not from the viewpoint of the scholar but from that of its broadest audience, then the influence of tradition and the intrusion of prejudice become more apparent. In historical writing and education for some general public, the viewpoint and needs of the audience all too often influence the presentation, which becomes ethnocentrically selective and implicitly or explicitly relies on traditional lore and values. Such presentation is relatively immune from criticism because the audience to which it is directed and which alone pays serious attention to it is predisposed, not to criticism, but to belief.

What is needed is a clearer distinction between history as a branch of knowledge and the selective use of historical knowledge to further the interests, identity, or religion of a particular group. The analysis of whatever in the past is relevant to explain the present characteristics of a given group is a legitimate historical activity. The history of a religion, the study of the interaction through time of a creed and its adherents, is a legitimate historical activity. But the arrangement of the past actions of a group in accordance with a particular religious belief, however legitimate as a branch of theology, is not history proper. And the selection of some but not all of the past actions of a group in order to strengthen the identity and pride of the present group or to mold its future action in specific ways, although it may be "history for *our* needs," is certainly not history proper. I should be the last to say that people should not use history as an aid in solving present problems or as part of the material from which they derive the values and meaning of their lives. And I would agree that these factors influence to some extent even the historian who is trying to do no more than to solve strictly historical problems. But as a historian, I would oppose purportedly historical work that consciously pursues these aims.

History that is written on the basis of the beliefs and needs of a particular group tends to emphasize groups more than individuals and falls easily into that stereotypy of groups that readily leads to prejudice. Not only does it emphasize the characteristics that individual members share at any one time at the expense of their variations, but it all too readily assumes the constancy of the group identity through time at the expense of change and discontinuity. Yet it is clear that medieval English people resembled medieval French people far more than they resembled present English people, and it is clear that present Jews in America resemble other Americans far more than they resemble Jews of the first century of the Common Era. Perhaps the most extreme example of a purportedly historical statement that embodies these faults is the statement that the Jews are responsible for the death of Christ.

Part 2
Anti-Judaism

3.

Anti-Judaism as the Necessary Preparation for Antisemitism

Anti-Judaism I take to be a total or partial opposition to Judaism—and to Jews as adherents of it—by people who accept a competing system of beliefs and practices and consider certain genuine Judaic beliefs and practices as inferior. Anti-Judaism, therefore, can be pagan, Christian, Communist, or what you will, but its specific character will depend on the character of the competing system. Voltaire's anti-Judaism differed from that of Augustine, as Augustine's differed from that of Tacitus. Of all forms of anti-Judaism, the Christian has been the most intense because of the intimate dependence of Christianity on Judaism.

Classical pagan anti-Judaism was neither universal nor homogeneous. Throughout the Roman Empire there was considerable objection to Jewish exclusiveness and peculiar customs, as these were imperfectly understood. In addition, in the east there was intense hostility provoked by violent military, political, and economic intergroup competition. None of this, however, led Romans to attempt to suppress Judaism or degrade the social status of Jews. For, since paganism shared few fundamental premises with Judaism, it did not recognize Judaism as a vital challenge but saw it rather as an alien alternative that attracted proselytes from the lower orders. Precisely because the character of pagan anti-Judaism depended on the character of classical polytheistic culture, it could not be transmitted to Christianity to any serious degree.[1]

Christianity, by contrast, grew out of Judaism amidst a conflict with non-Christian Jews, and that birth trauma was enshrined in Christian

revelation and central to Christian theology. The Christian acceptance
of Jewish scripture and the Christian claim to be the true Israel meant
that, for Christians, Jews were a central element of God's providential
plan. Moreover the continued existence of Judaism after Jesus was the
physical embodiment of doubt about the validity of Christianity. Unlike pagan anti-Judaism, Christian anti-Judaism was a central and essential element of the Christian system of beliefs. The elaboration of
anti-Judaic doctrine and polemics and the effort to prove that Christianity was foreshadowed in the Old Testament would be a major
theological enterprise for centuries.[2]

Christian anti-Judaism can be separated into three aspects: the doctrinal, the legal, and the popular. Doctrinal anti-Judaism attempted to
prove that Christians were the true Israel and that most adherents of
Judaism before Jesus and all of its adherents thereafter were at the least
inferior to Christians and, at the strongest, the polar enemies of Christianity. I need not rehearse the basic elements of the doctrine about the
willful rebels who disobeyed God, killed Christ, persecuted his followers, and obdurately persisted in their blindness, thereby serving as witnesses to the truth of Christian scripture and to the punishment imposed on Jews by God. Nor need I comment on the strongly defensive
tone that marks the initial elaboration of the doctrine, even in
Chrysostom.[3]

The legal aspect of anti-Judaism was the effort of Christians to
order society legally according to the implications of the doctrine, to
reinforce argument by physical sanctions. Foreshadowed within the
pre-Constantinian Christian communities, that aspect only became
prominent when Christians were able to influence or control secular
authority. From the time of Constantine, and particularly from that of
Theodosius I, ecclesiastical influence was successfully exerted to obtain
legislation that would inhibit contact between Jews and Christians,
diminish Jewish social status, and, in the extreme policy of Ambrose
and some other ecclesiastics, extirpate Judaism. Legal anti-Judaism had
little impact in the early Middle Ages, but one of its principles exerted
gradual pressure even though there was little feeling against Jews.[4]

A central proposition of legal anti-Judaism from the earliest days
had been that no Jew should be in a position to exercise control over
Christians, whether through public office, the institution of slavery, or
otherwise. Motivated by the desire to prevent Jewish proselytism and
manifest God's alleged punishment of Jews, it also provided a useful

justification for self-interested Christians who desired to monopolize social and economic advantages and to deprive Jews of the advantages they possessed. The prohibition of Jewish possession of Christian slaves on that basis made Jewish involvement in large-scale agriculture difficult. The same principle made exclusion of Jews from the feudal network almost axiomatic, and, by the twelfth century, it was serving to exclude Jews from membership in merchant guilds and other activities in the developing towns.[5]

Yet the legal implications of Christian anti-Judaism could not be fully developed until the bulk of the population identified profoundly with Christianity and accepted its cosmology in such a way as to desire to attack Judaism and degrade Jews. That condition did not obtain in the Christian Roman Empire or the early Middle Ages and was not reached in western Europe, I would argue, until the eleventh century. The failure of Agobard and Amulo's effort to win promulgation of a rigorous legal anti-Judaism in the Carolingian Empire indicates how slowly broad anti-Judaic feeling developed.[6] Only by the eleventh century, after nominally Christian Europe had repulsed the second wave of pagan invasions, does a profound identification with Christianity—as then understood—seem to have developed, and Europe to have cloaked itself in a new mantle of white churches and set a broad movement of religious reform in motion.[7] And only in the eleventh century is there indisputable evidence of broad, popular anti-Judaism.

At this point it becomes essential to distinguish northern from Mediterranean Europe and popular from legal anti-Judaism. Up to the eleventh century, the effort to implement anti-Judaism had been primarily episcopal and Mediterranean. But in the eleventh century, intense popular anti-Judaism emerged, and it appeared only in northern Europe and was not officially incited. Although Christianity was longer and more deeply rooted in Mediterranean Europe, and although the Jewish population was densest there, there was little violent popular anti-Judaism, possibly because a significant and diversified Jewish population had existed there as long as Christianity, the sense of Christian identity had developed more gradually, and the disruption of social institutions had been less, particularly of urban centers. In the north, however, major social institutions were in the formative stage, the revival of commerce was stimulating the reappearance of town life, Christianity was more recent, identification with it was more abrupt, and the less diversified and in many cases very recent Jewish population was a very small—and strange—minority. Moreover the sudden intensification of Christian consciousness here was paralleled by the great development of Jewish consciousness from Gershom to Rashi.

Whatever the reasons, the massacres of 1096 were almost entirely limited to the north, were perpetrated by lower levels of the population, and were overwhelmingly anti-Judaic.[8] Jews were killed because they continued to adhere to Judaism and rejected Christianity. Indoctrination in Christianity and its attendant anti-Judaism had here proved more explosive than its propagators had intended. And after 1096 and through most of the twelfth century, most ecclesiastical and secular authorities were more concerned to check than to develop popular anti-Judaic feeling. Papal bulls of protection, while reiterating basic anti-Judaic doctrine, reemphasized the obligation to protect Jews and Judaism; and secular authorities on the same basis took further measures to protect—and also to control—Jews.[9] Yet all these efforts were explicitly based on official anti-Judaic doctrine; they increased awareness of it and brought a further implementation of legal anti-Judaism.

In the twelfth century, the pressure of popular anti-Judaism, the implementation of legal anti-Judaism, and anti-Judaism's long appeal to Christian self-interest combined to set in motion the process known as the self-fulfilling prophecy whereby a group already assumed to be inferior is forced by the majority to engage in conduct that seems further confirmation of the minority's inferiority.[10] By the middle of the twelfth century in northern Europe, Jews were becoming stereotyped as usurers in addition to the older stereotype of Christ-killers.[11] The gradual exclusion of Jews from many social roles and the dangers of participation in long-distance commerce because of violent popular anti-Judaism drastically reduced the choices available to literate people who had heretofore enjoyed most of the privileges of freemen. And the need for credit in a rapidly expanding economy, the self-interested support by secular authorities of Jewish moneylending which made that occupation temporarily profitable, and the desire of the minority to come together behind the relative safety of town walls, all encouraged a disproportionate participation of Jews in the single social role of providers of the lesser and more unpopular kind of credit.[12]

That concentration was not intended by those who had propagated anti-Judaism any more than it was dictated by Judaism, and by the beginning of the thirteenth century the Catholic church was trying to reverse the undesired development. Nonetheless, it was the pressure of anti-Judaism which had restricted Jews to a specific and degrading role. That Jews were forced into a role that the church officially desired to eliminate was due to the specific character of medieval society, not to ecclesiastical intention, but the general principle that Jews should occupy a degraded social position had long been inherent in Christian anti-Judaism.

By the beginning of the thirteenth century, because of these developments, Jews were no longer simply dispersed adherents of an inferior religion but had been assigned a definite, collective, religious, legal, and social status in the organization of medieval society. They had become an institutionalized inferior minority, symbolized ecclesiastically by the distinctive clothing commanded by the Fourth Lateran Council, secularly by their unique legal status as Jews, and socially by their prominence in moneylending. And now, as a defenseless and institutionalized minority, Jews in northern Europe could also be manipulated by the majority not only physically but also mentally. The way was open for the development of a false irrational conception of the Jew.

Norwich, Pontoise, Blois, Fulda, Lincoln, Oberwesel, Röttingen, Chinon, the Armleder, the Black Death, Trent—the sequence symbolizes the appearance and development, chronological and geographical, of a new and deadly kind of persecution of Jews, and one very different from that in ancient Alexandria or in 1096. Whereas the old accusations that Jews were responsible for the death of Christ (as they acknowledged), that they obdurately rejected Christianity, and that they were peculiarly involved in moneylending had been faulty overgeneralizations reflecting a central core of truth, the new accusations of ritual murder, host desecration, and well-poisoning were not faulty and inflexible generalizations but false fantasies unsupported by evidence. In addition to anti-Judaism, antisemitism now appears, developing slowly until 1300 and then intensifying rapidly, starting in the north and only gradually spreading to the south of Europe.[13] It starts where the Jewish population was smallest and most defenseless, and where the pressure of majority anti-Judaism—doctrinal, legal, and popular—had most restricted diversity within the minority.

In the north by about 1200, Jews had become an ideal focus for all those individuals whose personal need to displace and project guilt and hatred sought a socially acceptable outlet.[14] There was a wide audience predisposed to accept accusations against a little-known group whose evil deviance had been so institutionally defined. There were self-interested individuals who sought calculated profit from purveying the rumors. And Jews no longer had the power to act as they wished, to demonstrate the falsity of stereotypes about their character and potential, or to disprove the irrational accusations against them.

These projections of ritual murder, host desecration, and well-poisoning inevitably assumed a religious coloration, but in fact they owed more to tensions within the majority society and the psychological problems of individuals than to the real conflict between Christianity and Judaism. They were not a necessary or predictable result of anti-Judaism as a body of ideas but rather a social and psychological reaction to the institutionalization of the inferior minority in a rapidly developing society whose stresses increased dramatically at the end of the thirteenth century.

Henceforth and for centuries, however, anti-Judaism and antisemitism would coexist and be mutually reinforcing. And antisemitism could persist even when social norms were non-Christian or anti-Christian, for antisemitism was neither a logical extension nor a simple vulgarization of Christian anti-Judaic doctrine[15] but an expression, made possible by the oppression of a minority, of darker and less ideational needs. To the extent that Christian anti-Judaism was responsible for making Jews an oppressed minority, it helped to create beliefs and attitudes that Christianity could not contain. They contaminated Christianity itself and were only generally condemned as unchristian in the second half of the twentieth century. A problem that yet remains to be solved is how Christians can remain Christians and avoid anti-Judaism.[16]

4.
The Transformation of Anti-Judaism

I

A generation has passed since the killing of over five million Jews in a campaign of genocide that received much tacit support from those not directly involved. Yet only very recently have non-Jewish historians begun to face the fundamental questions those killings raised. How recently attitudes have changed, and how reluctantly, can be seen from histories of the crusades published after 1945. In 1951, Runciman provided the following explanation of the first great massacre of European Jews in 1096:

> Their unpopularity grew throughout the eleventh century, as more classes of the community began to borrow money from them; and the beginnings of the crusading movement added to it. It was expensive for a knight to equip himself for a Crusade; if he had no land and no possessions to pledge, he must borrow money from the Jews. But was it right that in order to go and fight for Christendom he must fall into the clutches of members of the race that crucified Christ?[1]

The anachronism of referring to Jews as a race and depicting them as extensively engaged in moneylending in the eleventh century now needs little comment, and Runciman's intent to exculpate the killers and Christianity is obvious. A similar, erroneous, pejorative, and tendentiously exculpating explanation was given in 1955 by Duncalf in the other major recent history of the crusades.[2]

Exculpation of Christianity has also been achieved, without attacking Jews, by explaining that the popular crusaders who committed the massacres were moved to massacre Jews, not by their Christianity, but by their violent greed. That solution had already been put forward by Grousset in 1934.

> The antisemitic popular attacks in the valley of the Rhine, directed against the episcopal authorities by the populace of the region, were—under the pretext of the crusade—a simple *jacquerie* movement with which the knight-brigands of the region, the sworn enemies of ecclesiastical power, were only too happy to associate themselves.[3]

And in 1965, Meyer used the same explanation.

> As in the persecutions of the later Middle Ages, the argument that the Jews, as enemies of Christ, deserved to be punished was merely a feeble attempt to conceal the real motive: greed.[4]

The only explanation of the massacres of 1096 by historians of the majority that implicates Christianity is the one put forward by Alphandery about 1930 and published posthumously in 1954, that the popular crusaders were moved to massacre Jews by eschatological prophecies about the coming of Antichrist, the return of Charlemagne, and the millennium. This view was enthusiastically espoused by Cohn in 1957 and in 1969 by Prawer, who emphasized the Judaic roots of such apocalyptic ideas; but the extent of the influence of millennial ideas has been questioned since.[5] In any case, this view does not implicate central Christian beliefs and places responsibility partly on secular legends.

The accounts of the massacres of 1096 in most histories of the crusades have been brief, one-sided, and often based on false assumptions, yet that is almost the only place in which the understanding of non-Jewish historians can be found, for their tactic when discussing other subjects has been almost complete silence, as if the massacres were unrelated to any other significant medieval developments. But if we turn to historians of the Jews, how different the massacres look. For them, the massacres of 1096 were a decisive turning point in Jewish history, in Christian-Jewish relations, and in the history of antisemitism.[6]

As early as 1908, Caro had pointed out that the Jews who were massacred were not new in the area, did not differ in occupation from other town dwellers, and were not accused of economic misconduct; "the opposition that divided the inhabitants of the towns was not economic in character but religious."[7] But historians of the majority did not pick up the clue, and it was left to historians of Jews from Graetz to the present to insist, in Baron's words, that "in substance, the Crusades generally and their anti-Jewish aspects specifically can be understood only against the background of the extraordinary religious enthusiasm generated by revivalist preachers."[8] Yet if historians of the Jews have been predisposed to assert that the character of European religiosity, not Jewish conduct or Christian greed, was the root cause of the massacres, they have been reluctant, for many reasons, to probe too deeply into the character of that religiosity.

The patent disagreement between historians of the majority and historians of the Jews cries out for resolution. Were the religious beliefs of some Christians directly responsible for the attacks on Jews or were those beliefs merely used to conceal other, secular motives? On the one hand, it can be argued that those who committed the first great massacre of Jews in Europe in 1096 were not acting from religious motives because the fundamental Catholic theology about the significance of Jews after Christ had been established by the late fourth century, had not caused massacres of Jews, and had changed little by the end of the eleventh century. On the other hand, it can be argued that hostility against Jews did vary greatly from 400 to 1100, and that hostility against Jews as a group was expressed almost exclusively in religious terms throughout the period. Hence the increase in hostility by the eleventh century, especially in northern Europe, must have been a result of the gradual Christianization of Europe.

Was Christianity responsible for the massacres of 1096, and if so, how? The subject is sensitive. Fortunately, changed relations between Jews and non-Jews since Auschwitz have facilitated more objective analyses. In the following interpretation, I shall use some rather cumbersome sociological categories of analysis in an effort to augment neutrality and to focus attention on how Christians conceived of their society and hence of the position of Jews in it.

II

By a religion I mean what people are commanded to believe by those exercising social authority; and by religiosity I mean what individuals do in fact believe about themselves and their universe—which can vary greatly and may or may not be in harmony with what they have been told to believe.[9] Both religions and religiosities depend on people's conviction that there are contacts between their empirically known existence and the supra-empirical reality in which they believe, contacts through which they can gain understanding of how the two are related (rituals, miracles, the elders of a tribe, prophets, priests, kings, psychological states). That belief in particular modes of communion or contact connects people's knowledge of empirical reality with their understanding of supra-empirical reality and makes them interdependent. Religions and religiosities are, therefore, inescapably molded by the social experiences that shape the believers' mentality and their understanding of their identity. Hence, both religions and religiosities have a social dimension that reflects people's trust in—or distrust of—prevailing social relations. Since the adherents of a religion believe that those who prescribe their beliefs—whether the elders of a tribe, a king, or a priesthood that is differentiated from the normal government of the society—have a privileged contact with the gods or god, their religiosity supports the authority of those leaders. Religions and religiosities can therefore be distinguished by the social authorities they acknowledge or deny.

A religion and the religiosity of its adherents may sacralize a tribe, a biologically connected ethnic group, as in ancient Israel. When it does, we may speak of the religion and religiosity of a people. Or, if the ties of such a society become seriously weakened, we may speak of a religion and religiosity that is only closely supportive of a people, supportive of the ideal rather than a reality, as was the case for Judaism in the Roman period, when Jews were widely dispersed and many gentiles were converts or partial converts to Judaism. But the religiosity of some individuals may reject existing religions and tend toward universality if those who share that outlook defy existing social authorities and admit people who share their beliefs from any society, as was initially the case for Paul of Tarsus and his followers. And, as was the case with the formation of Christian churches in the first two centuries, people with such religiosity may create new religions, new religious societies with their own authorities, which differentiate themselves sharply from the larger society in which they live and may oppose the authorities of the larger society.

But if such a religion then becomes officially accepted by the rulers of a complex, role-differentiated society, as was the case for the Catholic church by the fourth century, then the religiosity of its adherents may support both the social authority of the priesthood and the social authority of the political rulers of the society. Thus, by the fourth century, Christians in ever-increasing numbers were integrating their beliefs about Christ and their beliefs about the Roman Empire, some of them believing that the adherence of citizens to Christianity would unite and strengthen the empire.[10] Their religiosity was supportive of the differentiated authorities of a complex, ethnically diverse society, not the elders or priests of a people or tribe. The difference is that indicated by Ferdinand Tönnies's distinction between a *Gesellschaft* and a *Gemeinschaft* or Max Weber's distinction between rational-legal and traditional authority.

When a religion is made official in such a role-differentiated society, there are now two different social authorities claiming supremacy, the priesthood and the government, and tension can arise in the religiosity of its members. On particular issues, the religiosity of individuals may now support either the secular elite or the priesthood as the ultimate authority in society and the best contact with supra-empirical reality. Yet so long as there is a relatively stable equilibrium between the two social authorities, each will support the other against any dissidents who threaten the social order. Even when the balance is changing and open conflict breaks out, as in the Investiture Contest, neither side will seek the elimination of the other, only its subordination, for both are concerned with the preservation of social authority.

The success of a religion in a differentiated society, its syncretic adaptation to the surrounding culture and acceptance by the government, can also breed another type of religiosity, a religiosity of withdrawal from the larger society in reaction to what is seen as a dilution of the original religious ideals. With the spread of Christianity in the Roman Empire, a new form of Christian religiosity appeared, the religiosity of withdrawal of the desert fathers and monks. Important in the late Roman world, it became so dominant after the fall of Rome that we often speak of the subsequent centuries in western Europe as the Benedictine Age. Yet the dominant religiosity of that age was in fact very different; it was a Christian religiosity supportive, often closely supportive, of peoples, for example, the Franks.

Religions and religiosity are thus influenced by their social context, and can be differentiated accordingly, and Christian religions and the religiosity of Christians has consequently varied greatly. Religions and religiosities also vary in another way. In common parlance, distinctions are drawn between otherworldly and worldly, spiritualistic and materialistic, or pure and corrupt religions, and sociologists have distinguished between consummatory and instrumental or between high and practical religions.[11] To avoid the evaluative connotations of many of those terms, I shall refer to this distinction as that between supra-empirical and empirical religions and religiosity.

By supra-empirical religiosity I mean the attitude that proper belief and practice only affect that believer's relations to supra-empirical reality and not his or her empirically verifiable well-being here on earth. And by empirical religiosity I mean the attitude that proper belief and practice bring rewards *both* in the supra-empirical realm *and* in the empirical realm, for example, success in battle, wealth, health, or the simpler satisfaction of belonging to a mutually supportive community. Most religiosity falls somewhere in between these extremes, and once again it is obvious that Christian religiosity has differed widely along the spectrum.

I will now use these categories and distinctions to analyze the historical changes in Christian religiosity from the fourth to the eleventh century to see whether changes that were independent of the existence of Jews were correlated with marked changes in attitudes toward Jews.

III

When Archbishop Egilbert of Trier tried to protect the Jews of his city from forced baptism or massacre at the end of May in 1096, he could not know that Karl Marx would be born in his city in 1818 and voluntarily baptized at age seven. Almost equally certainly, he did not connect his problem with events that had occurred earlier in Augusta Treverorum, the northwestern capital of the late Roman Empire. Here it was that Athanasius of Alexandria was exiled from 335 to 337 and that Ambrosius Aurelianus, future bishop of Milan, was born to an aristocratic Roman family between 334 and 340. It was here that the emperor Gratian resided and that he received, for his instruction in the Nicaean faith, the treatise he had requested from Ambrose, bishop of Milan since 374, although it was in Milan that Gratian published his famous edict of 383 which disestablished paganism. It was at Trier also that Priscillian was executed in 385 by the fiercely Nicaean usurper, Magnus Maximus, who then descended on Italy in 387 and angered Christians by forcing them to rebuild the synagogue they had destroyed in Rome. And it was from Trier also that Ponticianus came to Milan in 386 to spark the decisive conversion of Augustine.

Theodosius I's edict against apostates from Christianity and his prohibition of pagan worship in 392 cannot be linked with Trier save through the influence of the bishop who had been born there, but these remarks may serve as a reminder that the legal victory of Nicaean Christianity over paganism and Arianism was a symptom of the profound changes that had been taking place not only in imperial government but also in Christianity. After the institutional development of the priesthood, and especially since the conversion of Constantine, the universal religiosity of early Christians had been displaced by the great increase in religiosity supportive of social authority. And it in turn had generated the reactive religiosity of withdrawal that sought to avoid what was felt as contamination by separating from normal procreative society.

Not surprisingly, the tensions between these three types of prevailing religiosity was a psychological problem for individuals as well as a sociological phenomenon. Some Christians who were sensitive to all three types were unable to choose between them. Instead they compartmentalized their minds and activities so that different stimuli evoked different dimensions of religiosity at different times. They would withdraw into contemplation to refresh their sense of the universality of their Christianity, and then, thus reinvigorated, they would go out, respond to the challenges of the world, and strenuously exercise their authority as holy men in the surrounding society. As a result of that mental compartmentalization, they were able to think thoughts in one sphere that were almost unthinkable in the other and that seem mutually contradictory. Hence the problem of reaching an unequivocal judgment about personalities such as Gregory VII or Bernard of Clairvaux, and hence the contrasting appeal of Francis of Assisi.

Other examples of that tension are not hard to find. It is fascinating in the holy men of Syria who enhanced their charisma by dramatic renunciation of social bonds and then exercised the authority so gained to resolve disputes in the surrounding society[12] or, less admirably, in the Egyptian monks who withdrew from society only to issue forth to destroy temples and lynch Hypatia. The tension is peculiarly obvious in Augustine, torn between his episcopal responsibilities and the attraction of a monastic life, between his psychological awareness of how he had come to believe and his advocacy of social coercion against those who disagreed with him. That compartmentalization, however, enabled, indeed encouraged, Christian leaders to act in ways that promoted Christian religiosity supportive of social authority and legitimated the use of social authority to promote their Christianity. They used their charismatic authority to pressure secular authorities to act against pagan, Arian, Donatist, and Judaic religiosity; and only the prophet Nathan's rebuke of King David, presumes to admonish Theodosius in Christ's voice.

> I have chosen you, the youngest of your brothers, and from a private person made you emperor. I placed your offspring on the imperial throne. I made barbarian people subject to you. I gave you peace. I delivered your enemy captive in your power. . . . And when there was great danger that the perfidious plans of the barbarians would penetrate the Alps . . . I brought you victory within the very ramparts of the Alps. Thus I gave you a triumph over your enemies, yet you give my enemies a triumph over my people.

Then, when he was preaching in Theodosius's presence, he sought to force the complete revocation of the order. Since this was a sermon,[21] there was no explicit mention of Callinicum; instead, the sermon described the love of Christ who offered his death that men might be forgiven and emphasized the correction of sin by love. A soiled conscience, he declared, defiled Christ's feet, and only the church could cleanse soiled consciences—a cleansing the Jews had refused despite all that God had done for them. Ambrose then repeated his adaptation of Nathan's rebuke and went on to tell the emperor directly to beware of God's censure, to submit to God and love his body, the church, by granting pardon: "because all are needed, guard the whole body of the Lord Jesus, that he also by his heavenly condescension may preserve your kingdom." And not until Theodosius had promised to revoke his order would Ambrose celebrate the Eucharist. He then offered the sacrifice and felt that the grace of the offering was so great that "we were in the presence of God. Thus, all was done as I wished." Ambrose's religiosity was such that it both contemplated God and distributed social authority on earth as if from on high.

For Ambrose, Christianity is universal in that individuals from all peoples and classes may, by true faith, become members of the mystical body of Christ, the church, and be saved by grace. The assurance of true faith is, however, social: membership in the congregation founded by Christ through his apostles, particularly Peter; and that congregation is empirically identifiable by its communion with the Catholic bishops, that is, the Roman church, which alone has truth.[22] But in that community all are not equal. In all religious matters, laymen are to obey the priesthood. All priests are distinguished from the laity by their detachment from secular ties and have their own nobility "which is preferable to that of prefects and consuls."[23] But it is the bishops who have been commissioned by Christ to transmit the faith, asceticism and desire for solitary communion with God.[18] Brown has emphasized the spiritual intensity of his sermons with their repeated insistence, according to Augustine, that "when God is thought of, our thoughts should dwell on no material reality whatsoever." This dimension of Ambrose's religiosity led Brown to declare that Ambrose's "religion was radically other-worldly."[19] Empirically, however, we can only observe that Ambrose related both his contemplation and his worldly action to his Christian beliefs and that he manifested both a religiosity of withdrawal and a religiosity supportive of social authority that was noticeably empirical in character.

As soon as he heard of the emperor's order, Ambrose wrote demanding its revocation.[20] "Which," he asked, "is more important, the formality of discipline or the cause of religion?" If the bishop were ordered to rebuild the synagogue, he would have either to apostasize by rebuilding the place where enemies of God worshiped or to incur the martyrdom of punishment for disobedience. Theodosius should rather charge Ambrose, for "I proclaim that I set the synagogue on fire, or at least ordered others to do so, that there might not be left a building in which Christ is denied." Ambrose says that he would have burned the synagogue at Milan himself had not God already started its destruction. He should have burned it anyway but had not because he had not expected to be punished for it and so obtain the reward of martyrdom. And although Ambrose had opened by admitting that the bishop of Callinicum might have been overimpetuous, he now asks that "no one call the bishop to task for performing his duty." He cites Jeremiah to justify imperial refusal to protect synagogues: "Therefore do not thou pray for this people, nor show mercy for them, and do not approach me for them; for I will not hear thee." Ambrose also invokes the law of nations to argue that since Jews had destroyed churches during the reign of Julian the Apostate and not been punished, Christians should not be punished for similar actions. But Ambrose does not mean by this that the emperor should treat religions neutrally or even-handedly.

The emperor is inescapably engaged in the cosmic struggle between good and evil. Maximus, Ambrose asserts, was overthrown because he ordered Christians to rebuild the synagogue they had burned at Rome. The Christian emperor must take sides in the ongoing war of the church against the Jews: "Will you give the Jews this triumph over God's church, this victory over Christ's people?" The empirical religiosity hinted here becomes fully explicit as Ambrose, echoing the retrospective illusion of history has enabled us to overlook how nearly Judaism came to sharing the fate of paganism, Arianism, and Donatism within the empire.

Jewish legal status had declined since Constantine; theological invective against Judaism reached a peak at the end of the fourth century; and Judaic religiosity was increasingly threatened by physical violence. Throughout the century and into the fifth, there were increasingly frequent attacks on synagogues—in Africa, Spain, Antioch, Rome, Mesopotamia, Alexandria, Syria, and Palestine—which "were usually made with the tacit agreement, even at the instigation, of the local ecclesiastical authorities."[13] Some historians, while acknowledging that a new and distinctively Christian hostility had appeared, have nonetheless argued that the attacks were, to a large extent, the result of the transmission to Christianity through pagan converts of the old pagan hostility against Jews. Thus even Simon speaks of "the animosity of the Greco-Roman world, now Christianized."[14] But this explanation is open to serious objections—for example, that pagans who were hostile to Judaism were likely to be equally hostile to Christianity—and the bulk of the evidence points clearly in the opposite direction, as Simon finally acknowledged.[15]

If Chrysostom's *Homilies* of 386–387 are the most famous of the verbal assaults on Judaic religiosity by churchmen, the destruction of the synagogue at Callinicum in 388 is the most famous physical attack. In itself, the attack in the relatively small locality in Mesopotamia differed little from other incidents of the kind. Incited by their bishop, the local Christian population seized the valuables in the synagogue and burned it down, while local monks also destroyed a chapel of the Gnostic Valentinians. When the incident was reported to Theodosius I, the emperor ordered that the Christians should be punished for breaking the law protecting synagogues, that the valuables seized should be restored, and that the synagogue should be rebuilt at the bishop's expense. What has made the affair famous is Ambrose's intervention to force Theodosius to rescind his order, and the fact that some Christian historians have condemned the intervention.[16] Yet however the action is judged by people with different kinds of Christian religiosity, it was an integral part of Ambrose's religiosity.

As Matthews has recently described him, "Ambrose was the complete politician; and he stood at the centre of a Christian court society of impressive style and accomplishment."[17] Yet in startling contrast with his involvement in society as a man of action was his personal and mere priests may only preach, and that exceptionally, when commissioned by the bishops.[24] They alone are the direct successors of the apostles, and Ambrose "emphasizes in every possible way the dignity and authority of the bishops."[25]

Within society as a whole, Ambrose distinguishes sharply between the authority of the bishops and that of secular government by moral rather than legal arguments[26] and insists on the superiority of the bishops. Only bishops could decide which matters were religious, and in religious matters not even the emperor could judge the decisions of bishops and priests. Both before and after Constantine, Christians had to be prepared to disobey secular authorities when they opposed the religious authority of the bishops and to suffer martyrdom in consequence.

Secular government was necessary, legitimate, and autonomous in its own, lesser sphere, but it also had a religious legitimacy. Secular government is ordained by God to control the desire of sinful humans to dominate their fellows. To the Roman Empire, however, Ambrose attributed a higher mission: it is willed by God as a means to spread the true faith; it will prosper so long as it serves that end; Roman victories and the political successes of emperors have been given by God; and the fall of the empire will signal the end of the world.[27] So ineradicable a part of Ambrose's identity was his Roman citizenship that he could declare that "everyone is your brother, first of all those of the faith and then those under Roman law."[28]

Ambrose's religiosity was supportive of the superior social authority of the priesthood but also of secular social authority. Even though Roman law and the emperors had persecuted the martyrs still so vivid in Christian memory, Roman secular authority had always peculiarly served the true faith by its other proper activities; and now that the emperors were Christians, the Roman imperium could become the fully conscious instrument to serve and spread the faith. For Ambrose made no distinction between the emperor as a private person within the church and his exercise of imperial authority. In matters deemed religious by the bishops, the Christian emperor should use his power to execute episcopal imperatives, to enforce the decrees of councils, banish deposed bishops, and punish heretics.[29] Indeed, as Ambrose's excommunication of Theodosius for the massacre at Thessalonica demonstrates, even when religious issues were not directly involved, the emperors should be made to act in accordance with the bishops' sense of morality.

The conversion of the emperors from unwitting agents of divine providence to conscious, if unreliable, executors of religious imperatives pronounced by the bishops made it easier for Ambrose to reconcile the supra-empirical and empirical poles of his religiosity, to connect Christ and Rome. For the pre-Constantinian period, he had had to develop a theological interpretation or rationalization to overcome the obvious empirical contradictions, but by his own time, despite Julian the Apostate's actions when Ambrose was about thirty, he could feel that pagan persecution was a thing of the past. Indeed, before he died, and in no small part because of his efforts, paganism had been dethroned and his Nicaean Christianity made the official religion of the empire. By his own efforts and those of other bishops in communion with Rome, he could now influence secular authority so that there would be little obvious discrepancy between the faith he attributed to the apostles and the special religious mission he ascribed to the empire he had formerly served as governor of Aemilia-Liguria.

Ambrose's religiosity was that of a confident, aristocratic, politically active Latin bishop in communion with Rome of the late fourth century, and it was somewhat empirical and very supportive of Roman social authority in general and of the superior social authority of the priesthood in particular. But what were the implications of that type of religiosity for Jews? Ambrose's attitude toward Jews was ambiguous and the treatment of Jews he favored was oblique. On the one hand, he equated Jews with Cain and did not advocate that the emperor or anyone else expel or kill them. Had there been a great massacre of defenseless Jews, he would doubtless have condemned it, just as he opposed the massacre at Thessalonica and the execution of Priscillian, whose ideas he condemned. Nor, so far as we know, did he himself incite direct attacks on Jews or their synagogues. On the other hand, he encouraged the gradual elimination of Judaic religiosity through the physical action of others. He exhorted Theodosius not to protect synagogues, prevented him from punishing those involved in the destruction at Callinicum, asserted that the bishop of Callinicum had only done his duty, and probably persuaded Theodosius to delegate his authority to protect synagogues to local officials who were more open to local pressures.[30] Moreover, he or his influence may have been responsible for the fact that, by 423, Jews were prohibited from constructing new synagogues except to replace those destroyed by Christians, and from repairing or expanding existing synagogues without special permission.[31] No wonder attacks on synagogues continued until the Germanic conquest.

Ambrose seems to have felt that the direct involvement of bishops in physical attacks on Judaic religiosity and its symbols was inappropriate episcopal conduct, perhaps aware that such involvement tarnished their charismatic detachment. Nor, so far as we know, did Ambrose and his fellow bishops try to have Judaism declared illicit, in marked contrast with their attitude toward paganism. But Ambrose was not outraged when lay Christians destroyed synagogues in defiance of the law, or even when a distant bishop was directly involved. He looked forward to the elimination of all places of worship in which Christ was denied and was manifestly pleased when a synagogue was destroyed. Although he never destroyed one himself or encouraged other bishops before the fact to do so, he tried to ensure that those who did would not be punished. He seems to have interpreted uncommanded but obliquely encouraged violence by laymen against Jews as a manifestation of divine providence that would gradually ensure the punishment and elimination of Judaic religiosity.

If Ambrose's influential religiosity is any indication — and thirteenth-century papal policy suggests that it is — Christian religiosity supportive of the superior social authority of the priesthood would acknowledge Pauline theology about Jews by tolerating the existence of Judaic religiosity in principle, but it would encourage secular rulers to stunt its expression, condone violent verbal attacks by ecclesiastics, and turn a blind eye to all but the most flagrant attacks by lay people.

IV

A moratorium was imposed on Ambrose's providence for Jews by the fall of the Roman Empire in the west, for whatever else was involved in the fall, it meant a profound transformation in the character of society, social authority, dominant mentality, and Christian religiosity. If, as Cochrane has argued, Christianity introduced through Augustine a new vision of personality to classical culture,[32] it was largely lost in the early Middle Ages when the identity of the individual was conceived primarily in terms of social membership.[33] The Germans neither eliminated all they found nor established themselves as tribes, but tribal attitudes and institutions were fundamental in maintaining some cohesion among the conquerors and in shaping the new

kingdoms—albeit less so in southern than in northern Europe. The
character of kingship, the personality of law, and the importance of the
kindred and blood feud are obvious examples of the reliance on primitive social techniques in new and more complex conditions. Although
few of the invading groups were movements of a whole or single people, the invaders reacted to their new situation in the light of what they
had known before and, despite their dilution and admixture, attempted to reconstitute their old sense of identity as peoples. To use
Tönnies's and Weber's terms, a series of *Gemeinschaften* that operated
by traditional authority replaced the Roman *Gesellschaft* with its legal-
rational authority. And these efforts to reconstitute biologically connected peoples with a common culture enabled the invaders to preserve
much of the social dimension of their former religiosity after they had
accepted a Christian creed.

The religiosity of the invaders had been polytheistic, highly ritualistic, emphatically empirical, and supportive of peoples. A people
should properly have one common set of beliefs and rituals that were
those of their chiefs or kings, the sacralized intermediaries between
them and their gods. That form of religiosity, which legitimated the
religious decisions of kings and elders, made possible the mass conversions to Christian beliefs. But the medium of conversion affected the
message, for the invaders understood their new beliefs according to the
presuppositions of their former religiosity.

Germanic Christian religiosity was closely supportive of peoples and
highly empirical. We could point to King Sisebut's insistence on the
material advantages that Visigothic kings gained by acceptance of Nicaean beliefs or to Isidore of Seville's celebration of Gothic virtues, a
religiosity summarized by Fontaine as *Gott mit uns*.[34] We could quote
Clovis's conversion as described by Gregory of Tours. More explicit,
however, is the eighth-century prologue to the Salic law: "Long live
Christ who loves the Franks. May he guard the kingdom, fill their
leaders with the light of his grace, protect their army, accord them the
defense of the faith."[35]

Yet the amplest short expression is perhaps to be found, at the
peak of the Carolingian Empire, in Alcuin's assertion to the king of
Northumbria that the prosperity of the whole folk, military success,
good weather, abundance of land, plentiful sons, and the health of the
people depend on the king's righteousness.[36] This religiosity was nicely
summed up by Delaruelle: "One knows that the Carolingian civilization was in many ways a civilization of liturgy. There was a *populus*

Christianus, veritable Holy People, who recognized themselves by the collective practice of the same liturgy."[37]

Germans were not attracted to Christianity by its rich revelation and sophisticated theology or by the supra-empirical and universal religiosity described in books they could not read. Nor were they forced to convert, although the Roman aura may have impressed them. Their own collective religiosity was the firm base that made the conversion possible; and the fundamental change that occurred in it, I would suggest, was stimulated by the socially unsettling experience of the migrations and was their conversion from polytheistic beliefs that tended to emphasize one high god to monotheistic beliefs that acknowledged subordinate supernatural figures. As millennia of human history indicate, humans do not come easily to the idea of monotheism, but once adumbrated and actively disseminated, monotheism has demonstrated amazing power to displace polytheism when preached to people whose contact with more complex societies has given them broader and unsettling horizons. The extended social and geographic distance seems to have distanced the gods also and encouraged their merger into a single superior supra-empirical reality.

Even though Germanic Arianism has been interpreted as a preservation of polytheistic attitudes, the subordination of Christ to the Father can equally be understood as an insistence on divine unity rather than trinity.[38] That, rather than a lack of theological sophistication, may be what lay behind the assertion to Gregory of Tours by Oppila, the lay Visigothic ambassador of King Leovigild: "I believe that the Father, the Son, and the Holy Spirit are the virtues of a single God."[39] After all, the Nicaean Germans also modified the concept of the Trinity to suit their predispositions. The attraction of a unitary god is obvious in the Franks who compressed the Trinity so far as possible into the single figure of Christ, understood as the omnipotent creator, wrathful judge, majestic king, and triumphant warrior. As Fichtenau has said, "Christ was thus made almost the sole representative of the Holy Trinity."[40]

Germanic Christianity thus tended toward a rigorous monotheism, was highly ritualistic rather than contemplative or theological, and was extremely empirical. As that suggests, it was also very closely supportive of particular, biologically and ethnically linked, peoples. Of course no Germanic people could make Christian religiosity its exclusive property, but each group's Christian religiosity was kept as closely supportive of its own people as possible.

The domination of Christianized Germanic peoples was, as Blumen-kranz has carefully described,[41] a pleasant change for Jews after their controlled oppression in the Christian Roman Empire. The Germanic acceptance of Jews seems to have been the result of two characteristics of their religiosity. In the first place, the monotheistic, ritualistic, empirical Christian religiosity closely supportive of the Germanic peoples notably resembled that of ancient Israel, and Germans consequently resonated more to the Old Testament, which recorded the battles of a people chosen by God, than to the New Testament messages of pacifism, individualism, and disruption of people and family. They could view Judaic religiosity tolerantly as the prototypic monotheistic religiosity of a people and be highly insensitive to the emphasis on conflict between Jews and Judeo-Christians enshrined in parts of the New Testament. In the second place, Germanic monotheistic religiosity seems to have preserved some of the polytheistic tolerance that expected each people to have its own gods and rituals.

The Germans did lose much of their former tolerance when they converted to monotheism. To the extent that they were convinced that there was only one god, they no longer accepted the polytheism of other peoples as valid even—or perhaps particularly—when those people were similar in culture to themselves, as is suggested by Charlemagne's military conversion of the Saxons or Alfred's military conversion of the Danes after Chippenham. But they do not seem to have been overly disturbed by other peoples who worshiped the one god in their own distinctive way, provided those people were not a military threat. Religious difference seems to have had little influence, for example, on the relations between the Arian Visigoths and Nicaean Frankish kings.[42] And although personal sophistication may have influenced Theoderic's Arian toleration of Catholics in his Ostrogothic Italian kingdom, the absence of any significant persecution or proselytizing of Catholics by the much less sophisticated Visigothic Arian kings before Leovigild suggests that a commonly shared Visigothic attitude was more decisive. And that general tolerance of other people's monotheistic religiosity can only have strengthened the acceptance of the people of the Old Testament.

The one great exception was the Visigothic kings' persecution of both Arian and Judaic religiosity after King Reccared had abjured Arian beliefs for the peoples whom he ruled in 589 and was promised present and eternal glory. To explain that sudden change in treatment of Jews, it has been suggested that since Arian Ostrogoths, Visigoths, and Lombards were not hostile to Jews, there must have been something about Arianism that enabled its adherents to get along well with Jews,[43] and by implication that Nicaean belief involved much greater hostility. But since those indisputably Nicaean and emphatically concerned Christians, Charlemagne and Louis the Pious, treated Jews very favorably, that explanation is untenable, as is also the simple explanation that King Sisebut was inspired to command the forced baptism of all the Jews in his kingdom about 616 by his "Christian piety."[44] The new attitude was not a consequence of Nicaean beliefs per se but of the royal rejection of one Christian credal symbol for another, for the changes in the social dimension of Visigothic religiosity had made credal uniformity a crucial issue for Visigothic identity.

It has also been suggested frequently that the Visigothic kings converted to Catholicism primarily to gain the support of the Hispano-Romans and unite their kingdom politically, and that they persecuted Jews as the one remaining obstacle to that unity. Now it is indisputable that the kings assumed that religiosity and the unity of a people were inseparable, an assumption peculiarly explicit in the seventy-fifth canon of the Fourth Council of Toledo and the seventh canon of the Fifth,[45] but that does not prove that they persecuted Jews from purely political motives and consciously regarded religion simply as a useful instrument.

That explanation, sketched by Parkes,[46] has recently been restated in the strongest terms by Bachrach.[47] Whereas Parkes argued that the kings persecuted Jews to win the support of the clerical party, Bachrach affirms that the kings were not particularly religious and that the Jews were sufficiently powerful so that most kings were quite willing to defy the church's anti-Jewish policy and favor Jews in order to win their support. In reaction, however, their rivals in the frequent struggles for the throne, although equally irreligious, persecuted Jews to punish them for supporting their opponents and to win the support of anti-Jewish churchmen.

The explanation implies that, after 589, Visigothic kings no longer believed in a superior, supra-empirical reality and had been converted into seventeenth-century *politiques*, an idea that flies in the face of everything we know about the period and is directly contradicted by the royal insistence on religious unity, by the peculiar institution of the Councils of Toledo, and by the purely religious character[48] of royal invective against Jews. The argument also neglects the fact that many churchmen, including Isidore of Seville, disapproved of Sisebut's extreme actions against Judaic religiosity. Nor does it explain why there were no persecutions before 589 when dynastic disputes were also endemic. There remains the obvious alternative, that the kings remained religious in their own way but consciously modified both the credal and social dimensions of their religiosity in a way that had direct implications for the existence of Judaic religiosity in the kingdom.

By the second half of the sixth century, the reality of a biologically linked Visigothic people with a common culture was visibly crumbling. Vastly outnumbered and surrounded by the more sophisticated Hispano-Roman culture, Visigothic nobles and even princes were intermarrying with Hispano-Romans, and converting in significant numbers to Nicaean Christianity. No longer could kings depend on Visigothic solidarity as Nicaean Hispano-Romans supported Arian kings against rebellious Nicaean Visigoths.[49] The connection between royal authority, the Visigoths, and their god was becoming obscure.

King Leovigild (568–86) knew this far better than we do, and his personal ambition, sense of responsibility, and religiosity converged to demand a resolution of these patent contradictions that would confirm his conception of himself as king of the Visigothic people. On the one hand, he married his son to a Catholic, annulled the old prohibition of intermarriage between Visigoths and Hispano-Romans, was willing to accept that a Nicaean turned to Arianism did not need to be baptized again, and was willing to accept that Christ was in some way equal to the Father. But on the other hand, although he thus facilitated the conversion of the Hispano-Romans to a Visigothic identity, he retained the personality of law that maintained the distinction between the identity of the conquering and the conquered peoples.[50]

Leovigild modified both the credal and social dimensions of his own religiosity, but there seems to have been little change in his basic understanding of human nature, human relations, and the relation of peoples to their god. Faced by empirical challenges he could not deny to the social dimension of his religiosity, to his conviction that Visigothic identity demanded the people's unity in religion, he responded by making minor adjustments in both the credal and biological dimensions of Visigothic identity that acknowledged what Visigoths were actually doing, diminished the difference between the Visigoths and the conquered population, and potentially made possible the submergence of the Hispano-Romans in Visigothic identity. To preserve

Visigothic identity, he followed a policy that implied the ultimate inclusion of all the people he ruled in a broadened Visigothic people and
the reconstitution of that people's unique relation to their god.

His solution to the tensions in his religiosity failed because he could
not persuade the vastly larger number of Hispano-Romans to accept
the Arian creed and Gothic liturgy and hence achieve the religious
unity presupposed by his understanding of a united kingdom and people. Although he used force halfheartedly to coerce conversions, he
lacked the power to succeed. Nor could he use the normal Germanic
form of conversion in which kings, relying on the religiosity of a people of their followers, led their people in conversion, for he had no
such religious authority over Hispano-Romans.

Leovigild's intolerance was mild, but it was the first significant
breach in the pattern of Visigothic tolerance and was not the result of
any decisive change in the king's creed. It was a reflection of Leovigild's unwillingness or inability to depart far from his conception of
who he was, who Visigoths were, and how peoples were connected
with their god. Yet his action did imply that the changes in the empirical reality of Visigothic identity necessitated a credal change by
someone. And only three years after his death, Reccared formally converted Visigothic religiosity from Arian to Nicaean beliefs.

He encountered no serious opposition from his Visigoths because of
the other characteristics of their religiosity, while the Nicaeans could
only rejoice, particularly since they were increasingly influenced by
Visigothic culture. And whether they were influenced by the late Roman religiosity supportive of social authority or by the Germanic religiosity supportive of a people, they could now view the king's power
as religiously legitimated, and did so with enthusiasm.

Because of that support from Hispano-Romans who were barely
connected biologically with the Visigoths, it might seem that royal
religiosity had changed from being supportive of a people to being
supportive of social authority, primarily that of the king. But whatever
the case for the Hispano-Roman bishops, the kings' mental adjustment
did not go that far. The fundamental assumptions of Reccared, Sisebut,
and their successors seem little different from those of the Arian Leovigild. They could not conceive of abandoning the Visigothic identity
that socially legitimated their presence on the throne. The authority
they protected was their own and that of the Visigoths over the
Hispano-Romans. And despite Roman trappings, authority in the

kingdom more resembled the undifferentiated authority of a traditional society than the differentiated, legal-rational authority of the
Roman Empire.

The conversion was, in fact, a very one-sided compromise. If the
Goths gave up their credal distinctiveness and accepted the dilution of
their biological identity, the Hispano-Romans gradually lost their cultural identity and converted to the religiosity supportive of the people
of their Visigothic kings. Isidore of Seville glorified the Goths; the
Councils of Toledo supported the kings; the power and number of
Visigothic bishops increased dramatically; and Chintilla decreed in the
Fifth Council that only a noble Goth could become king.[51] Despite the
incorporation of Hispano-Romans, authority was still transmitted by
biological descent; and secular and religious authority were not differentiated but fused in the Councils of Toledo and—at least by 672—
in the anointment of the kings.[52] The effects of this compromise were
plain to see by 654 when Recceswinth prohibited the use of Roman
law and promulgated a single code applicable to both Goths and Romans that also removed Hispano-Romans from most important judicial positions. In Thompson's judgment, the effect of Chindaswinth's
and Recceswinth's policies was to "deprive the Romans of practically
all political, executive, and ecclesiastical powers."[53]

The kings had been able to submerge the identity of the Hispano-
Romans as a group in the reconstituted people of the Visigothic kingdom and to make Nicaean beliefs and Latin liturgy supportive of that
people and its king. The cultural fusion in fact neither successfully
integrated the kingdom nor significantly reinforced royal authority,
but there was no important challenge to one principle on which the
existence of that weak kingship rested: the connection between the
Visigothic people and their god through their kings and priests. The
kings had been able to reconstitute in enlarged form the social dimension of their religiosity. They therefore had no reason to question its
underlying assumption, that the king and his people had to be one in
religiosity.

That the kings were both the focus and most ardent supporters of
that religiosity is apparent not only from their relations with the bishops in the Councils of Toledo; it is apparent also in their excessive
concern, clearly exceeding that of the bishops, to eliminate Judaic religiosity. Sisebut's law of 612 prohibiting Jews from having Christian
slaves and regulating mixed unions and their offspring was apparently

not inspired by the bishops; and his decisive precedent of forcing baptism on Jews was later criticized by the bishops. Moreover, although only some of his successors pursued that policy vigorously, those who did, including as impressive a figure as Recceswinth, could not rely on episcopal, to say nothing of lay, support.[54]

The royal persecution did encourage the bishops to insist on the anti-Judaic measures of the late empire—and more—in order to prevent Jewish proselytism, stunt the expression of Judaic religiosity, and retain the converts. But although the bishops heartily supported an Ambrosian approach, they stopped short of accepting baptism by royal force as part of God's providence, which does not mean that that policy was not religious, only that it was a feature of royal rather than episcopal religiosity. The kings sought to eliminate Judaic religiosity, unsuccessfully, because they felt that they and their Goths had modified their own religiosity, and that their modified religiosity supportive of the people of their kingdom should apply to Jews as much as to anyone else.[55] The bitterness of royal intolerance toward Jews probably reflects the kings' awareness that while both Goths and Hispano-Romans had been willing to give up part of their former distinctive identity, the Jews with their much older religiosity of a people would not and stood out as the only serious empirical contradiction of the social premise of royal religiosity down to the fall of the kingdom in 711.

V

If we now move northward, it becomes very obvious that Germanic Nicaean religiosity was not by nature intolerant of Judaic religiosity when its social ground was not threatened. In the Merovingian and Carolingian kingdoms, where Romanization was superficial and Germanic culture dominant, there was almost no intolerance, and most of what little there was was clerical intolerance of the Mediterranean kind. Between 558 and 629, three or four bishops in central and southern Gaul gave Jews of their cities the choice of baptism or exile,[56] but there was almost no royal action. King Chilperic did order Jews to be baptized about 580, but that seems to have been the reaction to a face-to-face theological disagreement of a peculiar personality and to have affected few Jews, and that only briefly. As for the alleged expulsion by Dagobert about 629, it almost certainly did not happen since it left no traces in the canons of later councils, and when we have evidence for Jews later, we find them comfortably established in the Carolingian Empire.[57]

The only frequent actions against Judaic religiosity were the irregular efforts of bishops assembled in councils from 517 to 888 to prevent Jewish proselytism. They spasmodically forebade Christians to marry or eat with Jews and prohibited Jews from mingling with Christians at Easter, exercising authority over Christians, or possessing Christian slaves. Yet, although the councils were frequently summoned by kings, these canons were rarely supported by the kings. Childebert I (511–558) apparently forebade Jews to mingle at Easter, and Clothar II in 615 prohibited Jews from holding positions of authority and claimed any slaves whom their Jewish masters had misused or converted to Judaism. But the evidence is meager and its significance is further diminished by the fact that Louis the Pious stopped Archbishop Agobard of Lyons's campaign against Jews, and Charles the Bald refused to ratify the anti-Judaic canons of the council of Meaux and Paris in 845–846.[58]

The Franks, including almost all their kings and most of their bishops, were not disturbed by the presence of Jews. In this they were no different from the Arian Goths and Lombards. Where they differed from the Arian Germans was that the social dimension or base of their religiosity was not threatened until much later. Since the monotheistic belief they had accepted in their new surroundings was the same as that of those they had conquered, and since their numbers and military strength were sufficiently great that their culture was not immediately threatened by the conquered, they never felt their identity menaced, nor were they forced to pay serious attention to credal differences as challenges to their identity.

It would be a serious misunderstanding to think that the Carolingian Franks tolerated Judaic religiosity because they were not really Christian. That is implied, for example, by Fichtenau's assertion that "laymen were only too often of the comfortable opinion that knowledge of the Gospels was the business of the clergy alone" and that the commands of scripture applied only to monks.[59] The assertion implicitly judges one form of Christian religiosity by the norms of another. It might be countered by asking how illiterate believers in Christ could have known the Gospels in that sense, but it is more important to ask what role the Bible, that affirmation of contact with God, played in their religiosity.

Even in the monasteries, the Gospels were no more emphasized than the Old Testament, and both were valued more as a symbolic means of deepening the connection with God than as texts that only yielded their meaning after systematic analysis.[60] As for the distinction between laymen and monks, that was not a fissure in, but an integral part of, their religiosity. What had started as a religiosity of withdrawal from society to preserve the sense of the universality of Christianity had gradually become an institution of society in which religious virtuosi did not so much study the Gospels or follow the commands (which?) of scripture as obey the Rule and the abbot and perform rituals for the benefit of the society that supported them. If this was the Benedictine Age, it was so because both laymen and clerics believed that monasteries and the symbolic action within them, including the use of scripture, were their most immediate, direct, and continuous connection with their god, who supported their people so long as their king—their other primary contact—acted properly.

However Frankish Christianity be described, it was not threatened by Judaic religiosity. With few exceptions, Christians of all ranks in northern Europe were not hostile to Jews, in striking contrast with the churchmen of the late Roman Empire and the Nicaean Visigothic kings. Only toward the end of the Carolingian period do we hear a new and threatening voice that had come from the Mediterranean. Agobard of Lyons opposed the belief that events were caused by magic or people in the sky rather than by God's cosmic government, and he condemned the judicial ordeal. He also opposed the personality of law, holding that all, as Christians, should be under one law and able to testify for each other "where there is neither barbarian nor Scythian, Aquitanian nor Lombard, Burgundian nor Alemanni, slave nor free, but all are one in Christ."[61]

The paraphrase of Paul's striking expression of Christian universal religiosity contrasts sharply with the prevailing highly empirical religiosity supportive of the Franks. Yet the paraphrase was used in the context of the Carolingian Empire with its stabilization of social order, and it was employed to support the superiority of the social authority of the priesthood over secular authority, an intention that can be seen from Agobard's actions against Louis the Pious as well as from his words. Like Ambrose, Agobard envisioned a Christian government of a society of Christians in which secular rulers would obey bishops in religious matters.

Agobard stands out in that period as a rare and clear exponent of an older—and future—type of Christian religiosity. It is, therefore, significant but not surprising to find that he was also unusually sensitive to, and critical of, the prevailing tolerance of Jews and tried energetically to get Louis the Pious to treat them less favorably.[62] Although neither he nor his successor at Lyons, Amulo, was successful, Agobard nonetheless represents the first clear expression in northern Europe of the old attitude toward Jews of the Mediterranean priesthood. Yet, like Ambrose, neither he nor Amulo advocated the official destruction of synagogues or the expulsion of Jews. Christian religiosity supportive of the priesthood had never directly advocated such extreme measures, and that basic toleration had been firmly established by the authorities of the church well before Agobard appeared.

Toleration had continued in Italy after Ambrose because of the countervailing imperial tradition of Roman law and the fact that no intolerant Germanic kingdom like the Visigothic had developed there. Gregory the Great had made that tradition part of papal practice and canon law at the end of the sixth century in words that would echo through the centuries in protection of Jews;[63] and although his stand did not prevent the Visigothic persecutions of the seventh century, it did establish the principle at Rome, and it was reinforced by Frankish practice. It was even supported by the canon of the fourth Council of Toledo that condemned forced baptisms in reaction to Sisebut's action. Even more ironically, it was supported by the very canons of the earlier Frankish councils that Agobard and Amulo sought to have enforced, for those canons to prevent Jewish proselytism assumed that the presence of Judaic religiosity was to be tolerated. Hence, when Calixtus II drew on Gregory's words about 1120 and issued the bull *Sicut Judeis* to protect Jews from massacres and forced baptisms like those of 1096, he was only explicitly commanding general obedience to a rule that had long been established in principle and practice.

VI

What had spurred Calixtus to action was the first massive effort to eliminate Judaic religiosity since Visigothic Spain, a persecution that differed dramatically from what had gone before. Since Constantine, the attacks on Judaic religiosity had occurred in Mediterranean Europe, had been inspired from above, primarily by ecclesiastics, and had had little lay and popular support. The massacres of 1096, however, occurred in northern Europe in what had been the heartland of the

Carolingian Empire; they were conducted almost exclusively by lay people from the lower ranks of society; and these people acted in open defiance of both ecclesiastical and secular authority.

This novel expression of hostility coincided with fundamental changes in European society which made the eleventh century a watershed. The second wave of pagan invasions of the ninth and tenth centuries had, with the aid of civil war, destroyed the Carolingian unity of Europe but made people more conscious of themselves as Christians. Even without the invasions, the stresses in Carolingian society might have led to a gradual breakdown and reorganization. But as it was, the rapidity of the breakdown, the sudden hunger for social order, and the frantic search for local solutions divided the social map of Europe in new ways, disturbed people's sense of their identity, and laid the basis for the rapid political, social, and economic development after 1050.[64]

That reorganization brought the end of the Benedictine Age. Although the vast development of the Cluniac order in the eleventh century might seem the apex of Benedictinism, it was a death knell. The organization of a vast network of houses under a single abbot responsible only to the pope tended to dissociate those monasteries from their surrounding societies and particular peoples, while the reforms within the houses reduced the similarity in mentality to the surrounding world by reinvigorating the religiosity of withdrawal that had been the original basis of monasticism but had been drastically modified by the religiosity supportive of peoples of the Benedictine Age. At the same time, however, the success of the Cluniac order throughout Europe provided a model for the integration of Latin Christendom by a centralized priesthood.

The paradox of the eleventh century is that, while the extreme decentralization of European society provoked local solutions to disorder, people began to think of Europe as Latin Christendom and to support the development of a centralized papal church that would give it administrative and executive integration. While in secular matters people cooperated more or less willingly to develop the regional political societies that destroyed old ethnic unities and would split Europe enduringly into territorial governments, in religious matters they cooperated, willingly or unwillingly, in the development of the papal monarchy that would be the most impressive government of all for several centuries.

The political, social, and religious reordering of Europe in the eleventh century could hardly fail to provoke grave tensions in many people's sense of their identity and their relationship with their god. Diverse people reacted in diverse ways and reinterpreted their inherited religiosity more or less consciously. There is no more explicit expression of changing consciousness than Gregory VII's famous affirmation: "The Lord . . . did not say 'I am custom,' but 'the truth.' " As Tellenbach recognized, Gregory was a revolutionary,[65] but he was far from alone.

> It often happens at critical moments in history that ideas which have long held the field almost unchallenged are suddenly discovered, not to be wrong, but to be useless; then almost everyone can see they are absurd. So it was around the year 1100.[66]

Although Southern is here referring to the papal victory over royal claims to sacral authority, his description applies to many changes wrought in the eleventh century by the realization that the customary understanding of human conduct, which had defined the social dimension of people's religiosity, had been seriously undermined both by events and by new conceptions of the supra-empirical.

Well before Gregory VII, some monks had read the Bible with a new sensitivity that made them aware of the discrepancy between monastic religiosity—even as reformed by Cluny—and the life described in the Gospels. The most lapidary expression of that new consciousness was formulated a century later by Etienne de Muret, the founder of the order of Grandmont: "If someone asks you to what order you belong, reply to that of the Gospels, which is the foundation of all the rules."[67] The earliest clear symptom of the change can be seen in the increase in eremetical life in Italy, which can be conveniently dated from the foundation of the order of Camaldoli by Romuald about 1012 and of Vallambrosa by Gualberto about 1039. These orders, however, had no direct effect across the Alps, for the foundation of new orders in the north only started with the foundation of the Carthusians by Bruno of Cologne in 1084 and of Cîteaux by Robert of Molesmes in 1098.

The new sensitivity to the Gospels did, however, cross the Alps and spread across Europe before the new orders were founded in the north. Individuals who had been attracted to the new religiosity of withdrawal but found it insufficiently universal left monasteries and hermitages to preach to lay people. This is the phenomenon that Chenu has called le reveil évangélique, a return to the Gospels and the apostolic model of religiosity that had greater impact on lay people than on the clergy because of the latter's institutional indoctrination.[68] These people denied religious significance to the divisions and institutions of society. They insisted through their emphasis on poverty on their liminal status between the society they had devalued and the eternal salvation they sought as individuals.[69] But they remained in society and profoundly disturbed it.

Our knowledge of these movements is unfortunately limited and distorted because we learn of them primarily from their enemies, clerics of different religiosity who sought to classify the resurgence of the apostolic model as some ancient heresy. Yet thanks to the work of Chenu, Delaruelle, Grundmann, da Milano, Morghen, Manselli, Russell, Violante, and others, their contours have become much clearer.[70] And although the movements did not all have the same ideas, their family resemblance is obvious despite a difference in social attitudes between south and north.

There were doubts about either the divinity or humanity of Christ; there were denials of the efficacy of the Eucharist, prayers for the dead, and infant baptism; there were attacks on the sanctity of churches, crosses, and the clergy; and there was a countervailing insistence on the Gospels, the inspiration of the Holy Spirit, individual faith, evangelical preaching, real poverty, and chastity. A more direct attack on the dominant religiosity of the Benedictine Age would be hard to imagine, and it was met by brutal persecution from 1022 onward, primarily by lay people and lower clergy,[71] but also by more moderate official efforts at repression.

These people denied the right of social authority, whether ecclesiastical or secular, to control their religiosity and accepted the alternative of poverty and marginality. They differentiated their religiosity sharply from the claims of the surrounding society, and their appearance, much more than the Investiture Contest, marks the frontier between two phases of medieval religious history. They emerged before the papal reforming movement in northern as well as southern Europe. Although their numbers were limited, we have evidence of movements at Limoges about 1018, at Orléans between 1015 and 1022, at Liège and Arras about 1025, at Monteforte in Alpine Italy about 1028, across France in 1049, and at Milan and Florence around 1060. By the mid-twelfth century, they had grown remarkably in numbers and prominence. I need only mention Tanchelm, Henry of Le Mans, Peter of Bruys, and Arnold of Brescia, to say nothing of the appeal of Manichean ideas.

But if these people differentiated their more universal religiosity from the surrounding society, their reaction to that society, or the appeal of those ideas to different classes in society, differed in southern and northern Europe. The Italian and southern French movements— the Montefortians, Patarines, Arnoldists, and even the later Albigensians—appealed to members of all classes. Indeed the Patarines and Arnoldists sought a social revolution that would deny ecclesiastics secular authority and hence desacralize secular society in accordance with their own alienation from it. In the north, however, the movements seem to have been restricted almost exclusively to the lower rural and urban classes, and their members, whatever they may have wished, seem to have had little hope of changing the social order. That may be why the peculiarly northern groups which Russell has typified as eccentric[72] so blatantly defied normal mores, as in the case of the movement led by Tanchelm. In any case, the socially restricted appeal of the new religiosity in the north, and the aristocratic turning to the new monastic orders, indicate that in the north the new evangelical religiosity appealed particularly to people who felt disadvantaged as compared with others by changes in the social order.

These movements were still small in the eleventh century when they were suddenly overshadowed by a more famous change in medieval religiosity. The council of Reims of 1049 is far better known for Leo IX's use of the relics of St. Remi to reinforce his own authority than for its declaration that heresy was rampant throughout Gaul. And the council may be considered to mark the beginning of the papal campaign to define and control European religiosity that sparked the Investiture Contest.

Typically described as the culmination of earlier movements of local ecclesiastical reform, the Gregorian reform has been interpreted as a struggle to free religion from the social contamination, such as *Eigenkirchen*, wrought by the Germanic invasions and the religiosity of the Benedictine Age. Supported by the reinvigorated religiosity of withdrawal whose exponents did not hesitate to act in the broader society, the popes sought to reverse history, to overthrow the sacral authority of kings that was supported by Germanic religiosity, and to replace it with a religiosity supportive of the supreme social authority of the priesthood that obeyed the bishop of Rome.

A religiosity reminiscent of that of Ambrose reappeared, and our sense of a sequence reversed is sharpened when we recall that the Investiture Contest reintroduced a sharp distinction between the sacred and the profane and between the priesthood and secular rulers. That distinction stimulated the development of a complex, legal-rational society with differentiated roles. It in turn provoked a gradual assertion of the distinctive and autonomous character of secular authority which prepared the way for the reemergence in the twelfth and particularly the thirteenth century of a religiosity supportive of the superior social authority of secular rulers.

Since popes from Gregory VII to Boniface VIII insisted emphatically on the universality of Christianity and their authority, and since the centralized Latin church did not coincide with any single ethnic group or political society, it is easy to view the reformed Catholic church as the reestablishment of Christian universality. In fact, however, that church arrested and tried to suppress the new expressions of universal religiosity and defined its exponents as heretics unless they were willing to obey the priesthood, as we can see even more clearly in the later reaction to the Franciscan movement. In the last analysis, a heretic was a person who obdurately refused to obey the pope.

Yet once sensitivity to the appeal of universal religiosity had been awakened in an increasingly complex society in rapid development, it could not be eradicated. Consequently, the Investiture Contest was only one of the two main contests provoked by the vigorous assertion of papal authority. As Innocent III's career would remind us, papal religiosity supportive of the priesthood was opposed from two very different directions: by kings and by those branded as heretics. And as Ockham's career would remind us, the two could even ally by the later Middle Ages.

The two types of opposition varied in importance regionally. In urban areas in northern Italy, southern France, and the Rhineland, where complex social regulations in increasingly abstract terms were rapidly being developed for compact town populations in areas without any corresponding development of strong royal government (in contrast with Paris and London), the conflict of religiosities was between ecclesiastical authorities and heretics, between religiosity supportive of the priesthood and universal religiosity. But in much of Germany, then England, and finally France, where strong monarchies existed or developed, the salient conflict of religiosities was between religiosity supportive of the authority of the priesthood and religiosity supportive of the authority of kings, whether as leaders of the people or later as secular social authorities in increasingly legal-rational societies. A map of the differences would correspond closely to the map of the activity of the papal Inquisition, which pursued heresy where central authority was weak, and particularly in urbanized areas. And it is worth noting in passing that both types of polarization provoked by the thrust of papal authority were so strong that, as indicated by the gradual monastic decline and the later prominence of the friars, the appeal of the intermediate religiosity of withdrawal was radically diminished.

Since religious tensions varied according to regional social structure, there was a marked difference between Mediterranean and northern Europe. In Mediterranean Europe, where no great Germanic kingdoms had developed, there were no kings of peoples or royal touch for scrofula, only kings of territories. Nor, save embryonically in Naples and Sicily, were there any strong central governments. Consequently, these fragmented political societies had little significance of their own as religious symbols. Dispersed through them, however, was a richness unknown in the north of other symbols of contact with God: Rome, relics, popes, pilgrimage places, bishops, priests, and monasteries. And since these were associated with the clergy rather than with political societies and their secular rulers, religious tension generated reactions against the priesthood rather than against lay authority and social structure.

Largely because of its Roman legacy and urban continuity, the Mediterranean world had preserved the distinction between the sacred and the profane to a degree unknown in the north. In the superficially Romanized north, however, that distinction had almost been obliterated by Germanic religiosity. Indeed, if we can speak of a church in northern Europe around 800, in the sense of a religious institution with an effective central authority, we have to talk about the Carolingian or Frankish church, for religious organization and practice was controlled by Charlemagne, not the pope, and the dominant religiosity was that supportive of a people and its leaders. By 1096, the dominant religiosity in the north was still, despite the Investiture Contest, a religiosity supportive of the people, whether the Germans, the French, or the English. Consequently, those in the north around 1096 who responded to the evangelical revival and reacted against the religiosity supportive of peoples or social authority had to react, not just against the authority of the priesthood, but also and primarily against secular authority and the religiosity supportive of the social structure and its elite. That dual tension in the north goes far toward explaining why the northern response to Urban II's call to holy war in 1095 differed so noticeably from the southern.[73]

VII

The First Crusade indicates that popular religiosity in the north differed considerably from that in the south. Most of those who took the cross in 1095 and 1096 came from southern France and Italy; they were led by their recognized secular rulers who were already familiar with, and involved in, Mediterranean international politics; they moved as socially integrated groups, the poorest being incorporated in the official contingents; and these contingents did not massacre Jews. In the north, however, the crusaders were fewer; the kings did not participate; the movement was divided between the official contingents and the popular crusaders; and some of the bands of popular crusaders massacred many Jews.

The official contingents from the north were much like the contingents from Mediterranean Europe. They included almost all the crusaders of knightly rank; they were led, if not by the kings, at least by dukes and important counts who legitimately exercised local authority over the crusaders in normal times; and they did not depart until 15 August 1096, the date set by the pope. The striking difference in the northern reaction was the so-called peasants' or popular crusade, a phenomenon unknown in the south. These northern popular crusaders came overwhelmingly from the lower rural and urban classes; they followed charismatic figures who had not previously exercised authority over them; and they set off well before the official date. And whereas in Mediterranean Europe, where there were many Jews, there were no significant massacres, in the north, where there were relatively few, there occurred the first great massacres of Jews in the history of western Europe. Since the call to holy war was the catalyst that produced the massacres, and that call resounded throughout Europe, it has often been implied or asserted that there were massacres throughout Europe. It should therefore be emphasized that although the call to holy war was general throughout Europe, it galvanized only a small minority in a limited area of northern Europe to try to eliminate Judaic religiosity. The obvious question is why those people were excited to massacre Jews when most others were not.

Throughout the eleventh century, there was a mounting emphasis on the earthly Jerusalem and on holy war against unbelieving enemies of God in Spain. By the end of the century, there was a new concern with the suffering of Christ, and the Cross had acquired a new emotional significance. The thought that the Jews had killed Christ was therefore more likely to arouse passionate reactions. But there was as yet no widespread profound hostility against Jews in 1095. Despite the call to crusade, most people who stayed at home did not kill Jews, and some defended them. Hostility was heightened in the north, as indicated by the report that Godfrey de Bouillon, duke of Lower Lorraine, had sworn to kill Jews before leaving for the Holy Land and was only bought off by Jewish bribes. But the emperor and bishops opposed such actions, and none of the official contingents was involved in a major massacre—whatever individual members may have done at Rouen or elsewhere. Nor was the largest group of popular crusaders, the followers of Peter the Hermit, collectively responsible for any massacre. Great massacres were committed only by some, apparently a minority, of the popular crusaders. That contrast in response to the symbols of holy war and Jews indicates that there was something significantly different about the religiosity of the popular crusaders, both those who followed Peter the Hermit and those who committed the massacres, however hard it may be to say anything about the latter because of the paucity of evidence about them.

Those who joined the official contingents in the north were not moved by a new theological insight and were not rebelling against the social order. Although younger sons of the knightly class may have been disturbed by recent social changes, the official crusaders neither defied established authority nor rebelled against the prevailing northern religiosity supportive of peoples. They maintained their empirical religiosity and strong sense of ethnic identity. The deeds of God were done by the Franks of sweet France: Gesta Dei per Francos. Like Roland and Oliver, they were off to war against powerful enemies of Christ, expecting that Christ would give victory, booty, and new lands to his chosen people as he had in the past. True, their horizon had expanded to include the earthly Jerusalem, and they were now more self-consciously Christian, but their conception of the nature of their god and the way they were connected with him seems little changed. If anything, the official crusaders may have felt that the expedition to Jerusalem was a way to overcome their fragmentation since the dissolution of the Carolingian Empire and to reaffirm their collective identity as Franks, the people loved by God. In any case, those who

enrolled in the official contingents seem rather adventurous opportun-
ists than religious radicals or social rebels.

For people with this religiosity, Jews were important only when seen
as a military or social threat, as allies of the Saracens or, like heretics,
as menacing religious conformity by their proselytism. The scattered
efforts by northern authorities to expel or baptize Jews around 1010
occurred when al-Hakim was persecuting Christians in the east with,
according to rumor, the help of Jews,[74] and when churchmen and lay
people were becoming bothered by new forms of Christian religiosity.
In 1063, when the northern contingents went to join the campaign
against the Saracens in Spain, they attacked Jews only after they had
left their own lands and were approaching their enemies, and the attack seems to have been limited and brief.[75] Similarly, the official contingents of the First Crusade did not attack Jews until the slaughter in
Jerusalem in 1099 in the heat of victory.

Very different was the religiosity of the popular crusaders. They
came from the area between the Seine and the Rhine where decentralization and rapid social change had most disrupted older social patterns, and where the language frontier raised disquieting questions
about Frankish and Germanic identity. Their collective action deviated
so flagrantly from the normal conduct of peasants and poor towns-
people, and from the prevailing hierarchic norms, that we can only
assume that they eagerly welcomed the alternative to their normal
lives. In Victor Turner's terms, their movement could be seen as a
desire to pass from their present identity to a new one, as an anti-
structure by which they sought to move from the constriction of their
assigned social roles into a broader, more equal, and more satisfying
community.[76]

The catalyst that moved the greatest number was Peter the Hermit,
a man poorly dressed who rode barefoot on a donkey, was believed to
bear a revelation received directly from Christ, preached repentance
and sacrifice, and summoned them with papal approval to abandon
their homes, take up the Cross, and go to the earthly Jerusalem. The
appeal of the universal religiosity inherent in this apostolic model demonstrated amazing power to detach large numbers of people in that
area from their social bonds in 1096. Peter's evangelical preaching had
fleetingly opened a passage out of the normal social structure—as Innocent III's authorization would later open one for those attracted by
Francis of Assisi.

Yet when we remember that the northern peasants of 1096 were largely ignorant of the new developments in theology and had grown up in a culture impregnated with the religiosity supportive of a people, and when we remember how empirical their crusading religiosity would be, we may suspect that most were attracted only very partially or incompletely by the appeal of universal religiosity inherent in Peter the Hermit's preaching. It seems more likely that most interpreted that militant appeal rather as a broadening of their own religiosity, as an invitation to become members of a greater people, of the people of Christendom whose leader, the pope, had summoned them to war. Of course, those who followed Peter the Hermit must have had many motives, but they had some strong sense of social ties. Their cohesion, very relative orderliness, and arrival at distant Constantinople indicate the restraining influence of a common purpose that encouraged social cooperation, as do some of the later reactions of the lower ranks of the official contingents against the self-interested and disintegrative polit-ical conduct of their leaders of the official crusade which delayed the capture of Jerusalem.

The fact that these groups did not massacre Jews not only corrob-orates the existence of some fragile consensus but also says something about its nature. People who had felt constricted, degraded, and alien-ated in a rapidly changing society, and who were sensitized to the appeal of a more universal religiosity and society, were not initially predisposed to attack Jews—as would also be true of the early Fran-ciscan movement. Doubtless they were newly aware that Judaic reli-giosity was a denial of their own, but they do not seem to have felt menaced by it. They were leaving their old society with its Jews; their identity and religiosity was now that of their new community that had no territory and contained no Jews; and they were marching toward a future triumph.

Those who did feel threatened and used force to extirpate Judaic religiosity by baptism or death followed other leaders. Our knowledge of them is scanty, and we may concentrate on Emicho of Leiningen and his followers, for they were indisputably responsible for the great-est massacres. Unfortunately, we have little reliable knowledge about them. We do know that, although they had been excited by Peter the Hermit's preaching, they did not join him but collected after his de-parture. They were led, not by a hermit or priest, but by a Rhineland count of dubious reputation who now claimed to be physically marked with a cross and was joined by a handful of French and German knights. From the outset, they defied both secular and ecclesiastical authority as they plundered and massacred, even delaying their trip to the Holy Land to attack Jews. When they did set off, they were so disorderly and rapacious, despite the leadership of some experienced knights, that they were attacked by the Christians along the route and never reached Constantinople. And if the reports about Emicho's cross and the goat and goose inspired by the Holy Spirit to lead them may be believed, their religiosity was remarkably empirical.

Their conduct suggests that social ties meant little to them and that the social dimension of their religiosity had disintegrated, either because their satisfaction in the identities assigned them by society had been undermined by social change, or because personal incapacities prevented them from fulfilling the roles assigned them satisfactorily. Like Peter the Hermit's followers, they left their old society without waiting for the official contingents that embodied the norms of Frankish religiosity. But unlike Peter the Hermit's group and like the official contingents, they seem to have been little affected by the appeal of universal religiosity or the vision of a greater people of Christendom and very easily deflected by possibilities of plunder. And, unlike either, they had immediate recourse to violence, not only against Jews but also against the authorities of their own society.

It is hard to believe that Emicho and his followers were moved to repentance and sacrifice by Peter the Hermit's appeal or the Gospels; they were anything but intropunitive. Yet it is undeniable that they oriented themselves by religious symbols, whether Jerusalem, the Cross, Jews, or a goat inspired by the Holy Spirit. They were the products of a culture deeply impregnated with Christian symbols, not Nazis bathed in nationalism. Nor were they atheists. Almost all must have believed unthinkingly in the existence of a superior, supra-empirical reality which they designated by Christian symbols. Despite Meyer, they did not attack Jews simply out of brutal greed. Whatever the attraction of booty, what they sought to extirpate was the Judaic religiosity that incarnated doubts about their own faith: Jews were not killed if they would accept baptism. It was because they were Christians that Emicho and his followers focused their anger on Jews. But what were the other characteristics of their religiosity that made them react so differently from the other crusaders?

They seem to have been catalyzed by religious symbols to react collectively and violently against their society without any vision of a new society, of a satisfying life in this world. In contrast with people like Robert of Arbrissel and Peter the Hermit and his followers, they seem to have been unwilling or unable to reintegrate the empirical and supra-empirical poles of their religiosity, unable to find a new Christian way of life, whether social or individual—other than that of destruction. If so, we are faced with the conclusion that, if their religiosity seems weaker than that of others, it was not because they disbelieved in Christ. It was because their trust in the connection between God and any earthly society they could conceive had weakened so drastically—and with it their assurance of the value of their own earthly identity as individuals—that they were prepared to take any action, however extreme, that seemed to reconnect them with God and reassure them of the value of their existence.

When the call to holy war offered that opportunity, they seized it feverishly and tried to reorient themselves by Jerusalem, a leader, Emicho, allegedly stamped with the Cross, the Jews, the infidels, and the goat inspired by the Holy Spirit. These Christian symbols were concrete realities, accessible without intermediaries; through them, they felt directly reconnected with their god from whom they had felt estranged; they were present realities that could be reached and utilized more or less immediately by people whose tolerance for frustration was low. And therein lay the seeds of the tragedy from which Archbishop Egilbert tried to save the Jews of Trier in May of 1096.

The preaching of the crusade had excited some of the most alienated, frustrated, and aggressive individuals, who sought immediate gratification, to give new meaning for their lives through violence that was connected with Christ through Christian symbols and that would, they had been told, save them. The symbolically designated object closest at hand was the relatively defenseless Jews, "God's worst enemies," a central symbol for Christians but also real humans who could be subjugated or killed. Horrible as it was, Emicho and his followers' campaign of militant conversion differed in style from Charlemagne's military conversion of the Saxons primarily in its lack of social legitimation and shortsightedness and in the relative defenselessness of those who suffered from it.

My analysis might seem open to the criticism that I have exculpated Christianity in much the same way as Grousset by questioning the Christianity of Emicho and his followers. So let me reemphasize that it was people who believed in the divinity of Christ and sought connection with him who brought death to Rachel, daughter of Isaac, to her young sons Isaac and Aaron, to her beautiful daughters Bella and

Madrona, and to the hundreds of other martyrs of Mainz, Worms, Cologne, and other cities. Indeed, these people massacred Jews because, despite their disorientation and alienation, they still believed in Christ and had been affected by the new emphasis on the historical life of Jesus and the role in his death ascribed to Jews. They were able to do so, moreover, because few other Christians would oppose them when Christendom was fighting its enemies.

Nor should we forget that although Emicho's band would have its successors in the followers of Rindfleisch in 1298 and the Armleder in 1338 and others, the effort to eliminate Judaic religiosity would meanwhile be pursued less violently but more effectively and constantly by Christians whose religiosity was supportive of social authority. After 1096, Christian anti-Judaism became increasingly general and violent. By 1500, western Europe would be nearly *judenrein* without papal protest, not because of voluntary conversions from Judaic to Christian religiosity, but because of the physical coercion—exercised without papal protest—by people such as Edward I of England, Charles II of Anjou, Philip IV of France, the authorities of many German towns, and Ferdinand and Isabella of Spain. It may be possible to exculpate Christianity from the persecution of Jews by defining Christian religions abstractly in carefully chosen normative terms, but if Christianity is defined empirically by the religiosity of its adherents, no sweeping dissociation is possible, only distinctions between different kinds of Christians.

5.

Doubt in Christendom

When faith is affirmed in words, it becomes belief, and the obverse of belief is doubt or disbelief. When people begin to think about their faith, to formulate their beliefs for themselves and assert them to others, that need is accompanied by—often impelled by—the recognition that not everyone believes as they do, that their beliefs may be or are consciously rejected by others, and that they may even have doubts about some of their beliefs themselves. That is certainly true of Christianity. Through the centuries, Christians have formulated their faith as beliefs against the pressure of other people's doubts or disbelief and had doubts themselves. That pressure affected the development of Christian beliefs and conduct in fundamental ways, most evidently in the division of Christianity into different religions and most tragically in the persecution of those considered heretics and of Jews.

It would take volumes to describe and analyze all the doubts that bothered Christians through the centuries and to trace their consequences.[1] Here I will only discuss them schematically in order to distinguish different kinds of doubt, to argue that, beginning in the eleventh century, many Christians began to be bothered by a new kind of doubt, and to suggest how that new kind of doubt affected attitudes toward Jews.

Since there have been many Christian beliefs, what Christians doubted has varied. Their doubts have varied not only in specific content but also in kind, provoking different kinds of reaction. Doubts differ in kind because there are different ways of thinking. Thus Christian thinkers—and not they alone—have used the terms "reason" and "faith" to distinguish between two very different ways of thinking about reality, and consequently they have had at least four different kinds of doubt. While accepting that reason is a common and defining characteristic of all human beings save infants and idiots, Christian thinkers have thought of faith as a different mode of understanding derived from a different source. As Aquinas put it,

> It was necessary for man's salvation that there should be a knowledge revealed by God, besides philosophical science built up by human reason .... [for] the end must first be known by men who are to direct their thoughts and actions to the end. Hence it was necessary for the salvation of man that certain truths which exceed human reason should be made known to him by divine revelation.[2]

Although I would express it differently and insist that faith is as much a characteristic of non-Christians as of Christians and that Aquinas was using "truth" in two different senses, I think a broad distinction of that kind is necessary for any analysis of religious phenomena, especially religious doubts. Since I have discussed my own conception of the difference at length elsewhere,[3] I need only indicate it briefly here. One kind of thinking is the rational empirical thinking, be it pretheoretical and practical or sophisticated and scientific, that is constrained by logic and observation, is a common human property, and enables us to solve the practical problems that must be solved for physical survival. The other, nonrational thinking, often referred to as symbolic thinking, is the kind that finds expression in art and affirmations of belief. This mode of thinking is also or even more a universal human characteristic, for it precedes rational empirical thinking. It is the resultant of the totality of our experiences, a resultant that we express in the dominant beliefs that guide our purposive conduct, including our use of our capacity for rational empirical thinking to solve specific problems.

Expressions of nonrational thinking differ most obviously from rational empirical propositions in that symbols or words are not used unambiguously to denote the same entities or processes. As is evident in poetry, symbols are used polysemically and connected with each other without regard to logic in changing ways that evoke and associate wide ranges of disparate experience. Rather than dealing with specific phenomena or practical problems, nonrational thoughts express our sense of the global meaning and value of our diverse experiences. Yet, if this kind of thinking is not logical, neither is it irrational, for it uses logic and observation in a subordinate role. Thinking only becomes irrational when the interplay between nonrational and rational empirical thinking is inhibited, when people repress their capacity for observation and reality-testing in an effort to protect cherished nonrational beliefs that are menaced by available rational empirical knowledge.

If poetry is an obvious example of this kind of thinking, a particularly rich example is biblical exegesis, which might be called second-level nonrational thought, that is, nonrational thinking about expressions of thought. As Beryl Smalley so well put it,

> One finds, as did Alice, a country governed by queer laws which the inhabitants oddly regard as rational. In order to understand medieval Bible study one must live there long enough to slip into their ways and appreciate the logic of their strict, elaborately fantastic conventions. Philo admits that anything in Scripture may signify any other thing provided that it obeys the rules of an intricate pseudo-science, the allegorical interpretation.[4]

Smalley's ironic tone indicates that the relations asserted by this mode of thought are not in fact rational; if she speaks of logic, the term is used metaphorically to refer to the conventions that govern the resulting fantastic associations. To take one example, if we read Caspary's extensive and fascinating analysis of one instance of biblical exegesis,[5] we can see that Origen's conscious elaboration of nonrational symbolic relations was indeed governed by complex conventions. But whether or not the conventions were the structures of thought detected by Lévi-Strauss or Dumézil, they were not the rules of logic and empirical inquiry.

That broad distinction between kinds of thinking enables us to differentiate at least four kinds of doubt. One kind, the rational empirical doubts about rational empirical propositions so frequent in everyday life and among scientists, will not concern us here. The other three are directly relevant to religious thought and action. Religious doubts may be caused by the appeal of competing beliefs or religions, by awareness that beliefs as formulated are logically self-contradictory, or by the recognition that religious beliefs clash with empirical knowledge. The first is what I shall call nonrational doubts, for example, doubts about whether the Holy Spirit proceeded from the Father and the Son or from the Father alone. The second, with which I will be less concerned here, is the rational doubts that arise when theologians find logical contradictions in their formulations of beliefs, as Thomists and Ockhamists did in the Middle Ages. The third is the rational empirical doubts about beliefs that can arise when affirmations of faith are stated as empirical propositions and seem contradicted by empirical knowledge, for example, doubt about the dogma that priestly consecration changes bread and wine into flesh and blood.

Christians had their uncertainties from the beginning, and they inspired many debates between Christians in the first centuries, but initially and for centuries after, their doubts were almost entirely nonrational. When the Marcionites, Gnostics, Montanists, Arians, Athanasians, Donatists, Pelagians, and others argued with each other about the nature of God, his actions, his providential plans, and the conduct he commanded, what they were arguing about was unobservable save as beliefs in their own minds; their disagreements and doubts were not amenable to rational empirical discussion and only very secondarily to logical resolution.

True, Christians based their faith on something they claimed was, or had been, observable, the resurrection of Jesus of Nazareth. But Jesus was no longer there, and though his resurrection could be asserted on the basis of reports, as Paul insisted, that event could no longer be observed and could be doubted, as Paul also recognized.[6] And as Paul knew only too well, and as Christians would be reminded through the centuries by the New Testament—the majority of Jews at the time, including Jews who had encountered Jesus, had rejected that cornerstone of Christian faith, as most Jews would continue to do for centuries after. Thus, in addition to any uncertainties Christians might have had amongst themselves, such as those of doubting Thomas, they were confronted from the outset by the challenge of Jewish nonrational, rational, and rational empirical disbelief.

To protect their faith, Christians not only had to develop their own expressions of it, they had to explain why most Jews had not believed. And the need only became greater when Christians sought to persuade non-Jews of the truth of their gospel and had to explain why most Jews rejected it. In the first centuries, however, Christians did not advance rational empirical explanations of Christian belief and Jewish disbelief. They were not social psychologists searching for an objective explanation of why they believed as they did; they were seeking to understand what had happened according to their new beliefs. In any case, since the minority of Jews who had believed in Jesus and the majority who did not had shared broadly the same physical, cultural, and social environment and the same religious beliefs, and had heard the same message from Jesus, the knowledge available in the period did not provide any obvious empirical explanation of the cleavage. Moreover, any effort to explain rationally and empirically why Jews had not believed Jesus would imply that Christian belief could similarly be explained away by this-worldly arguments. Hence, not surprisingly, Christians produced nonrational arguments.

To put it in my terms, they explained the Jewish refusal to believe in Jesus and to understand scripture as the Christians did by the belief that Jews were unable or unwilling to utilize their nonrational capacities properly. That explanation came in three somewhat different forms. Christians asserted that most Jews had not understood because Jesus' message was divine but obscure and accessible only to a select group; that God had deprived most Jews of the necessary mental—or spiritual—capacity to understand; and that most Jews refused even to try to understand because they were immoral. The first explanation appears in the earliest Gospel.

> And when he was alone, those who were about him with the twelve asked him concerning the parables. And he said to them, "To you has been given the secret of the kingdom of God, but for those outside everything is in parables; so that they may indeed see but not perceive, and may indeed hear but not understand; lest they should turn again, and be forgiven." And he said to them, "Do you not understand this parable? How then will you understand all the parables?"[7]

The second and most influential explanation was created by Paul. If anyone needed an explicit explanation of Jewish disbelief, it was Paul. He who had been a Pharisee and persecutor of Christians not only became a Christian but the apostle to non-Jews. He had to try to understand what had happened to him and to explain why it had not happened to so many other Jews. His answer is the earliest extant formulation of what would become the main explanation of Jewish disbelief. As he put it, paraphrasing Deuteronomy and Isaiah, "What then? Israel failed to obtain what it sought. The elect obtained it, but the rest were hardened, as it is written, 'God gave them a spirit of stupor, eyes that should not see and ears that should not hear, down to this very day.' "[8]

Or, as he interpreted a passage in Exodus,

> But their minds were hardened; for to this day, when they read the old covenant, that same veil remains unlifted, because only through Christ is it taken away. Yes, to this day whenever Moses is read a veil lies over their minds; but when a man turns to the Lord the veil is removed.
> And even if our gospel is veiled, it is veiled only to those who are

perishing. In their case the god of this world has blinded the minds of the unbelievers, to keep them from seeing the light of the gospel of the glory of Christ, who is the likeness of God.[9]

By the time of the fourth Gospel, a third explanation appeared that explicitly attributed the alleged blindness to Jewish immorality in words attributed to Jesus.

> Why do you not understand what I say? It is because you cannot bear to hear my word. You are of your father the devil, and your will is to do your father's desires. He was a murderer from the beginning, and has nothing to do with the truth, because there is no truth in him.[10]

If Christians and Jews had disagreed only about Jesus' preaching about the kingdom of heaven and his divinity, the disagreement would have been purely nonrational, a debate about unobservable matters that no rational empirical argument could settle. But another matter of disagreement could be directly and continuously observed by both sides, the writings that Paul referred to as the Old Covenant. Jesus had presented his message as a further intepretation of, or addition to, prior divine revelations to the Jews, and most Christians thereafter accepted that the Hebrew scriptures (as they incorporated them in their own Old Testament) were divinely inspired, that they revealed not only actions of God but even the words he had addressed to human beings directly or through his prophets. Save for the Marcionites, who cut the Gordian knot of Jewish disbelief by denying the validity of the Old Testament, Christians had to interpret the words of the Old Testament so that they could be understood as pointing toward Jesus of Nazareth and confirming his divinity. Not only that; they also had to explain why Jews interpreted scripture differently—the problem Paul recognized so early and wrestled with so ambiguously in his Epistle to the Romans.

For these and other reasons, there had to be a Christian understanding of Hebrew scripture. "When pressed for evidence of the supernatural origin of Christianity, the second-century Church sought an answer principally in the fulfilment by Jesus of Old Testament prophecy and in the universal diffusion of the faith."[11] Indeed, "for many centuries the exposition of prophecy continued to form the prime content of the instruction given to catechumens when they were taught about the person of Christ."[12] But there also had to be an explanation of why Jews did not interpret the same scripture, their scripture, as Christians did. Consequently, "virtually every major Christian writer

of the first five centuries either composed a treatise in opposition to
Judaism or made this issue a dominant theme in a treatise devoted to
some other subject."[13] Central to these polemics were arguments that
Jews misunderstood the meaning of passages in Hebrew scripture. As
Justin Martyr put it in the second century when talking to a Jew, they
are "your Scriptures, or rather not yours, but ours. For we believe and
obey them, whereas you, though you read them, do not grasp their
spirit."[14]

What linked Jews and Christians so closely, but also ensured enduring disagreement, was that they agreed on one thing: that Hebrew
scripture was divine revelation and that it had one, divinely authorized
meaning. Today, scholars who do not adhere to a Judaic or Christian
religion, and even many who do, analyze the text very differently.
Thanks to the evidence of centuries and to the work of the semioticists
and deconstructionists, we have recognized the extent to which the
meanings stimulated by a text, particularly a text as full of allegorical
and poetic language as the Bible, necessarily differ between author and
reader and from reader to reader or from one school of thought to
another. But the Jewish and Christian canonization of a work whose
ultimate author was thought to be the one God implied that it could
have only one correct meaning, and that properly disposed readers
would discern that meaning. Neither Jews nor Christians believed
there could be valid conflicting interpretations of scripture (although
there might be different layers of meaning), and both Jews and Christians believed they understood what Hebrew scripture meant, that is,
what God meant. But since Christians had developed a radically different belief about God, indeed worshiped as god someone Jews did
not, their interpretation of Hebrew scripture differed irreconcilably
from that of Jews.

The standard Christian argument, repeated ad nauseam through the
centuries, was nonrational: that Jews understood only the literal meaning of their Scripture, not its spiritual meaning. Of course, the Old
Testament had been written by Jews and was replete with nonrational
expressions and poetic or metaphorical language, and Jews did not
interpret their scripture only literally. But that fact was concealed because Jews and Christians could not agree on what was literal and
what was spiritual or metaphorical. Contributing greatly to that confusion was the fact that both sides made assertions about God or his
actions as if they were empirical propositions, literally true in the way
any empirical proposition was true. What each side refused to recog-

nize was that many passages they understood as referring to divine attributes or action could not have a literal meaning, if by literal we mean a fixed meaning. The meaning they gave these passages depended on the meaning they gave the symbol "God," but "God" was a polysemic symbol, not an observable phenomenon. Consequently, the meanings both sides gave to the disputed proof texts depended on their own nonrational thinking and differed because they had different nonrational convictions. Each side could attribute its own literal and symbolic meanings to the crucial passages.

In arguing against Jewish interpretations, Christians attributed their own literal meaning to many poetical passages and attributed their own allegorical meanings to many literal passages. One technique was to take a metaphorical passage, give it a literal interpretation that made it seem absurd, attribute that reading to the Jews, and then put forward a Christian spiritual meaning. Since nothing in revelation could be absurd, Christians could argue that the literal-minded Jews had misunderstood the passage, that it could only be understood spiritually or metaphorically, and that, when so understood, it supported Christian beliefs. Nowhere was that more the case than in the treatment of metaphorical passages from the prophets and the Psalms on which Christians relied so heavily to demonstrate that their Christ was foreseen in the Old Testament.

A good example[15] appears in the earliest extant polemical treatise against Jews, Justin Martyr's *Dialogue with Trypho*, a real or fictional Jew. Justin quotes at length from Psalm 72 (Vulgate 71), which, according to Jews, was a prayer for Solomon. It asks that God give to "the king's son" justice to judge, life as long as the sun endures, peace, dominion from sea to sea and from the river to the ends of the earth, the service of all nations, a name blessed forevermore, and many other things. But Justin takes this hyperbolic, nonrational prayer or expression of hope literally as if it were a prophecy of empirical events, points out that none of the things foretold in the Psalm happened to Solomon, and then declares that that demonstrated that "the words clearly proclaim that they were spoken of the eternal King, that is, Christ."[16]

In brief, Jews engaged in a hermeneutical interpretation of the totality of their scripture, and Christians engaged in a hermeneutical intepretation of the totality of their scripture—but these were different scriptures and different interpretations, for the text that the Christians interpreted as a whole included the New Testament. If the common ground that both Christians and Jews accepted, Hebrew scripture,

made dialogue seem possible, the scripture that only Christians accepted made enduring disagreement certain—and bitter. For nearly
two millennia, Christian apologists and polemicists were unable to
recognize that their nonrational intepretation of expressions of Judaic
nonrational thought as if they were empirical assertions made agreement impossible. But the Jewish interpretation of Hebrew scripture
was by no means the only challenge Christian thinkers faced in the first
centuries. They also had to confront Greco-Roman thought and society and, particularly after Constantine's toleration of Christianity, develop a Christian explanation of the history and future of the non-
Christian society in which they were now tolerated. Once again, their
explanation was nonrational.

Of all these efforts to explain their earthly existence in the light of
Christian beliefs, the most impressive, and the one that most influenced
the Middle Ages, was that of Augustine of Hippo, who found the
Trinity reflected in his psychology and reorganized all known history
in accordance with his Christian beliefs in the *City of God*. His depiction of the dynamics of history was not the result of rational empirical analysis but of faith seeking understanding. Though he incorporated much of the historical knowledge of his time, he explicitly
subordinated what he knew to what he believed, a subordination mir-
rored in his fundamental distinction between the history of the two
cities and the primary role he attributed to divine providence.

Yet if the meaning he gave to history was a direct expression of his
beliefs about his god and by no means what might be considered objective history, it was not irrational; he used the historical knowledge
of his time without seriously distorting it. Even if, for example, he
explained the destruction of Jerusalem and the dispersion of Jews from
Palestine by the Romans as a divine punishment for the death of
Christ, that was a nonrational association that in no way denied the
events he and others knew had happened. The belief only associated
the Roman Empire nonrationally with God as his unwitting agent, a
correlation also used by Ambrose to explain the indisputable fact of
the amazing spread of Christianity. Ironically enough, even Augustine's explanation of why God had permitted the continued existence
of Jews in a degraded condition—so that they could serve the truth of
Christianity by demonstrating that the Christians had not fabricated
their scriptures—was a nonrational interpretation of the empirical fact
that Jews continued to exist and that Christians were now able to

exploit Jews so as make their existence serve as an argument for Christianity.

By the end of the fourth century, some Christians, particularly ecclesiastics, had become increasingly hostile toward Jews, but their accusations were nonrational, not irrational. If they blamed Jews bitterly for the death of Jesus and their refusal to convert to Christian beliefs, the facts on which they based their charge were accurate. Since Jews did reject the Christian message and freely acknowledged that they had condemned Jesus as a heretic, the accusations did not falsify the known facts; they simply placed a Christian evaluation on them.

It is very hard to find any examples of Christian irrational hostility or irrational accusations against Jews in the Roman period. In general, and in marked contrast with what would occur later, Christians did not accuse Jews of conduct in which Jews did not engage, nor did they condemn Jews for any conduct other than their disbelief in Christianity or maintenance of Judaism. Despite the inflamed biblical rhetoric that some Christians, most notably Chrysostom, used to express their hostility, they perceived contemporary Jews realistically—so far as their limited knowledge, for example, of rabbinic Judaism, permitted. They disagreed with, or hated, Jews for what they really were, people who challenged and looked with contempt on Christian beliefs.

There are at least three obvious explanations of why Christians in the Roman period were not impelled toward an irrational conception of Jews. In the first place, Christianity had developed within an environment, the Roman Empire, that Christians had not created but had to recognize. Even after Christianity had become politically influential, Christians knew that they were a minority throughout the empire and could not change that environment radically. They had to accept it as an imperfect given, as the city of earth. What they could and did do, however, was to devote massive efforts of nonrational thought to transforming its significance so that they could understand their present world as a passing stage in providential history. And since they believed that things as they were were not what they should be and finally would be, they could recognize immediate realities they disliked, such as Jews, for what they were and deal with them, not by denying or distorting their reality, but by evaluating them according to their beliefs, which promised a better future. There was little pressure to distort or repress what they knew empirically.

A second and related explanation is that Christians lived in a world of religious pluralism. Not only were they a minority surrounded by polytheists, philosophers, Mithraists, and others, they were also divided among themselves and very aware of those divisions. Accustomed to living surrounded by disagreement and disbelief, they did not start from a presupposition of conformity that made religious dissent a sign of other kinds of aberrant conduct. Well aware that their message was spreading but that the mission was by no means complete, they were more concerned to assert their faith than to think of those who disagreed with them as social deviants or criminals in the secular sense. They probably also recognized that it would weaken their efforts to make converts if they gave a picture of Jews that non-Christians knew was false.

A third, more abstract explanation—and one applicable particularly to the more sophisticated Christian leaders—may be found in the prevailing epistemology, which favored nonrational thought and diminished the likelihood of a head-on clash with rational empirical thought. The most prized goals of Roman education were literary culture and rhetorical skill in persuasion—with all their reliance on metaphor and polysemic symbols. Although people were familiar with the basic elements of Aristotelian logic, the Aristotelian concern with rational empirical analysis had long since declined. Not only had philosophy been divorced from science but it had been perniciously influenced by rhetoric.[17] Those who considered themselves philosophers were more concerned with seeking wisdom concerning god and determining the best way of life, in other words, with second-level nonrational symbolizing and moral evaluation, than with the kind of systematic logical thought about empirical reality often pursued by Aristotle.

To the extent that Christian thinkers did not dismiss philosophy, it was primarily Middle Platonism and Neoplatonism that attracted them, not surprisingly since those schools of thought maintained that the highest reality was immaterial, that the material world was an imperfect reflection of eternal ideas in the mind of God, and that truth was achieved by an internal awareness of having come into contact with those ideas. And if the heuristic value of that epistemological stance for psychological self-analysis may have been great, it was not conducive to logical analysis of empirically observed phenomena. For in their eyes, truth did not come through such analysis; it came from above through mental contact with God or, as Augustine would have put it, through the divine illumination accorded to men whose will was, thanks to grace, well disposed.

Hence, although Augustine continually distinguished between reason and authority, or reason and faith, what he meant by rational knowledge differed radically from what it meant to Aristotle or a modern scientist. *Curiositas*, the pursuit of knowledge for its own sake, was to be avoided. Scientific knowledge was of no interest in itself. Scientific findings were useful only to furnish illustrations for an argument about a higher truth,[18] in other words, to buttress a highly sophisticated form of second-level nonrational thought. It was therefore very unlikely that Augustine or those who thought like him would ever have to face an insoluble conflict between their nonrational thought and their rational empirical knowledge. What they sought was ultimate certitude about the universe as a whole, and what they found was so internal and immaterial as to be almost immune to empirical invalidation.

Whatever the precise reasons, Christians in the late Roman Empire were able to achieve a highly sophisticated form of nonrational thought that utilized much of the prevailing rational empirical knowledge and did not conflict with it in a way that might have impelled some to irrationality. And that was true also of Christian ideas about Jews. Christians did not accuse contemporary Jews of possessing characteristics or engaging in conduct they did not manifest. And after the fall of the Roman Empire in the West, such a conflict became even less likely because of changes in the character of Christian religiosity. More primitive social conditions rapidly lowered the level of education of the sub-Roman aristocracy, and with the conversion of the Germanic invaders and the rural sub-Romans and Celts, the literacy rate among all Christians declined radically. Even more important, the preconceptions according to which the new converts assimilated the Christian symbols and ideas that were presented to them were very different from those of the Christian thinkers of the fourth century.

From about 500 to 1000, the primary expression of Christian religiosity in the West was through ritual. Christians had faith in the sense of unreflecting trust in their god's power and were very concerned to propitiate him properly through ritual. There was little concern for assent to propositions about the nature of that god beyond the acceptance of a creed that they understood in their own way and used mainly as a ritual. Among the few who were literate, there was, of course, second-level nonrational thought in commentaries on scripture and the like. But, with the exception of a few thinkers in the ninth century, such as John Scotus Erigena and Ratramnus of Corbie, neither of whose ideas was accepted, there was no Christian thinker who could be compared with those of the Roman period. Hardly anyone engaged in the kind of rational empirical thinking that might have made him aware of a conflict between his Christian beliefs and his empirical knowledge.

Even Erigena, who insisted that only scripture was to be accepted as absolutely authoritative and that everything else, including assertions of the church fathers, should be accepted only if consonant with reason, considered reason to be, not the application of logic to empirical observations, but the discipline of disputing properly in a Neoplatonic way.[19] Ratramnus was almost alone in his awareness of a conflict between what Christians were told to believe and what he could observe. Yet if the religiosity of the overwhelming majority of Christians made awareness of a conflict between their beliefs and their knowledge extremely unlikely, it had another characteristic that had the potential to arouse that conflict in a way unknown in Roman times.

Christian religiosity from 500 to 1000 was highly empirical in the sense that believers firmly expected that their trust in, and propitiation of, their god would bring immediate and observable rewards on earth as well as in heaven—a position diametrically opposed to that of Augustine. God was in direct and amazingly detailed control of what went on on earth. Belief in frequent very concrete acts of God— miracles—became a far more prominent part of Christian religiosity than it had ever been in the third and fourth centuries. We might describe this attitude as the objectifying of the supernatural or the materializing of the divine, an objectification most obvious in the insistence that Christ was really present in the bread and wine of the Eucharist but equally obvious in the cult of relics, a practice so central to medieval people that Luchaire described it as the true religion of the Middle Ages.[20]

That predisposition of Germanic or "primitive" religiosity was reinforced by the triumph of Christianity throughout western Europe, by the fact that by 1000 almost all western Europeans had placed their trust in Christ the King, that all political authorities avowed and supported Christian religiosity, and that western Europe was divided into dioceses and parishes and covered by churches and monasteries as it never had been in the Roman period. Except for the presence of pagans and Moslems on the borders and of some Moslems and Jews within, there was no religious pluralism, not even the variety of Christian dissent so familiar in the Roman period. In that overwhelmingly and monolithically Christian environment, Christ's sovereignty and control of all events seemed very real, a fact, not a faith.

To us, the empirical religiosity of the period may seem mere superstition, as it did to Luchaire, yet it was not irrational. If people believed that their kinglike god was all-powerful, had created the world, and would save those who worshiped him properly, and if their knowledge of natural forces was minimal in comparison with ours or that of the Greeks, there was nothing irrational about understanding inexplicable rewards on earth for which one had prayed as the result of divine action. After all, that attitude was by no means limited to the Middle Ages; the religiosity of Constantine and Ambrose was also, if to a lesser extent, empirical, and many people today still pray for help in this world.

But the religiosity of almost all Christians between 500 and 1000 was empirical to a degree unknown in the Roman period. Consequently, people expressed many nonrational beliefs flatly as empirical truths, and therein lay the potential for a new and most unsettling kind of doubt, rational empirical doubts. If, for whatever reason, Christians developed their ability to think rationally and empirically and increased their knowledge of natural processes, they might become uneasily aware of conflicts between the affirmations of their empirical religiosity and their rational empirical knowledge. And that is precisely what happened.

A striking change in mentality began in the late tenth century, whose radical effects are obvious by the later eleventh century. Though there has been little scholarly agreement on the causes and character of the change in outlook, there is general agreement on many of its effects. The most dramatic effect was the Investiture Contest, which involved the first conscious debate over the proper organization of medieval society. Almost equally striking was what has been called the "renaissance of the twelfth century," the new intellectual mastery of the works of Christian and non-Christian thinkers of the Greco-Roman period such as Augustine and Aristotle, and the new way in which that material was used by the Scholastics. Equally obvious is the economic "take-off" of Europe, the political reorganization of Europe under relatively effective central governments, and the outward thrust of the crusades. Hence, whether scholars locate the watershed around

1000, 1050, or 1096, they agree that the Middle Ages can be divided into two periods with very different characteristics. But as yet there is no consensus on why those changes occurred as they did.

The easiest answer is that after 950—with the end of the Viking, Saracen, and Magyar invasions, favorable climatic conditions, and new technologies—political and economic conditions improved rapidly, permitting demographic growth and providing a surplus of goods and people that allowed more and more people to engage constructively in activities such as commerce, government, and scholarship. The result was a recovery or renaissance of old learning and a religious reformation and renewal that built on earlier models of Christianity. The continuous development of Western civilization, interrupted by the fall of the western Roman Empire, the Germanic invasions, and the second wave of invasions from 850 to 950, began again. Against that view, however, it can be argued that what developed in Europe after 1000 was more a radical innovation than a rebirth, renewal, or further development of what had gone before.

The social and political breakdown between about 850 and 950 not only disrupted old patterns of social organization; it led to new ways of thinking. As the traditional social structures of western Europe were radically undermined, adventurous and fearful individuals were forced to think in new ways about their changed environment in order to survive.[21] In reaction to the weakening or disappearance of central government in northern Europe, the more powerful developed webs of feudal relations that were agreements sworn between individuals, not a system imposed from above. To compensate for the loss of opportunities for booty, the elite developed new relations with peasants, banal lordship, in order to exploit agrarian production. And to satisfy that dispersed elite's needs, commerce and towns, which had had little place in northern Europe before, expanded rapidly, placing a premium on their inhabitants' ability to calculate numerically and to estimate the reactions of others.[22]

By 1050, as a result of that strenuous effort to adapt to new conditions, the extreme decentralization of Europe was being reversed, and the major political, social, and economic features that would characterize society in the future were settling into place. That reorganization of life at the practical level was achieved by decentralized experimentation, by an ingenious utilization, modification, and recombination of known techniques in new ways. Not surprisingly, that pioneering outlook also stimulated new ways of thinking about religious matters.

Quantitative change and exploitation of the legacy of the past there was, but even more striking was the qualitative change in the character of religious thought, action, and social organization. To take the most striking example, though there had been scattered and ambiguous verbal claims of papal authority before 1046,[23] there had never been an effectively centralized church controlled by the bishop of Rome. At the end of the fourth century, Bishop Ambrose of Milan had exercised more authority than Bishop Siricius of Rome. By 1195, however, only fifty years after the beginning of the Investiture Contest, the bishop of Rome was able to launch a European army toward Jerusalem and was exercising heretofore unheard-of authority over churchmen and laity throughout Europe.

A new kind of church, indeed a new Christian religion, was being created, one whose structure and prescriptions would be carefully defined by popes, theologians, and canon lawyers in the course of the twelfth and early thirteenth centuries. Theological expression also changed radically. One has only to compare a medieval summa with any writing of Augustine or Bede to realize how radically the approach of theologians had changed. And while all that was going on, a new kind of secular government was being developed that differed greatly from the city-centered polities of antiquity: legal rational government (to use Weber's terminology) centralized by a single person whose authority depended on the cooperation of a widely dispersed rural elite.

Though there was significant continuity, it seems difficult to explain those changes as primarily a recovery and renewal of what had been going on before, made possible by more favorable economic and political conditions. A different line of explanation is suggested by several well-known features of the period after 1000: the new image of Christ, the proliferation of evangelical ascetics, the appearance of popular movements considered heretical by the Catholic church, theological debates among the learned, a new mastery of nature and interest in investigating it, and a new kind of doubt about fundamental Catholic beliefs. A major change in mentality began to occur well before the Investiture Contest, and with it came an upsurge of religious doubts.

As Chenu and Southern have made clear in different ways,[24] people began to think of their god in a dramatically new way, Romuald,

Damian, Anselm, Bernard, and Francis of Assisi being the most salient. Instead of the former conception that largely collapsed the Trinity into the single image of Christ and portrayed him as an all-powerful king and judge, resembling the God of the Old Testament, people began, starting in the last quarter of the tenth century, to think of Christ—or Jesus, as he was more frequently called now—in a strikingly new way. Although the whole Bible had been available and read by some for centuries before, the Gospel stories of the observable events that were the foundation of Christian faith had received remarkably little attention before 1000 and been understood very differently. But starting around 1000, for reasons that have never been adequately explained, an increasing number of people began to read the Gospels literally as reports of observable human events, to think of Jesus as a suffering human, and to empathize with his sufferings and those of his mother. Thereafter, that new understanding spread remarkably, finding magnificent expression in Cistercian religiosity and supreme expression in Francis of Assisi.

The new conception of Christ was closely connected with another well-known novelty, the multiplication of eremetic ascetics such as Romuald, Damian, and Robert of Arbrissel, who were deeply moved by their new sense of closeness to Jesus through the humanity they shared, and who were impelled to spread that good news to others by evangelical preaching. Not only that, several of them rejected the triumphant form of ascetic life of the Cluniac order as inadequate and founded new monastic orders whose way of life accorded better with their new vision of Jesus and new sense of purpose. No wonder Southern declared that this period has the characteristics of an "age of conversion."[25]

New ways of thinking and the doubts they produced are even more obvious in the popular religious movements that appeared before the Investiture Contest and were condemned as heretical by ecclesiastical authorities.[26] About 1000, a highly eccentric and otherwise unimportant individual in northern France named Leutard apparently rejected the authority of the Old Testament, relied only on the authority of the Gospels, and attracted a number of followers. Some twenty years later some people farther south at Limoges apparently denied the efficacy of baptism and images. Far more striking, however, was the thought of some canons and laity at Orléans between about 1015 and 1022. They apparently held that Christ was not really born of Mary, did not really suffer to save humanity, and did not rise from the dead. They are said to have justified their position by arguing that they had not been there to witness Christ's life and death and did not believe something just because it was written down. They also seem to have denied the efficacy of baptism, the Eucharist, and prayers for the dead. They apparently based their argument on a premise that could be taken as the motto of the new kind of doubt: "what nature denies is always out of harmony with creation." They were burned by King Robert the Pious of France in 1022, the first execution for heresy in western Europe since that of Priscillian in 385.

Other localized religious movements appeared before 1050. Usually inspired by some clerical leader, they had in common a tendency to rely on the Gospels, to reject infant baptism and the Eucharist, to deny either the humanity or divinity of Christ, and to emphasize their inspiration by the Holy Spirit. By 1049, the council held by Pope Leo IX at Reims observed that heresy was rampant throughout Gaul. Evidence of such movements disappears in the second half of the eleventh century, possibly because of the excitement engendered by the Investiture Contest. But the so-called peasants' crusade of 1096 demonstrates that many at the lower levels of society were thinking about their god in new ways and acting in an unprecedented fashion. And in the first half of the twelfth century, the spreading impact of new ways of thinking on lay people is very obvious in fairly large popular religious movements that emphasized the Gospels and denied the efficacy of the sacraments and the authority of the clergy.

We know most about the movements in southern France led by Peter of Bruys and Henry of Le Mans or Lausanne, thanks to Peter the Venerable's polemic against the movements and to the monk William's account of a debate he had with Henry of Lausanne.[27] Henry rejected the authority of the church fathers as merely human and relied only on the New Testament to support his beliefs. Peter apparently rejected not only the fathers but also the Old Testament and any parts of the New that were not the reports of eyewitnesses. Both rejected infant baptism. Henry held that unworthy priests could not make Christ present in the Eucharist, and Peter denied that priests had any sacramental power. He also condemned the use of the Cross as a symbol because it was an instrument of torture, and he denied that there had been any supernatural intervention in the world since Christ, save for the impalpable working of the Holy Spirit. Like the group at Orléans, Henry and Peter clearly preferred to modify radically the nonrational beliefs with which they had grown up rather than to suppress their ability to think for themselves about what they could observe.[28]

There were several such movements in the twelfth century, and Brian Stock has argued that they were "textual communities," communities whose activities centered around texts made available orally by the literate interpreters who led the movements, and that this contact with the texts induced their unlettered followers to adopt "a type of rationality inseparable from the text," which in turn led them to a critique of the nature of observable reality.[29] He also argues that people in illiterate or oral cultures take the empirical reality of nature for granted, but that in these textual communities they now saw nature as something that had to be interpreted and authenticated by texts. "How could the given physicality of things be reconciled with forms of thought which suggested a more real existence at their core?"[30]

It seems to me that the causal sequence was almost precisely the reverse. The fundamental question for these people seems rather to have been: How could traditional formulations of empirical religiosity that had long been transmitted textually and orally be reconciled with what people knew empirically and refused to deny? There had been "textual communities" of literate and not very literate people in and around monasteries and cathedrals for five hundred years before this challenge, and they had not asked these kinds of questions. Why had this challenge not arisen before the eleventh century? Moreover, if we distinguish mentality from literacy, it is by no means certain that the literate leaders of these movements were very different in mentality from their illiterate audience.

What is most striking about these popular movements is their denial of so many widely prevalent and solidly textualized beliefs. In 1000 and for some time after, there had been a massive flow of capital to monasteries, especially the Cluniac order, because almost everyone believed that the prayers of the monks and the masses for the dead conducted by their priests assured salvation after death for the monks and their lay donors. But these dissenting movements denied the sacramental powers of priests, rejected the Eucharist, objected to infant baptism, and asserted that prayers for the dead were useless. They thus called in doubt fundamental beliefs and rituals on which people had long relied unquestioningly for their ultimate salvation. How could they?

Medieval thinkers typically spoke of the intellectual tensions of this period as the conflict between reason and authority that resulted from the new mastery and use of logic, and modern scholars have similarly written about the conflict between reason and faith or reason and revelation. That usage of "reason," however, masks the difference between logical thinking about metaphysical propositions and rational empiricism. Dialectical argument was not only the application of logic to the premises of faith and passages in revelation; it also encouraged and employed empirical arguments. And what seems decisively new in this period is the increasing reliance on empirical knowledge in religious thought.

If we examine the change in outlook of the popular religious movements of the eleventh and twelfth centuries, its novelty does not seem to lie in these people's insistence on logical thought but rather in their trust in their own concrete empirical knowledge. As their frequent emphasis on the Holy Spirit and rejection of infant baptism suggests, they were placing increasing trust in what they believed to be their divinely given ability to think for themselves as individuals about what they experienced. And when they thought for themselves, they found that their empirical knowledge conflicted with beliefs prescribed by their religion. They rejected those beliefs and sought beliefs that were consonant with nature, that is, with what they could observe with their own eyes, or thought they could have observed had they witnessed an event in the past.

As Chenu observed, as people gained some control of natural forces, there was a new attitude toward nature, a "realization which laid hold of these men . . . when they thought of themselves as confronting an external, present, intelligible, and active reality as they might confront a partner . . . whose might and whose decrees called for an accommodation or a conflict."[31] As they differentiated themselves from nature, they viewed it in a new light. According to Chenu, one result of that more scientific view was a desacralization of nature that produced a crisis in the old symbolic intepretation of nature.[32] It could be argued to the contrary, however, that what happened was just the opposite, a sacralization of nature in the sense that the empirical reality of nature gained an importance for religious thinking it had not had before.[33]

Christians were now confronting a new kind of doubt, rational empirical doubts. Increasingly, people were thinking that long-held religious beliefs, expressed in many texts, had to be authenticated, discarded, or reformulated according to what they knew about nature from their own direct experience. Their empiricism far more than their

logic threatened traditional beliefs. And though Chenu places the appearance of the new attitude in the twelfth century, it was already
apparent in the first half of the eleventh century, well before Berengar
had made his highly literate doubts heard throughout Christendom
and forced his fellow theologians to confront them. It was expressed
in the so-called heretical movements by people at a low social level
who knew nothing of Boethius or Aristotle.

The impact of doubts on theologians came a little later, but when
it came, it was pervasive. If we focused purely on intellectual history,
we might be tempted to think that the widespread debate about the
relative importance of reason and authority in the first half of the
twelfth century was simply a result of the new mastery of logic and its
application to traditional theological assertions, and that the doubts
the new use of logic occasioned were therefore purely rational doubts.
For there can be no doubt that the use of the new logic raised many
theological questions that could be argued logically but not resolved
empirically. But theologians also recognized increasingly that their formulations had to be couched in language that recognized the validity
of empirical knowledge—as the nominalists stressed. However much
they may have deployed their logic in abstact metaphysical arguments,
there was also an effort to reformulate expressions of belief so that
they not only did not defy logic but also did not conflict with what was
known empirically. An obvious example is the development of the
doctrine and dogma of transubstantiation with its distinction between
observable accidents and unobservable substance.

Rational empirical doubts about the Eucharist were first expressed
by a theologian in the Carolingian period, but they had little immediate impact. Though there were controversies about the Trinity, pre-
destination, and Iconoclasm in the Carolingian period, these were over
unobservable matters and were conducted primarily by arguments
from authority. But a new kind of doubt is apparent in the debates
over the virginity of Mary and the Eucharist between Ratramnus, a
monk of Corbie, and Radbertus, who later became abbot of Corbie. As
Pelikan describes the Marian controversy, Ratramnus declared that "a
preoccupation with the miraculous aspects of Christ's nativity beyond
'established nature or the authority of Holy Scripture' was a concession to 'heathen superstition,' by which the virgin birth would not have
been a genuine birth but a 'monstrosity.' "[34] That new concern with
what was natural is even clearer in the debate over the Eucharist.

In 831, Radbertus published his treatise *On the Body and Blood of the Lord* and sent a revised copy of it in 844 to King Charles the Bald. As Laistner noted, "the question of the Real Presence had never before been the theme of a formal treatise,"[35] but now it evoked interest. The king then asked Ratramnus, also noted as a theologian, for his opinion, and Ratramnus wrote a treatise of his own with the same title. Radbertus had proclaimed that in the Eucharist "nothing takes place under a figure, under a hidden symbol, but it is performed with a naked manifestation of reality itself." The consecrated bread and wine were the historical body and blood of Christ. In reaction to that flat-footed assertion of a nonrational affirmation as a rational empirical proposition, Ratramnus responded that the Eucharist was a mystery in which "it is one thing which appears to the bodily sense and another which faith beholds." For Ratramnus, the Eucharist "exhibits one thing outwardly to the human senses and proclaims another thing inwardly to the minds of the faithful." Ratramnus thus distinguished nonrational meanings sharply from empirical knowledge: the faithful did not eat the historical body of Christ.[36]

However isolated, the reappearance of relatively sophisticated second-level Christian thought in a northern European environment thus displayed a new and potentially very troubling awareness of conflicts between beliefs as formulated and empirical knowledge. It did not go farther because intellectual advance was suddenly arrested by civil war, the invasions of the Vikings, Saracens, and Magyars, and the breakdown of the Carolingian Empire. But after the invasions had ended, the intellectual climate changed radically as more and more people, even at the lower levels, began to think in a new way.

Soon after the appearance of a new emphasis on personal experience and the first popular religious movements, and in apparent contrast with them, a new systematic and impersonal body of law and theological teaching began to be developed in the schools. Southern found that coincidence paradoxical,[37] but when we focus on the appearance of doubts, there are obvious connections. If the evangelical ascetics doubted that the traditional forms of holy life were the best road to salvation, and if some "heretics" doubted what had been accepted as fundamental beliefs, it is not surprising that theologians were also affected by the more objective approach to observable events and were themselves troubled by doubts.

The beginning of the intellectual approach known as Scholasticism might be traced back to Gerbert of Aurillac (d. 1003) with his interest in logic and science, or to the great teacher Fulbert of Chartres (d.

1028), who placed great emphasis on grammar and dialectic but was Platonic in philosophy and held that human reason could only analyze theological problems to a very limited extent. But in a culture where many individuals were thinking freshly for themselves without central control, that interest in the proper use of language and in basic logic could also lead thinkers in the direction anticipated by Ratramnus, that is, to the recognition of conflicts between Christian beliefs and empirical knowledge.

It was Berengar of Tours (d. 1088), Fulbert's pupil and himself a renowned teacher, who made that new kind of doubt a central problem on the agenda of Christian theologians. He probably developed his ideas about the Eucharist in the course of the 1040s and formulated them explicitly about 1047 after becoming familiar with the arguments of Ratramnus, which were then attributed to John the Scot (Erigena).[38] By 1050, when his theses were officially condemned at the Council of Vercelli, they had attracted wide attention. Toward the end of his career, he had, on his own count, been condemned by fourteen synods. His opposition included some of the most celebrated thinkers of the day, Humbert of Moyenmoutier, Peter Damian, Lanfranc, and Guitmund of Aversa. As a result, it was now known throughout Europe that one of the most highly educated of clerics had challenged the assertion that the consecrated bread and wine of the Eucharist became Christ's true body and blood. It was even said that he had so many supporters that "the whole church everywhere has been infected . . . with this poisonous leaven."

"A portion of the flesh of Christ cannot be present on the altar . . . unless the body of Christ in heaven is cut up and a particle that has been cut off from it is sent down to the altar." For Berengar, so long as what could be observed was bread and wine, there was nothing physical on the altar but bread and wine, although the bread and wine had been made symbols of Christ for the faithful. Berengar was saying in effect that there was no empirical change in the bread and wine themselves, but that, through consecration and faith, they gained an added dimension that made Christ present to believers. By contrast, Cardinal Humbert, his most powerful opponent, forced Berengar to say (obviously with mental reservations) that "the bread and wine are the true body and blood of our Lord Jesus Christ . . . handled and broken by the hands of the priests and ground by the teeth of the faithful." As a later cardinal would declare, what was received at the altar was "no other flesh than that which he took to heaven for us, no other blood than that which flowed from his side."[39]

In the terms used here, Berengar distinguished between nonrational affirmations and rational empirical propositions, and he refused to accept a formulation of nonrational belief that would have forced him to deny his rational empiricism. When he became aware of an undeniable conflict between what he knew and what he was told to believe, he did not abandon his faith; he modified the language by which he expressed his beliefs in order to eliminate the conflict. His opponents and the authorities of the church, however, were far less willing to listen to empirical reason, for there were other considerations at stake. Maintenance of the literal interpretation of the Eucharist was of supreme importance for the priesthood, since its authority depended primarily on its monopoly of sacramental power.

Another very different but crucial consideration was the belief that the Eucharist differed from all the other sacraments in that it was a sacrifice, the distinctive sacrifice of Christianity, and a real sacrifice unlike those of the Old Testament. As Rupert of Deutz, who also wrote a treatise against Jews, insisted somewhat later, "if it consisted only in the sacrament, that is in bread and wine that had been consecrated but not changed, there would be no reason why the sacrifice of the New Testament would be superior to that of the Old Testament."[40]

Consequently, from Berengar to Aquinas, immense intellectual efforts were made to correlate Christ's invisible presence and the empirical reality of the bread and wine without denying the validity of empirical knowledge. The appearances were saved by the theories of concomitance and transubstantiation, which were so explicit—and so sensitive to empirical questions—that they even permitted an answer to as apparently empirical a question as whether a mouse could eat Christ's body and, if so, how long the body of Christ continued to exist within the mouse.

With Berengar of Tours, the medieval conflict between what is usually called reason and faith or reason and revelation began in earnest. After Berengar had insisted on an apparent conflict on a fundamental matter and resolved it by modifying his formulation of his faith, his opponents could not avoid the challenge. In responding on the specific issue, they were forced to face the general problem of the relation of human reason to faith. Cardinal Humbert, who took formulations of nonrational correlations very literally and then developed logical arguments from them that paid no attention to empirically obvious practical difficulties,[41] seems simply to have insisted on the logical consequences of taking the words of consecration literally. Peter Damian, who opposed Humbert on that issue, held that reason or philosophy did have a role in theology, albeit a very subordinate one, but he insisted that an omnipotent god could do what was rationally and empirically impossible. Damian could therefore hold that Christ was really and substantially present in the Eucharist despite the apparent rational and empirical impossibility. Lanfranc of Pavia was more favorable to the use of reason or dialectic in theological matters. Although he defended the traditional interpretation of the Eucharist, primarily by citing traditional authorities, he believed that reason or dialectic, when properly used, did not menace faith but rather confirmed it.

That limited legitimation of the use of reason sufficiently encouraged Lanfranc's most famous pupil, Anselm of Aosta, so that he reasoned about the most fundamental beliefs of his faith. Although he held that true understanding could only derive from true faith, he nonetheless developed his famous ontological argument for the existence of god. What is not always emphasized in discussions of that famous argument is that Anselm developed his argument in 1077–1078 because he was bothered by his awareness that he did not know of a single argument that was sufficient by itself to prove the existence of god and was obsessively determined to find one.[42] However untroubled his faith, something in his mentality made him painfully aware that he had no rationally convincing proof of the existence of his god. He even expressed a yearning for empirical proof as he asked God in prayer, "If you are everywhere, why do I not see you present?"[43] But that did not trouble him deeply, for he believed firmly in the god he could find in the inner chamber of his mind, where, he believed, all thoughts save those of god could be excluded. Twenty years later, however, he was still seeking rational arguments to buttress his faith.

In 1098, Anselm completed *Cur Deus homo*, which Southern considers a greater intellectual achievement than his ontological proof of god. In it, Anselm argued the necessity for human salvation of god becoming man. He was moved to write it partly by Roscelin's application of logic to the Trinity, which had raised the question of whether the Incarnation was a fact or a figment of the imagination. But he was also directly inspired by his awareness of Jewish disbelief, thanks to his knowledge of the polemical treatise, *Disputation of a Jew and a Christian*, by his friend Gilbert Crispin.[44] Moreover, as Anselm noted, not only did Jews reject that belief; many Christians wondered about the Incarnation in their hearts.

Such disbelief could be based on different kinds of argument. It could appeal to authority (i.e., God never revealed that he would become man in Hebrew scripture), to logic (i.e., humanity cannot be ascribed to God because the definition of God is logically incompatible with the definition of humanity), or to empirical observation (i.e., Jesus' life and death are fully explicable in normal human terms and support no supernatural explanations). Anselm dealt only with the logical problem. Because he accepted the premises of faith provided by the New Testament and its intepretation of the Old as the basis for his argument, he did not appeal to authority or respond with an empirical argument; he produced his famous logical argument. Nevertheless, it was his awareness of doubt that had moved him to recognize that there was a problem in equating god and empirical humanity.

If Anselm remained safely within the bounds of orthodoxy, his great achievement demonstrated a mastery of logic that only strengthened the obvious trend of the period and encouraged others to develop their own rational capacities and apply them to religious problems. And when someone of great capacity appeared, someone whose mentality found rational arguments more attractive than nonrational meditation, perhaps because he had not received a monastic indoctrination, the problem of the relation between reason and faith became a burning issue across Europe. As Bernard of Clairvaux, that master of the exposition of nonrational thought, put it with considerable insight if less accuracy,

> Master Peter Abelard . . . speaks iniquity openly. He corrupts the integrity of the faith and the chastity of the Church. He oversteps the landmarks placed by our Fathers in discussing and writing about the faith, the sacraments, and the Holy Trinity; he changes each thing according to his pleasure, adding to it or taking from it. . . . He is a man who does not know his own limitations, making void the virtue of the cross by the cleverness of his words.[45]

How far Abelard had gone is perhaps most obvious, not from his emphasis on the apparent contradictions in the writings of the church fathers or from his theological interpretations, but from his awareness of the observable sociological roots of the conflicts between faiths and between faith and reason. In his *Dialogue of a Philosopher with a Jew and a Christian*, the philosopher asks the Jew and the Christian, "Did some rational consideration induce you into your respective religious schools of thought, or do you simply follow the opinion of men and the love of your own people?" The philosopher then puts forward a strong empirical argument that upbringing had been more important and continues,

> But youths as well as adults, the unlettered as well as the lettered, are said to feel the same way about faith, and the one who does not go beyond the common understanding of the people is said to be the most steadfast in faith. Surely the result of this is that no one is allowed to inquire into what should be believed among his own people or to doubt what everyone affirms, without fear of punishment. For it is embarrassing for men to be questioned about that to which they are incapable of responding. . . . These even frequently burst into such insanity that they are not ashamed to declare that they believe what they admit they are unable to understand, as if faith consists in the utterance of words rather than in the understanding of the mind, and as if faith were more a matter of the mouth than of the heart. . . . The attachment of each to his own school of thought even makes them so presumptuous and proud that whomever they see separated in faith from themselves, they judge to be estranged from the mercy of God, and with everyone else condemned, they will declare that they alone will be blessed.[46]

We have no good reason to doubt Abelard's Christian faith, but he was thinking about faith and formulations of belief in a new way that implicitly raised the question of why, empirically, people had faith or believed as they did. He was twice condemned for his theological positions, and after his last condemnation, he was sheltered by Peter the Venerable. In striking contrast with Abelard, Peter the Venerable was steeped in monastic meditation and not a product of the cathedral schools. But even he (perhaps stimulated by Abelard?) would ask the same question about faith even more explicitly and try to answer it empirically, with peculiar results that demonstrate the gravity of the challenge posed by new, more empirical attitudes.[47]

It is unnecessary for my present purposes to examine at greater length the conflict between those who opposed the examination of beliefs in the light of reason and empirical knowledge and those who favored the effort to harmonize them. By the time of Aquinas, the recognition of doubts and the magnitude of the effort to overcome them without denying rational empirical knowledge could not be more manifest. To the extent that the medium is the message, the monotonous organization of Aquinas's *Summa theologica* is a monument not only to faith but also to doubt and the effort to overcome it. Each of its thousands of articles is most explicitly organized as a list of possible doubts, a contrary affirmation, and a refutation of the opposing positions. The centrality of questions, disputations, and determinations in the university curriculum bore the same message. And the activities of the Inquisition are evidence that questions and doubts were not restricted to intellectual circles, and that efforts to overcome or repress them were only partially successful. But there was another and very different kind of reaction to the appearance of rational empirical doubts.

When some people became uneasily aware of doubts or disbelief that challenged beliefs central to their sense of identity, they reacted irrationally. Irrational reactions are first obvious in connection with the Christians burned at Orléans in 1022. Although those condemned were clearly thoughtful people devoted to a very moral life, a contemporary chronicler accused them of engaging in sexual orgies and of a form of ritual cannibalism, of consuming the ashes of the infants produced by their orgies. Unable to face the challenge of their arguments directly, the chronicler protected himself by asserting that those whose thinking so challenged his own could not be normal human beings. The menace of the heretics' ideas was thus demonstrated, not by careful argument, but empirically, so to speak, by allegedly observable physical conduct that deviated so radically from normal human conduct as to demonstrate that their thoughts must be evilly wrong. During the next two centuries, other people would make similar allegations, and, in 1233, Gregory IX gave this kind of fantasy official backing in the bull *Vox in Rama*.[48] But worse was to follow.

Once Christians had begun to be bothered by a new kind of doubt, it was almost inevitable that their awareness of their own doubts would affect their thinking about Jews, the incarnation of disbelief in their midst. Between 600 and 1000, Jewish disbelief had troubled Christians very little. So long as Christians expressed their faith in Christ the King confidently, unreflectingly, and primarily through liturgy, they were little disturbed by the presence of Jews and not hostile to them.[49] Although some bishops occasionally tried to implement the laws established in the Roman period to restrict intercourse with Jews, their actions had little effect on general attitudes toward Jews. If pejorative statements about Jews by Christian writers of the Roman period were repeated in the commentaries of churchmen in this period,

polemic treatises against Jews were rare. Several were composed in
Visigothic Spain in the seventh century, when forcibly converted Jews
posed a special problem, but from then until about 1070 the only
polemical treatise specifically devoted to refuting Jewish arguments
was the anonymous *Altercatio Aecclesie contra Synagogam*, which was
apparently written in England about 950 and did not become widely
known.[50]

Discussions and arguments did continue, perhaps all the more easily
since relations between Christians and Jews were generally amicable.
Thus we hear of a debate between a Jew and a Christian in Pavia about
760, and Rabanus Maurus in the first half of the ninth century was
familiar with many of the Judaic arguments against Christianity. But
the most striking polemics were not treatises concerned with Jewish
disbelief as a general or pervasive problem; they were epistolary arguments between individuals occasioned by dramatic conversions. In
840–841, Paul Alvarus, a Christian converted from Judaism, argued
with Bodo/Eleazar, a Jew who had been a deacon at the court of Louis
the Pious; and about 1020, Henry, a cleric of Henry II of Germany,
argued with Vecelin, a Jew who had also been a cleric.[51] Thus, although there seems to have been considerable informal discussion,
Jewish disbelief provoked strong reactions only when something dramatic happened. But after the appearance of the Christian movements
that challenged old beliefs, and after Berengar had made it impossible
for theologians to avoid the challenge of empiricism, reactions to Jewish disbelief changed rapidly.

The new sensitivity to Jewish disbelief is obvious. The eleventh century ended with the massacre of Jews in northern Europe in 1096, the
first great massacre ever of Jews in Europe, and massacres would accompany later crusades.[52] The attacks in the Rhineland in 1096 were
an effort by illiterate people to extirpate Judaism by forced baptism or
massacre. They justified their conduct by the accusation that Jews had
killed Christ, and that thinking, like the crusading focus on Jerusalem,
seems in large measure a result of the new familiarity with the story of
Jesus' life in the Gospels as it was disseminated by Peter the Hermit,
Robert of Arbrissel, and other ascetic preachers of the new understanding of the Gospels. But the new sensitivity to Jewish disbelief was
by no means limited to illiterates or expressed only in physical attacks.
Between 1070 and 1150, at least seven major and several minor treatises were written with the explicit purpose of refuting Judaic belief
and hence quelling any doubts that Jewish disbelief might arouse, as

well as a famous treatise on the Incarnation which had Jewish disbelief openly in mind.[53]

About 1070, a cleric asked Peter Damian to write something so that he "could by rational arguments block the mouths of the Jews" who often argued with him, and so that he could triumph when arguing concerning Christ by deploying the manifest testimonies of Holy Scripture.[54] Damian felt that the cleric could better spend his time fighting the sins of the flesh and the machinations of the Devil, since Jews had been almost annihilated from the face of the earth. Indeed, Damian seems to have had little contact with Jews himself and little knowledge of Jewish arguments except from the polemical writings of the church fathers. Nonetheless, Damian approved the cleric's intent.

> It is certainly dishonorable that a man of the church be silenced through ignorance by those outside who make false accusations, and that a Christian, not knowing how to reason about Christ, should depart beaten and confused by insulting enemies. It often comes to this, that harmful inexperience of these things and innocence that is to be guarded against not only increases the audacity of the unbelievers but also begets error and doubt in the hearts of the faithful.[55]

Since Damian believed that faith was the foundation of all virtue and that, when the foundation was shaken, the whole edifice was threatened, he answered the cleric's plea with a little treatise. In the first two chapters, he brought together a large number of the passages from the Old Testament which Christians had long interpreted to demonstrate that God was a Trinity and that Christ was the fulfillment of the prophecies of the Old Testament. This long section concludes with an expression of amazement at the density of Jewish blindness. In the next section, Damian explained why Christians do not follow the legal prescriptions of the Old Testament. He then cited yet more passages from the Old Testament which he interpreted as foretelling Christ.

Yet, since he feared that the testimonies he had drawn from scripture would not draw Jews to faith in Christ (or protect inexperienced Christians), he tried briefly to convince Jews of their error by a quasi-empirical argument. He asked what grave sin Jews had committed so that God in his anger had punished them with dispersion and subjugation. According to the Old Testament, though they had sinned gravely before, they had always repented, their punishment had been limited, and God had shown mercy on them. Since then, however, as their own Josephus had described, thousands of Jews had been killed and thousands taken into captivity by Titus and Vespasian, and the remainder had been subjected to other peoples. For a thousand years there had been no Temple, king, or priests in Israel. They had incurred this great punishment because they had killed Christ and refused to repent. Damian therefore called on Jews to repent and abandon their blindness, but he doubted that this—hardly novel—argument would convince them either.

In fact, although Damian allowed his hypothetical Jew to ask why the Christians had abandoned certain practices of the Law, he did not present any difficult Jewish arguments against his own position. Indeed, he seems to have had no great interest in converting Jews and was inclined to leave that difficult task to his god. It seems probable that he wrote this treatise at a very busy time not so much to convert Jews as to protect Christians from "error and doubt." And if the diffusion of this unoriginal treatise owed much to Damian's great reputation, it also indicates that people were feeling a new need to refute the arguments of Jews.

Far more original, better informed, and more influential was the *Disputation of a Jew and a Christian* written about 1090 by Gilbert Crispin, abbot of Westminster, and submitted by him to Anselm.[56] However reworked after the fact to ensure that Christianity would emerge triumphant, it demonstrated familiarity with the fundamental objections of contemporary Jews and was apparently the outcome of real and amicable arguments between Gilbert and a Jew who had been educated at Mainz. It differs noticeably from Damian's treatise in that it seems a genuine effort to convince a Jew of the truth of Christianity by an open and intelligent discussion of how scripture should be interpreted and of why Christians intepreted the Old Testament as they did. Although the Jew is not allowed to have the best of the debate, he is nonetheless permitted to voice highly intelligent objections.

Various central issues are discussed: the validity or fulfillment of the Law, the immutability of God, the conception of God as a trinity, the possibility of God taking on humanity or of a human being God, the belief that the divine infinity could be circumscribed in the body of a human or a woman's womb, the idea that a virgin could either conceive or bear a child and remain a virgin, the question of whether the Messiah had or had not yet appeared, the Christian veneration of images in defiance of the biblical prohibition of images, especially the (for the Jew) horrifying image of Christ on a cross. As usual, the debate is carried on largely by reference to the authority of the Old Testament, and the Christian relies heavily on the distinction between the literal or human sense of various passages and their spiritual or divine sense. But whereas Damian, for the most part, simply quoted passages from the Old Testament as if their meaning were self-evident and did not try to justify his interpretations, Crispin argued his interpretations at some length, thereby acknowledging that there were problems inherent in understanding scripture.

Crispin's treatise is remarkable because it betrays no hatred of Jews, nor, we should note, does it stray into irrationality. The same is true of Anselm's *Cur Deus homo*. Having read Crispin's treatise, Anselm was well aware of the principal Jewish objection and opened his argument by summarizing their central objection, which struck at the core of Christianity.

> The unbelievers deride our simplicity, objecting that we do God an injury, and disgrace him, when we assert that he descended to a woman's womb, was born of a woman, was nourished with milk and human food, and — not to mention many other things unbecoming to God — suffered weariness, hunger, thirst, scourging and death on the Cross among thieves.

Though not a treatise against Jews in form or fundamental purpose, *Cur Deus homo* was nonetheless an argument to counter Jewish disbelief.[57] In contrast with Crispin, Anselm did not argue about passages in scripture but tried to find necessary arguments that would make the Incarnation rationally intelligible, given the premises of original sin and God's justice and mercy. Significantly, when confronted with the challenge, he rejected the older soteriological belief about the Devil's role and developed his own new and magnificent soteriology that focused on human capacity or incapacity. Faith seeking understanding had thus led him to doubt a centuries-old Christian formulation of belief and replace it with a new formulation.

Very different was another treatise that recognized that the age-old arguments between Christians and Jews about the meaning of passages in scripture would never lead either side to change its mind.[58] Peter the Venerable's *Against the Inveterate Stubbornness of the Jews* (ca. 1144) is perhaps the richest polemical treatise against the Jews. But Peter's mind worked in almost exactly the opposite way to Anselm's; he looked for empirical evidence rather than philosophical arguments to overcome challenges to his beliefs. When confronting the challenge of Jewish disbelief, he devoted most of his treatise to something jointly observable, the Old Testament, trying at length to demonstrate the validity of the Christian interpretation. But Peter seems to have recognized that even his careful restatement of the Christian interpreta-

tion of the Old Testament would not convince Jews, for he suddenly
threw up his hands and changed his argument dramatically.

He asked himself the basic question that underlay the whole dispute: How do any people come to have right faith? And he tried to
answer his question by a rational empirical argument about faith and
by asserting that the correctness of faith in Christ was proved by a
miracle he asserted anyone could observe. Even then, however, he recognized that his novel argument would not change the minds of the
Jews. And that so angered him that he proclaimed that Jews were not
rational human beings but animals who had lost the power of reasoning. Thus, whereas the first Christians had accused Jews of being
literal-minded people who lacked spiritual understanding, now, after
rational empirical doubts had appeared among Christians, Peter was
impelled to assert that Jews were neither spiritual nor rational, perhaps
not human.

Peter stands on the borderline between anti-Judaism and antisemitism, and not he alone. The new empiricism was not only affecting the
way Christians thought about nature and their own beliefs; it was
changing the way they thought about contemporary Jews. The emphasis on the historicity of Jesus' life and death and the role attributed
to Jews in the Christian account directed attention to the reality of
contemporary Jews. Jews, however, did not seem obviously blind or
evil in a way that supported Christian beliefs. Of course, Jews differed
saliently in their disbelief in Christ and were willing to challenge Christian beliefs openly so long as it was safe, as Peter the Venerable well
knew. Yet if people knew that contemporary Jews had different beliefs
and customs, the Jews they encountered spoke the same languages as
Christians, thought very similarly, and did many of the same things.
Their very normality made it hard to think of them as damned killers
of Christ. And their numbers were so small that they hardly seemed a
serious threat to the functioning of society[59] or any present religious
danger to individual Christians who were secure in their faith. But not
all Christians were, as Peter, who wrestled with his own doubts, also
knew all too well.

Christians in increasing numbers were challenging traditionally central Christian beliefs, some even doubting the reality of Christ's humanity. Those doubts could only be reinforced by awareness of the
normality and humanity of contemporary Jews, who lived in the midst
of an apparently triumphant Christendom yet still did not believe.

Their presence was officially tolerated, as Innocent III, echoing Augustine, would insist, because they served as a *proof* of Christianity. But in daily life, the very normality of Jews could seem a challenge to Christian beliefs rather than a proof of them. Christians who were seriously troubled by their own doubts were therefore predisposed to believe any charges that buttressed their own beliefs by depicting contemporary Jews as eternally deficient and evil, not only Christ-killers but also an immmediate, if camouflaged, danger to contemporary Christians.

Peter the Venerable took a long mental step in that direction, but his treatise had almost no influence. Other people, however, attributed cosmic evil to Jews in a different but also apparently empirical way that proved all too influential. Since the challenge of doubts had stimulated irrational fantasies about the Christians condemned as heretics, it is not surprising that irrational fantasies were now projected on that incarnation of disbelief, the dispersed minority of Jews. In 1150, for the first time in the Middle Ages, Jews were accused of conspiring to crucify Christian children to gain revenge on Christ and win back their freedom. Other similar charges soon followed. The economic and legal developments that now distinguished Jews in daily life from all Christians and encouraged Christians to think of them as a people apart facilitated their dissemination and credibility.[60] More and more people came to believe that Jews engaged in secret, though physically observable, conduct whose inhumanity demonstrated their cosmic evil and confirmed threatened Christian beliefs. By the end of the thirteenth century, irrational fantasies about Jews were widespread, and from then on, not calls to crusade but accusations of ritual murder, host profanation, and well-poisoning would arouse people to massacre thousands of Jews.[61] In addition to anti-Judaism, antisemitism had become part of medieval culture.

Part 3

Jewish Legal Status

6

"Judei Nostri" and the Beginning of Capetian Legislation

I

The ordinances on the Jews of 1223 and 1230 are generally described as the beginning of effective general legislation by the Capetian kings of France, yet agreement on the constitutional importance of the ordinances has not yet produced agreement on their precise meaning and significance. On the one hand, historians such as Esmein, Viollet, Declareuil, Chénon, Perrot, Fawtier, and Olivier-Martin, who followed Flammermont and Luchaire's analysis of royal legislation, have held that all the provisions of both the 1223 and 1230 ordinance bound both those who had consented and those who had not, and were applicable throughout the kingdom.[1] On the other hand, an older view stemming from Brussel and Petiet, followed hesitantly by Glasson, and most recently advanced by Petit-Dutaillis has maintained that, although the 1230 ordinance was applicable in its entirety throughout the kingdom, the ordinance of 1223 either applied in its entirety only to those who had consented to it, or else contained only one provision applicable to those who had not sworn to observe it.[2] This disagreement results partly from ambiguities in the texts, but also from a failure to set the ordinances in the context of their avowed purposes.

Both groups of historians have one characteristic in common: a lack of concern with the problem that occupied the men who drew up the texts. The importance of royal regulations concerning the Jews for the development of general legislation in thirteenth-century France has been taken for granted by legal and constitutional historians, and with good reason.[3] Unfortunately, historians concerned with royal policy toward the Jews have not been interested in the development of royal legislative power; and historians concerned with royal legislative power have paid too little attention to the immediate purpose of the ordinances under discussion, which was the implementation of policy concerning the Jews rather than the assertion of royal power over the magnates. Yet any assessment of the constitutional significance of these ordinances must take that purpose into account. It is unnecessary to unravel here all the complicated history of royal-baronial policy toward the Jews, for a description of one crucial aspect of that policy will clarify the constitutional status of the ordinances of 1223 and 1230.

An examination of the struggle of the king and certain barons to assert their possessory rights over Jews[4] shows that the ordinance of 1223, either in whole or in part, was intended to bind only those who had sworn to observe it; was not intended to be valid throughout the kingdom; and was not treated as binding even by those who had sworn it. It reveals the existence of another ordinance on the Jews of 1227 never discussed in this context. And it suggests strongly that not even the ordinance of 1230 was applicable throughout the kingdom in its entirety; that only one of its provisions was applicable to those who had not consented; and that that provision only affirmed as law a principle which had largely been accepted as customary and which had the support of several magnates. Although the development of royal power was reflected in the promulgation and implementation of these ordinances, the ordinances themselves do not seem to have constituted as great an innovation and imposition of the royal will as has sometimes been suggested.[5] Reexamination of the ordinances makes it apparent that there has been a tendency to exaggerate the extent to which royal power had developed by the first decades of the thirteenth century. If we concentrate on control of Jews rather than royal control of magnates, the beginning of effective legislation appears in a new light.

In Carolingian times, Jews were important as imperial merchants and slave-traders, not as usurers. Then, as later, the Catholic church was concerned with the cohabitation of Jews and Christians and with the religious implications of trade in Christian slaves; but at this time the church showed no concern with the Jews as usurers. Although as religious aliens the Jews stood apart from the mass of Carolingian subjects, their status was assured by imperial charters of protection.[6]

With the breakdown of Carolingian authority and the economic decline of the ninth and tenth centuries, the economic activity of many Jewish groups became almost indistinguishable from that of the communities in which they lived, although their adherence to their own religion, laws, and language set the Jews noticeably apart.[7] The religious revival of the eleventh century made their religious status all the more apparent and unpopular. The massacres incited by Volkmar, Gottschalk, and Emicho of Leiningen at the time of the First Crusade expressed the deep hostility of many peasants and simple priests toward the Jews, as compared with the more benevolent attitude of burgesses such as those of Mainz, princes such as Henry IV of Germany, and prelates such as the archbishop of Mainz.[8]

The massacres raised the problem of the status of the Jews under the new conditions of the twelfth century. The church, while intent upon keeping Jews in an inferior position and apart from Christians, and despite eschatological tradition associating Jews with Antichrist, nonetheless sought to protect Jews as a witness to their crime and because their remnant was to be saved at the end of the world.[9] After the massacres, from about 1120, successive popes issued a bull, *Sicut Judeis*, frequently known as the *Constitutio pro Judeis*, which confirmed Jews in the enjoyment of their privileges of worship and forbade illegal violence against them.[10] And, if the monk Ralph and Peter the Venerable incited action against Jews at the time of the Second Crusade, Saint Bernard denounced the persecution of the Jews with his usual uncompromising severity.[11] Papal protection and the protection of individual churchmen, however, could be only intermittently efficacious. The normal status of the Jews depended upon the protection which secular rulers, for a variety of motives, were willing and able to extend.

Massacres of Jews were unofficial acts of violence and, as such, the concern of rulers. In Germany, Henry IV reacted to the massacres of 1096 by attempting to punish the offenders and by placing the Jews under the protection of the imperial Land Peace of Mainz in 1103. By 1179, the Jews were designated by Frederick I as persons *qui ad fiscum imperatoris pertinent*; Frederick II's privilege of 1236 treated all Jews in Germany as serfs immediately pertaining to the imperial chamber or fiscus.[12] The German king had reasserted royal responsibility for, and the supremacy of royal rights over, all Jews in Germany. In England, there seem to have been no Jews before the Conquest, but those who came over thereafter rapidly fell under royal authority. Their status was probably based on a charter of Henry I, no longer extant, which "confirmed the community, in short, in a position of privilege as a separate entity—existing for the king's advantage, protected by him in all legitimate transactions and answerable to him alone."[13] Stephen tried to protect them during the Second Crusade, and the reign of Henry II was a period of security and prosperity that made possible the colossal fortune of Aaron of Lincoln. In France, however, because of the limited sphere of effective royal power up to the end of the twelfth century, there was no central authority to protect and profit from the Jews. The kings of France could not and did not claim a monopoly of ultimate rights over the Jews of France. Protection and control of the dispersed communities remained by default with local magnates.

After the First Crusade, economic motives led secular rulers increasingly to protect and control Jews. Jews had been profiting from the economic revival, as had other favorably placed elements of the population, but the hostility unleashed by the crusades against the enemies of God and the development of Christian commerce apparently made many occupations uncertain for them. Increasingly they turned to moneylending in competition with Christian merchants and monasteries.[14] "It is only after the first Crusade that the word Jew comes to have any connection with money-lender, but within a century the two words became almost synonymous."[15] This development can be seen in canon law. Through the twelfth century, popes and councils condemned clerical and Christian usury with increasing severity, particularly in the Third Lateran Council.[16] But until 1198, although canonical regulation betrayed an increasing concern with Jews as a peril to the faith,[17] no attention was paid to Jewish usury. Then, in 1198, Innocent III's privilege for crusaders commanded Christians, under pain of excommunication, to have nothing to do with Jews who did not remit usury to crusaders.[18] In 1205, Innocent complained that Jews were taking usury upon usury, and in 1208 that Christian princes were using Jews to exact usury from their people.[19] The Fourth Lateran Council prohibited Jews from taking heavy or immoderate usury,[20] and this remained the basis of the church's regulation of Jewish moneylending until about 1230. At that time, Raymond of Pennaforte and others denied Jews the right to take usury from Christians and held that Jews ought to be compelled to refund usuries.[21] Thus church action on usury testifies to the growing importance of moneylending in the last half of the twelfth century, and of Jewish moneylending in particular by the end of the century. It is interesting to note that the period during which the church became concerned with Jewish usury and moved toward a prohibition of it was also the period in which massive royal regulation of the Jews developed in France, which finally prohibited Jewish usury and even attempted to prohibit the enforcement of Christian debts to Jews.

Kings and territorial magnates profited from the economic revival by the sale of privileges to merchants and towns, and by tolls and taxation. Few greater opportunities were offered than by the Jews. The church was protected from arbitrary taxation, and there were limits to the taxes which could be imposed on Christian merchants. Jews, however, had never acquired the freedom of Christian merchants, and popular hostility made them almost completely dependent on the uncertain mercies of their protectors. Jewish profits could be tapped in a way that Christian profits could not. Rulers could retain or expel Jews, tallage them completely arbitrarily, take over their credits, cancel debts owed them, and confiscate their possessions wholly or in part. For the reign of Henry II in England,

> it has been estimated that an average of £ 3,000 — that is, something like one-seventh of the total revenue — was derived at this period from the Jews every year in the normal course of taxation, without taking into account occasional windfalls when individual or community were amerced for some real or imaginary trespass.[22]

The reason for the concern of secular rulers to protect the Jews from their subjects, and even from churchmen,[23] in a period of rising hostility to the Jews is readily apparent. Not necessarily as apparent is the fact, noted by Innocent III, that the revenue acquired from Jews constituted a form of indirect taxation of those sections of the population which found borrowing necessary or profitable.

In France in the twelfth century, profits from Jews were divided amongst the various possessors of Jews, but no common law regulated the possession of Jews throughout the kingdom, nor was there any means of promulgating such a law. The competence of the royal court was too narrowly circumscribed to be the serious influence toward uniformity that it was to become in the thirteenth century.[24] Such approaches as there had been to royal legislation prior to 1180 had been pious wishes on problems related to religious ideals rather than effective general legislation on matters of primary concern to the magnates.[25] Under these circumstances both the king and magnates could only rely on their own power to maintain their control of Jews. The principle that Jews were to be controlled, profited from, and therefore protected from all save their protector was not in doubt. The

example of Germany and England and of local action in France ensured as much. The problem for the king or a baron was to obtain
general recognition of his right to his Jews, and to prevent other lords
from receiving or seizing his Jews. This problem became much more
intense as possession of Jews became more lucrative and as the increasing unification of northern France under Philip Augustus made
competition more intense. When, in 1230, a provision was promulgated protecting possessory rights over Jews throughout the kingdom,
it was the result of a fifty years' struggle of the king and various
magnates to establish their right to their Jews.

II

The accession of Philip Augustus marked the end of a long period
of security and royal generosity which had attracted Jews to the royal
domain and brought criticism on Louis VII. In 1180, Philip arrested all
the Jews of the domain and compelled them to pay fifteen thousand
marks for their release and the recovery of their possessions. In 1180–
1181, Philip released all Christians of his domain from four-fifths of
their debts to Jews, retaining the remaining fifth for himself. Having
acquired most of the liquid assets of the Jews, he proceeded to expel
them from the domain in 1182, thereby gaining possession of their
immovables.[26] Although Rigord attributed these actions to Philip's piety, fiscal considerations probably played a major role.[27] Aversion to
the Jews and naive impetuosity may also have affected his decision, for
he had killed the goose that laid the golden eggs, as he was to discover.
The young Philip of 1182 was not yet the cool calculator of later years.

The expelled Jews doubtless settled in the lands of neighboring magnates where there were Jewish communities until the next major dis-
turbance in 1198. In that year,

> there was a holy man in France named Folques of Neuilly, which Neuilly
> is between Lagny-sur-Marne and Paris, and he was a priest and had the
> parish of the village. And this said Folques began to speak of God through
> the Ile de France and neighboring lands.[28]
>
> In those days, moreover, the Jews were troubled with serious plundering
> and affliction. For since the lord Folques demanded the complete extirpa-
> tion of sins and implanting of virtues and utterly abhorred usurers, he
> detested the Jews in all ways, because many of us were weakened by infinite
> and heavy usuries. Hence, at his instance and fervent instigation, and
> through the striving of the bishops, it was brought to pass that half of all
> the debts owed to the Jews were to be repudiated and half were to be paid

at decreed terms. But some of the barons commanded that they be expelled from their lands; however, the expelled were received and retained by the king. Truly, that detracted no little from the king's reputation, while those whom he had expelled a long time back he admitted again.[29]

We have no other evidence of baronial ordinances remitting and prolonging debts at this date, but we know that Philip Augustus re-admitted Jews to the royal domain in July of 1198, despite ecclesiastical objections.[30] The Jewish migration of 1198 doubtless stimulated him to reverse the economic mistake of 1182. This reversal of royal policy inevitably increased the competition for control of Jews at a time of heavy borrowing, particularly competition between the king and the count of Champagne, whose Jewish communities were so close to the royal domain.

In September 1198, Philip Augustus and Thibaut III of Champagne drew up charters that are the first effort to regulate the distribution of rights over Jews in northern France that has come down to us.[31] Each granted that he would not keep the Jews of the other without the other's consent, and that the Jews of the one could engage in lending operations in the lands of the other only with the latter's permission. The reason for these charters is not far to seek. An order of Philip of the same date commands his bailiffs and provosts to ensure payment to Thibaut of legitimate debts owed to Thibaut's Jews as of 8 September.[32] For this purpose, the officials, with the help of the people of the count, may seize the property of the debtors. These charters of Philip and Thibaut are the first in a series of some eighteen such promises from 1198 to 1231 between the king and individual barons, or between barons.

In May of 1201, Blanche of Champagne, in the charter regulating the conditions of her regency of Champagne, promised to keep the conventiones of 1198 and not extort more from the Jews of Champagne than Thibaut had received.[33] In 1203/4, Philip confirmed an agreement between Blanche and a Jew, Cresselin, who was allowed to lend within the lands of the king but promised not to leave the dependency of the countess.[34] The acquisition of Angevin lands apparently led the king to further efforts to control and profit from his more numerous Jews. We have evidence of royal measures about 1204 to ensure that the Jews of Normandy and the Ile de France would not leave the royal lands, and the definition of the rights and duties of the seneschals of Anjou and Poitou in August 1204 provided for tallage of the Jews.[35]

The first extant regulation laying down a procedure for loans by
Jews is the *stabilimentum* of 1 September 1206, made by Philip Augustus with the consent and will of Blanche of Champagne and Guy of
Dampierre.[36] It prescribed a maximum rate of interest and periods for
repayment, and it ensured official knowledge and control by establishing officials to write and seal contracts and providing penalties for
misinformation on the amount and terms of the debts. To prevent the
reception of stolen goods, Jews were forbidden to take bloody or recently wet clothes as pawns. Ecclesiastical requirements were taken
into account by forbidding Jews to take church vessels or ornaments
as pawns or to lend against the security of church lands under the
jurisdiction of the promulgators without their consent. There is no
provision requiring the parties not to keep each other's Jews. The *stabilimentum* was apparently designed to ensure efficient lending, known
to and controlled by the authorities, and to afford some protection to
debtors and some consideration for ecclesiastical demands.[37] It clearly
demonstrates an increasing interest in Jewish lending activities.[38] The
stabilimentum was to last "until we and the countess of Troyes and
Guy of Dampierre, who made it, withdraw it by ourselves and those
of our barons whom we shall wish to call to it." We have no record
of other barons giving their consent and adhering to this regulation,
but the provision for later adherences was a precedent for the ordinance of 1223.

Although the preamble of the 1206 ordinance states that it was
made by the king with the consent of the two magnates, the provision
for withdrawing it says that it was made by the king and the two
magnates. Regulation of matters of economic importance was achieved
by mutual convention or treaties rather than by royal legislation. This
can be seen more clearly in the Villeneuve regulation of 1209 concerned with subinfeudation, which is clearly a joint convention:

> Philip king of France, Odo duke of Burgundy, Hervé count of Nevers,
> Renaud count of Boulogne, Gaucher count of Saint-Pol, Guy of Dampierre,
> and several other magnates of the kingdom of France unanimously agree
> and by public consent confirm that . . .[39]

Such conventions seem to have developed out of the usual charter
form, with its tradition of individual consent, rather than from Carolingian legislative precedents or religious conceptions of royal responsibility for the peace and welfare of the realm.

From 1210 to 1218, the king and others made further efforts to regulate the possession of Jews through individual charters. In May 1210, Philip Augustus exchanged charters with Gaucher count of Saint-Pol, with Hervé count of Nevers, and with Blanche of Champagne, in which each promised not to retain the other's Jews.[40] In October, Odo duke of Burgundy and Blanche of Champagne exchanged similar promises.[41] In June of 1210, Guy of Dampierre confirmed an agreement between Baldwin, one of Blanche's Jews, and Blanche, which was guaranteed by Guy's Jews: Baldwin and his wife acknowledged that they were the Jews of Blanche, and Guy took good care to state that certain Jews were his.[42] In 1214, Miles d'Ervy sold all his rights in Jews to Blanche.[43] In 1216, Archambaud of Bourbon promised for himself and his brother, William of Dampierre, that they would not retain Blanche's Jews for two years; in 1218 they made a similar promise for one year, while Blanche promised not to retain their Jews for the same period.[44] Evidently magnates were as concerned to preserve their Jews from the depredations of their neighbors as was the king.

While the king and magnates protected Jews in order to profit from their activities during a period of seigneurial financial embarrassment, the legate Robert of Courçon and Innocent III inveighed against the Jews as a peril to the faith and against the growth of Jewish usury, particularly in France.[45] The Fourth Lateran Council enacted regulations to limit Jews and Jewish usury.[46] Something of this agitation about usury is reflected in Philip Augustus's ordinance of 2 February 1219 for the Jews *potestatis suae*, of his domain.[47] It demonstrates little concern with the Jews as a religious peril, despite recent canonical legislation on that problem. It only repeats the 1206 provision against the acceptance of church ornaments as pawns, and forbids Jews to lend to certain clerics without the consent of their superiors, but it does not order Jews to wear the distinguishing mark ordered by the Fourth Lateran Council. The bulk of the regulation is concerned with Jewish moneylending and apparently constitutes an effort to protect debtors, particularly poorer debtors. It is difficult to say whether this concern was a reaction to the misfortunes of the debtors, an attempt by the king to organize the credit system he controlled on a sounder basis, or a response to the Church's appeal to prevent heavy and immoderate usury.[48] Whatever Philip's purpose, he made no effort to have other magnates enforce similar regulations in their lands, even though he was at least as firmly in control of northern France as Louis VIII was to be, or as Blanche of Castille was to be up to 1230.

Between 1219 and 1223, the effort of magnates other than the king to protect their possession of Jews continued. In June of 1219, Gautier of Vignory swore to protect the Jews of Blanche of Champagne who were coming to stay in his lands, and to return them safely to Blanche's lands whenever they wished.[49] In June of 1220, Henry, count of Bar-le-Duc, and Blanche of Champagne promised not to retain each other's Jews.[50] In August of 1220, Blanche of Champagne and Hervé of Nevers confirmed a compromise between four Jews, brothers, two of whom belonged to Blanche and two to Hervé.[51] All of these documents suggest the difficulty of maintaining rights over Jews when Jews lived and lent in lands other than those of their possessors. The mobility of these assets and the advantage to their possessors of permitting them to extend their financial operations to other lands made control and possession difficult, and therefore made insistence on possessory rights imperative.

The reign of Philip Augustus was a period of reasonable security and prosperity for the Jews of northern France as financially interested authorities became more organized and better able to safeguard their interests. Increasing regulation doubtless hampered Jewish activity, yet the status of the Jews was more clearly defined and enforced by more powerful rulers. There were no massacres in Philip's forty-four-year reign to compare with those accompanying the First and Second Crusades or those of Saint Louis's reign, but ecclesiastical concern with the Jews both as a religious peril and as usurers was mounting. With Philip's death in 1223, the calculating royal policy of profitable acceptance of the Jews ended. The ordinances of 1223, 1227, and 1230, not to mention later regulations, expressed a new royal policy toward Jewish moneylending which more closely reflected religious attitudes.[52]

III

Louis VIII was crowned on 6 August 1223, and on 8 November he promulgated a *stabilimentum* which, instead of regulating the moneylending of the Jews like the ordinance of 1219, attempted to suppress it.[53] The *stabilimentum* provided that no debt to Jews was to run at usury from 8 November on, that the authorities concerned would not enforce payment to Jews of usuries accumulated after that date,[54] and that outstanding debts to Jews contracted within the last five years were to be repaid within three years by nine payments to the lords of the Jews. The last payment was supposed to be made on 1 November 1226. The ordinance then declared that the king and "his barons" could not retain each other's Jews; and this particular provision included an interpretative rider, to be discussed later, which has caused considerable disagreement among historians. The remaining provisions denied Jews the right to have their own seal to seal their debts, required Jews to enroll their debts (i.e., credits) with their lords by 2 February 1224, and invalidated debts not enrolled by that date or contracted more than five years prior to the ordinance.

There has been disagreement about the motives behind this ordinance,[55] but whatever Louis's motives, the appearance of the ordinance only three months after his coronation must be attributed to royal initiative. It is less clear whether the ordinance, to which so many magnates consented, represented an imposition of royal authority on the magnates concerned or whether it was an expression of the common interests of king and magnates. It is not even certain whom the ordinance was intended to bind. Who made the regulation, and to whom did it apply?

At first sight, the preamble to the ordinance seems more than usually explicit on this point:

> Know that by the will and consent of the archbishops, bishops, counts, barons, and knights of the kingdom of France who have Jews and who do not have Jews, we have made this *stabilimentum* concerning the Jews which those whose names are written below have sworn to keep . . .

There follow twenty-five names, including only one ecclesiastic, William, bishop of Châlons and count of Perche. Petit-Dutaillis apparently believed that only those named in the ordinance were present, for he stated that only one ecclesiastic was present.[56] But the presence of only one ecclesiastic at an important assembly, at which Henry III's demand for the return of the Angevin continental fiefs was considered,[57] seems most unlikely. Indubitably all members of the ranks mentioned were not present, yet it seems likely that, as the words of the preamble clearly suggest, more people were present than those who swore to keep the ordinance. The preamble seems to say that a large number of magnates, lay and ecclesiastical, had been present and had consented to the making of the ordinance, while a smaller, named group of twenty-four of those present (Robert III, count of Dreux, swore for himself and his brother Peter, count of Brittany), composed primarily of royal officials and possessors of Jews, had sworn to observe the ordinance. Although wider consent was given to the making of the ordinance, its application was apparently explicitly limited to those named people who had sworn to observe it. Were this the only evidence of the range of application of the ordinance, its constitutional relevance would be merely that it was the first convention on matters of economic importance made by and applicable to the king and so many important magnates; but it would be no different in form from the Villeneuve convention of 1209.

The first substantive provisions—condemning usury, stating that "neither we nor our barons" will enforce usury from 8 November, and regulating the repayment of outstanding debts—raise no problems. They bind only those who had sworn to observe the ordinance, and "our barons" refers to the twenty-five magnates named in the act. Disagreement on the range of the ordinance arises only with the non-retention provision with its interpretative rider:

> And be it known that we and our barons have decreed and ordained concerning the status of the Jews that none of us can receive or keep the Jews of another; and this is to be understood as well for those who have sworn the *stabilimentum* as for those who have not sworn.

The remaining substantive provisions have no such inteprative phrases and, like the first provisions, bind only those who had sworn to observe the ordinance.

One interpretation of the nonretention provision and its rider, that of Flammermont, Esmein, Viollet, Declareuil, Chénon, Perrot, and Fawtier, may be dismissed at the outset: that the rider applies to the whole ordinance and makes the whole ordinance binding on those who had not consented.[58] The rider is clearly appended to only one provision in the middle of the ordinance, a provision of long and particular concern to possessors of Jews as we have seen, which adequately explains the special treatment accorded to it. Neither Vuitry nor Caro, who were primarily concerned with the policy implemented by the ordinance, thought that the rider applied to anything except the provision to which it was attached.[59] Nor did Petit-Dutaillis, who is the most recent constitutional historian to have examined the ordinance in detail, think that the rider applied to the whole ordinance.[60] Only a tendency to exaggerate the development of royal power can explain the interpretation of the whole ordinance by a rider to one provision.

There remains the question of whether the provision to which the rider was attached was meant to bind those who had not sworn the ordinance. Petiet, who also held that the rider referred to the whole ordinance, noted that the rider was ambiguous and held that it could be understood to bind either all the barons of France, or else all the barons present at the assembly, including those who had not sworn. He chose the latter alternative since "the other supposes an audacity in the king which was not justified by the position of the monarchy in 1223."[61] Whether or not we agree with Petiet's whole argument, there is considerable weight in this reason for trying to limit the meaning of the rider as narrowly as possible. Petit-Dutaillis, who perceived that the rider applied only to that one provision, held that the rider bound all barons, whether or not they had sworn or been present, to observe that particular provision.[62] But there is another, unnoticed, ambiguity in the text.

It has always been presumed that the rider meant that neither those who had nor those who had not sworn the ordinance could retain the Jews of anyone else, that is, the rider clarified an ambiguity as to who might not take another's Jews. But an alternative interpretation is possible. It would be well to have the provision in front of us:

> Et sciendum quod nos et barones nostri statuimus et ordinavimus de statu Judeorum quod nullus nostrum alterius Judeos recipere potest vel retinere; et hoc intelligendum est tam de hiis qui stabilimentum juraverunt quam de illis qui non juraverunt.

It is possible, and in the light of other evidence necessary, to interpret the rider as clarifying whose Jews were not to be taken. *Hiis* and *illis*, in this view, refer back to the nearest pronoun, *alterius*; they do not refer back to *nullus nostrum*. The rider is intended to remove an ambiguity in the provision. But *nullus nostrum* refers to *nos et barones nostri*; and *nos nec barones nostri* in the previous provision on the nonenforcement of usury, which binds only those who have sworn, clearly means the king and the magnates who have sworn to observe the ordinance. There is, then, no ambiguity about *nullus nostrum*, but there is considerable ambiguity about *alterius*, about whose Jews could not be retained. The previous charters promising not to retain Jews had protected the possessory rights only of those who had promised to respect each other's rights, as the jurors of the ordinance well knew. Therefore, although *alterius* could refer either to those who had sworn

this ordinance or to any possessor of Jews, it would have been understood to refer only to those who had sworn, unless a clarifying phrase
had been added. The rider was added to make clear that the king and
jurors would not keep the Jews either of those who had sworn or of
those who had not.

Such a provision seems at first an unlikely piece of altruism, but it
should be remembered that the king and several magnates had been
trying to ensure the sanctity of possessory rights over Jews for some
time, and that most major possessors of Jews[63] had sworn to observe
the ordinance. Furthermore, this provision was the outcome of a
broadening series of mutual conventions; by framing the provision this
way, the king and the jurors made it possible to secure later adhesions
to it without having to obtain fresh promises from the jurors that they
would not take the Jews of the new adherent. In fact, Thibaut IV of
Champagne, probably the most important possessor of Jews after the
king, was not among those who had sworn to observe the ordinance.
A major convention such as this which did not protect his rights would
have seemed a most unfriendly act, and Louis VIII wanted Thibaut's
service against Henry III. Far from being altruistic, the provision may
have been carefully framed to take Thibaut's position into account.

Fortunately there is evidence to confirm this interpretation. We have
a letter of November 1223 of the countess of Nevers, one of the jurors
of the ordinance, in which she informs the king that she has sworn to
observe the *stabilimentum* like the other barons, *sicut alii barones*.[64] (It
should be noted that a phrase as general, out of context, as *alii barones*, like *barones nostri*, could refer to a very specific group.) In striking contrast we have a charter of Thibaut, also of November but after
the 8th, in which he says only that from the past 8th of November he
will not and cannot retain the Jews of his dear lord, Louis, nor can the
king, from that day, keep any of his Jews.[65] Despite the ordinance, and
presumably with royal consent, although the royal charter is not available, Thibaut simply continued the twenty-five-year-old tradition of
promises of nonretention between two parties. Then, either because
Louis was not satisfied or because Thibaut saw a further advantage,
Thibaut issued another charter in December announcing that he had
granted that he would not retain any royal Jews or any Jews of *those
who had sworn to hold the ordinance*, and that neither the king nor
those who had sworn the ordinance (stabilimentum) could retain any
of his Jews.[66]

Thibaut obviously did not consider that a magnate was bound by that particular provision, or by any other provision of the ordinance, unless he had given his individual consent. Conversely, he clearly assumed that only those who had sworn were bound by any of the provisions. What Thibaut thought the rider meant—and he should have known—is also clear. Without any further promise from the jurors beyond the ordinance itself, he states that they, and only they, are bound not to take his Jews, in other words, that they had already bound themselves by the ordinance not to take anybody's Jews. Thibaut does not feel, however, that the ordinance bound him not to take anybody's Jews, because he carefully limits his own obligation to not taking the Jews of the jurors. Possibly less concerned with the promulgation of principle than the king, Thibaut refused to advance beyond the tradition of mutual promises by which the counts of Champagne had been trying to protect their possession of Jews for the past twenty-five years.

Special treatment was accorded to the nonretention provision in 1223 for the same reason that had led to the earlier nonretention charters: profit from Jews depended upon undisputed possession of them. In 1223, possessors of Jews were about to proceed to a profitable manipulation of debts to Jews which might prompt some lords to retain the Jews of others, and some Jews to move to the lands of lords who offered more favorable conditions. As broad agreement as possible among the most powerful possessors of Jews to respect each other's rights over Jews was a vital preliminary to the envisaged extortion, particularly since the Jews of one lord would have creditors in the lands of another lord. Until Jews ceased to have any real economic importance in the eyes of the magnates, the nonretention promise would remain the keystone of any joint regulation of the Jews.

The political importance of the whole ordinance lay primarily in the fact that Louis was able to obtain the cooperation of so many magnates for his policy, embodied in a royal ordinance. Whether all the jurors were as willing to dissociate themselves from the open enforcement of usury to Jews is debatable. Thibaut at least was not. But to the extent that Louis may have succeeded in imposing his will upon some of those who swore the ordinance, aided by the prospect of immediate profit offered by the other provisions of the ordinance, the ordinance expresses the increased political power of the monarchy.

Constitutionally, the ordinance was a stepping-stone rather than a watershed. It did not diminish the rights of the magnates over their Jews but presumed that magnates had the same rights over their Jews as the king over his, and it protected their rights as much as his. It was still a treaty between the king and a number of his magnates, validated by their individual consent and applicable only to them, like the Villeneuve convention of 1209.[67] Like the 1206 ordinance on the Jews, it provides for the possibility of later adhesions.[68] Although it did not introduce any new royal legislative rights over the magnates, it did bring the old technique of legislation by convention with provision for future adhesions to its highest development. It would be but a small step from the assertion of legal principle with the expectation of future adhesions, embodied in the nonretention provision of 1223, to the promulgation of a legal principle which all were expected to obey whether or not they had consented to its promulgation.

Promulgation, however, was one thing, enforcement and observation another. The ordinance of 1223 seems to have been more effective as a means for coordinating profitable pillage of the Jews—and their debtors[69]—than as legislation. Not even its central provision bound the parties who had consented with any finality. Despite the emphasis on the validity of possessory rights, the older tradition of individual charters promptly reappeared. Only a year after the ordinance, Louis VIII and Thibaut again issued charters promising not to keep each other's Jews after 8 November 1224.[70] In May of that year, we have evidence of a conflict between William of Dampierre and Thibaut, including a dispute over Jews.[71] Promises not to keep each other's Jews between Renaud of Charenton and Archambaud of Bourbon in 1226/27 show that the effort to protect rights over Jews was not simply the result of rivalry between the king and the count of Champagne, although similar promises between Louis IX and Thibaut in April 1228/29 indicate that that rivalry continued.[72] A similar agreement in April 1230 between Louis IX and John, son of the count of Soissons, demonstrates that the count of Champagne was not the only threat to royal rights over Jews.[73] Conflict over possession of Jews continued as if the ordinance had never been promulgated. It would seem that general statements which many people swore to observe were still regarded more as declarations of the immediate intentions of independent parties than as binding covenants to be enforced by all available power under the direction of the king.

IV

For the Jews, the ordinance of 1223 was the beginning of a series of disasters. Louis VIII died on 8 November 1226, and under the regency of Blanche of Castile, royal policy toward Jews became harsher. Between 8 November 1226 and 24 June 1227, a royal order commanded royal officials not to enforce payment of debts to Jews. Its existence is revealed by a later order, falling in the same period, which revoked the former order and commanded officials to enforce payment of debts contracted prior to the 1223 ordinance, but not to concern themselves with debts contracted thereafter, unless the Jews had letters of Louis VIII or Louis IX ordering enforcement of such debts.[74] The renewed enforcement of debts was to enable the Jews to make payments they owed the king. The refusal to enforce debts may have been a form of pressure to force the Jews to pay a fine in order to gain enforcement of their debts; it may have reflected royal uncertainty as to whether to enforce debts of 1223 which had not been paid by the assigned term of 1 November 1226; or it may have been a sign of hesitation about how to deal with new debts contracted since the 1223 ordinance. Whatever the original purpose, royal policy was moving from the refusal to enforce usury of the 1223 ordinance to the refusal to enforce debts at all, which appears in the 1230 ordinance. But, before 1230, another ordinance was issued in 1227, which Caro alone of recent historians has noticed and discussed.[75]

We know of the *stabilimentum* of 1227 only from references to it in a later ordinance, apparently only for the royal domain, of 31 May 1228.[76] The ordinance of 1227 was probably promulgated on 24 June 1227, for it decreed a prolongation by nine payments through three years of outstanding debts contracted between the ordinance of 1223 and 24 June 1227. The final payment was to be made on 16 May 1230. Only repayment of the principal was called for; in accordance with the ordinance of 1223, no payment of usury was to be enforced. The ordinance of May 1228 decreed that the provision of the 1223 ordinance for debts prior to 8 November 1223 and the ordinance of 1227 were to be observed. It also laid down a procedure for dealing with contracts that might conceal usury, provided for the recording of debts by chirograph, and prohibited the enforcement of usury from 1 June 1228.

Caro says that the ordinance of 1228 apparently applied only to the royal domain, without giving any reasons. Probably his main reason was that the ordinance never mentions any baronial action or cooperation. Thus, while the 1223 ordinance says that "neither we nor our barons" will enforce usury,[77] the 1228 ordinance says only "nor shall we" enforce usury. Also, the 1228 ordinance speaks of two good men elected *de mandato nostro* to receive proofs of the original amount of a loan, but men would not be elected for administrative purposes in the territory of magnates according to a royal order. There is little doubt, therefore, that the 1228 ordinance was for the domain only, and this makes some of the terminology it uses more interesting.

Although Martène called it a *stabilimentum* in his rubric, in fact the domain ordinance never calls itself a *stabilimentum*. Yet it speaks of the ordinance of 1223 as a *stabilimentum*, which is what that ordinance calls itself, and what Thibaut and the countess of Nevers called it. When we remember that the ordinance of 1206—which was a convention between Philip Augustus, Blanche of Champagne, and Guy of Dampierre—calls itself a *stabilimentum*, whereas Philip's ordinance for the domain of 1219 does not,[78] we may suspect that the term *stabilimentum* was used at this time for royal-baronial conventions, not for domain ordinances. This possibility is strengthened by the fact that the 1228 ordinance also refers to the 1227 ordinance as a *stabilimentum*, and there is additional evidence that the 1227 ordinance was not restricted to the domain.

Caro does not give his opinion as to whether the 1227 ordinance was only for the domain. Since we do not have a copy of the original, it is difficult to be decisive, but it is probable that its range was wider and that it was another convention of the 1223 type. The possible significance of the fact that it was called a *stabilimentum* has already been discussed. More interesting, if by no means conclusive, evidence of its range is a bull of Gregory IX of 6 April 1233 to the archbishops and bishops throughout the kingdom of France.[79] The Jews in France had appealed to the pope, and in response Gregory wrote that the Jews, "bearing the image of our Savior, and created by the Creator of all, are not to be destroyed by his creatures, that is Christ's faithful, for the Lord forbids it; for however great the perversity of their intermediate position, their fathers were created as friends of God, and the remnant shall be saved." Gregory then describes the plight of the Jews from information given him by the Jews and presumably by others.

The chronology of Gregory's description of the misfortunes of the Jews is not clearly consistent with other evidence of policy toward the Jews in this period. The bull describes a sequence of events: (1) measures decreed "in certain parts of the kingdom" prolonging through four years repayment of the principal of Christian debts to Jews, with partial payments each year, but without enforcement of usury despite public contracts to the contrary; (2) four years later a capture of the Jews, enrollment of their debts, and extortion together with an unwillingness to permit Jews to demand payment; (3) a period of torture extending to the recent past of those still imprisoned because they did not have the wherewithal to pay the amounts demanded by certain lords; (4) a recent oath by some lords not to enforce debts to Jews and the ejection of Jews from the lands of some lords; and (5) a period sufficient for the most recent events to have been reported to Gregory and provoke his reaction.

However confused the information received by Gregory, there seem clearly to have been at least two distinct measures, separated by at least three years: a prolongation of repayments without usury and an oath not to enforce debts to Jews. The latter corresponds to a provision of the ordinance of December 1230.[80] The prolongation referred to is apparently that of 1227. It is true that the ordinance of 1230, like those of 1223 and 1227, decreed a prolongation of three (not four) years extending through four calendar years, but the bull clearly places the prolongation at least three years before the oath not to enforce debts and, therefore, could only refer to the 1227 or 1223 ordinance.[81] But the 1223 ordinance did not prohibit enforcement of usury already due on the outstanding debts whose payment was prolonged; it only prohibited usury in the future, whereas the 1227 ordinance did prohibit payment of usury on the prolonged debts. The only problem here is that since the 1223 ordinance had prohibited Jewish usury and promised that it would not be enforced, it might be expected that thereafter there would be no such public contracts involving usury as the bull mentions. In fact, the ordinance of 1228 presumed that there were such usurious contracts, and there is no reason for us to attribute more efficacy to the ordinance of 1223 than did those who framed the ordinance of 1228.

It therefore seems that the prolongation of payments mentioned at the beginning of the papal account refers to the *stabilimentum* of 1227. Gregory's description of this measure as being decreed in certain parts of the kingdom, and the implication of the bull that the measure was carried out by certain but not all lords, strongly suggests that the ordinance was neither a regulation for the royal domain only nor a royal edict for the whole kingdom.[82] If this is correct, then the ordinance of 1227 was a convention between the king and several magnates, similar to the ordinance of 1223, and ought to be placed with the ordinances of 1223 and 1230 in the history of royal general legislation.

V

On 16 May 1230, the last of the payments commanded by the 1227 ordinance was due, and in December another ordinance was promulgated to regulate Jews and the debts owed them. The *statuta* on the Jews of December 1230 were decreed for the salvation of Louis IX, his father, and his ancestors, and for the utility of the whole kingdom;[83] in these provisions, as Caro has said, "the religious point of view had decisively influenced purely economic modes of action."[84] In this ordinance we also find for the first time the promulgation of a legal rule of direct economic concern to barons that was clearly and unambiguously intended to bind those who had not consented throughout the kingdom. The rule was, as we might expect by now, that no one may keep the Jew of another. It is not coincidental that a principle originally asserted by individuals for purely economic reasons was finally promulgated as law for the whole kingdom only when expressed as the fulfillment of religious imperatives.

The ordinance went beyond previous policy in its harshness to the Jews. The first provisions stated that the king and *barones nostri* would not enforce debts owed to Jews in the future,[85] that no one in the whole kingdom could retain the Jews of another, and that anyone could seize his Jew, like his serf, whenever found under another lord or even in another kingdom. The ordinance then provided that outstanding debts to Jews (presumably those contracted from 24 June 1227) should be repaid by three annual payments on 1 November, the last payment to be due on 1 November 1233, and that payment would be enforced only for debts enrolled with the lords by 1 November 1231. Neither the king nor *barones nostri* would enforce payment of usury to Christians, usury being understood as anything beyond the principal.[86]

Religious considerations are obvious not only in the preamble but also in the provisions. Usury, which had originally been viewed as a fiscal opportunity for royal government made possible by religious beliefs, had become a primarily religious problem, at least in the eyes of Blanche and her advisers, who now went beyond canonical prescriptions by refusing to enforce debts to Jews.[87] It is significant, as an indication of religious motivation, that this is the first extant royal enactment that reinforced canonical sanctions against Christian usurers.[88] The influence of canon law is also apparent in the statement that a man may seize his Jew *tanquam proprium servum*. The theo-

logical concept of *servitus Judeorum*, in the sense of spiritual serfdom
to Christian princes, goes back to the church fathers and was widely
accepted by medieval theologians.[89] It had been emphasized in Innocent III's bull of 1205 to the archbishop of Sens and the bishop of
Paris, which was included in *Compilatio III* in 1209/10.[90] Guillaume
le Breton had used the concept, probably between 1214 and 1217, to
deduce a specific consequence in secular law.[91] And in 1230 it appeared as a secular law applicable to the whole kingdom, assimilating
the status of Jews in France to that of serfs, six years before a similar
development in Germany.[92] Whatever the motives of Blanche and her
advisers, for many barons these religious justifications were but rationalizations to cover the extortion and torture describe in the bull of
April 1233.

It is generally held that all provisions of this ordinance were intended to be applicable throughout the kingdom; but it is probable
that only the nonretention provision, which explicitly says so, was
intended to be so applicable.[93] The reference to the utility of the kingdom in the preamble, on which Olivier-Martin's argument for the universal validity of the ordinance is based,[94] does suggest that the ordinance was meant to apply to the whole kingdom; but the phrase is
somewhat general and inconclusive. More detailed examination of the
language of the whole ordinance is necessary.

After mentioning the considerations of salvation and utility behind
the ordinance, the preamble goes on to state that the provisions were
decreed according to Louis's sincere will and the common counsel of
his barons (*barones nostrorum*). Then, after the substantive provisions
summarized above, comes the enforcement provision on which most
arguments for the general validity of the ordinance have been based. It
states that the king will enforce observation of the ordinance in his
lands, and his barons (*barones nostri*) in their lands; and if any barons
(*aliqui barones*) refuse to observe it, the king will compel them, and the
other barons (*alii barones*) are bound to aid the king to do so. The king
and the other barons are also bound to aid each other in compelling
rebels within the lands of the barons to observe it. After the enforcement provision, the king says that he wishes the *statuta* to be observed
perpetually by himself and his barons, and states that his barons (*barones nostri*) have similarly conceded that they and their heirs will observe it perpetually. There follows immediately a series of unusually
explicit statements of individual consent and adhesion in the following
form: "I, Philip of Boulogne have willed, counseled, and sworn those

things set down above."[95] There are seventeen such statements of important magnates, including most possessors of Jews with the exception of Peter of Dreux, who had just been deprived of his regency of Brittany and was still in rebellion.[96] The eighteenth statement is that of the king in almost identical language: "Moreover we have willed, counseled, and sworn this for the salvation of our and our ancestors' souls."

If we omit consideration of the nonretention provision for the moment and attempt to establish the range of application of the rest of the ordinance, the main problem to be settled is the meaning of *barones nostri*, *aliqui barones*, and *alii barones*, for it is they who were bound by the ordinance. We have already seen that in the 1223 ordinance and in the countess of Nevers's charter of 1223 *barones nostri* and *alii barones* refer only to those who had sworn the ordinance.[97] The same is true for the 1230 ordinance if it is credited with a consistent use of language. The ordinance was decreed by the king according to the counsel of "his barons," the king and "his barons" grant that they will observe it, and the general statement of baronial consent is immediately followed by seventeen very explicit oaths of individual barons. There is no reason to think that, in the eyes of the magnates present, *barones nostri* referred to anyone save themselves who had in fact counseled and sworn the ordinance; they were the king's barons, and *barones nostri* did not necessarily mean *omnes barones*. *Barones nostri*, therefore, probably refers only to those who swore the ordinance. *Aliqui barones*, who may refuse to observe the ordinance, are contrasted with *alii barones*, who do observe it. But in the countess of Nevers's charter of 1223, *alii barones* means the remainder of the barons who had sworn the ordinance of 1223.

There is, then, no necessity to interpret *barones* as referring to any other barons than those who had sworn. Indeed this is the only interpretation that makes the language of the ordinance self-consistent and consistent with the language of the 1223 ordinance. It may also be remarked that, in the enforcement provision, *aliqui barones* and *in terris baronum* are at best ambiguous. The addition or substitution of *in toto regno* would have made a wider meaning obvious and unambiguous, had that been desired; and Blanche and her advisers were quite capable of drawing up an unambiguous statement. The only ambiguity, it may be suggested, comes from an anachronistic interpretation of the ordinance in the light of later royal legislation, without a proper recognition of the limited range of royal legislative power in the early thirteenth century. Particularly in relation to matters of direct economic interest to the major magnates, there had been no tradition other than that of individual consent up to 1230.

There is no conclusive documentary proof of this interpretation, such as Thibaut's charter for the 1223 ordinance, but there is evidence within the ordinance of 1230 that an unambiguous provision applying to the whole kingdom could be drawn up when desired:

> nos et barones nostri Judeis nulla debita de cetero contrahenda faciemus haberi, nec aliquis in toto regno poterit retinere Judeum alterius domini, et, ubicumque aliquis inveniet Judeum suum, ipsum licite poterit capere tamquam proprium servum, quantumcumque moram fecerit Judeus sub alterius dominio vel in alio regno.

The contrast between *barones nostri* in the one provision and *aliquis in toto regno* in the other is evident. There can be no doubt about the nonretention provision: explicitly and unambiguously it states that no one in the whole kingdom can take the Jew of another lord. With the exception of the general reference to the utility of the whole kingdom in the preamble, this is the only use of *totum regnum* in the ordinance; further, it is the only use of the phrase in a substantive provision. Remembering the long effort of the king and major possessors of Jews to protect their possessory rights and the special treatment accorded to the nonretention provision in the ordinance of 1223, we might be led to expect special treatment of that provision in 1230. When we find such treatment, we may presume that it was not an unintentional result of loose draftsmanship, particularly when the provision included for the first time a reference to the theological concept of the *servitus Judeorum* to give it wider moral validity.

Possibly the strongest argument, on internal evidence, against the view that only the nonretention provision was binding on those who had not sworn the ordinance is that the provision against Christian usury was not made explicitly applicable to the whole kingdom, although it involved a principle of equally universal canonical validity.[98] But with the crude definition of usury as anything beyond the principal, this law lacked the legal precision of the nonretention provision, did not strengthen the economic position of the magnates, ran counter to the economic needs of the period, and therefore fell into the category of unenforceable pious wishes. In the second place, the provision against Christian usury draws attention to another peculiarity of the language of the ordinance. The king and "his barons" promise that they will not enforce usury to Christians as they promise not to enforce debts to Jews; they do not prohibit anyone else from doing so. These provisions are in the form of a mutual pledge rather than a prohibition. The nonretention provision, however, is in the form of a universal prohibition and a universal permission to those exercising governmental powers. Had all the provisions of the ordinance been intended to apply throughout the kingdom, they could all have been expressed as imperatives or permissions for all lords rather than as mutual promises. In fact, only the nonretention provision is couched in such terms. Thus examination of the Christian usury provision only reinforces the view that no provision except the nonretention provision was intended to be binding throughout the kingdom.

The bull of 1233 affords further confirmation of this interpretation.[99] Gregory speaks only of several lords who, intending to drive out their Jews, swore that they would not enforce contracts between Jews and Christians. He did not think that this measure had been promulgated for the whole kingdom, and presumably the Jews who had appealed to him would have been the first to inform him of such a universal restriction had it occurred. A more general consideration adds weight to this view. In 1230, the rebellion of Peter of Dreux was still continuing, Henry III's expedition had just returned to England, but there was no truce between France and England.[100] Although a series of baronial rebellions had been temporarily settled, and Blanche had regained control, it would have been highly unwise for her to jeopardize the prospect of a period of calm by an immediate attack on the rights of restive magnates. Yet an attempt to override the tradition of legislation by the individual consent of the magnates would have been just such an attack.

This consideration is strengthened by the form of the ordinance which, with the exception of the nonretention provision, emphasized the importance of individual consent by the series of very individual promises of the consenting magnates. When these statements of individual consent are linked with the immediately preceding enforcement provision, and if the enforcement provision is interpreted as referring to any barons in the kingdom, we get the paradoxical result that, in an interlude between rebellions, leading magnates most explicitly exercised their right of individual consent to deny that right to other barons who had not been present. I find this most improbable. It seems much more probable that the enforcement provision was not a futile attempt to enforce the whole ordinance throughout the kingdom, but a practical effort to make the provisions enforceable among those who had consented to them—a sufficiently difficult problem in itself at this stage, as can be seen from the results of the 1223 ordinance.

The nonretention provision, however, was intended to apply throughout the kingdom, as we know for the simple reason that it clearly says so. Here finally and indisputably was a law promulgated for the whole kingdom, binding upon those who had not consented, that was not merely a pious wish. Yet of all the provisions, it was the one whose extension to the whole kingdom would seem least incompatible with the emphasis on individual consent in the ordinance, for the provision was intended more to protect existing rights than to change them. The validity of rights over Jews and the ultimate royal monopoly of them had been accepted in England and Germany. In France also there had never been doubt that barons could exercise various rights over Jews. The problem for possessors of Jews had been to ensure their ability to exercise such rights over specific Jews when there was no central government capable of preventing one magnate from taking another's Jews. For some time the king and major possessors of Jews had been trying to gain recognition of their right to certain Jews. Finally, after the practical efforts of the king and individual magnates to control their own Jews, after a thirty-two-year tradition of mutual promises between individuals, and after the impressive covenant of 1223 between the king and many magnates, so drafted as to permit future adhesions, the king of France was able, with the support of interested magnates, to promulgate as law for the whole kingdom the rule that no one could keep the Jews of another.

To most of the magnates who exercised their right of individual consent to ratify a law intended to bind those who had not consented (even apparently in other kingdoms!), the provision can hardly have seemed more than a recognition and confirmation of acknowledged customary rights that had been imperfectly respected. For the provision did not give the king a monopoly of rights over Jews or change the nature of baronial rights over Jews; it merely safeguarded the existing rights of those who had such rights over certain Jews. The first piece of general royal legislation of secular importance was certainly no sweeping innovation impressively and unilaterally imposed by a masterful king or regent.[101] But we should never have expected that it would be; beginnings rarely look like conclusions.

There remains the question of whether the ordinance was effective. We may safely presume that the manipulation of debts was carried out with considerable brutality to the advantage of possessors of Jews, although the ejection of Jews from the lands of some lords, mentioned in the bull of 1233, was not envisaged in the ordinance. But not all provisions were equally observed. Hugh X of Lusignan, count of La Marche and Angoulême, was one of those who had sworn the whole ordinance. On 1 June 1232, he announced that two royal Jews and their families had been taken into his protection to live at Lusignan or elsewhere in his lands as they wished. For an annual payment of ten pounds of Tours—and he promises not to extort more from them— Hugh guarantees that he will enforce legitimately proven debts to them.[102] He also promises that, if at any time they should wish to leave, he will give them a safe-conduct to the lands of the king, whose Jews they are. It seems that the promise not to enforce debts to Jews was not observed very consistently by the jurors of the ordinance, not to speak of others.[103]

Hugh does seem prepared to observe the nonretention provision, however, for he acknowledges that they are royal Jews. And apparently the nonretention provision was successful in establishing an acknowledged legal principle. Although in November 1231 Hugh IV of Burgundy and William of Mont-Saint-Jean promised not to retain each other's Jews, this is the last of the long series of nonretention charters that has come to my attention.[104] Hereafter the principle that magnates had rights over those Jews who could be proved to have lived in their lands and been under their power seems to have been generally admitted. The right of magnates to particular Jews was now protected, not by the exchange of nonretention charters, but by inquests and court action.[105] The long struggle to establish a generally acknowledged legal rule distributing rights over Jews throughout France apparently came to an end after 1230.[106]

One reason for the effectiveness of the nonretention provision was a new factor of the first importance for the development of royal legislative power. For the first time, so far as our evidence goes, the king tried to enforce a legislative provision in the lands of another magnate. Robert III, count of Dreux, who died in 1234,[107] had not sworn the ordinance of 1230; Thibaut IV of Champagne had. In February 1235, Louis IX informed Thibaut that he had previously ordered Thibaut's people and bailiffs to return Jews of the countess of Dreux, which they had not done, contrary to the *stabilimentum* on the Jews. Louis therefore continued, "We order and require you to return to the countess of Dreux her Jews staying in your lands, according to our *stabilimen-*

tum concerning the Jews."[108] A step of great importance had been taken, if an obvious one in our eyes, toward the centralization of French society. The obligation of magnates to observe royal legislation applicable in their lands was not merely a moral obligation as Lot and Fawtier have suggested;[109] it was a legal obligation, at least whenever the king was willing and able to enforce observation. The claim that Jews were *Judei nostri* or *Judei mei* no longer rested on force and mutual conventions but on the law of the land promulgated by royal ordinance and enforced by the king. The Capetians had enacted their first measure of effective general legislation—over the bodies of the Jews.[110]

VI

In 1198 a magnate would readily claim that Jews were *Judei sui*, less easily admit the existence of *Judei eius*, and barely acknowledge that there might be *Judei eorum*. Twenty-five years later, after individual pacts, the king and twenty-five barons were willing to recognize Jews who were *Judei alterius*. From 1230 on, *aliquis in toto regno* was legally bound to acknowledge Jews who were *Judei alterius domini* as a corollary to his claim that a Jew was *Judeus suus*. There can be few less admirable examples of the development of distributive justice in the Middle Ages than this, *Judeum suum cuique tribue*; few less auspicious beginnings for that power to make explicit and immediate changes in the legal rules of a great society, which Langlois has called the principal attribute of public power.[111]

If we leave justice and turn to law, frequently a large step, we are struck by the amount of time and effort it took to move from the claim of *meum* to the admission of *tuum*, from the struggle for possession to the promulgation and acknowledgment of a general law protecting one type of rights throughout the kingdom. The basic process is plain: a widening series of individual pacts, a joint covenant, and finally the crossing of the chasm between an agreement of powerful individuals and the imposition of a law by a central authority with powerful support upon all, whether or not they had wanted or consented to the law. It seems an impressive and arduous way to gain recognition of a rule whose basic principle had been implicit in previous centuries. More important, it demonstrates both the extreme difficulty of legislating on matters of economic importance and the extent to which such legislation was a crystallization of the individual consent of magnates catalyzed by the monarchy and the Church.

Although the role of the monarchy and the increase of royal power have not been stressed throughout this discussion, the monarchy, recognized as the preeminent secular authority, was the necessary focal point for secular general legislation. And there is no doubt that royal initiative lay behind the major developments we have discussed. It is equally evident that no effective secular legislation could be promulgated until royal power and the royal administrative and judicial system had developed sufficiently to make wide and effective enforcement a reasonable possibility. But essential as was the role of the monarchy, royal power was far from self-sufficient; other support and other influences were necessary for this development.

The ordinances on the Jews depended heavily on baronial consent and were based, to a large extent, on the common interests of the king and several powerful magnates. Their promulgation and enforcement were made possible by that baronial support. Despite Luchaire's belief that the Capetians were as absolute and had as full legislative powers as the Carolingians,[112] these ordinances show that changes in the organization of French society since the last capitulary in 884 had altered the context and conditions of legislation. Whatever the case for legislation clearly religious in inspiration and purpose, on matters of obvious economic and political relevance, legislation in the early thirteenth century had to recognize the baronial independence of previous centuries by basing itself upon, and developing out of, the consent of individual magnates. Even if traditions of Carolingian power were cherished at the royal court, there is no reason to think that the magnates would support royal actions that flagrantly opposed their existing rights. Indeed the emphasis on individual consent in the nonretention charters and the ordinances on Jews is evidence that the magnates were guided by more recent custom.

Yet neither royal power nor the interests of several magnates are sufficient to explain the leap from conventions between individuals to general legislation on economically important problems, which involved not only innovation in the law but innovation in the form of law. For this, it seems, the influence of the church was necessary. The twelfth-century attempts at general legislation had been an expression of the monarchy's acknowledged religious duty of protecting the church and the peace and, unlike the ordinances on the Jews, had not developed out of a series of conventions.[113] The generality they claimed depended on the universality of the ideals they expressed, and they had the support of ecclesiastical sanctions. Secular regulation of the Jews in the early thirteenth century, despite the religious premises involved, did not fall into this category of religiously inspired ordinances for the simple reason that, at least until 1223, both king and magnates were well aware that they were inspired by fiscal, not religious, motives. But attitudes toward the Jews were changing.

The Jews had been protected by secular authorities for economic reasons and tolerated by the church for religious reasons, and their status depended on an uneasy equilibrium between those conflicting interests and authorities. The balance was disturbed as royal-baronial demands drained Jewish wealth and as the church, increasingly concerned with both the economic and religious activities of the Jews, defined their status more precisely by canonical regulation. By 1223, Louis VIII, Blanche of Castile, and their advisers were more concerned with the dangers and disadvantages of supporting the Jews than with possible profits from them. Many magnates, at least outwardly, took the same view, although in fact they seem to have used the religious view of the Jews as a convenient rationalization for more brutal treatment to extort the utmost from a declining source of revenue, a popular course at a time of heresy and wide indebtedness. Inspired by avarice or avid for blood, barons treated Jews in a way that rapidly went beyond canonical requirements and drew papal condemnation.

Where baronial self-interest and ecclesiastical ideas coincided most closely was on the principle that Jews, to whom ecclesiastical sanctions on usury did not directly apply, should be controlled by secular authorities—although from the church's point of view a major reason was to control Jewish as well as Christian usury,[114] while the desire to protect profits was uppermost in baronial minds. And when the Jews as a religious issue were becoming more important than the Jews as an economic asset, Capetian legislation was first able to move from covenant and individual consent to effective general legislation on the question of the right to control Jews, with explicit reference to a theological concept. Caught between the imperatives of a universal ideal and the assertions of individual self-interest, the Jews provided the ground on which two forms of legal change could meet and join to produce a new form. The ordinance of 1230 is a precedent for that overriding of individual consent by secular authority for the common good which would change, with the development of a new and political ethic, to the subordination of individuals to the necessity of reason of state.

7.

"Tanquam Servi": The Change in Jewish Status in French Law about 1200

I

The concept of "Jewish serfdom" dominates present historiography about the legal status of medieval Jews. "Crucial for an understanding of the entire Jewish position in the medieval world," Salo W. Baron has declared, "is the institution of 'Jewish serfdom.' "[1] And the recent *Encyclopaedia Judaica* explains the meaning of the term *servi camerae regis*, in Cecil Roth's words, as: "(Lat. 'servants of the royal chamber'), definition of the status of Jews in Christian Europe in the Middle Ages, first used in the thirteenth century."[2] Almost inevitably, this concept has influenced discussions of Jewish legal status in France in the thirteenth century, particularly discussion of one of the statutes concerning Jews which Louis IX promulgated in 1230, a statute of decisive importance both for the development of French legislation and for Jews.

> Nor can anyone in the whole kingdom retain the Jew of another lord, and wherever anyone may find his Jew he may lawfully seize him just like his own serf [*tanquam proprium servum*], no matter how long the Jew shall have stayed under another lord or in another kingdom.[3]

One article, primarily concerned with the legislative importance of the statute, has stated that its language assimilated the status of Jews to that of serfs and has alluded to the theological concept of perpetual Jewish servitude, *perpetua servitus*, as a partial explanation.[4] Salo Baron has asserted that the statute stressed the fact that "Jews were the *proprii servi* of their lords."[5] Simon Schwartzfuchs, although arguing

that the effort to "enserf" Jews did not succeed but only brought a
progressive contamination by servile status of the Jewish one, nonetheless viewed the statute as an effort to assimilate the Jew to the serf
and as important in the decline of Jewish status from that of free
men.[6] Since Bernhard Blumenkranz discussed Jewish legal status without referring to the language of the statute, he avoided the issue of
servility.[7] But Robert Chazan has recently maintained that the statute
was the "terminological culmination" of "the equation of Jewish status to that of serfs," which may have been influenced by "the earlier
adoption in English circles of overt expressions of Jewish serfdom,"
supporting his assertions with a reference to Baron's discussion of
"Jewish serfdom."[8]

The way we now understand the statute of 1230 depends not only
on the evidence that immediately surrounds it but also on the general
conception of "Jewish serfdom," that institution whose peculiarity is
underlined by the quotation marks within which it is placed by Baron,
the scholar who has most emphasized it. Hence, if we wish to clarify
our understanding of French developments, it would help to have a
clear idea of "Jewish serfdom." But that concept is difficult to sum-
marize. Prevailing formulations of what is apparently a legal phenomenon lack legal precision. They conflate perspectives and terminology
that should be kept distinct, such as those of canon law; of German,
English, and French law; and of interpretations of the historic role of
Jews. And the whole concept swims in analogical generalization.

The uncertainties that pervade it are partly explicable by its history.
The historians of the first half of the nineteenth century who discussed
the legal status of adherents of Judaism were concerned with the problem of the relation between the status of Jews and that of serfs because
some legal texts spoke of *servi camere* or *tanquam proprii servi* or *sicut
nostrum proprium catallum* in connection with Jews, and because the
drastic decline in Jewish status in the thirteenth century made the comparison with servile status seem obvious. Many of their interpretations
have since been rejected, yet the early scholars also hewed most of the
building blocks of the present conception of "Jewish serfdom." If the
idea of some early scholars that Jews in the Carolingian Empire were
aliens entirely dependent on royal privileges for their rights has now
generally been rejected,[9] the view that Jews then were free men under
Roman law with such modifications in that status as were necessitated
by religious differences had already been sketched by Jost, Depping,
Graetz, Stobbe, and Dubnow[10] and would be maintained by Georg

Caro, Bernhard Blumenkranz, and Guido Kisch.[11] And if the idea that the status of Jews became identical with that of serfs by the thirteenth century now finds little support, earlier scholars had also insisted that there was a marked difference.[12]

Another central proposition of the present conception of "Jewish serfdom"—that the term *servus*, when applied to Jews, was usually employed to protect, not to control or humiliate them—is also over a hundred years old. Most early scholars emphasized that Jews badly needed protection by the twelfth century and that the German kings or emperors made Jews their *servi* and assumed the duty of protecting them, although Eichhorn and Cassel stressed that such protection was an act of royal grace while Graetz, Stobbe, and Dubnow interpreted it as an imperial duty.[13]

One explanation, accepted by Graetz and Dubnow, of why German emperors felt obliged to protect Jews and called them *servi* was originally provided by Selig Cassel in his impressive, book-length article in 1850. He pointed out that Eike von Repgow, the author of the great collection of law, the *Sachsenspiegel* (1224), had explained the German emperor's protection of Jews by the tradition that the Roman emperor Vespasian had taken the Jews enslaved after the Jewish war of 67–70 under his protection; and that explanation has remained part of the present conception of "Jewish serfdom."[14]

Even more influential has been another explanation sketched by Cassel. Heavily influenced by Hegelian thought, Cassel was sensitive to the march of ideas and, in a perceptive analysis, argued that only after the Christianization of the mass of Europeans, the organization of the ecclesiastical hierarchy under the popes, and the development of a code of canon law could Christian ideas seriously affect Jewish secular status.[15] One sign that that stage had been reached by the end of the eleventh century was the massacres accompanying the First Crusade, which meant that Jews needed special protection. Another was the impact of theology and canon law on secular law in the twelfth and thirteenth centuries. "The formulation of imperial law in Germany at this time was stimulated by opposition to the activity of the collection of canon law."[16]

Of particular importance for Jews was the decretal of Innocent III in 1205 which incorporated the theological doctrine that Jews had been subjected to perpetual servitude to Christians because they had crucified Christ, a decretal included in Gregory IX's official code of canon law, the *Decretales*, in 1234. Cassel held that when Frederick II, the first emperor to use it, introduced the term *servi camere* in 1236, he drew both on the Vespasian tradition of the secular dependence on the emperor and on the religious doctrine of Jewish servitude to Christians, and used these counterbalancing ideas to justify his own claim to hegemony over Jews.[17]

Strangely enough, Graetz, Stobbe, and Dubnow neglected this explanation of the role of "perpetual servitude" in the development of chamber serfdom in Germany. Nonetheless, thanks to twentieth-century scholars,[18] Cassel's explanation has become perhaps the central element in the present conception of both chamber serfdom and "Jewish serfdom," the latter term owing its name through a misleading translation to the theological doctrine. Kisch considers the doctrine to have been one of the three main motivations of the development of chamber serfdom in Germany, the other two being the emperor's desire to strengthen imperial control and the social tendency to segregate Jews. He has even argued implausibly that Frederick II waited until the publication of the *Decretales* in 1234 had disseminated the theological concept before using the term *servi camere* himself in 1236.[19] And Baron has devoted an article to the thesis that papal insistence on Jewish servitude was part of the much broader papal drive for hegemony, for *plenitudo potestatis*, and that Frederick II's assertion that Jews were *servi camere* was an imperial counterclaim, a direct reaction to papal competition for jurisdiction over Jews.[20] He has also stressed the importance of the doctrine in his discussions of "Jewish serfdom" in other kingdoms and in general.[21]

There are presently two, considerably divergent views of the development of chamber serfdom—or "Jewish serfdom"—in Germany. Kisch holds that, from Carolingian times to the end of the eleventh century, Jews were free men under customary law, not aliens, a status strengthened by the inclusion of Jews in the imperial land peaces of the twelfth century. The development of chamber serfdom from 1236, however, brought a fundamental change and deterioration in Jewish status, or rather created a separate Jewish status. It placed Jews under an all-inclusive special law whose application was decided solely by the religious criterion of Judaism, so that Jews became a special class outside the common law applicable to others.[22]

Baron, however, supports the view that Jews were aliens in Carolingian times, albeit a peculiar kind of aliens who, because of royal protection, were "a new group of royal vassals, somewhat akin to Christian nobles."[23] He holds that a change came with the massacres of 1096 and the inclusion of Jews in the land peaces, since these emphasized Jewish dependence on imperial protection, which was construed by the emperors and their advisers "as a mark of that peculiar 'bondage' which the Church had been preaching from time immemorial."[24] And the development of Jewish status from 1103 to Frederick II in 1236 is interpreted primarily as an imperial reaction to the drive for papal hegemony and increasing papal insistence on controlling Jews through the doctrine of perpetual servitude.[25] But unlike Kisch, Baron does not see the introduction of the term *servi camere* as marking a fundamental change in Jewish status. Time and time again he insists that the main purpose of imperial actions was to protect Jews.

> In both the earlier and newer formulations defining the Jews' relationship to the imperial Chamber, the obvious intention was not a lowering of their status, but rather an indication of the particular causes that impelled the emperors to protect them.[26]
>
> It must not be forgotten, for example, that almost all the laws enacted by the German emperors in which the Jews are referred to as "belonging" to, or being "serfs" of, the emperor's Chamber were intended to benefit, not humiliate them.[27]
>
> It was, indeed, according to this widely accepted legal meaning of living as free men under royal protection that the Jews and most of their masters conceived of their status as royal "serfs."[28]

An obvious feature of both early and recent work on chamber serfdom or "Jewish serfdom" is its concentration on Germany. Some reasons are obvious. The eye-catching term *servi camere* was formulated and fairly frequently employed there, whereas the terms *servus* and *Judeus* were rarely conjoined in the laws of other kingdoms. The German king, moreover, was also emperor, an office surrounded by the halo of the Roman Empire and the traditions of Roman law and possessing a claim to superiority over Christian Europe which brought it into conflict with the papacy. As a result of that conflict, conscious debate about the organization of Christendom focused on Germany rather than other kingdoms, and the claims of the emperor, including those about Jews, were very carefully formulated in theoretical and legal terms. A very different kind of reason is the fact that modern Jewish historiography was born in central Europe, principally in Germany, and was practiced initially by people who were more at home in the history and languages of that region than of western Europe.

Whatever the reasons, the concentration on Germany encouraged a tendency to use the legal status of Jews in Germany as archetypical when discussing the legal status of Jews in other kingdoms, despite obvious differences. The early French scholars, such as Beugnot and Depping, had emphasized royal exploitation rather than royal protection of Jews in France. But Graetz and Dubnow, although agreeing on that difference, nonetheless used the German terminology to denote the legal status of Jews in France and England.

> The Jews had, in all essentials, been *servi camere* before in France and England; that is, they were half-and-half the property of the king or the barons, and under one or another title they constantly had to hold their purses in readiness to replenish the empty coffers of their lords. In Germany, however, they had in return the protection of the emperor.[29]
> Here [in France and England] the king, who considered the Jew's person and all his belongings as his own property, harshly exploited the commerce-serf—and when the serf's services were no longer needed, he was driven from the country mercilessly. In Germany, Jews were also regarded as belonging to the "King's Chamber" and in the 13th century the status of "serfs of the empire" . . . was legalized in official documents; but here this "serfdom" signified more the duty of the highest authority to protect Jews, and to see to it that they were not wronged, than the right to exploit their labor.[30]

The tendency to generalize German terminology and explanations is marked in recent scholarship. Yitzhak Baer declared that, "generally speaking, the Jews in Spain, as in all of Christian Europe, were regarded as the personal property of the king," and explained that "this principle followed directly from the teaching of the Church Fathers that the Jews were doomed to perpetual servitude"—even though the early evidence he cited to support that explanation for Spain antedated Innocent III's decretal of 1205.[31] Cecil Roth's generalization of German terminology to Christian Europe has already been quoted. More revealing of the dominance of preconceptions born in Germany, however, is his assertion in his detailed study of Jews in England. In England, *servi camere* was never in fact used in any legal text, nor were Jews ever stated to be, or be like, *servi* (or *villani* or *nativi*), yet Roth nonetheless asserted that, "as elsewhere in Europe in the Middle Ages, the Jews were reckoned *servi camere regis*, or Serfs of the Royal Chamber. Nowhere, indeed, was this laid down more explicitly."[32] And as we have seen, recent discussions of the status of Jews in France have referred to "Jewish serfdom" and used the explanation of the theological doctrine.[33]

The most sweeping generalization of concepts emanating from Germany has been made by Baron, who seeks to offset "the lachrymose conception of Jewish history" and believes that "the basic similarity of institutions governing Jewish life throughout medieval Europe becomes manifest to any observer."[34] Baron's discussions of the development of chamber serfdom in Germany precede his discussions of "Jewish serfdom" in other kingdoms. And when he turns to other kingdoms, he argues that their rulers and jurists were aware of, and reacted against, both the church's claim to control Jews on the basis of the doctrine of perpetual servitude and the imperial claim that Jews were serfs of the imperial chamber; instead they developed their own justification by relying on the doctrine of perpetual servitude but stressing their own independent authority.[35]

> They accepted the concept of the Jews' condemnation to "perpetual servitude" because of their guilt for having repudiated Christ. But they insisted that the Jews were serfs of Christian rulers, whoever these may be, rather than specifically of the Church or Empire. This royal interpretation appeared so simple that it did not require elaborations of the type found in papal or imperial letters.[36]

The vacuum indicated by the last sentence is used by Baron to support or impose his theses. The absence of any language stating that Jews were serfs in England is overlooked to maintain that English Jews were "the king's defenceless 'serfs' " and that the English kings had the underlying conviction that "the Jews really were *their* serfs."[37] But the same absence is also used to argue that Jews in England were *not* serfs or rightless,[38] despite the fact that Jews were far more drastically controlled and exploited in England than in Germany, where they really were called *servi camere*. For only thus can Baron assert the universality of "Jewish serfdom" and preserve his principal thesis to offset the lachrymose conception of Jewish history, the thesis that Jews were called or considered serfs because rulers sought to protect them.

> In the first place, it ought to give us pause that almost all early decrees mentioning the Jews' specific allegiance to the royal power were intended for the former's *protection*. For the most part Jewish "serfdom" was cited as a reason why kings felt obliged to safeguard the rights of their Jewish wards.[39]
> In this sense the Jewish "serfs" were indeed free men living under royal protection but enjoying a considerable measure of self-determination and individual mobility.[40]

And this is very much the view which Cecil Roth has canonized in the *Encyclopaedia Judaica*:

> The status of the Jews was above all that of serfs, and theoretically they were subject only to royal authority. The ruler had the right to tax them for the benefit of his treasury (*camera regis*), but at the same time he had the duty to protect them when they were in danger from others.[41]

As one attempts to disentangle the various strands of the present concept of "Jewish serfdom," one becomes aware of some striking reversals and antitheses. Whereas early scholars sought to explain why Jews in Germany were called *servi camere*, their explanation has now been applied where Jews were never called serfs in order to prove that they were really "serfs." What was originally seen—and still is by Kisch—as a crucial degradation of the status of Jews has been interpreted as an effort to preserve the rights of Jews as free men. And whereas the terminology of servility has usually been associated with exploitation—save for the rhetorical expressions of humility such as the papal title *servus servorum Dei*—it is now seen as a measure of protection. By a use of quotation marks that obscures the difference between a quotation of medieval evidence and a modern analogy, we are now told both that Jews were everywhere serfs and that they were nowhere serfs like any other serfs.

It is no wonder that "Jewish serfdom" itself is put in quotation marks by its major proponent, for it is a very paradoxical concept. And if paradox is an indication of previous error, then perhaps the crucial error has been the dissociation of modern definitions of the legal status of medieval Jews from the language of medieval law and the abandonment of the effort to discover why Jews were legally designated as they were in different areas. A secondary error has been the use of German conditions as archetypical for the status of Jews everywhere.

II

A reexamination of the legal status of Jews in France might well begin with an examination of the situation in England in order to balance the previous influence of historiography about Germany. England and France then had a common, French-speaking, governing class, both secular and ecclesiastical. And if the development of the ritual murder libel in England and France is any indication, there were some common attitudes toward Jews, whose moneylending was also better developed in those kingdoms than in Germany. Ever since Graetz, moreover, scholars have tended to contrast the exploitative treatment of Jews by English and French kings with the protective attitude of German kings. The recent suggestion that the equation of the status of Jews to that of serfs in France in 1230 may have been influenced by the earlier development of "overt expressions of Jewish serfdom" in England also suggests the need for a fuller analysis of any possibe influence.[42]

We cannot look to England for a direct explanation of why *servus* and *Judeus* were legally linked, since those terms were never conjoined in English law. But we can discover why they were not. The language of the law provides an immediate clue: legally, Jews were simply, consistently, and adequately designated as *Judei*. No need was apparently felt to compare them with serfs. The reason would seem to lie in the distinctive situation of Jews in England. Significant Jewish settlement in England occurred only after the Conquest of 1066; from 1066 to 1290, despite occasional civil war, the English monarchy was the most centralized and efficient in Europe; and from William the Conqueror to Edward I, English kings exercised an undisputed monopoly of jurisdiction over that small, recent, and defenseless element of the population.[43]

If the Jews' need for protection and the desire of strong kings to gain or maintain as many profitable rights as possible made that monopoly possible, what made it conceivable was the religious difference with its legal consequences that set Jews apart from others and made it possible to think of them as people who could be treated legally as a special group regardless of their occupations. On the Continent, at least since Carolingian times, Jews could substitute an oath for the judicial ordeals and could substitute a Jewish for a Christian oath; at least in northern France they could not exercise authority over Christians; they could engage in the most manifest usury; and they were not subject to the other great jurisdiction that ordered society, canon law. Since Anglo-Saxon law had said nothing about Jews, the Anglo-Norman kings were able to impose their own definition, with the consequence that in England the legal status of Jews had another peculiarity: they were protected, taxed, and judged only by the king and his officials.

That royal monopoly of jurisdiction is reflected in two frequently quoted texts. The first is a passage from the so-called Laws of Edward the Confessor, compiled about 1135. The second is two clauses from King John's charter of 1201 for the Jews of England and Normandy, a charter that was based on an earlier charter of Henry II and granted Jews the right to reside freely and honorably, among other privileges.

> It should be known that, since all Jews wherever they may be in the kingdom should be under the liege wardship and protection of the king, and since none of them can subject himself to any rich man without the king's permission since the Jews and all they have are the king's, if anyone shall detain them or their money, the king may claim [them] just as his property [*tanquam suum proprium*] if he wishes and is able.[44]
>
> And wherever the Jews may be, they may lawfully go wheresoever they wish with all their chattels just as our own things [*sicut res nostre proprie*], and no one may lawfully detain them or prohibit them from doing this. And we command that they be quit through all England and Normandy of all customs, tolls, and payments on the measure of wine just as our own chattels [*sicut nostrum proprium catallum*].[45]

Both texts say much the same thing. In order to protect Jews and the royal monopoly of jurisdiction over them, the king had forbidden any subject to retain them or their possessions. And to illustrate their unusual status, it was added that they could move with their possessions freely just as royal property could. The comparative adverbs *tanquam* and *sicut* do not introduce assertions that Jews *are* the king's property (the substantive *proprium*) or his own (the adjective *proprius*) things or chattels. They introduce a comparison that emphasizes that, should anyone detain Jews or their possessions, the subject who detains them will stand in the same legal relation to the king as if he had seized royal property, and that the king may therefore demand their return, not for himself, but for the Jews.

Another example, which can be read without presuppositions about Jewish status, confirms this interpretation. It is from a charter in which Henry II granted the privilege of *firma burgi*, with its greater autonomy, to the burgesses (*burgenses mei*) of Cambridge.

> For that reason, I order you [royal officials and subjects] to guard and preserve the said burgesses and all that is theirs just as my property [*sicut mea propria*] so that no one may injure or molest or harm them in anything. For I do not wish that they respond to anyone concerning these matters except to me and before my exchequer.[46]

By this language the king neither asserted that the burgesses were serfs nor implied that he conceived that they were really his "serfs," although he did assert that they were solely under his jurisdiction.

There is no reason to interpret the similes in the texts concerning Jews any differently — unless we are trying to force a thesis on them. To say that those texts are overt expressions of "Jewish serfdom," or to speak of the conception of Jewish servility and say that the passage from the Laws of Edward the Confessor was "the first clear enunciation of the principle in a secular context in the Middle Ages"[47] is to have been deluded by the prevailing conception of "Jewish serfdom."

The definition of Jewish status in England resulted from the concrete rights and obligations prescribed by English kings, not from such similes. And for most of the twelfth century, that status was high, with most of the rights of burgesses, some special privileges, some special restrictions, and not very onerous obligations. Toward the end of the century, however, the king tightened his administrative controls and increased his exploitation of his *Judei*. The development of the special justices of the Jews and the Exchequer of the Jews after 1190 both emphasized the distinctiveness of Jewish status and enabled the king to increase his exploitation drastically. King John's arbitrary exploitation and mass imprisonment of 1210 marked the beginning of a rapid deterioration of Jewish status, which only made that status even more distinctive.

By 1233, Jews were only licensed to reside permanently in certain towns and could not go overseas without special permission, and in that year the king commanded:

> No Jew shall remain in our kingdom save such as can serve [*servire*] the king and find good pledges of fidelity. Other Jews, indeed, who have nothing wherewith they may serve the king, shall leave the kingdom.[48]

By the middle of the thirteenth century, the rights of Jews had diminished and their obligations had increased so radically that a passage deceptively attributed to Bracton, the great English jurist, ascribed to Jews a status that sounded like that of slaves in the Roman Empire but bore no resemblance to that of serfs in England.

> A Jew, indeed, can have nothing of his own because whatever he acquires he acquires not for himself but for the king, because they live not for themselves but for others, and so they acquire for others and not for themselves.[49]

The author of this passage did not explain the king's right by asserting that the Jews were his serfs, for the consequences would not have followed. Indeed, no thirteenth-century Englishman would have confused Jewish and servile status because of the obvious differences in pattern of settlement, occupation—and law. Jews did not become, or come to be thought of, as serfs in England between 1066 and 1290. What happened in that period was that their distinctive status as Jews was, at first gradually and then drastically, degraded until the final distinction and degradation of the expulsion of 1290.

Yet whether Jewish status was high or low, English kings protected their Jews from third parties, save for temporary lapses. The desire or duty to protect dependents from molestation by others applied to any dependents. If one may speak of a political program of medieval kings, then perhaps its central plank was insistence on rights over dependents and protection of the rights of obedient dependents. Effective protection of dependents was a manifestation of royal power, while any breach in that protection was a defiance of royal authority and a threat to royal power, an attitude well expressed in King John's writ prohibiting attacks on Jews: "If I give my peace even to a dog, it must be kept inviolate."[50] The protection of Jews in England was a function of royal power, and it would not have been improved by speaking of them as serfs. In fact, English Jews were both better protected and more severely exploited in England, where they were never called or thought of as serfs, than in Germany where they were called *servi camere*.

III

When we turn to the legal status of Jews in northern France with the advantage of an English as well as a German perspective, the similarity between the language of the law in France and England is obvious. In French as in English law, Jews were designated consistently as *Judei*, although as competition for them developed in the twelfth century, a possessive adjective—*mei, nostri, sui*—was frequently added in recognition of the division of jurisdiction. French Jews were never described as *servi camere*; and only in the statute of 1230—and its repetition along with other ordinances in Louis IX's reforming ordinances of 1254[51]—was *servus* ever conjoined with *Judeus*. The terms were not linked in the other statutes of 1230, and, so far as I know, they were never linked in any other ordinance concerning Jews in the thirteenth century. If the language of the law is any guide—as perhaps it should be in legal matters—then the legal status of adherents of Judaism, so far as they acquired a distinctive status, was that of Jews, not serfs. But why, then, were *Judei* and *servi* linked by the comparative adverb *tanquam* in 1230?

To answer that question in particular and, indeed, to clarify the whole problem of "Jewish serfdom," we must be able to forget Jews for a while and discover what serfdom meant to non-Jews and how lords controlled their more defenseless dependents. What did *servus* symbolize to those who ruled northern France in the early thirteenth century, and how did they control their *servi* and other dependents?

In Roman law, *servus* denoted a slave, and it retained that meaning for a considerable time in the slave societies of the early Middle Ages. Slavery continued in the Iberian peninsula and along the Mediterranean coast of France until the fifteenth century, but by the twelfth century slaves were increasingly designated by other terms such as *captivus, saracenus,* or *sclavus.*[52] In northwestern Europe, however, slavery had disappeared by the twelfth century, and *servus* (or more typically *homo proprius, homo de corpore, villanus,* and the like, or their vernacular equivalents) was used to denote what was now the most extreme dependency in northwestern Europe, although it was milder than slavery and became progressively milder.

Servile status varied so markedly from region to region that it is difficult or dangerous to generalize about its characteristics even for the thirteenth century.[53] It bound people who had risen from more extreme forms of dependency and had fallen from greater freedom, whether collectively or through individual action and commendation. But whatever their origin, these people and their descendants had become personally, hereditarily, and involuntarily dependent on a single lord. "One was a serf, unless freed, from father to son, and not in any vague way, but very precisely serf of a specific lord."[54] Yet the obligations of serfs differed only in degree from those of immediately higher statuses, which were filled by people who were *de facto* almost equally bound to their lords by economic and social conditions; and serfs could cross that thin line by manumission. As a result, the contours of serfdom were vague, and it could be difficult to prove by their customary obligations who was a serf, especially with the improvement in servile status from the tenth century. The effort to overcome that uncertainty resulted in sharper definition by the thirteenth century. The three most typical obligations, whose performance was evidence that a person was a lord's serf, were *chevage, formariage,* and *mainmorte*, although their form and relative importance still varied considerably from region to region.

The increasing definition of servile status coincided, however, by the end of the twelfth century, with its decline in several areas and its virtual disappearance from some regions: Forez, the Mâconnais, most of Picardy, and Normandy—and from most towns.[55] A major cause of that regression was the demand for manpower, despite demographic advance, for agrarian and urban expansion. As lords sought to increase their revenue from rents and profits of jurisdiction by bringing their wastelands and forests under cultivation and developing their towns, they tried to attract settlers by offering advantageous legal and economic conditions. Prosperous free peasants were unlikely to respond, but serfs and poor free peasants saw an opportunity to better their condition, if they could leave their present position.[56]

Those who migrated, colonists or pioneers of internal expansion, were given a new status when they arrived, that of *hospites* or *hôtes*. Although usually distinguished from that of serfs,[57] their status was highly variable. Some *hôtes* differed little from serfs and seem to have been considered unfree, especially the *hôtes taillables*.[58] And some—or the rights over them—were sold or granted to other lords.[59] Those described as *couchans et levans*, a term also used for serfs, seem to have been free to leave their village and their lord if they found other *hôtes* to take their place.[60] Other documents, however, expressly specify personal liberty for *hôtes*.[61] Even if the line between servile status and that of *hôtes* was indistinct at the margins, the latter was freer and often much freer from onerous obligations and personal dependency, at least until the middle of the thirteenth century; and it was accompanied by economic opportunity. Nor should we forget that undetected residence of serfs for a year and a day in most towns meant indisputable freedom. These advantages accompanying the movement of internal expansion consequently attracted serfs and poor peasants to new villages and towns, and their former lords thereby lost manpower, jurisdiction, and revenue.

Evidence of the competition for manpower is fairly plentiful even if we restrict ourselves to royal documents between 1170 and 1215. In charters in which the king founded or confirmed another lord's foundation of a *villeneuve*, a clause might appear which forbade the reception or retention there of any of the king's men without his consent.[62] One royal charter is very explicit. The abbey of Saint-Melon agreed in 1196 to share with the king the foundation of a *villeneuve* in its woods, the king receiving half the profits in return for his support. The king agreed that no serfs or men of two other lords, who had surrendered their rights in this land, should be received in the village; and he promised not to make it a commune.[63] The king then granted favorable customs to the inhabitants with one major reservation.

> This, I say, we grant, with this condition that no one of our serfs, no one of our *hôtes*, no one from our communes, and no one of our burgesses shall be received to reside in the said *villeneuve* except by our will and consent.[64]

Similarly, when the greater liberties of the customs of Lorris or a commune were granted to an existing village or town, a clause prohibiting the reception or retention there of the king's men or serfs[65] or the serfs of other lords[66] might be included. Even a royal grant of arable land to a lord might include, along with a prohibition against erecting a fortress, another against reception of men from the royal domain.[67]

Clearly, the drain of manpower was a matter of some consequence to the king and other lords, not merely the loss of serfs but also the departure of *hôtes*, free peasants, members of communes, and burgesses. This concern prompted the king and other lords to go beyond *ad hoc* measures, which prevented the flight to a specific locality, and develop more general measures. These measures were more political than legal, for whereas lords who had rights in specific localities could demand that their rights be protected in the relevant charters, more abstract agreements involved bargaining.

In 1177/78, Louis VII reached an agreement with two brothers. The king wanted to regain the provostship of Flagy, which they held hereditarily by royal grant. To recover it, Louis made the following concession:

> We notify those present and future that we have conceded to Joscelin and Gautier de Thouri that neither we nor our heirs will retain any either of their male or female serfs in our *villeneuves* or in all our land. And if any male or female serf of the aforesaid Joscelin and Gautier shall withdraw to our *villeneuves* or our land and it shall be proven by witnesses worthy of faith, he or she shall be unconditionally returned.[68]

To stop the drain of their serfs, Joscelin and Gautier were willing to abandon the provostship.

Another example demonstrates how a localized conflict between the king and a powerful lord could lead to a more general agreement. The bishop of Nevers had tried to get serfs he claimed at Bourges and

Aubigny back from Philip Augustus by impleading them in church courts, but he settled in 1212 for a compromise in which he retained his claim to six and ceded the others to the king. A general agreement was then reached in the same year in which the king promised to return any present serfs of the bishop who should withdraw to the lordship of the king or his son after an inquest had proved that they were the bishop's serfs, although the king would nonetheless get half of their ransom.[69]

Both of these agreements were concerned with the flight of serfs and did not change their status but rather prevented them from changing it. But competition was not limited to serfs, and the same technique was applied to people of other statuses. About 1170, Ivo, count of Soissons, and Simon d'Epagny agreed, in order to maintain peace, that "neither could receive in his lands the hôtes of the other."[70] A more complex agreement of 1183 between Philip Augustus and the chapter of the cathedral of Soissons applied to both serfs and hôtes but carefully distinguished between them. As a result of much ecclesiastical pressure, the king agreed not to retain in his villages or communes within the diocese of Soissons any serfs or hôtes couchans et levans of the chapter. But should any such people come into his villages and communes outside the diocese, he did not promise to return them but only agreed that the canons could seize whatever the serfs, but not the hôtes, possessed within the lands of the cathedral.[71] The difference in status was not obliterated by the agreement for those who remained under the chapter's jurisdiction or within the diocese and even affected those who left the diocese. As for the emphasis on the limits of the diocese, it suggests that, like the bishop of Nevers and the abbot of Saint-Denis later,[72] the chapter had been using ecclesiastical sanctions to try to retain its peasants; and it emphasizes the political character of the agreement.

Charters for villeneuves and communes and general agreements also prohibited retention of people of clearly higher statuses. In 1175/76, Louis VII confirmed his wife's grant of the customs of Lorris to one of her villages with the condition that she not retain there any male or female serf or any person whatsoever from the royal domain.[73] Much more sweeping and explicit was Philip Augustus's agreement with Blanche of Champagne in 1209, during Thibaut's minority, when unusual legal and political conditions arose.

> Know . . . that we have conceded to our beloved and faithful Blanche, countess of Troyes, that, from the first Thursday of the coming September

to the Christmas coming in one year, we shall not receive within our domains or wardships or communes or free villages [or towns] any man or woman who is from her domains, wardships, communes, or free villages.[74]

And in the following year, Philip made the same promise, this time to last until Thibaut reached twenty-one, and Blanche promised in identical terms not to retain any such people from the king's jurisdiction.[75]

Like all other commands and promises not to retain the dependents of another lord, this agreement controlled people not by changing their status but by preventing their movement between the contracting jurisdictions. As the alternative use of *recipere* and *retinere* suggests, the legal basis of these prohibitions and promises was not the status of the people whose movement was impeded but the rarely used right of a lord to refuse to receive newcomers of any status under his protection and jurisdiction. These general agreements were, in effect, immigration treaties agreed to by independent parties in order to control movement between them.

For a variety of reasons, it was impossible or undesirable to make the principle of the nonretention of *hôtes* and free persons of other lords general by legislation; yet had it been possible, their status would have been changed in one, but only one, important way. Like serfs, they would have become involuntarily and hereditarily dependent on one lord and under his jurisdiction. But no other aspect of their status would have changed: unlike serfs, they would have been as free as before to move within their lord's jurisdiction, and they would not have been constrained to obligations typical of serfs such as *chevage*, *formariage*, and *mainmorte*. The old distinctions of status would have remained even had a law been promulgated declaring: "No one in the whole kingdom can retain the man or woman of another lord, and wherever anyone may find his man or woman, he may lawfully seize him or her just as his own serf."

IV

Our hypothetical legislation brings us back to what was in fact the first piece of general legislation for the French kingdom, the statute of 1230 concerning Jews. Although unnoticed before, it is evident that the nonretention agreements that sought to control the movement of Christian manpower provided the model for the nonretention agreements about Jews, which began in 1198 and culminated in the statute of 1230. The technique and purpose were the same: to obtain agreement between competing authorities to limit competition for valuable dependents. But this time the technique was used to control competition for people legally classified as *Judei*, a problem that never arose in England because of the royal monopoly of jurisdiction over Jews.

In France, because of the weakness of the Capetian monarchy and the extreme fragmentation of secular authority before 1200, full jurisdiction over Jews pertained to any lord with high justice who permitted them to reside under his jurisdiction. Jews could move freely with their possessions from one lord to any other lord who would receive them. The precise details of their status depended on the way each lord treated his own Jews, and since there was no central authority to impose uniformity, considerable variation was possible. But since there were as yet few legal restrictions on how Jews earned their living and led their lives, and since most of the few special privileges and restrictions were a reflection of general ecclesiastical pressure, the principal variation in status was the way they were taxed or exploited.[76]

Through most of the twelfth century, however, taxation does not seem to have been particularly arbitrary or notably disproportionate to the taxation of other townsmen. Consonant with previous custom and, since about 1120, with the definition of their proper treatment by the papal bull *Sicut Judeis non*,[77] Jews were not usually deprived of their possessions save by legal process and regular taxation. And through most of the twelfth century, although they were legally designated as *Judei* and almost completely excluded from the rising guilds and town governments, it is difficult to speak of a unique Jewish status that put them outside the general law applicable to others, for the bulk of their rights and obligations and legal actions were identical with those of others, and no one could impose a uniform, special status on them. But however that problem is resolved, Jews were freer than most peasants.

The striking decline in the status of Jews began in the last decades of the twelfth century, when credit operations had become highly profitable and religious and economic pressures had intensified anti-Jewish feelings. The decline initially affected only Jews under royal jurisdiction.[78] Between 1180 and 1182, the young Philip Augustus first arbitrarily despoiled his Jews of much of their movable wealth and then expelled them from the royal domain, taking the remainder of their property. There was no trial and no attempt to provide a legal justification, but there were rumors of Jewish misconduct and of the dangerous impact of Jewish credit. The king treated his Jews this way because they were Jews. No contemporary said that he did this because they were serfs; indeed, the king never could have treated his serfs this way and never did so.

Only later, between 1214 and 1217, after the king had readmitted Jews to the royal domain in 1198, did a chronicler, Guillaume le Breton, justify the initial partial spoliation of 1180 by writing that the king "could have taken everything from them had he wished . . . just like the goods and chattels of serfs [*tanquam servorum res et catella*]."[79] Guillaume's poem was no legal document, yet we should nonetheless note that even he did not say that these Jews were serfs; he only said that the king had the same right to the possessions of his Jews which he had—in theory—to those of his serfs.

The Jews expelled from the royal domain in 1182 were welcomed by neighboring magnates such as the count of Champagne, and their availability reduced competition for Jews. But when the king unexpectedly readmitted Jews to the rich possibilities of the royal domain in 1198, the distribution of the relatively small number of rich Jews was suddenly disturbed in northern France, and conscious competition to acquire, retain, and control them suddenly arose. The competition was similar to the earlier competition for agrarian manpower, and the response was identical. Immediately after the readmission, in 1198, Philip Augustus and Thibaut III of Champagne agreed not to retain each other's Jews.

> Know that we have granted that we shall retain none of the Jews of . . . Thibaut, count of Troyes, in our land, except with the assent of that count from his mouth, and none of our Jews can lend money to anyone of the land of the said count, except with the count's assent from his mouth. And the same Count Thibaut has granted to us that he will retain no Jew of ours in his land except with our assent from our mouth, and that no Jew of his can lend money to anyone in our land except with our assent from our mouth.[80]

By 1210, the formula for such nonretention agreements had become succinct.

> Know that henceforward we shall neither receive nor retain the Jews of our beloved and faithful Blanche, countess of Troyes, nor she ours.[81]
> I, Gaucher de Châtillon, count of Saint-Pol, notify all who shall inspect the present letters that henceforward I shall neither receive nor retain the

Jews of my dearest lord Philip, illustrious king of France, nor will he hence-forward retain my Jews.[82]

These agreements sought to regulate the rights of the contracting lords and prescribed no change in the status of Jews. But since most lords did not acknowledge the limitation, the effort continued. We have some eighteen such nonretention agreements between 1198 and 1231. By 1223, Louis VIII was able to broaden agreement by getting twenty-five lords with jurisdiction over Jews to join him in swearing not to retain anyone else's Jews, while the count of Champagne, who had not sworn, promised later in the year not to retain any Jews of the king and the twenty-five lords. And finally, in 1230, the king was able to make the principle of nonretention of another's Jews law for the kingdom.

These measures were one result of the changing socioeconomic position of Jews—and a reflection of the increase in royal power. Excluded from other major economic occupations, Jews had become stereotyped as moneylenders since the middle of the twelfth century, just when the church had begun to legislate seriously against Christian usurers. If Jews had been thought of at the beginning of the twelfth century as townsmen and, much more rarely, agriculturalists who had certain special privileges and restrictions because of their religion, by 1200 it had become much easier to think of them as a vocationally specialized, inferior group that lived apart in towns, a group for which a unique and inferior legal status would be appropriate. Such a development seems obvious in England about 1200 with the organization of the special exchequer for Jews and John's arbitrary arrest and spoliation of them in 1210.

The same development is apparent in France, starting with Philip Augustus's spoliation of 1180–1182 and developing more systematically with the royal exploitation from 1198 on. In 1206, the king began to record, regulate, and restrict Jewish lending. The nonretention agreements of 1210 were the prelude to the mass imprisonment and arbitrary expropriations of that year, influenced by John's example. Further restrictions on lending were imposed on royal Jews in 1219. The ordinance of 1223, which included the nonretention promise of the king and the twenty-five, seems also to have included an effort to suppress Jewish usury and, more certainly, to have been the preparation for another partial expropriation. If one of the statutes of 1230 made the principle of nonretention law for the kingdom, another, which affected only the contracting parties, promised that loan contracts of Jews would not be enforced in the future. And by 1234, Louis IX had indicated his intention of expelling from the lands under his control any Jews who continued to exact usury. The vocational specialization of Jews and its profits had as a legal corollary that the status of Jews was increasingly defined, seemed increasingly unique, and became increasingly inferior.

The degradation of Jewish status, especially by the kings, raised the question of who had jurisdiction over people with Jewish status because in France, in contrast with England, Jews could flee royal exploitation and seek lords who would treat them better. It was therefore in the king's interest to prevent his Jews from migrating. With the extension of the royal domain by Philip Augustus and Louis VIII, the king had come to exercise jurisdiction over many Jews, perhaps more than were under any other lord. But since the king could not claim a monopoly of jurisdiction over all Jews, he could strengthen his grip over his own only by recognizing and enforcing the principle that other possessors had as exclusive jurisdiction over their Jews as he claimed over his. The statute of 1230 marked the triumph of that policy, but if the result was novel, the means employed were not, and their implications should now be clear.

The nonretention agreements about Jews copied the technique developed to maintain control of Christian manpower. And just as that technique had not changed the status of serfs, *hôtes*, free peasants, and townsmen but only preserved jurisdiction over people of those statuses, so too the nonretention agreements about Jews sought to preserve jurisdiction but did not themselves make any change in Jewish status, other, perhaps, than emphasizing its distinctiveness. As English developments demonstrate, possession of jurisdiction itself, even of a monopoly of undisputed jurisdiction, was compatible with either a high status of Jews or a degraded Jewish status, although there can be no doubt that it opened the way for the latter. The degradation of Jewish status depended on how anyone who had jurisdiction exercised it in practice.

Yet with the statute of 1230, a single aspect of Jewish status was, indeed, changed. For unlike the nonretention agreements about either Christians or Jews, the statute made the principle of nonretention law for all the kingdom, with the result that, legally, people of Jewish status were now involuntarily and hereditarily dependent on a single lord who could seize his Jew who had fled just as he could seize a person who owed him servile obligations. To illustrate and emphasize that change in the rights of lords and consequently in Jewish status, the statute used the simile *tanquam proprii servi.*

Even as a simile, however, it was imperfect, for proof that a Jew was subject to seizure was not provided by evidence that he had performed typically servile obligations for a lord. And whereas any lord could have serfs, only lords with high jurisdiction could have Jews. Moreover, whereas serfs were overwhelmingly rural and might become free by fleeing undetected for a year and a day to a town, Jews, typically townsmen, could be seized after any length of time and anywhere—even, it was said, in another kingdom. Yet since the simile was not a definition of Jewish status, only an analogy to illustrate one aspect of it, it did not need to be very precise and was dropped after it had served its limited purpose of emphasizing the consequence of the new definition of rights of jurisdiction over people whose status was that of Jews.

Despite recent historiography, the statute of 1230 did not stress that Jews were *proprii servi* of their lords, nor did it assimilate or equate the status of Jews to that of serfs.[83] It did so no more than Philip Augustus's order that his barons and others should protect the lands, men, and things of the church of Notre Dame of Chartres *tanquam nostras proprias* meant that the cathedral belonged not to the Virgin but to the king.[84] What it did was to make one aspect of Jewish status similar to, but not identical with, one aspect of servile status; and, much more important, it made Jewish status clearly unique.

In law, *Judei* had originally designated people who adhered to Judaism and, because of their religion, enjoyed special privileges, were subject to special restrictions, and were not supposed to exercise authority over Christians, but could otherwise engage in most of the occupations and activities open to other people. The various measures around 1200 to regulate and exploit Jewish lending had further restricted the status of Jews and made it seem more distinctive, but they had applied only to those Jews who lent money. The statute of 1230, however, applied to all Jews, imposed on all Jews a restriction that was motivated by the desire to control and exploit Jewish lending, and thereby implied that all Jews were conceived of as a group that specialized in an occupation that was illegal when exercised by Christians. Not simply their Judaism but also their major economic activity now set Jews as a group apart both in society and in law.

V

Since the statute of 1230 did not assert that Jews were serfs, it is difficult to argue that the theological doctrine of perpetual Jewish servitude had any influence on its language. The principle expressed in the statute had, in fact, a completely different and secular origin. The statute only extended the technique of the nonretention promises that had preceded it, and that technique was copied from the agreements intended to control Christian manpower, which assuredly owed nothing to the doctrine of perpetual servitude or other religious considerations. Of course, the statute, which imposed on Jews a restriction that could not be imposed on *hôtes*, free peasants, and townsmen, and only partially on serfs, is inexplicable without reference to the general religious situation. The millennial ecclesiastical pressure and the more recent popular hostility and persecutions had set Jews apart, forced them into occupational specialization, and left them at the mercy of the authorities who protected them against others but exploited them themselves. Yet we cannot say that the doctrine of perpetual servitude had any influence on the statute of 1230 unless we use the relatively infrequent references to that doctrine in theology and canon law very loosely as a symbol for all the infinitely more numerous assertions and actions whereby churchmen and lay people expressed their contempt or hatred for Jews. Of any direct influence of that particular doctrine, there is no evidence at all.

In any case, neither theology nor canon law prescribed that Jews should be serfs in secular law. Although no one in Europe had been so long and so seriously concerned to define the status of Jews as had ecclesiastics, their goal was very different. The matters that most concerned them were those which distinguished Jews from Christians: that Jews not exercise authority over Christians, employ them as servants, eat with them, have intercourse with them, or be physically indistinguishable from them. Together with certain measures of protection, it was these restrictions which ecclesiastics repeated in canon after canon and council after council, as well as in papal decretals. And it was to this definition of Jewish status that the papal bull, *Sicut Judeis non*, referred when it declared, following Gregory I, that just as Jews were not permitted to do more in their synagogues than the law allowed, so also they should not be damaged in those things which were permitted to them.

Here, and not in occasional references to perpetual Jewish servitude, was to be found the ecclesiastical definition of Jewish status; and its purpose was to ensure that Jews would be distinguishable from all Christians of any status and inferior in liberty to any Christian. In America, whites could apply the term "slave" in its classical sense to people of different color without in any way equating the status of people of color with that of whites, because the status of slave was never ascribed to whites. In medieval Europe, ecclesiastics could not categorize Jews as serfs because many Christians were serfs, and ecclesiastics wanted to ensure that the status of Jews would be lower than that of any Christian.

Servitude can have many forms, and the perpetual servitude which ecclesiastics sought to impose on Jews as punishment for their disbelief in Christ and their role in his crucifixion was unique. It was a highly theological servitude from which the economic considerations so obvious in the case of serfs or slaves was almost entirely absent. Thus Gregory IX could speak of the yoke of perpetual servitude in 1233 and command one month later that lords who had imprisoned Jews should release them to their former liberty and observe legitimate contracts made with them.[85] From it, Jews could be liberated only by God through the presence of his grace in baptism; and unlike serfs or slaves, Jews could liberate themselves—by accepting what the church proclaimed as truth.

Although Aquinas wrote that "Jews are *servi* of the princes in civil servitude,"[86] this usage and other examples in theology and canon law should never be deprived of their theological context. The ecclesiastics who framed and sought to enforce their definition of Jewish status were the people least likely to confuse the perpetual servitude of Jews with any other kind of servitude, even though they sometimes referred elliptically to those condemned to it as *servi*. Indeed, the papal bulls that spoke of the yoke of perpetual servitude and referred to Jews as *servi* were usually those that exhorted secular authorities, who had direct jurisdiction over Jews, to give Jews a status clearly distinct from that of all Christians.

In expectation of earthly advantage and, more rarely, in hope of heavenly reward, most secular rulers were quite willing to implement this ecclesiastical demand by assigning Jews a unique status in secular law. When the duke of Normandy became king of England, he and his successors took advantage of the unusual strength of the English monarchy and the novelty of Jewish settlement to impose a monopoly of jurisdiction over Jews which had been unknown in northern France; and by 1210, or even more clearly by 1233, the status of Jews was unique in English law and Jews were uniquely exploited. Although the doctrine of perpetual servitude played no direct role in the formulation of that status, and the exploitation by the Angevin kings was hardly religious in motivation, the result was nonetheless a unique status for Jews.

In France, the development was slower, more uneven, and more influenced by ecclesiastical pressure, but the outcome was similar. The weaker Capetian kings, who had long used the support of churchmen within France and of the papacy in their effort to increase royal power over the barons, managed to combine self-aggrandizement with obedience to the church more successfully than other rulers. Thus, in his spoliation of Jews in 1180–1182, Philip Augustus managed both to base his actions on religious considerations and to make a profit for his treasury; but his action also indicated the extent to which he regarded Jews as a special group to which normal law did not apply. The peculiarity of Jewish status became more prominent after the readmission of 1198, with the nonretention agreements, the increased exploitation that even provoked papal complaints, the imprisonments, and the increased regulation, and, consonant with ecclesiastical pressures, the restriction of Jewish lending by 1219. And with the statute of 1230, Jewish status became clearly distinguishable from all other statuses.

There can be little doubt that the king who promulgated the statute of 1230, attempted to suppress Jewish usury and convert Jews, and was the only king to support energetically the condemnation of the Talmud thought of Jews not as his serfs but, precisely because he was aware of theological doctrine, as very different from all Christians. According to one biographer, Louis IX declared about 1250 that to the church belonged jurisdiction over usurers but to the king belonged jurisdiction over the usury of Jews, "who are subject to me by the yoke of servitude."[87] Louis knew that theological doctrine assigned Jews to his jurisdiction in a way that no other people came under his control. From more mundane motives, many of his barons agreed that the status of Jews was indeed unique, for it permitted barons to engage in unparalleled exploitation.

Canon law did not prescribe that Jews should be treated like serfs in secular law, and neither in English nor in French law were they said to be serfs. The reason the terms *Judeus* and *servus* were once conjoined in a simile in France was not that theologians used the terms *servitus* and *servi*. The reason was that, because of the prior weakness of the Capetian monarchy, the king and his barons had been engaged in unregulated competition for jurisdiction over *Judei*; and the resolution of that uncertainty under French conditions was, in striking contrast with England, to assign to each lord with high justice who had jurisdiction over Jews a right to seize his Jews which was similar to but not identical with any lord's right to seize his serfs. The use of the simile in France and its absence in England reflected something that had nothing ⋂ do with either the doctrine of perpetual servitude or even the existence of Jews: the different constitutional development of the two kingdoms.

More generally—although I cannot support the argument properly here—I would hold that divergent constitutional development also explains the use or absence of the term *servi* to explicate Jewish status elsewhere. When it was said in Aragon and Castile from the late twelfth century that Jews were *servi* of the king, or in Germany from 1236 that Jews were *servi camere*, the term *servi*, it may be suggested, functioned as a metaphor—or legal fiction—to assert a royal claim to a monopoly of jurisdiction that was not and could not be exercised in fact. Thus, in the empire, since only Jews were *servi camere*, that term was a synonym for Jews in which *servi* functioned metaphorically to claim that Jews depended involuntarily and hereditarily on the emperor alone, although jurisdiction was in fact irretrievably divided. Indeed, the metaphor was used precisely because it was so divided.

The analogy of *servi* was used in connection with *Judei* in early-thirteenth-century secular law where, because of the previous or present weakness of central government, jurisdiction over Jews was divided, there was competition to control Jews, and kings were seeking to assert their jurisdiction over them—and thereby indirectly over their magnates and the kingdom. The term *servi* did not characterize the rights and obligations of Jews, for the status that gave them their rights and obligations was denoted by the term *Judei*; their rights and obligations were those of Jewish, not servile, status. *Servi* was only employed analogically by kings to emphasize a disputed right to exercise sole or fundamental jurisdiction over *Judei*. But use of the analogy did mark a decisive turning point in the status of Jews: it was employed, as Kisch demonstrated, when the status of Jews was coming to be perceived, not as servile, but as unique, as Jewish status.

The stronger the monarchy, the less was the need to employ the analogy even merely as a simile—as in England and France—and the more sharply defined and worse was the nature of Jewish status. Conversely, the weaker the monarchy, the greater was the insistence on the analogy by metaphor—as in Germany and Spain—and the more undefined and better the status of Jews. Insistence on the analogy was an indication of the lack of a strong central government that could impose a uniform Jewish status and policy toward Jews. Consequently, Jews were earliest expelled from those kingdoms where insistence on the analogy was least and central government was strongest—from England in 1290 and from France for the first time in 1306. But where the monarchy was weak and the analogy emphasized, expulsion came late or was never complete—from Spain in 1492 and from Germany.

Far from being an indication that Jews, having been considered free men who differed in religion, were now thought of as some kind of serf, the appearance of the analogy indicated that Jews were being thought of ever more obsessively as Jews and that rulers were trying to control them by assigning a unique status to them. Nor were rulers thereby seeking to protect Jews and preserve their rights as free men. Although they might protect Jews from others, their primary purpose was to control their Jews and their kingdoms more effectively. Indeed, where they were successful in defining Jewish status and protecting Jews, they rapidly exploited Jews and degraded Jewish status drastically.

The French evidence, more clearly than any other, reveals that use of the terminology of serfdom to elucidate Jewish status in secular law did not mean that the status of Jews was equated with that of serfs or that the kings considered Jews their serfs. It reveals that kings and barons conceived of Jews, far more than ever before, as a separate class of people with a distinctive status outside the law common to others, a status whose members were unambiguously designated as *Judei* by rulers and their jurists. The status of Jews in secular law was not "Jewish serfdom" but Jewish status, and to speak of Jews as royal serfs or "serfs" only obscures legal reality.

Nor is "Jewish serfdom" an accurate translation of *perpetua servitus Judeorum*,[88] for that concept of theology and canon law bears little resemblance to what modern historians mean by serfdom or what servile status meant to medieval lawyers. Moreover, Jewish status according to canon law did not correspond to Jewish status in secular law. When secular authorities assigned Jews a distinctive status, most of them elaborated it, not to comply with the church's desires, but in order to exploit Jewish moneylending; and when those profits dried up, they expelled their Jews contrary to Pauline theology and the papal bull *Sicut Judeis non.*

Neither Jewish status in canon law nor Jewish status in secular law is accurately described as "Jewish serfdom." "Jewish serfdom" conflates a dubious translation of a theological term with a metaphor of German law to establish a perspective. By forcing a correspondence between the universality of the church's doctrine and the way Jews were treated in various kingdoms, it seeks to elevate the unity of Jewish history above the variations of general history, but it obscures the reality of both.

Part 4

Irrational Fantasies

8

Peter the Venerable: Defense Against Doubts

Since I am a Canadian and first presented this paper in Canada, a country whose motto is *a mari usque ad mare*, I could not resist the opportunity to take Psalm 72 (Vulgate 71) verse 8 as my opening text: "And he shall have dominion from sea to sea and from the river to the ends of the earth." In 1867, the geographical aptitude of that expression of the desirability of vast dominion had struck Queen Victoria's government and the fathers of Canadian Confederation as a providential description of their nationalistic claim to vast lands. Some seven hundred years earlier, however, for Pierre de Montboissier, abbot of Cluny, the text was neither a prayer for Solomon nor a prophecy of Canada; it was a prophecy that Christ, King of kings, would rule the whole world; and Peter believed it had been realized.

Born in 1092 or 1094 of a highly religious family, Peter had grown to manhood in the triumphant Christendom of the years following the First Crusade. As a Cluniac novice and monk, he had been molded in a demanding but highly protected and indoctrinating atmosphere, one whose norms he so successfully internalized and expressed that in 1122 he was chosen abbot of the greatest monastery in Latin Christendom, where he officiated with the greatest solemnity in the largest church in Christendom. Although there were problems at Cluny then, Peter had good reason to be confident of himself and of the success of the Christendom with which he so completely identified.

This confidence rings out in a little treatise he wrote about 1132 to a monk who had fallen into the Apollinarian heresy.

Monstrous indeed it is to dispute about the faith in this time, now when the prince of the world is ejected from the world, now when Christ has dominion from sea to sea, now when all are taught by God, after, as Isaiah says, the earth has been filled with the knowledge of God as the waters cover the sea, after Satan, long pursuing the faith of Christ with pagan attacks and heretical disputes, has thus emptied the quiver of his wickedness, so that now no arrow remains with which he can wound the faith.[1]

The same confidence was voiced in the letter about the papal schism that Peter wrote between 1130 and 1134 to a major supporter of Anacletus II or Pierleoni. To shorten his argument, Peter says that he will not discuss the sacrilege, simony, homicide, and so forth that fight for Anacletus.

So that all this . . . may be put aside, consider this one thing. . . . Where may the church be supposed to be of which it is to be believed that it is in all nations of the world? Is it in a corner of the city of Rome or in the whole world? In part of Aquitaine or from sea to sea? . . . Either the church is with us . . . or if the church is with you, the kingdom of Christ has been greatly contracted. If, I say, the church is with you, false is the voice of the father promising the son, "I shall make the peoples your heritage and the ends of the earth your possession." False is the voice of the prophet, "He shall have dominion from sea to sea and from the river to the ends of the earth." . . . False certainly is all that if his inheritance and possession have been so reduced that he possesses nothing save the towers of Pierleoni and the little fortifications of the count of Poitou. If this is true, Christ now relinquishes what he had accepted, and he who has now been made inferior in possessions to any kinglet also loses the name of king, nor may anyone dare to call him king of kings or lord of lords.[2]

The kingdom of Peter's king of kings was so much on earth, so much an observable geographic area subjected to Christ, that Peter left considerations of quality largely aside and based his case on tangible quantity. What Peter failed to recognize was that his confidence might be challenged by historical reality, by subversion within Christendom, and by attack from without. Very soon, however, he, like many others, had to confront the development of significant heresy.

In 1137, Peter became bothered by the radical challenge of Peter of Bruys and Henry of Le Mans to such basic Cluniac beliefs as the need for churches, masses, and prayers for the dead. Peter was so concerned that, between 1137 and 1141, he wrote his first major theological treatise, in which the same note is sounded.

You, therefore . . . masters of error . . . dregs of heresy, refuse of schismatics . . . I summon you to come forth from your hiding places to meet us publicly. Truth does not have corners, as the people say, nor does light want to hide under a bushel, nor does that which is catholic like to be made solitary, because that which, by Christ's command, is diffused throughout the whole world is not content with parts of the world.[3]

During the 1140s, however, Peter had to admit that Satan's quiver was by no means as empty as he had first thought. Some of his own monks were even suggesting that Christ had never said openly in the Gospels that he was God. Peter's little treatise to rebut that opinion is usually dated about 1140, but it may have been written after he had brought back the Islamic material from Spain in 1143, and after it had provoked discussions at Cluny. For here, for the first time in a polemic, Peter acknowledged the extent of Saracen competition. Satan, Peter declared, "has occupied nearly half the world by means of the Saracens," whom he has persuaded to believe that Christ, although born of the Virgin, sent from God, and the word and spirit of God, is "neither God nor dead,"[4] a position close to that of Peter's monks.

Since visiting Spain of the three religions, Peter had been forced to recognize that Christ's dominion from sea to sea was not self-evident. Between 1144 and 1147, when he completed his greatest treatise, *Against the Inveterate Stubbornness of the Jews*, he could imagine that an impudent Jew would question his interpretation of Psalm 71 because, five hundred years after Christ and after the spread of Christian knowledge, the Mohammedan heresy had been able to arise and infect so many parts of the world. And although Peter's new defense of Christ's dominion might have comforted Christians, it would never have convinced Jews, and it is a very lame rationalization compared to his triumphant affirmation in 1132.

To this I reply that . . . a particular error should be perceived in one way and a universal error in another. For, with the exception of the beginnings of humanity . . . there never has been and never will be a time in which darkness may not be mingled with light and truth with error. . . . Some parts of the world, therefore, may be infected with some error . . . yet the whole world cannot be. Like many other errors, it [Islam] has been able to infect some parts of the world; it has not been able to take over the whole . . . . The Christian faith, however, did not, like errors, bring under itself pieces or parts of the world; but as truth derived from the highest truth, which is Christ, it subjected the whole world to itself. The whole world I said, because although pagans and Saracens may exercise lordship over some parts, and although Jews lurk among Christians and pagans, nonetheless there is no part of the earth or very little . . . that is not inhabited by Christians, whether governing or subject, so that the truth of what scripture says about Christ might be seen: "He shall have dominion from sea to sea and from the river to the ends of the earth."[5]

If Peter did his best to combat militant Saracens and lurking Jews by writing treatises against their disbelief, he also supported open war. In a sermon that was probably given at a crusading assembly in 1147,[6] he praised the fierce first crusaders who had liberated the Holy Sepulcher and "with pious swords purged the dwelling place of heavenly purity of the filth of the impious." They had recognized Christ's dominion.

> You knew that the dead one, who once reposed in it, abides in heaven; you knew that now he rules angels and men from the seat of divine majesty . . . not now subjected to Jews and Romans but subjecting all to himself by the power of invincible divinity. You knew that . . . he was dominating all the earth and hell itself.[7]

The Second Crusade, however, was far from invincible, and in his disappointment, Peter turned his anger on Christians, on the schismatic Greeks whom he believed largely responsible for the failure.

> Were it necessary, so far as it is fitting for a monk, I would not refuse to die if the justice of God would deign by some of them to avenge the death of so many and so noble men, nay I should rather say almost all the flower of all Gaul and Germany, destroyed by deplorable deceits.[8]

Not only was Christ's dominion contracting internationally in the 1140s; all was not well at Cluny. Despite Peter's moderate reforms and his long defense of Cluny written to Bernard of Clairvaux in the 1130s, he felt it necessary to write another long defense in 1144. Moreover, his efforts to solve the financial crisis of the richest monastery in Christendom had not been successful. The monks of Cluny, who had developed the most expensive form of monastic life in Christendom under Abbot Hugh, had begun to find themselves short of money, food, and even wine in the early twelfth century because of new economic and political conditions. Yet, according to Georges Duby, it was only about 1125, shortly after the accession of Peter the Venerable, that the trouble became chronic and the monks became conscious of its gravity.[9]

To alleviate the crisis, Peter turned to the prosperous Jews of Mâcon and then to Christian financiers, particularly "those Christian merchants of Cluny who had collected the bulk of the money that the monastery dispersed."[10] Peter was also helped by a loan from Henry of Blois, the princely bishop of Winchester, whom he thanked effusively in 1135.

> And what [may I say] about the sublime peak of your works, that with royal largesse like Cyrus and priestly concern like Esdras, you have brought back to the temple the vessels of the house of the Lord, plundered by the Babylonians, and you have again clothed with protection the Christ whom the Jews of our time, as if crucifying again, had despoiled of his clothing.[11]

Cluny's difficulties continued, however, and again in 1149 Cluny had to be rescued by a loan from Henry of Winchester. The contract was guaranteed by Christian merchants of Cluny, including one Robert the Usurer,[12] whose name reminds us that Christian usurers abounded then. Yet Peter's anger was directed only against those whose disbelief killed his Christ. Like the popular crusaders of 1096, who had advocated dealing first with God's worst enemies before proceeding east to attack the Saracens, Peter dispatched a modest proposal to Louis VII in 1146.

> If the Saracens are to be detested . . . how much more are the Jews to be execrated and hated who, utterly insensible to Christ and the Christian faith, reject, blaspheme, and ridicule that virgin birth and all the sacraments of human redemption? Nor do I say this to incite the royal or Christian sword to slay their wickedness. . . . God wishes them, not to be killed, but to be preserved in a life worse than death, like Cain the fratricide, for greater torment and greater ignominy. . . . I . . . exhort that they be punished in a way suitable to their wickedness. And what more fitting way to punish those impious people than . . . that those who have been enriched by fraud be deprived of what they have wretchedly . . . stolen? What I say is known to all. For it is not by honest agriculture, by military service, or by any kind of honest and useful office that they fill their barns with produce, their cellars with wine . . . and their chests with gold and silver; but rather by that which they deceitfully take from Christians, by that which they furtively buy from thieves, do they acquire precious things at cheap price. If a thief in the night breaks into the church of Christ, if with sacrilegious defiance he carries off . . . even the sacred crucifixes or chalices, since he flees from Christians, he flies to Jews, and . . . what he had stolen from holy churches he sells to synagogues of Satan. . . . Christ now, through the insensible vessels consecrated to him, suffers directly the Jewish insults, since, as I have often heard from truthful men . . . they direct such wickedness against those celestial vessels as is horrifying to think and detestable to say. . . . Let their lives be spared and their money taken away, so that the audacity of the infidel Saracens may be conquered by the right hands of the Christians, aided by the money of the blaspheming Jews. . . . All this, deb-

onair king, I have written from love of Christ and of yourself and the Christian army.[13]

Even after Auschwitz, those who have studied Peter have been reluctant to face this passionate revelation of Peter's hatred for human beings he himself had seen. Although the letter clearly refers to all Jews, Jean Leclercq has affirmed that Peter was only attacking dishonest Jews.[14] Virginia Berry has spoken of moderation, since Peter did not advocate killing the Jews,[15] while James Kritzeck has even praised the letter as "instrumental in halting the murder of Jews" that was partially, if unintentionally, caused by Bernard's preaching of the crusade.[16] And Giles Constable has tried to protect Peter's post-Hitlerian reputation by stating:

> This letter is cited in many works on Jewish history . . . as evidence that Peter the Venerable was anti-Jewish. This is true only in a religious, not in a racial sense. . . . The suggestions made in this letter, however indefensible in themselves, were the result of Peter's religious sentiments.[17]

Yet was it belief in Christ that prevented Peter from distinguishing between Judaism and the human reality of Jews or from acknowledging that his financial troubles were caused more by Christians than Jews? The contrast with Bernard of Clairvaux is instructive. If Bernard also approved the hard captivity whereby Jews were to expiate their crime and testify to Christian truth, neither the crusading atmosphere nor his anti-Judaism blinded him to economic realities or moral issues. "I will not mention those Christian moneylenders, if they can be called Christian, who, where there are no Jews, act, I grieve to say, in a manner worse than any Jew."[18] Moreover, Bernard did not advocate plundering Jews but attempted to stop the massacres incited by charges like those Peter was spreading.

The reluctance of Peter's modern supporters to recognize that he was, in Bernhard Blumenkranz's words, an "implacable enemy" of Jews results, I believe, from their tendency to portray Peter in the terms by which he tried so hard to present himself to his ingroup, as an unchangingly unquestioning believer tranquilly dedicated to truth, love, and peace, as the man whom, according to Bernard, "all the world befriends."[19] Yet as Duby has reminded us, we must not view Peter through stained glass.[20] Peter was more complicated than hagiography would allow, and not immune to hate or—at some level—doubt.[21]

The horrible contrast between the substantial hatred of the letter of

1146 and its concluding love provides a fundamental clue to his personality and to the problem of why the great abbot of Cluny directed his greatest work against powerless Jews whose pretensions to have a king at Narbonne or Rouen he ridiculed.[22] Peter's love of Christ and Christians was counterbalanced by his fear and hatred of the menaces surrounding Cluny, Christendom, and his faith in Christ. The emotional dualism that is so evident in the passages already quoted is characteristic of his works as a whole: when Peter gave extended expression, other than liturgical, to his conception of the universe, he did so to counteract disbelief in Christ's domination.

Almost all his principal works are adversarial: against the Petrobrusians, against those who denied that Christ openly revealed his divinity, against the Jews, and against the Saracens.[23] Even his late treatise on miracles, his only other major work, was a defense against the opinion that miracles had declined, for miracles confirmed faith.[24] And even in his correspondence, two of his longest letters, 16 percent of the total pages, are defenses against Cistercian criticism.[25] What he said he so admired in the church fathers could be said of him, that he "could not suffer any or the slightest rejection of the Christian faith,"[26] that is, of his own beliefs; and interestingly enough, he was also highly sensitive to real or fancied criticism from his friends.[27]

Peter had not always been so sensitive to theological opposition. The only reaction of his early years is the tiny treatise against the Apollinarian heretic. But in 1137, when he was about forty-four, he became disturbed by the Petrobrusians. And then, between 1140 and 1147, he completed the treatise against the Petrobrusians and one against those who denied that Christ said openly that he was God; he visited Spain, commissioned the translation of the Islamic materials, and completed the treatise against the Jews; and he drafted and probably completed his summary of the heresy of the Saracens and perhaps began his refutation of that disbelief. Why this burst of concentrated thought?

It has been affirmed that Peter wrote out of love to convert the Petrobrusians, Jews, and Saracens.[28] Yet Jean Châtillon concluded that Peter did not expect to convert the Petrobrusians but sought primarily to protect others from contagion.[29] As for the Arabs, Peter himself said that he did not expect his Latin work to convert many of them but hoped to fortify weak Christians against their pestilential ideas and to "counteract the concealed thoughts of some of us, by which they might be led into scandal."[30] The same is clearly true of the treatise against

the Jews, which has been characterized by Salo Baron as "almost vi-
cious Jew-baiting" and by Robert Chazan as "viciously negative."[31] In
fact, not even many Christians seem to have read these works.[32] One
busy person, however, was completely familiar with them, their author, and, at least when he was thinking one way, he had doubts he
wanted to put to rest.

There is a surprisingly revelatory passage in De miraculis. William
of Roanne, prior of Cluny and a severe disciplinarian, died just before
Peter the Venerable left on a trip to Rome in 1145. It was thought that
William had been poisoned, but the investigation begun before Peter
set off for Rome had reached no final conclusion. Once in Rome, Peter
experienced one of the rare miracles he attributed to his own experience. After he had gone to bed one night, William appeared to him in
a vision.

> I decided to ask him quickly about certain matters. Moreover, so that
> the vision may be seen as true and not a fantasy, I had never before thought
> of the things I asked, but now, sleeping, by the command of God I believe,
> they came newly to mind, and I began to think about them. Therefore I put
> the four things that had come to my mind while sleeping, I know not why,
> as questions to him. "How are you, Lord Prior?" I asked, calling him not
> by his proper name but by his office. To which he replied briefly, for he was
> always short in speech, usually answering with two or three words, "I am
> well, I am very well." To this first question I added a second, "Do you now
> see the Lord?" And he answered, "I see him continually, I see him contin-
> ually." To these two I added a third and asked, "Isn't what we believe
> about God certain, isn't the faith we hold true without any doubt?" "Noth-
> ing," he said, "is so true, nothing so certain." And fourthly I asked, "Is it
> true as rumor has it, is it true as many believe, that you were killed by
> poison by certain people whose deceit you knew about?" "It is true," he
> said, "it is true."

Peter awoke from his dream or daydream, committed it to memory,
went back to sleep, and once more had the same vision. "I asked him
the same things as before and heard the same things as before concerning his condition, his vision of God, the certainty of the Christian
faith, and his death, and he replied in the same order in which he had
replied to my questions before and in no fewer words."[33] As a result,
Peter no longer had any doubts about the prior's fate. But he had also
heard that his Christian faith was true beyond any doubt, and we may
well ask whose doubts he had needed to quiet.

The mental itinerary of Peter's treatises is fascinating. First, in reaction to the Petrobrusians, Peter defended specific Christian practices

that were fundamental to Cluny by appealing to scriptural authority, taking considerable pains along the way to demonstrate that the authority of the Old Testament was confirmed by the New. Next, Peter reacted against the possibility that the New Testament did not conclusively prove that Christ believed that he was God. Then Peter wrote his largest work in order to prove that the authority of the New Testament was confirmed by that of the Old, and to demonstrate that Christ's divinity was demonstrated by the Old Testament and corroborated by miracles and the insanity of later Jewish beliefs. Then he abandoned authority and tried to argue by reason alone that the Koran was false because of the manifest error of its empirical assertions about the falsification of the Judeo-Christian scriptures, its consequent self-contradiction, and the failure of Mohammed to meet the criteria for a genuine prophet. Hence the very falsity of the Koran testified to the authenticity of the Judeo-Christian scriptures and to the divinity of Christ.

Thus Peter's ever-lengthening pilgrimage had taken him from a defense of specific Christian practices to confronting the possibility that both the Old and New Testaments might have been falsified. Along the way he had faced or imagined an amazing range of doubts that could be raised against his Christianity and about divine revelation. Although he had started with an appeal to the authority of the New Testament, he then appealed to the Old Testament to confirm the New, and he ended with an appeal to reason alone. His confidence that Christ's dominion was empirically self-evident had clearly been shaken as he entered his fifties.

His faith in the divinity of Christ remained, of course, firm. It was doubtless unquestioning in those hours of oasis and transfiguration when he officiated at Cluny, enveloped in the symbolic reaffirmation of his faith and surrounded by the consensus of his monks. Yet there were other activities in his life and other foci of his mind. When he moved from symbolic expressions of faith to examination of experience, he changed to a different and disquieting realm of discourse, one that conflicted with his symbolic indoctrination because of the way his own mind worked. He sought certitude not in metaphysical concepts but in rational arguments about observable events. That need for concrete, literal veracity is apparent even in some of his liturgical reforms—for example, his insistence that crucifixes be of wood.[34] And in the treatise against the Jews, one is struck by the literal-minded and legalistic quality of his arguments about hyperbolic, qualitative, and prayerful expressions in the Old Testament. He wanted to demonstrate rationally and empirically that Judaism was false and that his own faith was true, and since that was impossible, his arguments verged on irrationality.

The most striking feature of his greatest treatise is the bedrock on which his argument for Christ's divinity finally comes to rest. Almost all of the first four chapters is devoted to proving Christ's divinity by certain Old Testament passages. But at the end of the fourth chapter, as if acknowledging the inconclusiveness of the prior arguments, Peter suddenly introduces a strikingly new kind of argument to clinch his case, an empirical analysis of the roots of faith.

Religious belief, he argues, stems from authority, reason, miracle, force, or voluptuousness, or some combination of them. Force and voluptuousness, however, only produce false faith, as in Islam. Moreover, only those who have already gained faith will accept the authority of that faith's scripture and law. Nor will reason, however meritorious, produce faith by itself. True faith precedes the acceptance of authority and is initiated by the interaction of reason and miracle, by the encounter of the human and the divine. Since miraculous events cannot be explained naturally, reason recognizes that they are truly supernatural actions that reveal the true God and authenticate the revelations made to his believers.[35] And we should note here that true prophecy, which Peter uses heavily as an argument against both the Jews and the Saracens, is also a kind of miracle since it similarly defies natural explanation and therefore indicates true divinity.

After Peter has presented this epistemology of belief to his allegedly Jewish audience, he then adduces the miracles ascribed to Christ. But sensitive as always to all possible objections, he immediately recognizes that these miracles will be challenged as Christian falsehood or self-deception and triumphantly brings forth his ultimate proof, "one single work of all the heavenly and public work of Christ . . . that you cannot deny . . . since the whole world proclaims it. . . . Of it you cannot say that it is confined to Christians since both they and the Saracens and pagans are witnesses to it."[36] We wait with bated breath . . . and what Peter offers us is certainly something observable, the fire that inexplicably or miraculously lights the lamps in the Holy Sepulcher each year on Easter Saturday. That surprising event, which may have started in the fourth century and was known in the West by the beginning of the twelfth century, was explained by Arabs in 1009 as the result of a mixture of balm of Mecca and oil of jasmine, was condemned as a pious fraud by Pope Gregory IX in 1238, and continues to this day.[37]

What is surprising is not Peter's belief in this miracle,[38] but his use of it as a final proof of Christ's divinity. To this had he been brought by his need for proof that was, in his own words, "corporeal and solid,"[39] by his need to demonstrate that Christ's dominion, in which he believed, was literally and concretely obvious to any reasonable person. Yet there was one empirical obstacle that Peter could neither overlook nor overcome rationally: the continued existence of the Jews, who had seen Christ, experienced the spread of Christianity, studied the Old Testament as closely as Peter had, and witnessed the miracle of the Sepulcher. And he knew they were not convinced.

Peter hated the Jews because their informed and uncoerced disbelief was the living symbol of the core of rational doubts that confronted him. For if the Jews were reasonable, then it was reasonable to believe that Jesus was only a dead man and that Christianity was lifeless. But that Peter could not face. There remained only one way in which he could maintain his belief that his faith was corroborated by his reason, and he took it.

> It seems to me, Jew, that I . . . judge in these matters . . . as do all men. And if all men, then you also—if, nevertheless, you are human. For I dare not declare that you are human lest perchance I lie, because I recognize that reason, that which distinguishes humans from . . . beasts, is extinct in you or in any case buried. . . . Truly, why are you not called brute animals? Why not beasts? Why not beasts of burden? . . . The ass hears but does not understand; the Jew hears but does not understand. Am I the first to say this? Has not the same been said many centuries before [by your prophet]? . . . And although it is fully proved by these sacred authorities that you are a domestic animal or beast . . . and it has been sufficiently shown by me, nevertheless yet a fifth chapter will be added that shall expose, not only to Christians but to all the lands of the world, that you are truly a beast of burden and that, when I affirm this, I in no way exceed the bounds of truth.[40]

That fifth and final chapter, far from displaying the "profound knowledge of the Jewish mind" that Séjourné and Kritzeck have attributed to Peter,[41] is a bitingly sarcastic presentation of polemically selected and misunderstood examples of Talmudic thought intended to prove the irrationality of Jews, to depict the web of Jewish thought as so absurd that it could "deceive or capture no one save, like the most common fly, the Jew."[42]

The angry cry, "I'm right; you're crazy, you're an ass," has resounded millennially from people threatened by opposition they could neither dismiss nor understand. Perhaps that form of denial comes particularly easily to troubled believers because the analogic language of faith provides ready metaphors that can be applied literally to deny the humanity of their opponents. In any case, it was that kind of symbolic literalism, far more than any explicit association of Jews with the Devil, that encouraged the later fantasies that Jews ate humans and had a strange smell, strange diseases, and horns. It was that fantasy which replaced inexplicably blinded Synagoga with the Jewish swine of the later Middle Ages. And once embedded, the fantasy that Jews were subhuman could be stripped of its Christian camouflage and pass easily from Christendom to the Third Reich.

That belief in the divinity of Jesus was not the sole, sufficient, or main cause of medieval hatred of Jews can be demonstrated by the contrast between Peter's attitudes and those of Gregory the Great, Bernard of Clairvaux, Thomas Aquinas, and many others whose faith was unthreatened. More important for people's hatred of Jews were their personal reactions to social problems they could not understand and to fissures in their faith they could not acknowledge. In the last analysis, the "beastly Jews" that Peter hated were the products of his own mind, the result of his compulsive efforts to find rational empirical arguments to protect his faith from menacing doubts. He accused Jews of being irrational, but, ironically, his own defense of his faith against Jewish disbelief verged on irrationality.[43] Herein Peter was a product of his times, and though he may only have been on the borderline, other Christians almost immediately went beyond that boundary and created the indisputably irrational fantasies about Jews that would endure for centuries.

9.
Thomas of Monmouth: Detector of Ritual Murder

The detective story in which the investigator is an amateur without official standing is a peculiarly English genre. Perhaps the earliest example, telling of an investigation that was pursued unofficially by an individual who arrived on the scene after the crime, disagreed with the official stand, pursued his own investigation, and reported the results, is *The Life and Passion of Saint William the Martyr of Norwich*, which Thomas of Monmouth started in 1149/50 and completed in 1172/73.[1] Book 1 of the *Life*, apparently completed by 1150, is a flowing narrative of the events of Willliam's life and of his death in 1144 as Thomas had reconstructed them. And although books 2–6, written in 1154/55, consist primarily of descriptions of the translations of William's body between 1150 and 1154 and of the miracles attributed to him, Thomas devoted the first part of book 2 to a lengthy defense of the truth of his reconstruction of the crime, a defense in which he carefully marshaled the evidence or arguments that had led him to his conclusions. The last book, book 7, which was only completed by 1173, describes the further miracles attributed to William between 1155 and 1173.[2]

While the work obviously belongs to the genre of hagiography, the first two books are primarily a detective story—even involving international intrigue—because confidence in William's sanctity depended entirely on certainty as to who had killed young William and how they had killed him. The central drama of the *Life* is not William's heroic holiness—indeed he plays a singularly passive role—but the revelation of who murdered him and how and why they did so, as can be seen from the summary in a contemporary chronicle.

> In his [King Stephen's] time, the Jews of Norwich bought a Christian child before Easter and tortured him with all the torture that our Lord was tortured with; and on Good Friday hanged him on a cross on account of our Lord, and then buried him. They expected it would be concealed, but our Lord made it plain that he was a holy martyr, and the monks took him and buried him with ceremony in the monastery, and through our Lord he works wonderful and varied miracles, and he is called St. William.[3]

This brief report in the final continuation of the *Anglo-Saxon Chronicle* was written in or immediately after 1155 at Peterborough, not very far from Norwich, and is the earliest extant trace of William's death. It is not direct evidence, however. Few copies of Thomas's *Life* seem to have been made (the only manuscript presently known, written shortly before 1200, was discovered by M. R. James in 1889), but elements of Thomas's story spread rather rapidly by word of mouth and were soon incorporated in other chronicles. Since the continuation of the *Anglo-Saxon Chronicle* was written after 1150, it was written after, and was dependent on, the story created by Thomas and the rumors emanating from Norwich. Indeed the Peterborough chronicler does not even know that at Norwich it was believed that William had died on the Wednesday before Good Friday. Yet if the *Chronicle* is neither independent nor accurate evidence, it does confirm that the crucifixion accusation had been made by 1155; and it illustrates that what interested people then and long after was not William himself. What mattered was the divinely assisted revelation of the identity of his killers and what they had done. William's death had occasioned the first of the connected series of accusations from the twelfth to the twentieth century that Jews committed ritual murder.

Thomas's *Life* of William, which records the accusation, is a rich document. If it is an interesting reflection of ecclesiastical life and religious mentality, as well as our first evidence for the presence of Jews in Norwich, it is important above all for the general history of Jews, and of relations between Christians and Jews, for it is our most direct evidence for the first medieval accusation that Jews were guilty of ritual murder, a myth that spread, caused the death of many Jews in different localities, and influenced Luther and Hitler among others. It is not surprising, therefore, that it has been discussed at length by both Jewish and non-Jewish historians and mentioned by many more.[4] The fundamental question these historians sought to answer was whether

Jews had indeed killed little William, and how, or if not, who had. In this they were only pursuing the same goal as Thomas of Monmouth, who was also their only evidence. Yet the death of William was of little importance by itself. Even if he had been killed by Jews, that, like many other homicides committed by Jews, would have been of little historical importance. The event in twelfth-century Norwich that had broad historical ramifications was not William's death but the accusation—which many at Norwich at the time did not believe—that the Jews of Norwich had crucified him. The most significant question to be put to the *Life*, therefore, and the one that is not directly answered by it, is not who killed William but who first accused the Jews of crucifying a Christian child out of religious hatred, and why that accusation was made.

Since historians agree that Thomas of Monmouth's evidence is too unreliable or insufficient to determine with any certainty who killed William and have only been able to produce widely divergent hypotheses, we might expect that it would be even more difficult to establish from it who accused Jews of a crucifixion. In fact, the reverse is true. At the least, we know that Thomas himself accused Jews of a crucifixion; and if we keep our eyes fixed not on William's unknown murderer but on Thomas himself, we can reach a much firmer conclusion about how the enduring myth of Jewish ritual murder was created than we will ever be able to do about who killed poor William.

Before we locate the creation of the medieval and modern myth in twelfth-century Norwich, however, we must be sure that the accusation at Norwich was not merely the repetition of an older myth. Two accusations of ritual murder or something similar to it had in fact been made against Jews in antiquity, and Jessopp and James suggested that the historiographic transmission of one of these might have influenced the Norwich accusation.[5] Whether the idea for the accusation at Norwich came from antiquity or was a fresh creation of the twelfth century is a question of such importance for our understanding of what went on at Norwich that it must be examined at some length. All too often it has been assumed that confrontation with Jews has inspired similar reactions throughout the millennia, a perspective that foreshortens history and reads it backward. From that perspective, it does not seem surprising that Jews in the twelfth century should have been accused of crucifying Christians. Yet if Jews had not been accused of anything resembling ritual murder for seven centuries, and if there was no knowledge of the accusations in antiquity, then the accusation at

Norwich was an independent creation, and the myth that inspired deadly attacks against Jews for centuries to come was an expression of the distinctive culture of twelfth-century Europe.

The first known accusation of ritual murder against Jews is that attributed to the historian Posidonius in the second century B.C.E. He apparently recorded that when Antiochus IV Epiphanes invaded and desecrated the Temple in 168, he found a Greek captive in the Temple who told him that every seven years the Jews captured a Greek, fattened him up, killed him, ate parts of him, and took an oath of undying enmity against Greeks.[6] Since the story is completely unbelievable, it has been suggested that it was fabricated as propaganda to justify Antiochus's desecration or was invented, probably at Alexandria, to express Greek hatred of Jews. Whatever the precise explanation, we can be sure that the accusation was not an immediate reaction of people on the spot at the time but was created afterward, possibly by Posidonius himself.[7] It certainly circulated in literary circles thereafter.

The rhetorician Apollonius Molon apparently repeated the story in Alexandria in the first century B.C.E., as did Damocritus, probably in the first century C.E.[8] It was also repeated by Apion in Alexandria in the first century with the modification that the ritual was an annual affair; and toward the end of that century, Flavius Josephus described the charge in *Against Apion* and denied it.[9] Josephus thereby ensured its preservation, yet the way he reacted to the charge indicates that he considered it a historical or literary fable rather than a belief widely current among Greeks in Alexandria that endangered contemporary Jews. And if the story had little currency in Alexandria, where anti-Jewish attitudes were strongest, it was apparently unknown outside of Alexandria, for no Roman writer, not even Tacitus, repeats it. Charges of ritual cannibalism were widely made against Christians in the second century, but not against Jews. And in the later centuries of the Roman Empire, though Christian writers were familiar with Josephus's works, they never referred to Apion's charge as preserved in Josephus.

Josephus was also well known in the Middle Ages, but if much attention was paid to his *Antiquities* and *Jewish Wars*, little was paid to *Against Apion*, even less to book 2 of that work, and still less to sections 89–96 of book 2, which contain the discussion of Apion's charge. In the first place, all extant Greek manuscripts of *Against Apion* derive from a single manuscript of the eleventh century which lacks sections 51–113 of book 2;[10] none consequently contains the accusation of ritual murder. Moreover, although Eusebius quoted or referred to Josephus so frequently that he was another major channel of transmission, he never referred to those sections; indeed no one seems to have done so.[11] Our knowledge of the sections missing from the Greek manuscripts of *Against Apion*, like that of medieval scholars, depends entirely on the Latin transmission of Josephus's works commissioned by Cassiodorus about 578.[12] Yet if all of *Against Apion* was thereby available to medieval scholars, they were little interested in it and concentrated on the *Antiquities* and *Wars*. Franz Blatt lists 171 Latin manuscripts containing the *Antiquities*, but only seventeen of these also contain *Against Apion*, and one of these contains only the first book.[13] Moreover, of the twenty-six manuscripts containing the Latin *Against Apion* that Carolus Boysen listed for his edition of that work, only five contain *Against Apion* by itself.[14]

Interest in *Against Apion* for its own sake seems to have been very late. Of the seventeen manuscripts of the Latin *Antiquities* listed by Blatt that also contain *Against Apion*, only seven are dated before the fourteenth century. Only six of the twenty-six manuscripts of the Latin *Against Apion* listed by Boysen are dated earlier than the fourteenth century; and the five manuscripts that contain only *Against Apion* without any other work by Josephus all date from the fifteenth or sixteenth century. Manuscripts containing the complete *Against Apion* were apparently very rare in the middle of the twelfth century when the medieval accusation of ritual murder against Jews appeared; and in the manuscripts in which *Against Apion* did appear then, it was always accompanied by other works of Josephus which attracted all the attention. Thus Peter Comestor (died c. 1179), who used Josephus more often and more explicitly than any other church writer, never referred to *Against Apion*.[15] Indeed, so far as Schreckenberg has noticed, the only medieval Latin author ever to cite the work, and that only for a single passage in book 1, was Sicard of Cremona, who died in 1215.[16] Nor is there any allusion to the story in Yossipon.

Since the first medieval accusation against Jews appeared at Norwich in England about 1150 and soon spread to northern France, the geographical dispersion of the manuscripts is also of interest, and one manuscript immediately attracts attention. It is an Italian manuscript in the Lincoln cathedral library which was given to the cathedral about 1150 by Bishop Robert of Chesney,[17] possibly a relative of John of Chesney, the sheriff of Norfolk who protected the accused Jews of Norwich. But the manuscript does not contain *Against Apion*. Indeed, none of the manuscripts that Blatt characterizes as the Anglo-Norman family does.[18] Similarly, in Boysen's list of five manuscripts of the work in English archives, our attention is immediately attracted to a manuscript of 1145 in the Bodleian Library, one of the best early manuscripts of the work.[19] But it is part of the great Canonici collection, which only came to Oxford from Italy in 1817. The only other one of these five manuscripts (now at Tübingen) that is dated before 1300 is also Italian and did not leave Italy during the Middle Ages.[20]

It seems reasonably clear that although Josephus was well known in the Middle Ages, copies of *Against Apion* were rare, particularly in the north, and of no interest. The absence of references to the work by medieval authors confirms that conclusion; and, so far as I know, there is no reference to Apion's story by any medieval writer in connection with a medieval accusation of ritual murder. The accusations of ritual cannibalism against Christians deemed heretical in the eleventh and twelfth centuries drew on an entirely different tradition.[21] So far as we can tell, there was a complete discontinuity between the first accusation against Jews in antiquity and the first medieval accusation.

The second and only other relevant accusation against Jews in antiquity is the charge against the Jews of Inmestar (Syria) about 415 in connection with the celebration of Purim. This is the charge that some have thought may have influenced the Norwich accusation. Before the alleged incident, Jews had been accused of burning an effigy of Haman that was made to resemble Christ, and in 408 Theodosius II had prohibited Jews from burning such an image or mocking the Cross during the Purim festivities.[22] Moreover, at least according to a Christian writing much later, forcibly baptized Jews at Alexandria had crucified a statue of Christ, mocked Christians, and provoked a riot.[23] Then, about 415, drunken Jews of Inmestar allegedly took a Christian boy, tied him to a cross in place of an effigy of Haman, and so mistreated him that he died. Our only evidence for the incident is a contemporary Christian historian, Socrates, and modern historians have disagreed about the truth of the report. Parkes and Simon accept that the Jews were drunk and did kill the boy in this fashion;[24] Juster was suspicious of the story;[25] and Roth and Blumenkranz are hesitant to pronounce.[26] Given the bitterness of relations then, the incident might have happened, but it could equally have been imagined by Socrates or others.

Socrates' story about the Inmestar incident was available to the Latin West during the Middle Ages in the work known as the *Historia tripartita*, the translation of the histories of Theodoret, Sozomen, and

Socrates commissioned by Cassiodorus. Manuscripts of the work were widely disseminated; yet of the 138 known manuscripts, only two early ones are found in England, and they date from the late twelfth or early thirteenth century.[27] The *Historia* was, however, cited or used by such universal chroniclers of the eleventh and twelfth centuries as Marianus Scotus, Hermann Contractus, Sigebert of Gembloux, and Otto of Freising, but none of them referred to the Inmestar incident. That may be because their treatment of fifth-century events in the Eastern Empire was very scanty and annalistic, and their attention was focused on major events of political and Christian history. Yet they did carry forward some stories of marginal events with miraculous implications such as the existence of a gigantic woman or Siamese twins.[28] Of this genre was the story about a Jew which comes right after the Inmestar story in the *Historia*. It concerned a Jew who, apparently about 416, got himself baptized by several Christian groups, presumably to collect the financial rewards offered adherents. But when he went to a church of Catholics to be baptized once more, the water in the font miraculously disappeared on each of the three times they tried to baptize him—thereby demonstrating the power of God and the bad faith of the Jew.[29] Now there was a story of religious significance, so Sigebert copied it, and through him it passed to the *Annals of Waverley*—but neither Sigebert nor the *Annals* mentions the Inmestar incident.[30]

Those who borrowed from the *Historia tripartita* did so sparingly and most selectively, and the Inmestar incident did not interest them. Marianus, Hermann, Sigebert, and Otto did not mention it, nor does it appear in other well-known early chroniclers, whether because they did not use the *Historia*, started their chronicle after 416, or were primarily concerned with Western or regional history. The incident is not mentioned by Prosper of Aquitaine, Isidore of Seville, Gregory of Tours, Bede (in *De temporibus* or *De temporum ratione*), the *Anglo-Saxon Chronicle*, or Hugh of Flavigny. In fact, Blumenkranz found no reference to the incident in any of the Latin Christian authors up to 1096,[31] nor does Yossipon mention it. And since the first medieval accusation against Jews appeared in England about 1150, it is significant that the incident does not appear in such Anglo-Norman or English chronicles as those of St. Edmunds, Florence of Worcester, Orderic Vitalis, Robert of Torigni, or Roger of Wendover. Moreover, to the best of my knowledge, the Inmestar incident is not mentioned in any medieval discussion of ritual murder. Certainly, Thomas of Monmouth does not allude to either the Inmestar incident or Apion's charge in his account of the Norwich accusation. Thus, to conclude our long digression, it seems as certain as such things can be that the two accusations in antiquity had no influence on the first medieval accusation. We can now return to the evidence provided by Thomas of Monmouth, secure in the knowledge that the accusation he recorded was an independent creation.

What we know of Thomas himself is limited to what he discloses incidentally in the *Life*. But because in book 2 he engaged in an angry defense of his reconstruction of the crime, he tells us more about how he acquired his information than do many medieval hagiographers. As his name indicates, Thomas of Monmouth was born in Wales and was, judging by his writing, a respectably educated man when he arrived at Norwich sometime after 1146 and probably not long before 1150 to become a monk in the cathedral priory. The city in which he settled was one of the largest in England, but its cathedral was recent, a consequence of the Norman Conquest.[32] In 1096, the see of Thetford and its bishop, Herbert of Losinga, had been transferred to Norwich. Herbert began the construction of the cathedral and, following English custom, established a priory of Benedictine monks as canons of the cathedral over which he presided until his death in 1119. He was succeeded by Bishop Eborard, who died in 1146 and was succeeded in turn by Bishop William Turbe, who was bishop when Thomas of Monmouth arrived. Another Norman innovation that confronted Thomas was the castle under the control of the sheriff of Norfolk, John of Chesney, member of a Norman family that supported King Stephen and provided him with three sheriffs and possibly a bishop of Lincoln.[33] The Conquest had also brought the settlement, beside the original Danish and Anglo-Saxon inhabitants, of a substantial number of French merchants, particularly in the new burgh beside the castle. More recent French-speaking residents—if it is true that no Jews resided outside of London before 1135[34]—were the relatively few Jews who lived primarily in the new burgh. Outside of Norwich, on the opposite side from the new burgh, lay Thorpe Wood; and it was there that the body of William, a twelve-year-old apprentice skinner, had been found on Easter Saturday, 25 March, of 1144.

When Thomas of Monmouth arrived, William had been dead for about four years, and his alleged marytrdom had drawn very little attention. Thomas, however, was attracted by the story and became obsessed with William's sanctity. He collected all the information he could about William, was highly influential in the development of his cult, became sacristan of his shrine, and wrote his *Life*. Since the *Life* is our only independent evidence for that first accusation, which was probably responsible for the accusations that followed fairly soon after, and since it may well be also the longest and most detailed account of any medieval accusation of ritual murder by a contemporary at or near the scene of the alleged crime,[35] it is somewhat surprising that there has been little effort to analyze it to discover how the accusation appeared at Norwich. The few modern scholars who have examined the *Life* closely were distracted from that problem by their concern to decide whether the Jews had in fact killed William. Indeed, they were so seduced by the urge to play detective, or so influenced by cultural predispositions, that even after they had recognized that the evidence was entirely insufficient to determine guilt, they went on to make strange conjectures.

Thomas of Monmouth would have been grateful for their failure to pursue the emergence of the accusation, for he wanted his readers to take it for granted as manifest truth. Book 1 describes events from William's birth to his honorable burial in the monks' cemetery, but most of it is devoted to a closely woven, melodramatic re-creation of what happened between 20 March and 24 April of 1144. We observe William's disappearance with a stranger who takes him to a Jew's house, we watch him being tortured and crucified by Jews, we listen to the murderers talking among themselves about how to dispose of the body, and we are told how they did dispose of it and how it was found.

Thomas thus ensures that his readers learn that William was crucified well before any of his protagonists, other than the murderers and their victim, do. Consequently, when readers who shared Thomas's preconceptions read that the boy's family accused Jews after the body had been found, they would not have been predisposed to ask why the family had suspected Jews of the crime, and it would seem only appropriate that the boy's uncle should accuse the Jews before an episcopal synod, and that the boy's body should be buried in the monks' cemetery. The crucifixion is thus presented as the fundamental and indisputable core of the drama.

Thomas does mention in passing that some elements of his story were not known until later, but there is only a single hint in book 1 that anyone in 1144 had doubted the basic accusation. The truth of the story is taken for granted, and the narrative is so dramatically circumstantial that it is easy to forget that Thomas wove it together out of hearsay five or six years later. Even when readers discover in book 2 that much of the story of book 1 was not known for some time after 1144, and that many people in 1144 and for years after did not believe the accusation, it is hard to abandon the perspective so compellingly imprinted by book 1, hard to set Thomas's convictions about the crime aside and view his words simply as data with which to establish, so far as possible, what did go on in Norwich in those years. It is much easier and seems more important to focus on the issue made central by Thomas himself. Did the Jews crucify William? Or—since credence in that myth has waned—did they do something else that explains why people then accused them of ritual murder, something that might justify, in some measure, all those who repeated that accusation later?

Granted that centuries of cultural conflict have made those questions important to many people for various reasons, the question the historian should first ask is: What can be established with certainty or high probability from the data of Thomas's words? We see events only as they were refracted through Thomas's mind, and the first step is to determine how Thomas acquired his conception of what happened. We cannot accept that something happened just as Thomas asserts that it did; indeed, we should be most suspicious of the assertions he most wants us to accept. Thomas was a monk of the twelfth century, concerned with his status on earth and in heaven, and convinced that loyal service to William would benefit him in both realms. His primary purpose was to praise William and edify others. So far as was compatible with those aims, he probably tried to be honest in the sense that he wrote nothing that he knew was certainly false. But his standards of evidence and analysis were not those of a modern historian. He had no disposition to be skeptical of his story, and he accepted anything he heard that could be used to support his conviction that William was a saint. He was sure—and badly wanted to be sure—that he had discovered what had happened to little William. The *Life* tells us what he wanted to believe happened, but not necessarily what really did happen.

Fortunately for us, the exigencies of his narrative—and his fellow monks' criticism of it—forced Thomas to reveal things that enable us to question his reliability. Many of the events between 1144 and 1150 that had to be mentioned in any description of William's death and later fame were so much a matter of public knowledge that neither Thomas nor anyone else could falsify them in obvious ways without

losing credibility. Thomas could wishfully distort them by vague rhetoric or avoid emphasizing them, but they could not be made to disappear entirely. An illuminating example is the body itself. Thomas
would have us believe that the wounds indicated a crucifixion, but he
cannot help revealing the manifest lack of concern with which the
body was treated for a whole month until someone suggested its potential as a relic. Similarly, he may distort accusations or testimony
produced in public to suit his thesis, but he cannot insert striking
assertions that people knew had not been made. Chronology is particularly revealing. The only sequence Thomas was concerned to establish precisely was the drama of William's disappearance, death, discovery, and honorable burial as he had reconstructed it. He does,
however, give dates or indications of chronology for many other
events; and if we establish the sequence of events that we can be fairly
sure happened, and disregard dubious assertions, a very different picture from that of Thomas's reconstruction appears. The general picture
of how events unfolded and of Thomas's role in them that emerges
from this procedure is as follows.

A priest named Wlward had two daughters, Leviva and Elviva. In
1144, Leviva was married to a priest, Godwin Sturt, and had a son
Alexander, who was a deacon, and a small daughter. Elviva had married one Wenstan and had two sons—Robert, who later became a
monk at Norwich, and William. William had been apprenticed to a
master skinner at age eight and was twelve in 1144. He lived with "a
certain Wulward" (apparently not his grandfather) and had occasion
to visit Jews in the course of his work. According to the Sturts, in Lent
of 1144 Godwin and Wulward had prohibited William from visiting
Jews any more.[36] Then, on the Monday of Easter week, 20 March
1144, a man who said he was the archdeacon's cook came with William to ask his mother's consent to take the boy to work in the kitchen.
Elviva, who can only have taken him for a Christian, consented after
receiving some money. Then, according only to Leviva, a highly biased
source as we shall see, the man and William briefly visited her, apparently on the Tuesday.[37] Thereafter, William disappeared from public sight until Easter Saturday, when his body was discovered in
Thorpe Wood.

The body was first seen by a nun and a peasant, and the latter
informed a forester, Henry of Sprowston, who came and saw the body
on Saturday but decided to do nothing about it until after the weekend. The news spread, and other people came out from Norwich on

Saturday and Easter Sunday to look at the body but also did nothing. On Monday, Henry of Sprowston came back and buried the body where it had been found. Meanwhile, some friends of William who had recognized the body told Godwin Sturt. Godwin, his son Alexander, and William's brother Robert came out on Tuesday, dug up the body, and recognized it. Instead of carrying it back for burial in consecrated ground[38] and seeking justice, they reburied it on the spot and returned to tell Leviva. According to the Sturts, she immediately told Godwin about a dream she had had two weeks before, in which she was in the marketplace when Jews ran at her, surrounded her, broke her right leg with a club, tore it off her body, and ran away with it. She then reminded Godwin that he had warned her that she would lose someone dear because of the Jews. When Elviva arrived and heard what the Sturts had to tell, she ran around crying that the Jews had killed her son, but her actions did not provoke an attack on Jews, nor did they seek refuge in the castle.[39] And although William's relatives must have talked a lot about it among themselves and with others, nothing worthy of note seems to have occurred for some three weeks thereafter.

Around the middle of April, Godwin arose in the synod being held by Bishop Eborard and accused Jews of the crime. Since Godwin spoke before many witnesses, some of whom were still alive six years later when Thomas wrote book 1 of the *Life*, Thomas could not falsify the accusation unduly. As Thomas has him speak, Godwin first exonerated all Christians from so cruel an act and accused the Jews. He justified the charge by referring to "the practices which the Jews are bound to carry out on the days specified," "the manner of the punishment inflicted and the character of the wounds," "the many confirmations of circumstances which agree together," his wife's "very remarkable vision," and "the crafty tricks of a very cunning messenger of the Jews."[40] It should be emphasized here that Thomas does not allege that Godwin explicitly accused the Jews of a crucifixion, striking as such an assertion would have been at the synod, and valuable as it would have been for Thomas's thesis. Instead, he puts some highly ambiguous words in Godwin's mouth that seem to accord with the lurid description of William's crucifixion that Thomas had already provided the reader. It hardly needs to be added that it is inconceivable that that highly unreformed priest, Godwin Sturt, had read the *Historia tripartita*.

Bishop Eborard replied to Godwin—and this is the only hint of doubt in book 1—that what he had alleged "is so far clearly uncertain to us."[41] Yet to ensure justice in this religious matter, Eborard thrice summoned the Jews to come and answer the charge. Obeying the sheriff, the Jews refused. But once the synod was over, the bishop again summoned the sheriff and the Jews, who came this time but departed without submitting to judgment. This dramatic event finally stirred up the inhabitants of Norwich, and for the first and only time the sheriff brought the Jews into the security of the castle. Thomas does not, however, mention any looting of houses.[42]

The excitement increased William's posthumous importance, which was first recognized by a visitor. Prior Aimar of the distant abbey of St. Pancras at Lewes had attended the synod for some unstated reason and stayed after. At some point he took a single priest aside (presumably Godwin) and got the details of what had happened from him. He then declared publicly that he wanted to take the body back to St. Pancras, where he would make it famous and a precious treasure for his monastery. Bishop Eborard recognized the possibilities and refused. He ordered that William's body be exhumed on 24 April 1144 from Thorpe Wood—where it had now lain for a whole month in unconsecrated ground—and be buried, presumably as a potential relic, in the monks' cemetery. He did not treat it as the relic of an indubitable martyr by burying it in the cathedral.[43] When the body was brought to the priory, according to Thomas writing well after the event, the monks washed it and, examining it as a potential relic, discovered thorn wounds in the scalp and even "pieces of the actual thorns," together with evident signs of martyrdom in the hands, feet, and side and plain indications that the body "had been plunged into boiling water." They then buried it with psalms and praise.[44]

Despite the assured tone of book 1, book 2 reveals that many of the clergy attributed no sanctity to William in 1144 and for years after. Indeed, William's first translation did not even arouse much faith among the lay folk of Norwich, for hardly any miracles were reported. When Thomas sat down about 1154 to record the miracles that had occurred before the second translation in 1150, he could assemble only five stories.[45] Since three of these, including a long-blooming rose bush, are attributed to 1144, only two were reported in the five years from 1145 to April of 1150. The fourth of these miracles occurred "some considerable time" after 1144, when Thomas was already present, and Thomas had to admit that before the fifth miracle, remembrance of William had almost died out.[46] It was the fifth miracle that

revived interest, Thomas informs us. Since interest had certainly revived when William's body was translated for the second time to the
chapter house on 12 April 1150, an event followed by many miracles,
and since no miracles intervened between the fifth miracle and the
translation, that fifth miracle was almost certainly reported in 1149 or
early in 1150.

The miracle concerned a beautiful virgin from Dunwich who had
been persistently pursued by an immodest but remarkably handsome
incubus. She was saved by a vision in which Herbert of Losinga, carefully announcing himself as the bishop who had founded the church at
Norwich, instructed her to bear candles to William's tomb. She came,
told her troubles to Wicheman, Bishop William's deputy for confessions, took her candles to the grave in the cemetery, and was
delivered.[47] Since we may doubt that young virgins of Dunwich were
ecclesiastical historians, it would seem that Wicheman had interpreted
the virgin's vision for her and thereby revived interest in Norwich's
potential relic. But that was by no means his only contribution.

In 1149, Aelward Ded, one of the richest citizens of Norwich, made
his deathbed confession to Wicheman, who told Thomas of Monmouth about it. As Thomas reports it, Aelward had said that on Good
Friday of 1144 he had encountered a prominent Jew named Eleazar
(who was safely dead by 1149) and another nameless Jew on the out-
skirts of Thorpe Wood. Wondering for some reason what was in the
sack one of them was carrying on his horse's neck, he approached,
touched it, and recognized it to be a human body, whereupon the Jews
fled into the wood. Aelward did nothing about them, however, because
he was distracted from his suspicions by devotional thoughts appropriate to the day! The Jews, however, fearing their crime had been
discovered, dropped the body in the wood, and hurried to—of all
people—the sheriff. They took John of Chesney aside, bribed him with
a hundred marks to keep their great secret, and then told that Christian and prominent official—on Good Friday—what they had done.
They persuaded him to summon Aelward and somehow compel that
substantial citizen and Christian to swear not to tell anyone about his
discovery.[48] And keep quiet Aelward Ded did, even after Godwin had
publicly accused the Jews, even after the body had been translated to
the monks' cemetery, even after John of Chesney died in 1146, and
even for three more years until he himself was dying in 1149. Or so
Wicheman alleged.

The story is superbly imaginative and unbelievable, but it provided "a lawful witness" to link Jews directly with the crime. We might try to explain it as the fantasy, based on some earlier encounter with Jews, of a senile old man on his deathbed, but it is far too coherent and too obviously serves a purpose for that. Not only does it link Jews solidly with the crime, but it explains away the uncomfortable fact that the sheriff, who should have investigated the accusation had there been any reasonable evidence, not only had not done so, but had protected the Jews after Godwin had accused them. Together with the virgin of Dunwich's story, it must have contributed greatly to the revival of interest in William that resulted in his second translation the next year. But Wicheman was by no means solely responsible for William's new fame. Thomas of Monmouth was now at the monastery.

The earliest date that Thomas provides for his presence is Lent of 1150, when he had the visions that were the immediate cause of the second translation, and he seems to have known of the events of 1146 only by hearsay. He was present when the fourth miracle was reported[49] and when interest in William was almost dead before the fifth miracle, of about 1149. Given the strength of his obsession, which occasioned the translation, it is hard to believe that he could have been long at the priory without trying to enhance William's fame. It therefore seems probable that he arrived in or a little before 1149 and, inspired by Wicheman or in conjunction with him, worked to revive interest in William.

Between his arrival and the second translation, Thomas was busy interviewing people and gathering testimony to demonstrate Jewish guilt and thereby confirm William's sanctity. He doubtless first sought out the Sturts and was predictably rewarded. The glaring weakness in Godwin's case against the Jews had been that no evidence connected them with William's disappearance and demise. Godwin had only been able to adduce Leviva's dream of losing her leg, to ascribe the craftiness of the self-styled cook to the Jews, and to refer vaguely to circumstantial evidence. No wonder Bishop Eborard had been dubious. Leviva's dream of course proved nothing, although it does indicate, in a way that invites psychoanalytic examination, her unusual fear of losing her leg and of Jews even before William's disappearance. But by 1149, Leviva had more to offer. She could tell Thomas that when William and the "cook" had visited her on the Tuesday, she had—for no recorded reason—been suspicious and had told her little daughter to follow them. She did and saw them enter a Jew's house and close the door.[50] Since Godwin did not mention that important testimony in his original accusation, although it would have greatly strengthened his case, and since there would have been far more decisive action against Jews had it been known that William was last seen entering a Jew's house, we can be sure that the story only surfaced later. Surprisingly, Thomas gives no name for the daughter, describing her only as a little girl; she may well have been dead by the time Thomas arrived. It is conceivable that as Leviva developed the family fantasy after 1144—and how many times she must have retold it—she drew in some story from her small child, who might sometime have seen William enter a Jew's house with someone. Since little attention would have been paid to so dubious an addition from so suspect a source, there is no way of telling when Leviva first told it. But just as Wicheman had produced the testimony of a lawful witness to connect Jews with the crime after the fact, so Leviva's story produced a link before the fact.

There was still a great gap, however. What had the Jews done to poor William between his disappearance and the disposal of his body? That could only be surmised by a free interpretation of his wounds. Thomas set out to fill the gap himself. After diligent inquiry, he discovered a Christian woman who had worked in 1144 as a servant in the house of a prominent Jew, Eleazar, who had died about 1146. She took Thomas to the house and they discovered the marks of the crucifixion. The woman said that on that fateful Wednesday she had been told to bring boiling water from the kitchen and, with one eye through a chink in the door (another invitation to psychological analysis), she saw with horror a boy attached to a post. She had done nothing, however, because she was afraid she would lose her wages, and she feared that the Jews would kill her since she was "the only Christian living among so many Jews."[51] Since there were relatively few Jews in Norwich, and they lived in leased houses, none of the houses could have been very far from houses and streets with Christians, and she could easily have slipped out to find help. She could also have come forward as soon as Godwin had accused the Jews in the synod. But she did nothing—shades of Aelward Ded—and only told her story some time later, apparently after being questioned by Thomas of Monmouth. The story is completely unbelievable, and presumably she told it to excuse herself for having worked for Jews and to bask in William's reflected glory.

It was also Thomas himself who acquired the most famous testimony of all. He heard it "from the lips" of Theobald, who said he had been a Jew in Cambridge in 1144, had converted when he heard of the glorious display of miracles worked through William, and had become a monk. Where Thomas met Theobald we do not know. Had he become a monk at Norwich, known to all as Theobald, we would have expected Thomas to say so and thereby guarantee the authenticity of this striking evidence "uttered by one who was a converted enemy, and had also been privy to the secrets of our enemies."[52] But Thomas does not. Thomas may have met him elsewhere, or he may have visited William's shrine at Norwich and been warmly questioned by Thomas. We can be sure, however, that Theobald's revelation delighted Thomas.

Theobald told Thomas that the Jews of Spain assembled every year in Narbonne, where their royal seed and renown flourished, in order to arrange the annual sacrifice prescribed in the ancient writings of their fathers. To show contempt for Christ, to revenge themselves because Christ's death had made them slaves in exile, and to obtain their freedom and their return to their own land, they had to shed blood annually by sacrificing a Christian. Each year, the Jews of Narbonne cast lots to determine the country in which the sacrifice would take place that year, and the Jews of the metropolis of that country then similarly determined in which town of their country the sacrifice would be performed. The lot fell on Norwich in 1144, and all the synagogues in England knew and consented to the act, which was why Theobald had known about it in Cambridge.[53]

The falsity of the fable is manifest. Not only is it in contradiction with everything we know from massive evidence about classical, medieval, and modern Judaism, but something known, as Theobald claims, to every Jew in Europe would have left many more traces. It is so obviously false that scholars have wondered whether Theobald is a product of Thomas's imagination. But as Joseph Jacobs pointed out in 1897, Theobald must have been a real person and said something like this because Thomas would not have known about the *nasi* of Narbonne.[54] Why Theobald said it is harder to answer. To express his hatred for the community he had left or from which he had been expelled? To prove the sincerity of his recent conversion? We shall never know. But what has not received attention is the fact that in this crowning testimony, even as reported by Thomas, there is no reference to a crucifixion, only to a sacrifice. When a Christian thought about sacrifice, particularly in connection with Easter week, he or she would immediately think of a crucifixion.[55] But a former Jew who wished to defame the community he had left or to prove the sincerity of his conversion by revealing some evil Jewish habit would be more likely to distort something genuinely Jewish such as the sacrifices of the Old Testament. And it is noteworthy that the only essential of the sacrifice mentioned by Theobald is the shedding of blood, and that this is the only place in the whole *Life* where the shedding of blood is given a religious significance.

Thomas does not introduce Theobald and report his fable until book 2, but there are allusions to him in the narrative in book 1. Just before the self-styled cook appears on the scene to lead William away, we are told that the Jews had been planning to kill some Christian, as Thomas had learnt "from certain Jews, who were afterwards converted to the Christian faith."[56] This can only refer to Theobald's revelation, even though he is made nameless and multiplied to sound more convincing. Another reference appears when the Jews are uncertain what to do with the body. They assemble the next morning and, "as we afterwards learnt from one of them," when they are still undecided after considerable discussion, one of them who had greater authority gives a speech, which Thomas presents in direct discourse, to warn of what will happen to Jews if such a horrible crime is discovered. He counsels that the body be disposed of far away, where it will not implicate Jews.[57] Thomas refers here only to a single Jew, and the construction of the sentence implies that it was a Jew present at the killing, but it is extremely unlikely that any Jew of Norwich would ever have said anything like that to Thomas. And if he had, Thomas would certainly have said more about him in book 2, where he assembles all his proofs and tells us about Theobald and his fable, but never mentions any other Jewish informant. It is far more probable that when he was getting as much as he could out of Theobald, Thomas had asked Theobald to explain why the body had been found in Thorpe Wood on the other side of Norwich far from Jews and their synagogue. Then, when writing the narrative, Thomas molded Theobald's answer and put it in the mouth of a leading Jew of Norwich. Theobald did lasting damage to Jews, but he served Thomas's search for sanctity well.

By 1150, Wicheman and Thomas had collected new and apparently damning evidence of Jewish culpability and effectively revived interest in William's sanctity. And now Thomas becomes an even more important figure in the drama. He tells us that he had three visions in Lent of 1150 in which Herbert of Losinga, duly identifying himself again as the church's founder (Wicheman's influence?), appeared and commanded Thomas to inform the bishop and prior that William's body must be transferred to the security of the chapter house. Thomas did so, and though Prior Elias seems to have been skeptical, Bishop William Turbe commanded the second translation. On the Wednesday of Easter week, 12 April 1150, Thomas was one of the six monks designated to open the sarcophagus, an occasion from which Thomas profited to steal two of William's teeth for his private relics.[58] Doubtless he felt he had a right. He had caused the translation, and thanks to his own devoted labors he could envisage William's martyrdom as no one else could unless he described it to them—as we can be sure he did when the rule of silence permitted.

Thomas had every reason to feel humbly proud. Indeed, he was so elevated that on Easter Sunday, four days after the translation, on the advice of some of his companions, he took a carpet from the church, placed it on William's tomb, and set a great candle at the head of the tomb without the authorization of the prior. Elias immediately ordered their removal, at which "the greater part of the convent was scandalized."[59] Three monks promptly reported two healing miracles and a vision in which the Virgin herself stood warranty for William.[60] To the monk who had the vision, one of the virgins accompanying the Virgin explained its meaning: "Behold, the queen of heaven and mother of the Lord has come to visit the patron so long assigned to this church, the martyr William, her truly beloved friend; she has crowned him and granted him the power of healing at his will."[61] The brethren paid more honor to the tomb, four more miracles were reported, and a monk had a vision in which William, referring to Thomas as his personal sacristan, appeared and commanded that candles be placed at his tomb.[62] Elias gave in; visitors to the tomb increased greatly; and on 22 October 1150, Elias died, perhaps from chagrin or, as Thomas suggests, as a punishment for his skepticism.[63] Prior Richard, Elias's successor, then personally took the carpet from the church and placed it again on the tomb.[64]

William had finally received the honors appropriate to a martyr, and to his tomb came a press of visitors, two-thirds from Norwich itself.[65] Their presence in the chapter house so disturbed the monks and so increased William's fame that the body was translated for a third time on 2 July 1151 to a place beside the high altar of the cathedral.[66] That signal honor brought further miracles, but after the peak in 1150/51 reports of miracles dropped sharply.[67] Although Thomas says that the fourth translation on Easter Monday, 5 April

1154, to the martyrs' chapel in the apse was done because the press of visitors was again inconveniencing the clergy,[68] it seems that miracles had been falling off, and that the fourth translation may have been intended to revive William's fame and revenues.

William's fame was slow in coming; and although the story about him would ultimately spread throughout Europe, his miracle-working powers at Norwich soon diminished sharply. His alleged martyrdom had attracted very few believers in 1144 and was almost forgotten by 1149. He attracted wide interest only in Norwich itself in 1150 and 1151 after Thomas's visions and the second translation, which inspired more miracles in one year than in the preceding six. But Thomas's contribution to William's sudden fame may have been much more substantial than those visions, for it is very probable that he wrote his narrative of the life and passion of William before the second translation and incorporated it later as book 1 of the larger work.

Although M. R. James believed that the whole work had been composed in 1172 or 1173, because the opening prologue and the last miracle story in book 7 were written then,[69] there are several indications that the work was not all written at one time. The last book, book 7, which was not completed until 1172/73, stands apart. It is the only book to have its own prologue, and Thomas there states that he had stopped writing in 1155, but that the revival of miracles thereafter had impelled him to take up his pen again.[70] Book 6 must therefore have been completed by 1155; and since book 2 alludes to King Stephen as dead,[71] books 2–6 must have been written after 25 October 1154 and no later than 1155. They were written at Bishop Turbe's command to preserve the record of the miracles,[72] and they also describe the second, third, and fourth translations. They were probably written after the fourth translation in April of 1154 as part of the effort to restore interest in Norwich's saint.

Book 1 seems to have been written earlier. The only time that Thomas opens a new book by referring explicitly to a prior one is at the beginning of book 2, where he states that in the previous book he had presented William's childhood and death.[73] Later in book 2, Thomas argues against many people who were hard of heart and did not believe in William's sanctity even though they had seen his cruelly wounded body or read about his cruel death *in presentibus scriptis*,[74] in what Thomas had written, which indicates that the narrative of William's life of book 1 had circulated for some time before Thomas wrote book 2. And whereas in book 2, when he refers to the king, he feels it necessary to specify that he is referring to the dead King Stephen, not Henry II, in book 1 he refers three times to the king without specifying that he means Stephen.[75]

Book 1 also differs markedly in content and tone from all the other books. It is a self-contained saint's life that begins with William's conception and ends triumphantly with his burial in the monks' cemetery. In marked contrast with the other books, Thomas here hardly ever refers to himself, doing so only briefly in a few places where he notes that he had learned of certain events from later testimony. The narrative itself only deals with events of 1144, and although there are passing allusions to later events such as Aelward Ded's death in 1149, there is no allusion to the second translation. Indeed, were it not for the mention of 1149, the reader might think that the narrative had been written shortly after the burial in the cemetery. Moreover, in striking contrast with book 2, where Thomas immediately departs from his stated purpose to launch a bitter attack on those who doubted William's sanctity, book 1 narrates his martyrdom as if no one could doubt its truth. Bishop Eborard's initial uncertainty is mentioned but soon seems canceled by his decision to order the first translation, and the book ends on a note of triumphant confidence.

Book 1 was just what those who wanted to promote William's reputation in 1149 would have wanted, whereas book 2, certainly written after October 1154, sounds very much like a defense of book 1 against those who had criticized it. And it is remarkable that the second translation occurred on the Wednesday of Easter week of 1150, precisely six liturgical years from that Wednesday of Easter week in 1144 which Thomas's reconstruction of the crime had established as the day of William's death. It is highly probable, therefore, that book 1 was written late in 1149 or early in 1150 to increase the new interest in William's powers and provide a compelling justification for his translation to a tomb more worthy of a martyr.

The dating of book 1 is important because it provides us with a *terminus ad quem* for the crucifixion accusation. We know that the accusation had been made and was known at Peterborough by 1155. If, as seems highly probable, book 1 was written about 1150, it had already been made by then. But when was it first voiced? And by whom? Where did Thomas get the idea, and how did he "know" that William had been crucified? The only evidence he adduces that might seem to support the accusation is: the nature of the wounds; the servant's story of what she had seen in the Jew's house; the marks in the house; and Theobald's story. But none of these items explains the emergence of the accusation.

What Thomas says about the state of the body is highly suspicious. In the first place, the wooden gag or teasel—whose miraculous powers Godwin Sturt later made available for a price—and the knotted cord used to torture the victim have nothing to do with a crucifixion, nor does the boiling water.[76] If we then turn to examine the words about the wounds attributed to Godwin at the synod, we are struck by their vagueness. Apparently Thomas could not assert that Godwin had claimed in the synod that William had been crucified and had had to be content with paraphrasing Godwin's words about cruel wounds so that they seemed open to such an interpretation. Equally suspect is Thomas's description of what the monks who washed the body had found. The body must have been in remarkably poor shape by then. William had been killed, apparently cruelly, and left exposed to the elements and the animals for three days; his body had then been buried, dug up, and reburied in the following two days; and then it had lain buried in the wood for a month and been dug up again before being examined. Given the state of the body and the medical ignorance of the period,[77] nobody could have said accurately what had been done to the boy. Thomas, writing six years later, could impose his interpretation on the wounds without fear of contradiction.

Before Thomas arrived in Norwich, at least up to 1146, there had apparently been no crucifixion accusation. About that year, the squires of an indebted knight named Simon de Novers had murdered the Jew Eleazar. Thomas provides an avowedly fictitious speech that William Turbe, who became bishop in 1146, might have made to King Stephen in defense of Simon, his vassal. Thomas has Turbe argue that Christians ought not to reply to a Jewish accusation until the Jews had purged themselves of William's murder. But Turbe is not made to say that William had been crucified, though such an accusation would have greatly strengthened the defense. He is only depicted as saying that Eleazar and other Jews did "as report says, miserably torment, kill, and hide in a wood a Christian boy."[78] Thomas apparently knew that Turbe would not have referred to such an accusation in 1146.

In fact, Thomas knew that the wounds had not manifestly indicated a crucifixion. When he discovered the servant and the house where the crime supposedly happened, the marks the woman showed him did not fit a proper iconographical crucifixion. In his narrative of the crime in book 1, he therefore states that the Jews nailed William's left hand and foot but tied his right hand and foot, so that if the body were discovered, its condition would not be recognized as evidence of a Jewish crime.[79] Since no one in 1144 thought that Jews crucified children, the motive alleged is ridiculous, but what Thomas unintentionally reveals is that no one could have known from the wounds that William had been crucified.

Interestingly enough, the only other evidence to support the accusation was obtained by Thomas himself in private conversations long after the crime. It was Thomas who discovered the Christian servant after he had made diligent inquiry, and she told him she had seen the boy attached to a post and pointed out some marks. But her story is completely implausible, and even Thomas does not claim that she spoke of a crucifixion. We should note, moreover, that it was only after Thomas had found the woman and looked at the marks on the posts that he discovered precisely how the "crucifixion" had occurred. And although the marks contradicted the accepted conception of a crucifixion and, consequently, Thomas's conviction that a crucifixion could be detected from the wounds, he nonetheless persisted in his belief. Obviously, he was already convinced before he visited the house that William must have been crucified and was determined to maintain that conviction at any cost.

Finally, there was Theobald, Thomas's only and prized source of information about what Jews did in secret. But Theobald had not been in Norwich when the crime was committed. Moreover, there is no mention of crucifixion in Thomas's lengthy report of Theobald's revelation; and had Theobald told Thomas that Jews annually crucified a Christian, Thomas would have recorded it with delight to confirm William's martyrdom and confound his critics. It remains true, of course, that Theobald introduced the myth of ritually required annual murder, yet we may wonder whether even he would have invented that myth had not Thomas eagerly asked him to explain why Jews had killed William so cruelly. In any case, without Thomas, Theobald's fable would have had no influence, for it came to be known to contemporaries and to us only because Thomas reported it in the *Life*.

Who, then, first accused Jews of crucifying William? Although people in the twelfth century were accustomed to brutal homicides, particularly during the civil war that was raging in England in 1144, crucifixion was not a contemporary form of cruelty, and people would be most unlikely to think of it when confronted with a damaged corpse and no solid evidence of who committed the crime or why. Only after

the accusation had been invented at Norwich would that possibility
spring readily to some people's minds. The accusation had apparently
not been made by 1146 and seems to have emerged only after Thomas's arrival. And it is striking that the testimonies that come closest
to supporting it—the stories of the Christian servant and Theobald—
were Thomas's personal discovery. It is even more striking that
Thomas never has any of the people whose stories he reports refer
explicitly to a crucifixion. Instead, he attributes ambiguous words to
them that could be interpreted as referring either to great cruelty or, as
Thomas wants the reader to think, to a crucifixion. In fact, so far as
the *Life* reveals, the only person at Norwich up to 1150 who had
explicitly asserted that the Jews had crucified the boy was Thomas
himself.

It is conceivable that Wicheman or some other supporter of
William's sanctity suggested to Thomas that the Jews might have crucified the boy. Once Godwin Sturt had made his accusation of cruel
murder, the association of Jews with the cruel killing of an innocent in
Easter week could easily have brought that image to mind. But no one
was more obsessed with William's sanctity and more likely to make
that connection than Thomas himself, especially since it made William
a Christlike figure, thus elevating him above most martyrs—as some
miracle stories make explicit. Certainly no one devoted more energy to
proving the accusation than Thomas; and when his thesis was challenged, he defended it vehemently as if his pride had been injured. For
it was his own detective work that had revealed precisely where and
how William had died, thereby greatly augmenting his fame. And certainly it was Thomas who did the most to publicize the accusation. So
far as we are ever likely to know, Thomas created the accusation. Since
he had not acquired all the elements of his story until 1149, and had
apparently written book 1 by 1150, we may feel reasonably sure that
the fantasy that Jews ritually murdered Christians by crucifixion was
created and contributed to Western culture by Thomas of Monmouth
about 1150.

So flushed with confidence was Thomas in 1150 by his great discovery that he placed the carpet on William's new tomb without Prior
Elias's approval. But once the excitement had died down and the results were published for all to read, Thomas discovered, as many others have, that the wider audience he sought included critics. Prior Elias
was only one of many. Five years later, when Thomas sat down to
write book 2, he was still very bitter. Although Elias had died in 1150,

others in the priory still doubted. Thomas angrily tells us in book 2 that "many . . . mocked at the miracles when they were made public" and "many suggested that the blessed boy William was likely to be of no special merit after his death, who they had heard had been a poor and neglected lad in his life." And some "though they saw with their own eyes that he was cruelly murdered . . . yet say: 'We are indeed sure that he died somehow, but we are utterly uncertain as to who killed him and why and how; hence we dare not say he is a saint or martyr.' "[80] Despite the common desire for a precious relic, many who were far more familiar with the events at Norwich than we can ever be, and who had read Thomas's account, found his story unbelievable. The modern scholar who views Thomas's account with deep skepticism has good company from the allegedly credulous Middle Ages.

We should be grateful to those medieval skeptics, because their criticism so angered Thomas that instead of simply recording the miracles and translations as he had announced he would, he spent most of book 2 in bolstering his argument for William's sanctity and setting out his proofs of Jewish guilt,[81] thereby enabling us to see more clearly how weak his case was. Only in book 2 do we learn that his detailed description of the murder depends primarily on the Christian servant's story, that the anonymous converted Jews of book 1 were only Theobald, and that Theobald told his fable to Thomas alone. Without book 2, we should not have known about the case of Simon de Novers and the words Thomas felt were appropriate to put in Bishop Turbe's mouth. Indeed, Thomas is so determined to prove his case that he gives us every proof he can think of, which reassures the modern investigator that Thomas's certainty did not depend on some information he forgot to include. He even proffers an early example of Jewish black humor as "a most effective proof," although he does not see the joke. Apparently some Jews later said to Christians, "You ought to have rendered us thanks, for we made a saint and martyr for you. . . . We did something for you that you couldn't do for yourselves."[82] And without book 2, we would have assumed that the first translation to the monks' cemetery had been followed by many miracles, instead of which we discover that there were amazingly few between 1144 and 1149, and that William was almost forgotten by the latter date. But above all, we would never have known that many people who had witnessed the events and read the results of Thomas's detection could not believe his story.

If those informed contemporaries were completely uncertain about who killed William or how, modern scholars, with only the data of Thomas's biased account to go on, will never know. The most likely candidate remains the self-styled archdeacon's cook who was never seen again, for he was the last person seen with William by witnesses whose testimony was available when the Jews were first accused in 1144. Nothing other than Godwin's suspicions connected the "cook" with Jews, and even Thomas recognizes that he cannot say whether he was a Christian or a Jew.[83] It is, moreover, impossible to believe that Elviva or Leviva would have let someone they suspected might be a Jew go off with William under false pretenses, or that Godwin would not have said in the synod that he was a Jew if he could have. Nothing connected Jews with the crime in 1144 except the Sturt family's fear and hate of them and the fact that William had been killed in Easter week. It also seems all but certain that no one accused Jews of crucifying William until Thomas of Monmouth did so about five years later and thereby ensured William's enduring fame.

Yet whatever the skepticism of many of Thomas's contemporaries at Norwich in the ten years after William's death, many began to believe in 1150 and have miraculous cures. The news spread, and although interest in William declined at Norwich after 1151, more people came from a distance in search of a cure.[84] By 1155, the Peterborough chronicler knew of the crucifixion accusation and the miracles. By 1170, the rumor that Jews crucified Christians had crossed the Channel and was known at Cambrai.[85] Slightly later, the abbot of Mont-Saint-Michel recorded that the Jews had crucified not only St. William at Norwich but also young Richard at Pontoise, a boy at Gloucester, and a boy at Blois.[86] And in 1255, England acquired its most famous mythical victim of ritual murder. Although no evidence linked Jews with the death of young Hugh of Lincoln, Jews were accused of crucifying him, which led to the execution of nineteen Jews by King Henry III and a new saint for Lincoln cathedral.[87] What evidence could not do, accusation had, thanks to the desire to think evil of Jews and thereby find confirmation of Christian beliefs.

Thomas of Monmouth was an influential figure in the formation of Western culture. He did not alter the course of battles, politics, or the economy. He solved no philosophical or theological problems. He was not even noteworthy for the holiness of his life or promotion to monastic office. Yet with substantial help from an otherwise unknown converted Jew, he created a myth that affected Western mentality from the twelfth to the twentieth century and caused, directly or indirectly, far more deaths than William's murderer could ever have dreamt of committing. Those deadly consequences should not blind us, however, to the creative imagination with which Thomas manipulated religious symbols and his perception of events in his environment in order to reinforce his religious security, turn murder into a miraculous cure for disease, and mold the religiosity of others to support his own. For Thomas was more concerned to strengthen his own Christian faith than to destroy Jews.

Strange as it may seem, Thomas does not appear to have had any unusual animus against Jews compared with other Christians of his day. To be sure, he depicts them as impudent and avaricious and as cruel and blasphemous killers, but he dwells on their alleged evil qualities only when the exigencies of his proof of William's sanctity demand it. He betrays no overriding obsession with Jews. He does not interrupt his narrative with irrelevant outbursts against them, nor does he inject further abuse when reporting the miracles. The Sturts did hate Jews and first accused them of cruel murder; and Theobald, the converted Jew, introduced the idea of an annual sacrifice. But Thomas only used the material provided by the animosity of others to achieve his own objective: to assure himself of a local supernatural protector and to gain prestige on earth by his successful labors to ensure recognition of William's sanctity. Thomas did, however, make his own fundamental contribution to the creation of what he believed to be the patron saint assigned by God to Norwich.

So long as William was seen only as a poor boy who might have been cruelly killed by some Jews out of religious animus, he could be viewed as a passive victim but hardly as a saint; and in fact he attracted little attention. One small modification, however, could and did radically change the significance of his death. If an innocent boy of twelve was crucified by Jews during Passover and in Easter week for no other reason than that he was a Christian, that he was a symbol of Christ's truth, he would seem Christ in microcosm. He would also seem representative of all those who felt as defenseless as a child against the little-understood forces that menaced their existence, and who turned for comfort to their faith that Christ might intervene here and now to protect them, or at least to ensure a better life hereafter. Only a little imagination was needed to make William a symbol of comfort and ultimate victory, and Thomas did not lack imagination. He crucified William and thereby made him a notable saint.

Thomas never described William's ultimate reward in his own

words. Or he did so only in words he ascribed to others. He tells us about a very young virgin of Mulbarton who was very religious for her tender age and had a vision of hell and heaven. Guided by a dove, she saw Christ in heaven with Mary at his right hand and, very close to him, a small boy of incomparable beauty whose robes were nearly identical with Christ's in all respects, in color, jewels, and gold, "as if the one garment had been cut from the other." The dove told her that this was William, the blessed martyr of Norwich, slain by the Jews. "Because he truly copied Christ in the passion of his death, Christ did not disdain to make him equal to himself by the honour of his purple robes."[88]

What Thomas heard about William after his arrival in Norwich excited him to wishful thinking about earth and heaven and himself; and William's image as reflected through Thomas has maintained its power to excite wishful thinking right down to the twentieth century. Modern scholars have been fascinated by the problem of who killed William and have exercised amazing ingenuity to provide a possible solution. But the evidence is so biased and inadequate that they had to rely heavily on dubious assumptions and produced strange and contradictory conjectures that tell us more about their authors than about William's death.[89] Yet if Thomas's *Life* of William will never reveal who killed poor little William, it is rich and rewarding evidence for something much more important, the creation of the crucifixion accusation, for the *Life* was written by the myth's creator.

10.

The Knight's Tale of
Young Hugh of Lincoln

Chaucer's prioress tells the tale of the young "clergeon" in an Asian
city who expressed his devotion to Mary by singing *Alma redemptoris*,
especially when walking to and from school through the Jewish
quarter.[1] The enraged Jews cut his throat and threw his body in their
privy, but his mother discovered him because Mary miraculously enabled him to continue singing. The singing body was then transported
in great procession to the nearest abbey; the provost had the Jews
drawn and hanged; and the boy-martyr was buried after his singing
had been miraculously explained and stopped. The prioress concludes
her story with an invocation that reminded her audience of another
tale of the same genre.

> O yonge Hugh of Lincoln, slayn also
> With cursed Jews, as it is notable,
> For it nis but a litel whyle ago;
> Pray eek for us, we sinful folk unstable
> That, of his mercy, god so merciable
> On us his grete mercy multiplye,
> For reverence of his moder Marye. Amen.

The history of the legend of the singing boy has been traced with
assiduity by Carleton Brown as part of the search for Chaucer's
sources and analogues. He divided the known versions of the legend
into three groups, and pointed out that Chaucer's version belonged to
group C and most resembled the earliest version in the group.[2] That

version, C 1, comes from an English collection of tales that was compiled between 1200 and 1216, probably about 1215.[3]

The ultimate source of the prioress's concluding invocation was, of course, the events surrounding the death of Hugh of Lincoln in 1255, for which nineteen Jews were executed by King Henry III. Those events inspired two quite different literary and popular traditions. In the first place, the alleged ritual murder was described in three contemporary chronicles and an Anglo-Norman ballad,[4] and Hugh's shrine at Lincoln and these writings preserved the memory of his fate for centuries. The event did not seem distant to Chaucer some 135 years later. It was doubtless in Marlowe's mind when he had Friar Jacomo ask what Barabas, the Jew of Malta, had done: "What, has he crucified a child?"[5] In the early eighteenth century, the Bollandists in the *Acta Sanctorum* established 27 July as the blessed martyr's day, his *acta* being provided by a fifteenth-century version of Matthew Paris's account.[6] And in the early nineteenth century, the traditional story of Hugh's death made Charles Lamb fearful of entering a synagogue.[7] A brochure published at Lincoln in 1911 directed the reader to the very well in the Jew's house in which Hugh's body had been thrown.[8]

The second tradition inspired by the events of 1255 was the ballad of "Sir Hugh" or "The Jew's Daughter," of which Francis Child was able to collect twenty-one divergent versions at the end of the nineteenth century.[9] The ballad bears scant resemblance to either the legend of the singing boy or ritual murder. The basic plot is that a Jew's daughter cajoles a boy, Sir Hugh, into her house to pick up a ball he had kicked through the window, sticks him like a pig, and throws his lead-encased body in "Our Lady's draw-well" in the house, where his mother discovers him because the body spoke. Although the version that Thomas Percy included in his *Reliques* in 1765 did not mention Lincoln, Percy noted the resemblance to both the Prioress's Tale and the "known" story of Hugh of Lincoln, which he, unlike Lamb, dismissed as groundless along with all other tales of ritual murder.[10]

The one source of the Prioress's Tale that has not been intensively examined is the "known" story of the events of 1255 that influenced English literary and popular culture from 1255 to the twentieth century, to say nothing of its use by nineteenth-century polemicists who sought to prove the truth of the ritual murder charge. Nor has the knight most responsible for the enduring fame of young Hugh of Lincoln ever received his due credit.

Historians concerned above all with the history of the non-Jewish

majority of thirteenth-century England—such as Lady Stenton, Christopher Brooke, and even Sir Maurice Powicke—do not even mention
the affair.[11] Only one recent historian of the majority has discussed it
at any length. Sir Francis Hill's study of medieval Lincoln has five
pages on little Hugh, an unavoidable topic from Hill's perspective, and
they constitute the fullest account widely available at present. Yet Hill
did not go into the affair at all deeply. His description is achieved
primarily by quotation of a page and a half of Matthew Paris's unreliable account and a very short paraphrase of the longer and more
reliable account in the annals of Burton. He is most valuable for the
history of "the Jew's house" where the murder was supposed to have
occurred. It was discovered in 1928 that the famous well where the
body was supposedly thrown had been built by a workman then living
to augment the antiquarian value of the house.[12]

Predictably, the only careful analysis of the affair—published in final form in 1896—was made by a Jewish historian, the indefatigable
Joseph Jacobs.[13] Utilizing the evidence of chronicles, ballads, governmental records, and archaeology, Jacobs concluded that little Hugh,
the eight-year-old son of a widow, Beatrice, accidentally fell into a
cesspool attached to a Jew's house on 31 July 1255. The body putre-
fied for some twenty-six days and then rose to the surface to dismay
Jews who had assembled from all over England to celebrate a marriage
in an important family. They surreptitiously dropped the body in a
well away from their houses where it was discovered on 29 August.
Among the crowd that collected was a canon of the cathedral, John of
Lexington, who brought up the rumor that Jews crucified Christian
children, and the body was forthwith buried in the cathedral with the
honors due to a martyr. John of Lexington then extracted a confession
from a Jew, Copin or Jopin, that there had been a ritual murder; and
when Henry III arrived in Lincoln some time later, he had Copin executed. The remainder of the Jews were imprisoned in London, eighteen were executed for refusing to throw themselves on the verdict of
a Christian jury, and the remainder were liberated in 1256. Jacob's
conclusions are accepted in Cecil Roth's brief account, save that Roth
does not mention John of Lexington, whose central role attracted Jacobs's and Hill's attention, and that Roth accepts Matthew Paris's
assertion that the body was found near Copin's house, which Jacobs
rejected.[14]

Jacobs provided an elegant solution to what he called a "pretty
problem." Yet he was hampered by the fact that relevant documents

had not been published and indexed and by a certain narrowness of perspective. It is now possible to correct and add substantially to his account and, in the process, to throw new light on an aspect of administrative history, on the local history of Lincoln, and on the Prioress's Tale.

I

Had the fantasy of ritual murder never developed, young Hugh would have remained but one of thousands of unrecorded victims of homicide or accidental death. That fantasy was created and initially most fully developed in England, which contributed it to the Continent, where it brought death and suffering to Jews down to the twentieth century. We may define ritual murder as the killing of a human, not merely from motives of religious hatred, but in such a way that the *form* of the killing is at least partly determined by ideas allegedly or actually important in the religion of the killers or the victims. From 1150 to 1235, the ritual murder accusation against Jews was that they annually crucified a Christian boy to insult Christ and as a sacrifice. In 1235, a second type of ritual murder accusation appeared by itself or in conjunction with the older accusation, that Jews killed a Christian child to acquire blood they needed for their rituals or medicine.

The crucifixion fantasy first developed around the discovery in 1144 in a wood outside Norwich of the body of little William. Secular authorities took no action, and there was considerable skepticism even among the monks of the cathedral where William was buried and became a notable focus of miracles. When fully developed by the 1150s, the Norwich fantasy proclaimed that European Jews annually conspired to crucify a Christian child at Easter or Passover to insult Christ and carry out the sacrifice necessary for the liberation of Jews and their return to their homeland; the crucifixion was accompanied by additional cruelties, and the state of the body revealed a Jewish crime.[15] In 1168, Jews of Gloucester and Jews from other communities, who had gathered to celebrate a circumcision in a prominent family, were accused of torturing and crucifying young Harold, whose body had been found in the Severn after he had been missing for twenty-two days. The body was thereafter enshrined in the cathedral.[16]

Before 1171 and possibly as early as 1163, some such accusation led to the establishment of the shrine of Richard of Pontoise at Paris.[17]

And in 1171, Stephen, count of Blois and Louis VII's seneschal, burned thirty-one Jews for killing a child, but no shrine could be established because there was not even a *corpus delicti*.[18] We know no details of the story surrounding the shrine of Robert at Bury St. Edmunds, who was supposedly killed secretly by a certain Jew in 1181. A similar rumor may have been current in Bristol in 1183 and certainly circulated in Winchester in 1192, but neither led to a shrine.[19] Indeed, from 1181 to 1244, nearly two generations, no new shrine was established although the fantasy became widespread in northern France and England.

Prior to 1179, Philip Augustus had heard from playmates that Jews annually killed a boy secretly in the catacombs under Paris to insult Christ and as a quasi-sacrifice.[20] In 1205, Innocent III reported in all seriousness that Jews in France evilly seized the opportunity of living among Christians to kill their hosts secretly, "as is recently said to have happened to a poor scholar found dead in their latrines."[21] At Lincoln in 1202, Jews were suspected of killing a child whose body had been found outside the walls. The accusation at Stanford in 1222 that Jews had played a game that mocked Christianity, possibly a Purim masquerade, does not seem to have been taken seriously by higher authorities. In 1225, however, a jury found two Jews of Winchester guilty of murder, possibly of a child, but since four others were freed and no chronicle mentions the case, there was probably no charge of ritual murder. Another Jew of Winchester was accused in the same year of killing a child but was freed on pledge because it was reported that the girl was still alive. One's suspicion that Winchester wanted a ritual murder shrine is strengthened by the imprisonment of Jews there in 1232 on suspicion that they were responsible for the death of the boy whose broken body had been discovered. They were freed, however, before their trial, whereas the mother who had also been arrested was kept in prison.[22]

The predisposition to accuse Jews whenever a child was missing or a child's body was found finally produced another shrine at London in 1244. A baby's body was found in St. Benet's cemetery, and marks on the body were thought to be Hebrew words. Suitably adjured converts were brought to translate them, and the case was popularly believed to be one of ritual murder, but no Jews were executed. Our unreliable informant, Matthew Paris, noted that such crucifixions are "frequently said to have happened" and that many said that God had operated miracles for the boy.

> And because it was discovered that Jews had formerly perpetrated such villainies, and that the holy crucified bodies had been ceremoniously received in the church, and miracles had broken forth, although the stigmata of the five wounds in the hands and feet and side did not appear on the said little body, nevertheless the canons of St. Paul's seized it and solemnly buried it near the high altar.[23]

In 1250, London—or Matthew Paris—produced an even wilder story. According to Matthew, Abraham of Berkhamsted, one of the richest Jews in England, bought an image of Mary with Jesus in her lap, placed it in his latrine, used it like the latrine, and ordered his wife to do likewise. When she, moved by her sex, cleaned the image's face, he killed her, and the crime was discovered. The story is highly dubious because, although Abraham was on trial in this period on some charge, he was released on pledge before his trial and was finally condemned to lose his chattels but freed on the condition that he avoid the king's presence for a year—hardly the penalty we would expect for murder or striking blasphemy.[24] Matthew Paris seems to have believed a preposterous rumor about what had happened.

Thus, by the middle of the thirteenth century, five shrines to alleged victims of ritual murder had been established, of which four were in England, the land where the fantasy had originated. Jews were widely believed to commit secret blasphemies and ritual murders, and local ecclesiastical authorities had fully supported the truth of the rumors. Yet no responsible secular authority had acted on the charge. Louis VII had not believed the charge at Blois, and no English king had condemned Jews for ritual murder despite many opportunities. All that changed dramatically in 1255.

II

The English fantasy of Jewish ritual murder by crucifixion achieved its classic form in 1255 because of Henry III's intervention and because little Hugh's story was vividly described by Matthew Paris, the most famous English thirteenth-century historian. His was probably the version known to Chaucer, Marlowe, Percy, and Lamb. And because of Matthew's fame, his version received first attention from modern historians and deflected them from other evidence. Both Jacobs and Hill quote his account almost completely, while only paraphrasing other versions—even though Jacobs realized that the Burton annals were more reliable. Yet Matthew should be suspected *a priori* because of his general carelessness, inaccuracy, unreliable dating of events within a given year, his stereotyping of non-English peoples and credulity about Jews, and his firm belief in the miraculous.[25] His ability to tell a compelling story is indubitable, but even his basic chronology of the Lincoln affair is wrong.

According to the Burton annals, Hugh disappeared on 31 July, was kept alive for twenty-six days, and killed on Friday, 27 August; his body was discovered on Sunday, 29 August; and the king arrived in Lincoln about 29 September. The Anglo-Norman ballad of Hugh of Lincoln, which demonstrates greater knowledge of local detail than any other source, also puts the disappearance about 31 July. Little Hugh's day in the calendar of the Use of Lincoln was established as 27 August, the presumed date of his martyrdom,[26] which indicates that the body was found after 27 August. And Henry III in fact arrived in Lincoln on 4 October.[27] One of the most significant features of the affair is that a month elapsed between Hugh's disappearance on 31 July and the discovery of his body on 29 August, and that another month passed before the king intervened on 4 October.

That feature is completely camouflaged in Matthew Paris. The only specific date he gives is for the public event that was least a matter of general knowledge, Hugh's disappearance, which he places about 29 June. He says that the boy was kept alive for ten days and fed on childish foods so that he would support the torture, while Jews were summoned from communities across England, *quasi ad Paschale sacrificium*. When they arrived, a parody of the Crucifixion was enacted during which each Jew punctured the boy with knives called *anelacii*, whereafter he was pierced to the heart and disemboweled for magical arts or augury. The Jews buried the body, but the earth cast it forth, so they threw it in the well of the house, Copin's house. Meanwhile Hugh's distraught mother asked neighbors and Hugh's friends where her son was and learned that he had last been seen entering Copin's house. Entering suddenly herself, she saw the body in the well, went and cautiously summoned the bailiffs, and only broke into lamentations when she returned with them. Matthew's account of the actions of both the Jews and Beatrice implies that the body was discovered no more than fifteen days after the disappearance, that is by 15 July—yet Hugh did not even disappear until 31 July.

Matthew's account of what happened next is even more misleading.

Perhaps because he felt that prompt action against Jews who were so obviously guilty must have been taken before the king arrived, he says that when the body was found, one Sir John of Lexington, who was among the crowd attracted by Beatrice's lamentations, "a certain wise and prudent man, moreover of elegant learning," declared, "We have heard that Jews sometimes, to dishonor our crucified lord Jesus Christ, have not shrunk from such assaults." John then offered Copin, the Jew most threatened since the body had been found in his house, personal immunity if he would confess, obtained a confession, and kept Copin in chains until the king arrived. When Henry heard the confession, he was so horrified that he overrode the promise, had Copin drawn and hanged, and had the remainder of the Jews captured and taken to London.

It is a convincingly circumstantial description, complete with vivid dialogue, although we may wonder why more Jews were not arrested after Copin's confession. Jacobs also noted that all other accounts placed Lexington's intervention and Copin's confession after the king's arrival, but he concluded that Lexington had intervened when the body was discovered. Jacobs's suspicions were sounder than his conclusion, for John of Lexington was in fact far from Lincoln when the body was discovered. Matthew was more concerned with spinning a striking anti-Jewish yarn than with accuracy. What then did happen in the month between Hugh's disappearance and the discovery of his body?

The Waverley annals say nothing about public events prior to the discovery. Instead they record that Hugh was tortured and crucified at Lincoln by Jews who had incredible difficulties in disposing of the body. They threw it in a river, but the water continually cast it forth on dry land; they buried it, but to their horror they found the body above ground on the morrow; finally they threw it in a well of drinking water, but even then its presence was revealed by a light of heavenly splendor and the fragrant odor that filled the area. When these marvels led to the discovery of the body, its hands and feet were found to be perforated, around the head like a crown were punctures made by something pointed, and the whole body was covered with wounds. Plainly it was a Jewish crime, and we may note that it was the state of the body, not the well where it was found, that revealed a Jewish crime.

The Burton annals are more helpful. Here the basic story is that Hugh was seized by Jopin, prince and priest of the Jews of Lincoln, and starved for twenty-six days until he could barely utter a word.

Meanwhile, leading Jews from other communities were summoned, and when they arrived Hugh was crucified. Before killing him, the Jews also cut off the cartilage of his nose and upper lip and punctured him with sharp points until his skin was like the hide of a hedgehog. Knowing they were suspect, they carried the body out secretly on a stormy night and dropped it in a well where it would not incriminate them. While all this was going on, Beatrice made inquiries of her neighbors and Hugh's playmates and heard where he had last been seen, which made her suspect the Jews. Suspicions were increased (or initially aroused) by the presence of a large number of Jews from outside Lincoln. When asked, the Jews explained that they had come to celebrate a marriage in a prominent family. Very implausibly, but emphasizing the vengeful role of the mother, the annals say that Beatrice then went to Scotland to complain to Henry III, who ordered an investigation. When the body was discovered by searchers in a certain well, it was immediately believed that Hugh had been martyred by the Jews.

The Anglo-Norman ballad agrees so closely with the Burton annals but includes so much more local detail that both probably reflect the full version current in Lincoln. According to the ballad, Hugh was abducted by Peitevin (in fact an important Jew of Lincoln), but the crime took place in Copin's house, and it was Copin (who has never been reliably identified) who played the role of Judas, leading Hugh by a rope into the assembly and selling him, whereupon he was crucified. The Jews buried the body, but it reappeared and was then thrown in a privy. Fearful of discovery, however, the Jews had the body thrown in a well behind the castle by a Jew's former nurse. Here a woman found it the next day on the ground beside the well, so covered with ordure she could barely touch it. The body was inspected by the coroners and taken back to Lincoln. A converted Jew, Falsim (also unidentified and possibly fictitious), advised them to wash the body to discover the manner of death, and it was immediately recognized as a case of ritual murder by the wounds.

Without exception all versions agree that the body was found in or near a well, and all agree that the well was not in or appurtenant to a Jew's house—except Matthew Paris, whose story of the discovery is implausible on other grounds. Neither Copin nor any other Jew would have left the body of a Christian boy in a well on his property where anyone could enter and see it without being noticed by the household. Equally implausible is the picture of Beatrice restraining her crowd-gathering lamentations until she returned with the bailiffs. Why did

Matthew replace the fact that the body was found elsewhere by the fictitious drama of maternal discovery in the Jew's house?

One immediately remembers that in the two main versions, A and C, of the legend of the singing boy, including C 1, it is the mother who discovers her son in a Jew's house. Our suspicion that Matthew embellished his yarn with touches from the earlier legend is strengthened by his allegation that Hugh was disemboweled for augury or magical purposes, a striking detail conspicuously absent from all other accounts. Yet C 1 says, "For you see, cutting the innocent boy's belly in the form of a cross, they extracted his insides and threw them together with the body in a privy (cloacam)."[28] Whatever be the origin of Matthew's addition of a disembowelment, his assertion that Hugh's mother found her boy in the Jew's house had enduring influence, for it reappears in the ballad of "Sir Hugh" or "The Jew's Daughter," which otherwise bears little resemblance to any other account, and it supported the tourist trade in Lincoln in 1911. In the same year, the eleventh edition of the *Encyclopaedia Britannica* asserted that Hugh's body had been found in the well of a Jew's house, and in 1964 Roth repeated that the body had been found in a cesspool near Copin's house.

Matthew's motive for inventing the discovery in a Jew's house, like the motive for the miraculous irrepressibility of Hugh's body, was the problem of connecting concretely with Jews a body found in a wood (Norwich), in a river (Gloucester), in a cemetery (London), or in a well (Lincoln). The central plot of the Prioress's Tale is a solution to the embarrassing question of why the Jews had not been able to do something as simple as getting rid of the body where it would not directly incriminate them. Our most reliable account of Hugh of Lincoln, the Burton annals, is noteworthy because, without any reference to miracles, it acknowledges that the body was found far from Jews and explains, plausibly if unverifiably, that the Jews had disposed of the body secretly. The Waverley annals and the Anglo-Norman ballad, while acknowledging that where the body was found did not incriminate Jews, nonetheless insist on the miraculous difficulties the Jews faced in trying to dispose of the body. Matthew Paris, however, made doubly sure: he described the miraculous refusal of the body to stay buried, and then flatly falsified the known facts of the discovery—with enduring success.

We are not done with the well, however. All the accounts, even Matthew's, agree that Hugh's body was found in a well, not a privy.

The Waverley annals explicitly mention a well of drinking water, and the ballad of "Sir Hugh" has the body dropped in a well fathoms deep. Yet Jacobs and Roth state that the body was in a cesspool for many days! They may have been affected by Matthew's account, believing that a *puteus* in a house would be a privy rather than a well, but more probably they were influenced by the medieval association of Jews with privies. As we have seen, Innocent III in 1205 lent credence to the report that the body of a scholar had been found in the latrines of Jews in Paris. The 1215 version, C 1, of the legend of the singing boy has the body thrown into the Jews' privy, as do all other versions of group C save one, and as does Chaucer. And Matthew Paris's story of Abraham of Berkhamsted demonstrates the currency of the association in England. Yet the only contemporary account of Hugh of Lincoln to mention a privy is the Anglo-Norman ballad, which alleges that the body was temporarily secreted there, but acknowledges that it was discovered elsewhere. Either the author borrowed from the legend of the singing boy, or he simply yielded to the attraction of the current association. But Jacobs and Roth accepted the idea, and the privy of legend became part of the modern history of Hugh of Lincoln.

The next problem is whether Hugh died on 27 August or whether he died a month earlier, as Jacobs concluded. However embryonic medieval forensic medicine may have been, people should have been able to distinguish readily between a month-old and a two-day-old corpse, had they wanted to. The description of the state of the body and the holy odor around the well are suspicious. Very probably, the desire to accuse Jews, who could not have killed the boy before they had assembled, induced people to repress or falsify the state of the body, as had happened with Harold of Gloucester. His obviously very badly damaged body was found in the Severn after he had been missing for three weeks, yet he was said to have been killed by an unusual assemblage of Jews only shortly before the body was found. We may assume that 27 August was settled on as the day of Hugh's martyrdom because, although remote from Easter or Passover, it was a Friday, the Sabbath, and because a story of long suffering and recent death had the strongest emotional impact. In any case, when the damaged body was discovered, it was immediately believed that the boy had been ritually murdered.

That accusation was no novelty in England by 1255, nor was the next development novel. All accounts agree that as soon as the body was discovered and Jews accused by rumor, the canons of Lincoln promptly sought possession of the body. The Burton and Waverley annals and the Anglo-Norman ballad describe a miracle, which occurred either when the body was discovered or when it was being carried to the cathedral, and the joy of the city at this renewed proof of divine concern. When Richard of Gravesend, dean of Lincoln, and the canons heard what was going on, they came and demanded the body. Overriding the claim of the priest in whose parish Hugh had been raised, they bore the body back to the cathedral in solemn procession with song and candles and buried Hugh as a holy martyr near Grosseteste's tomb. Powerfully assisted by the popular thirst for a new source of supernatural succor, their effort to promote Hugh to the ranks of the martyrs was highly successful. Thereby the dean and canons confirmed the truth of the rumor with the weight of their authority, as had the monks of Norwich, Gloucester, and Bury St. Edmunds and the canons of St. Paul's. The impact of such ecclesiastical confirmation is evident from Matthew Paris's description of its importance in the case of the baby of St. Benet's cemetery in 1244. Doubtless the precipitous decision of the dean and canons stemmed from the same motives as the similar actions of their precursors, the desire to enhance the reputation and revenues of their church. When Chaucer described the bearing of the singing boy's body to the nearest abbey, he was merely reflecting standard English practice.

However surprising it may now seem, what happened for the next month also followed precedent. Although the shrine doubtless became the scene of further miracles, there is no evidence of any action by secular authorities until Henry III arrived on 4 October, nor even of any popular attacks. Matthew Paris's story of the immediate intervention of John of Lexington is a fabrication; he intervened only after the arrival of the king. The Burton annals state that, when Henry came to Lincoln, he ordered an investigation and the capture of the Jews. Those captured were interrogated "in diverse ways"; Lexington offered Copin personal immunity and obtained a written confession; but when Henry heard the horrible confession, he immediately had Copin executed. The Anglo-Norman ballad simply says that after the investigation had been ordered, a wise man who was there induced Copin to confess.

The results were immediate. Not only was Copin executed, but on 4 October Henry ordered the sheriffs of Norfolk, Suffolk, Kent, Sussex, and Hampshire and the wardens of the Cinque Ports to prevent any Jews from leaving the realm, to imprison any Jews who sought to cross the seas, and to inform the king of what they had done.[29] On 14 October, the king ordered that the Jews who had been guarded at Lincoln be dispatched to Westminster.[30] Henry acted as had no king of England before him, and what moved him to decisive action was the confession that John of Lexington presented to him. It is now time to introduce the knight whose tale brought tragedy to Jews and lasting fame for Hugh of Lincoln.

III

Who was Sir John of Lexington? Jacobs thought he was a canon of Lincoln, and Roth does not even mention him. Hill, although he felt that John had put the confession in Copin's mouth, failed to recognize a prominent local figure. Sir Maurice Powicke knew who he was but failed to discuss the Lincoln affair. Matthew Paris does not identify him in connection with Hugh of Lincoln, but does so elsewhere in his chronicle, as the index reveals. Yet John's identity has always been clearly revealed in that connection by the Burton annalist, who described him strikingly as "a wise and prudent man and learned in both laws, to wit, canon and civil"—and as the king's steward. John of Lexington was a major figure.

Tout felt that it would be going too far to regard him as the first lay keeper of the royal seal, since that was not his principal office; yet John was a real keeper who used the seal, not a mere custodian, and he held the seal for considerable periods.[31] He was active during the period of Henry III's personal government and was not simply a petty administrator. Powicke mentions Ranulf Brito, Lawrence of St. Martin, Geoffrey of Despenser, and John of Lexington as examples of the well-lettered knights and clerks who stayed most closely by the king and most influenced royal policy.[32] Yet despite John's prominence, the only historian to identify the royal favorite with the prosecutor of Jews has been William Hunt. His brief articles on the Lexingtons in the *Dictionary of National Biography* also reveal that John belonged to a remarkable Nottinghamshire family peculiarly connected with Lincoln Minster.[33]

Lexington (now Laxton) was a mere fifteen miles west of Lincoln, the center of a barony held by Matilda of Cauz from 1202 to 1224.[34] John's father, Richard of Lexington, seems to have been a relatively unimportant knight employed by King John on local matters and supported by Brian de Lisle. From 1204 to 1207, when he fell under royal displeasure, Richard was a forester and custodian of the manor of Lexington while that center of the barony was retained in John's possession, which was the price Matilda had to pay to avoid remarriage.[35] Although Hunt, following Dugdale, described Richard as a baron, he never achieved that prominence. But he and his wife produced two daughters and six sons, four of whom were to play significant roles in English and even Continental affairs: Robert, John, Henry, and Stephen.[36]

Robert of Lexington, cleric, rendered account for his father for the farm of Lexington in 1206 and 1207, and in 1210, now described as Brian de Lisle's clerk, he did the same for Brian.[37] Brian and Robert rendered account of their custody of the bishopric of Lincoln in 1212 and of the honor of Peverel in 1214.[38] In 1214, Robert had custody of the archbishopric of York.[39] After the tumultuous years from 1215 to 1217, Robert can be found active in the service of Hubert de Burgh and as a justice in eyre.[40] He rose rapidly in Henry III's service to become one of the foremost royal judges.[41] We need not follow his legal career further save to note that he was active as a judge in Lincoln in 1232 and again in 1240, when he and his fellow judges provoked Bishop Grosseteste's wrath for hearing capital cases on Sunday— dubious conduct for a man who, perhaps, nearly became a bishop.[42]

Robert had held a prebend at Southwell Minster, eight miles south of Lexington, since 1214, and by 1238, when he received an indulgence for pluralism, he was a canon of Salisbury. In 1239, according to the Dunstable annals, he was one of two men unsuccessfully elected to the see of Coventry and Lichfield. In 1241, he founded the first chantry at Southwell, at the altar of Thomas Becket, for the souls of King John and Brian de Lisle and of his own father, mother, brothers, and sisters, and all his benefactors.[43] He was paralyzed shortly before his death and died on 20 May 1250. Matthew Paris provided a fitting epitaph: 'Robert of Lexington, cleric, who, long remaining in the office of justice, acquired for himself a famous name and most ample possessions."[44] For Robert was the real founder of the family fortunes through royal favor and personal shrewdness.

By 1232 he had acquired considerable holdings around Lexington from Maud of Cauz, her heirs, and many others. In 1231 he had also acquired a manor at Tuxford, three miles north of Lexington, from Olive, daughter of Alan, and in 1233 he acquired her manor of Warsop (now Worksop), some ten miles northwest of Lexington. Nor were his acquisitions limited to Nottinghamshire. By 1229 he had land at the Peak in Derbyshire and had spread out into Oxfordshire, obtaining land at Horley and Hornton from Hugh Bardolf for a term of eight years, land which he held in fee by 1232.[45]

Some light on the character of such transactions is thrown by his dealings with John Joscelin. In 1230 Robert lent John fifty marks, in return for which Robert received John's manor of Aston for a term of twenty years. If John did not repay within a year, Robert was to have the land outright, subject to paying John an additional seventeen marks; but even if John repaid on time, Robert was to hold the manor for twenty years. By 1232 Robert held the land in fee from John.[46]

Since Robert died in 1250, he was not involved in the tragedy at Lincoln. Nor was Master Peter, probably the second son, who was apparently dead by 1248. A cleric, he was presented to half the church of Gedling by King John in 1206, received the Master's degree by 1237, and witnessed a family charter in 1241, but is not mentioned thereafter and was presumably dead when William of Lexington was presented to Gedling in 1248.[47] Nor was the youngest brother Stephen connected with the events of 1255, although he is a notable example of the family's talents. A canon of Southwell in 1214, he pursued studies at Paris and Oxford, fell under the influence of Edmund Rich, and became a Cistercian in 1221 together with seven companions; they were the last students from Oxford "to hear the call of Cîteaux."[48] He rose rapidly, becoming abbot of Stanley about 1225, abbot of Savigny in 1229, and abbot of Clairvaux in 1243. Here he aroused considerable controversy by his establishment of the college of Chardonnet at Paris for student monks from Clairvaux. He was deposed or resigned about 1257 and died at Ourscamp in 1260.[49]

Henry, the fourth brother, was also a cleric and hardly unsuccessful. Canon of Southwell by 1237, he had become treasurer of Salisbury by 1241, doubtless aided by his brother, Canon Robert. In 1245, however, he moved back to his native region to become dean of Lincoln and, on Grosseteste's death in 1253, was elected bishop and confirmed in 1254.[50] In 1256, he obtained a collective papal dispensation for pluralism for William of Lexington, for his nephews Stephen and Oliver of Sutton, and for his kinsman Richard of Sutton, three of whom very shortly appear as canons of Lincoln in the extant evidence: Richard of Sutton in 1257, Oliver in 1259, and William of Lexington in 1260.[51] Henry's brief episcopate was otherwise thoroughly unremarkable, save that while he was bishop his cathedral acquired a new saint in 1255, a fact worthy of more attention than it has received—which is none. He died in 1258, leaving his estate to his nephews William of Sutton and Richard of Markham, and was succeeded as bishop from 1258 to 1280 by Richard of Gravesend, the dean who had acted so promptly to acquire little Hugh's body.[52]

Before we come to John of Lexington himself, the connections revealed by the 1256 dispensation and Henry's heirs repay study. William of Lexington is not described as a relative of Henry in the 1256 dispensation or elsewhere, yet his connection with the Lexingtons and the Suttons was very close. Vicar of half the church of Rauceby in 1232, Master William of Lexington was rector of Waddun by 1245, when he received a dispensation for pluralism. He benefited from Henry of Lexington's collective dispensation in 1256, and was a canon of Lincoln by 1260. He became precentor and almost immediately after was elected dean in 1261 and confirmed in 1262. He was presented to the Lexington-Sutton church of Warsop in conflict with a royal nominee in 1268 and died in 1272.[53]

The tight connection between the Lexingtons and the Sutton family is already clear. Hervey of Sutton (Sutton-on-Trent, two miles southeast of Lexington) had three sons: Robert, Richard, and Roland.[54] Roland, an itinerant justice and possibly sheriff of Nottingham about 1230,[55] had married a sister of the Lexingtons, and they apparently had four sons, all therefore nephews of the Lexingtons: William, Robert, Stephen, and Oliver. William inherited part of Henry of Lexington's estate in 1258; when he died in 1268, it passed to his son Robert; and on Robert's death in 1274, it passed to his son Richard.[56] Roland's other son who remained a layman, Robert, apparently died in 1286, and his estate was administered by his brother, Stephen.[57]

Stephen, a cleric, was appointed to the church of Stanlegh in 1233, was one of those licensed to hold an additional benefice in 1256, and was a canon of York by 1268.[58] In 1272, on the death of William of Lexington, he was presented to Warsop by his nephew, Robert of Sutton the younger, the son of William, and when Robert died in 1274, Stephen bought custody of his lands and heirs from the royal escheator.[59] Stephen held Warsop until 1280, the year he became archdeacon of Northampton, and then, as custodian of Robert's estate, presented Nicholas of Apeltre to Warsop. In 1286, Nicholas acted as Stephen's attorney for the administration of the estate of Stephen's brother, the elder Robert.[60] Stephen died in 1290, and his nephew, Thomas of Sutton, succeeded him as archdeacon of Northampton.[61] In

1291, his brother, Bishop Oliver of Lincoln, granted indulgences for prayers for his brother's soul.[62]

Oliver of Sutton, who occasionally styled himself Oliver of Lexington up to 1259, was rector of Schalford in 1244, when he received a dispensation for pluralism, doubtless to support his studies at Oxford, where he had become a master by 1249 and was teaching in 1260. In 1256, however, he gained a further dispensation through Bishop Henry of Lexington and became a canon of Lincoln before July 1259, dean from 1275 to 1280, and bishop from 1280 until his death in 1299.[63] In 1282, he had custody of the lands and heirs of Robert of Sutton, junior, possibly because Stephen had relinquished the custody of their nephew after becoming archdeacon of Northampton. In 1268, Oliver had also been the executor of another Sutton, Canon Richard of Lincoln.[64]

This Richard of Sutton was a kinsman of Henry of Lexington and the son of Robert, for whose soul and the soul of his wife Alice, Richard had arranged prayers at Southwell in 1260.[65] The Robert in question was most probably Roland's son, in which case Richard was a nephew of William, Stephen, and Oliver of Sutton. In 1241, Richard received the prebend at Southwell formerly held by Henry of Lexington, and after he received a dispensation for pluralism in 1244, he was presented to Warsop in 1245 by John of Lexington.[66] After receiving a further dispensation through Henry of Lexington in 1256, he became a canon of Lincoln by 1259, when he was granted a royal license to hunt in the forests of Nottinghamshire and Northamptonshire.[67] After his death in 1268, his executor, cousin Oliver, established a chantry for him at Southwell, and his uncle Stephen succeeded him at Warsop.

These genealogical investigations, however tedious, are revealing. They show that the Lexington-Sutton connection accounted for four canons of Southwell and, between 1244 and 1280, for four canons, three deans, and two bishops of Lincoln. Indeed, the years from 1258 to 1262 saw Henry of Lexington as bishop, William of Lexington as dean, and Richard and Oliver of Sutton as canons. When we remember that four of the five Lexington brothers were clerics, it seems something of an understatement to say that the Lexington family had a clerical tendency and came to focus its ambitions on Lincoln Minster. The only known Lexington who did not become a cleric was John, and even he made a major contribution to the cathedral.

IV

John of Lexington is by far the most mysterious of the brothers. Almost certainly he was the second or third son, for he was Robert's heir, and Henry was his heir. Moreover, however unreliable the indication may be, Robert died in 1250, John in 1257,[68] Henry in 1258, and Stephen in 1260. If Robert was 20 when we first meet him acting for his father in 1206, he was born in 1186 and was 64 when he died. John was therefore probably about 45, certainly no less than 35, when we first hear of him in 1235. In October of that year, Henry III granted him twenty pounds annually from the exchequer until he could be provided with the equivalent in escheats or wardships.[69] He would seem to have been landless until 1237, when Robert granted him the lands he had acquired at Tuxford, Warsop, and, apparently, at Aston, Horley, and Hornton. Robert retained his holdings around Lexington and stipulated that his grants to John should revert to himself should John die without heirs.[70]

This landless man in his forties was rapidly given major responsibilities by Henry III. After minor duties in 1236, he and Peter Grimaud were ordered to Rome in 1237 as royal envoys and used later in that year as collectors of the thirtieth.[71] In July of 1238, John and Master Simon the Norman interposed an appeal before the archbishop of York about the election to Durham. In August, Henry sent John to the king of Scotland, asking that king to trust what John had to say on Henry's part. And in September, when Henry in anger took the seal from Ralph Neville, John may have been one of those entrusted with its custody.[72]

Unmentioned in the royal records prior to 1235, John became an important member of the royal household in his first three years of service. Where had he been before 1235? The character of his responsibilities confirms that he was indeed, as Tout put it, one of the "rare phemonena of that generation, the *miles literatus*, the knight who could read and write Latin."[73] But, as Tout did not realize, his assignments also suggest unusual familiarity with church matters and canon law, and we are reminded that Matthew Paris and the Burton annalist emphasize his learning, the latter even saying that he was learned in both laws. Given the educational and clerical bent of his family, this suggests that he might have been studying somewhere, but I have been unable to find any trace of him at Oxford, Paris, or Bologna prior to 1235. Between 1249 and 1254, he did make a grant to

his brother Stephen's controversial college of Chardonnet of half the
right of patronage in the church of Roderham, styling himself lord of
Aston.[74] The grant may indicate an interest in education aroused by
earlier studies in Paris, but that can only be speculation. The evidence
does suggest, however, that John may have spent some time at a major
center of learning, perhaps outside England and possibly with a clerical
career in mind, and that he may have returned to England in 1235 to
seek his fortune instead in royal service with the help of his brother
Robert.

Once launched, John proved quite capable of proceeding on his
own. The year 1239 finds him issuing writs of *liberate* and receiving
royal grants, for example, of free warren in his lands, of the right to
hold a weekly market and an annual fair at Warsop, and of freedom
for life from service as a justice or on regards, perambulations, assizes,
and the like.[75] From February to about November 1240, he and Simon, dean of Chester, were custodians of the county of Chester.[76] By
February of 1241 he had been sent with Masters Alexander of Parma
and John de Dya, and Nicholas of Boleville, to Rome for the general
council summoned by Gregory IX. On the way he joined his brother
Stephen, then abbot of Savigny, and was responsible for saving him
from death or imprisonment when Enzio and his Sicilians attacked the
Genoese clerical convoy. Matthew Paris, who records this item and
probably heard it from John himself, describes John on this occasion
as a most vigorous and elegant knight. In September John had returned
and was busy escorting hostages from Henry III's Welsh campaign
back to London.[77]

It was about this time that Stephen wrote to Robert, recommending
that Robert's younger brother, the knight, be encouraged to marry a
woman of good morals and suitable body, even if of mediocre possessions, rather than a sterile woman or one prone to miscarriages with
three or four times the land. Ironically, by 1242 John had married
Margery of Merlay, daughter of Richard of Umfraville, who brought
him land but no heirs and survived him by some thirty years.[78]

John was one of the four commissioners appointed by Henry in
1242 to supervise amendments of the truce with the king of France, a
truce which Henry sought to denounce in preparation for his proposed
campaign.[79] The truce was denounced, and John stayed with Henry
during the campaign in 1242 and 1243. He was authorized to receive
scutage from his knight's fees, was granted half a manor, and was
pardoned a debt of ten marks he owed to Leon, Jew of York.[80] While

in France, John became keeper of the seal for the first time from 7 July 1242 to an uncertain date, and again from 28 September 1242, probably until 12 August 1243, when he fell sick.[81]

John's activities after his return from France in 1244 and 1245 have left little trace.[82] But in January 1246 he and three others were commissioned to investigate royal administration in Chester and discover who had sided with the Welsh, which was so threatening to the men of Chester that many fled and had to be reassured by the king that the commissioners were not justices for all pleas. In the same year, when the English prelates assembled to consider Innocent IV's demand for a subsidy, John appeared before them with Master Lawrence of St. Martin to prohibit their making any grant.[83] On 19 September 1247, John again became keeper of the seal, apparently until 10 May 1248, when he left the court briefly.[84] He became keeper again from 15 October 1249 until 21 February 1250, when he left the court and the seal was committed to Peter des Rivaux and Master William of Kilkenny. John returned to the court and the seal on 28 May 1250, was away from the court briefly in April and left the court on 28 May 1250, giving up the seal for the last time, again to Peter and William.[85] He had held the seal intermittently for over a year in France and for a year and a half in England. In the latter period of his keepership, if not before, he was also steward of the household. He is referred to by that title on 8 December 1247, but the title drops from the records after June 1248.[86] Since titles were infrequently recorded, he may have remained steward until his appointment as justice of the forests beyond Trent in 1252, or until 1253 when he failed to accompany Henry on his Gascon expedition, although the Burton annals still speak of him as steward in 1255.[87]

In 1250, John had inherited the lands of his brother Robert, including Lexington, and his brother Henry had been dean of Lincoln since 1245. John's interests now seemed to have turned to the region of his birth. On 23 November 1252, he was appointed justice of the forests beyond Trent and, in 1253, keeper of the castles of Scarborough, Bamborough, and Pickering, offices he held until June of 1255, except for custody of Scarborough, which he only gave up in November.[88] And while the king was in Gascony from August 1253 to December 1254, John remained in England, occupied by his northern duties, which included considerable judicial work. He had received a grant in 1250 that acceptance of judicial office would not prejudice his prior privilege of exemption from such offices, and as early as September of 1250 we find him sitting as one of the justices for the pleas of London, and the following years find him active as a judge in the north.[89] Absence from court did not mean loss of royal trust, however, for between October 1254 and January 1255, John journeyed several times to Scotland to prepare for Henry III's coming interview with Alexander III, the minor king of Scotland, married to Henry's daughter, whose affairs were a matter of much interest to Henry.[90]

We have come again to the year 1255. That summer Henry III traveled north to meet Alexander, and as we would expect, John accompanied the king to the interview he had helped prepare. The king was at Newcastle from 24 August to 1 September, and on 29 August, a writ was issued there by Henry of Bath and John of Lexington.[91] On the day that little Hugh's body was discovered and carried to Lincoln cathedral, John was—despite Matthew Paris—a good hundred miles north of Lincoln. Moreover, on 1 September, assuredly in total ignorance of Hugh's fate, the king was already planning to be in Lincoln about 22 September.[92] After the interview at Wark-on-Tweed from 8 to 21 September, Henry journeyed south by way of Newcastle, Durham, York, and Pontefract. On 2 October he reached Scrooby, some thirty miles from Lincoln, and on 3 October he was at Laneham, ten miles from Lincoln and nine miles from Lexington. The following day he was at Lincoln, Copin was executed, and ninety-one Jews were imprisoned.[93] Since there is no evidence of previous secular action, one may wonder sadly whether the miscarriage of justice would have occurred had Henry III not passed through Lincoln that autumn with John of Lexington.

By 4 October little Hugh's shrine and the fantasy that justified it had had a month to take firm root. Bishop Henry of Lexington, Dean Richard of Gravesend, and the canons had obvious motives for not wishing to see the fantasy questioned and must have hoped that it might be strengthened. Strengthened it was. What distinguished the Lincoln affair from other accusations of ritual murder was that the king took personal cognizance and had one Jew executed immediately and eighteen others spectacularly executed later. That royal substantiation of the truth of the charge was probably decisive for Hugh's fame, which far overshadowed that of William of Norwich, Harold of Gloucester, Robert of Bury St. Edmunds, and the poor anonymous infant of St. Paul's.

Whether or not Henry was persuaded to investigate by John of Lexington, the king chose to entrust the investigation to John.[94] How

John extorted the confession from Copin remains mysterious, since the body was not found in his house as Matthew Paris alleges, nor does Copin seem to have been the leading Jew of Lincoln as the Burton annals declare. The statement in these annals that the Jews were interrogated "in diverse ways" is ominous but not explicit. Torture was not permitted by English law, but singularly violent interrogation has occurred in twentieth-century jurisdictions that do not authorize torture, and such a confession is inconceivable without massive intimidation. Yet both Matthew Paris and the Burton annalist, who diverge on so many other points, stress that Copin confessed because he was promised personal immunity. It sounds very much as if John had identified Copin as a particularly weak man who was so frightened by threats about what was going to be done to Jews that he would do anything to save himself.

What Copin confessed is revealed in broad outline in the chronicles: the kidnaping, the summons of other Jews, the parody of the Crucifixion, and the miraculous difficulty in disposing of the body. Any confession had to accord in all essentials with the fantasy that had surrounded Hugh's tomb with the odor of sanctity for over a month. Both John and Copin knew what that story was, so it is immaterial whether John elicited it by pointed questions or Copin proffered it. Indeed, Matthew Paris has Copin's confession begin with the all-too-revealing statement: "What the Christians say is true." Copin "confessed" a Christian fantasy.

Once John had obtained a written confession from a Jew, the fame of Lincoln's new saint was assured. The impact of the confession on Henry III has been described; it figures in different ways in all three chronicles and the Anglo-Norman ballad; and it must have been central in the subsequent judicial proceedings. After Copin's execution, ninety-one Jews were taken to the Tower and inquiries were made about those who had fled. On 22 November, eighteen Jews who had refused to submit to the verdict of a jury composed only of Christians were drawn through the streets of London before daybreak and hanged on specially constructed gallows. All three chronicles note the event, although the Waverley annalist thought that it was these Jews who had confessed. A London chronicle that pays no attention to the events at Lincoln gives a brief but vivid description of the execution— which must have strikingly spread Hugh's fame.[95]

The remaining seventy-three prisoners were reduced to seventy-one when two were released. At the instance of Garcias Martini, knight of

Toledo, Benedict son of Moses of London was pardoned in December because he had only been accused of complicity after the fact by the inquisition made by John of Lexington, had submitted himself to the verdict of a jury, and had been declared guiltless by Hugh's mother. He was a prominent scholar and the father of Belaset, very probably the unfortunate girl whose marriage had brought Jews to Lincoln and death in 1255. In January of 1256, John, a Jew who had converted to Christianity while in the Tower, was pardoned at the instance of John of Derlinton, a Dominican active at court.[96]

For the trial of the remainder, the king on 7 January 1256 ordered a jury of twenty-four local knights and twenty-four citizens of Lincoln to be at Westminster on 3 February.[97] The seventy-one were condemned to death together, apparently, with all Jews of England who had consented to the crime. But then, to the surprise and shock of many, either the Franciscans (according to Matthew Paris) or the Dominicans (according to the Burton annals) interceded, and the king's brother, Richard of Cornwall, to whom Henry had temporarily ceded his financial rights over Jews, intervened. In May the remaining seventy-one were liberated.

Since these Jews had not converted and had, in Matthew Paris's words, "been found guilty by the jury according to the assertion of the Jew first hanged at Lincoln," doubt must have developed about their guilt. The friars would not have intervened unless they had believed the charge false. And although Richard of Cornwall may not have wished the economic condition of English Jews weakened, it is very dubious that he would have tried to save the seventy-one had he genuinely believed them guilty of crucifying a Christian child.[98] Moreover, Henry III's own belief must have weakened, for he alone had the authority to free them. Apparently once the initial excitement had died down, cooler heads had introduced a note of skepticism and, at the least, dispelled belief in a general Jewish conspiracy. Indeed, what is strange is that the king and his advisers had ever believed the charge in the first place. Educated men in high authority had not generally been receptive to the more outrageous accusations against Jews. No king, other than Henry III, had ever executed Jews for ritual murder, and Frederick II and Innocent IV had already officially declared their disbelief in the related blood libel.

Significantly, however, the crucifixion accusation had never been officially rejected. When Frederick II in 1236 denied the truth of the blood accusation raised at Fulda, no question of crucifixion was involved. When Henry III at Frederick's request sent two converts for the investigation of the charge, Henry remarked that he had never heard of an accusation like that at Fulda.[99] Since England then gloried in three shrines to supposed victims of ritual murder, he can only have been distinguishing the blood libel sharply from the crucifixion accusation. Innocent IV did so also.

In reaction to the horrible tragedy at Valréas in 1247,[100] Innocent produced the first papal pronouncement on ritual murder. He was some 125 miles north at Lyons at the time and knew that Jews had been accused of attempting both a crucifixion and a communion with human blood. He had also received a complaint from the Jews of Germany in 1247 that wherever a body was found Jews were accused of cannibalism and other imaginary crimes.[101] Yet when, in consequence, he officially forbade all the faithful to make false accusations against Jews, the only accusation specifically prohibited was that Jews shed human blood in their rites.[102] He said nothing about what was still the best-known charge, the accusation that Jews crucified Christian children. That charge was supported by four shrines and had just been raised anew at Valréas and apparently corroborated there by confessions obtained from Jews through torture during the investigation conducted by two Franciscans. Then and for centuries to come, churchmen were not prone to exculpate Jews from a charge of crucifixion, and Innocent's silence could easily be interpreted as tacit permission to continue crucifixion accusations.[103] Henry III and his advisers doubtless knew of Innocent's prohibition of the blood accusation, but its formulation was so narrow that Henry would not be inhibited by religious scruples in 1255.

The absence of any papal condemnation of the crucifixion fantasy may have been decisive for the nineteen executed Jews, for Henry III was a man who eagerly sought ecclesiastical support and divine favor to bolster his self-esteem.

> His nature was resilient and his moods of pious exaltation were frequent, seeking divine sanction for his rapid changes. A later chronicler, whose evidence is confirmed by the casual remarks of others, wrote of Henry: "The less he was clever in his actions within this present world the more he indulged in a display of humility before God. On some days he heard mass three times, and as he longed to hear even more masses, he had them celebrated privately."[104]

Powicke has also depicted Henry as a suspicious person who flung charges of treason recklessly, was credulous and poor in judgment, and often appeared like a petulant child.[105] When to these qualities we add his addiction to touring the shrines of England, it becomes easier to understand why he acted as he did, both when he heard Copin's confession and when the friars and cooler heads intervened later. Yet even Henry might not have believed the accusation initially had not a learned man he trusted presented him with a written confession.

Whichever road we take to Lincoln in October 1255, we meet John of Lexington at the crossroads by Copin's gallows. We shall never know whether he himself believed the tale he told the king. He had been at court when Henry III wrote to Frederick II about the Fulda accusation, and he was keeper of the seal in 1247 when Innocent IV promulgated the new prohibition of the blood accusation. He was a learned man whose horizon was European, and he had had considerable judicial experience. Yet he supported an accusation that was practically unsupported by evidence. Hugh's body had been found in a place that did not inculpate Jews, and nothing but the suggestions of neighbors and children, proffered amid the suspicions aroused by the presence of an unusual number of Jews, connected Hugh in any way with Jews. We may be sure that had there been any solid evidence that Hugh had last been seen entering a Jew's house, there would have been decisive action against Jews long before the king's arrival two months later. John conducted the investigation himself and must have known better than anyone how flimsy the evidence was, and how strangely the accusation resembled the legends of Norwich and Gloucester. He must also have interrogated several Jews before he found Copin, the weak reed, and it is hard to believe that he did not recognize that Copin was either insanely spiteful or a man so frightened that he would say anything to try to save himself.

A strong case can be made that John did not believe the confession but sought to bolster the reputation of the new saint in his brother's cathedral. Yet by the same token, he must have wanted to believe the fantasy, to overcome his doubts if only he could find some confirmation. His was a very ecclesiastical family with strong local ecclesiastical interests, and the most impressive support for the fantasy to date had come from local ecclesiastics at Norwich and other places who had sought new saints. He himself was an unusually clerkly knight and a ready believer in new local saints and their miracles. Matthew Paris cites John, "a man of great authority and knowledge," as his authority for the miracles attributed to Thomas of Hereford, archdeacon of Northampton, who died in August 1253 and was buried in a Carmelite

house.[106] With these motives and beliefs, John may well have suppressed any skepticism and sought vigorously only for confirmation. A
third possibility is that intially he wanted no more than a confirming
confession but was overtaken by Henry's credulity, was then forced to
rationalize his deed, and ended by believing the story himself. For if,
as is quite possible, Hugh fell by misadventure into a well, the only
murder in the Lincoln affair was the judicial murder of nineteen Jews
caused by John of Lexington.

Whatever John thought, what he did powerfully affected those predisposed to think evil of Jews then and for centuries to come. He
incited the weakly credulous Henry III to give the ritual murder fantasy
the blessing of royal authority, and he inspired Matthew Paris to write
a vivid garbled yarn that would ring in men's minds for centuries and
blind modern historians. A century and a half later, Geoffrey Chaucer,
after letting the legend of the singing boy slip from the prioress's lips,
would inevitably be reminded of England's most famous proof of Jewish evil and conclude with an invocation to young Hugh—whose alleged fate neither he nor his audience was likely to question.[107] John
of Lexington died in January of 1257, and his elegant learning will not
be described in any history of medieval thought, yet his tale of young
Hugh of Lincoln became a strand in English literature and a support
for irrational beliefs about Jews from 1255 to Auschwitz. It is time he
received his due credit.

11.
Ritual Cannibalism

I

The famous German monastery of Fulda was founded in 744 by
Sturmi, a follower of St. Boniface, and it was there that Boniface was
buried after his martyrdom in 754. Fulda's English connections were
renewed in the reign of Charlemagne, since its abbot, Hrabanus Maurus, was a pupil of Alcuin. By then, Fulda was a highly favored imperial abbey, blessed with great immunities and some fifteen thousand
hectares of land[1] that stretched from the Alps nearly to the North Sea.[2]
Although independent of episcopal authority, its land fell mostly
within the diocese of Würzburg but partly in the diocese of Mainz,
whose cathedral was about a hundred miles to the west. And as Hrabanus's name would remind us, Fulda was one of the two great centers
of learning in Germany, the other being Reichenau. In addition to its
excellent collection of biblical and patristic manuscripts, it possessed
so many works of classical and late classical authors that Laistner felt
its role in the transmission of classical and postclassical Latin writers
might fairly be called "unique."[3]

By the twelfth century, Fulda's scholarly fame had declined, but it
retained its riches, and its secular importance continued to increase. In
1220, its abbot Kuno, along with twenty-eight other abbots and ab-
besses, was raised to the rank of prince of the empire with high justice
over all the lands of Fulda, subject only to appeal to the emperor.[4]
That jurisdiction was exercised over the town of Fulda, which Abbot

Markward I had established around 1160 and which had grown considerably by the early thirteenth century. Outside the town walls, on the river Fulda, there were several mills, and on Christmas Day of 1235 the miller of one of these mills and his wife went to church in the town. While they were gone, their mill burnt down and the bodies of their five sons were found in the ruins. It was a sad day for the miller and his wife, but much sadder for the thirty-four Jews who lived in Fulda and for millions of Jews thereafter.

According to the Dominican annalist at Erfurt,[5] some 60 miles to the northeast of Fulda as the crow flies, the Jews of Fulda were accused of killing the boys; they confessed that two of them had killed the boys and drawn off their blood into waxed bags; and on 28 December 1235, thirty-four Jews were cruelly killed. According to the Erfurt annalist, they were killed by crusaders, but the more distant annalist of Marbach, some 120 miles south, wrote that they were killed by the citizens of Fulda.[6] And while the Erfurt annalist had given no explanation of why the Jews had wanted the blood, the more distant Marbach annalist reported that the Jews had drawn the blood *ad suum remedium*, an ambiguous word which could have been used with either religious or medicinal connotations.

The annalist of Marbach apparently wrote his account somewhat later, for his account is inextricably combined with later events at Hagenau, some 70 miles from Marbach. He informs us that in order to incite the emperor to act against the crime, the boys' bodies were brought from Fulda to the great imperial castle at Hagenau, a distance of at least 150 miles. That the bodies were brought to Hagenau is supported by the later, highly garbled account of Richer of Sens, which says nothing about either blood or Fulda. According to Richer, the Jews of Hagenau had killed three seven-year-old Christian boys whom they had treated too roughly in some mockery during Passover. Since the emperor was not then at Hagenau, the Christians who had discovered the crime waited until he came back and then brought the bodies before him, but Frederick II only said, "If they are dead, go bury them, for they aren't good for anything else."[7]

In fact, as we know from Frederick's own words, because of books he had read and Jewish converts he knew, he did not believe the charge. Nonetheless, because rumors were flying around Germany, he summoned the magnates of the empire to discuss the charge. Since they expressed diverse opinions, he then sent letters to the kings of Europe, asking them to send converts from Judaism to Christianity to determine the truth.[8] He did all this very quickly, for on 24 February 1236 Henry III of England wrote back to Frederick, remarking that he had never heard of such a crime before.[9]

When the converts Frederick had requested assembled in Germany in the spring of 1236, they declared that both the Bible and the Talmud made clear that Jews were not greedy for human blood, but rather considered any blood to be polluting, and human blood even more so. Nor, as they commented acutely, would Jews endanger themselves by such conduct. Frederick then proclaimed the accusation false. In July of 1236 at Augsburg, Frederick issued the famous imperial bull that extended to all Jews of Germany the privileges granted by Frederick I to the Jews of Worms, and which categorized the Jews of Germany as serfs of the imperial chamber. At the end of the privilege, he reported the results of his investigation, absolved the Jews of Fulda and Germany of the charge against them, and forbade any cleric or layman to make such accusations against Jews in the future.[10] But that did not stop the accusations.

In March of 1247, the Jews of Valréas on the French boundary of the empire were accused, apparently by two Franciscans, both of crucifying a child and of taking its blood for ritual purposes.[11] Several Jews were tortured and many killed. The survivors appealed to the pope; and on 28 May 1247, Innocent IV condemned the persecution in strong language.[12] Then, on 5 July 1247, he responded to the pleas of the Jews in Germany who were being attacked in various localities because they were alleged to share the heart of a murdered child while solemnizing Passover. Innocent declared the accusation false,[13] and four days later, on 9 July, he reissued the general papal bull of protection for Jews with a new addition. Noting that Jews had been killed at Fulda and in several other places because they were accused of using human blood in their religious rites, he expressed his disbelief and strictly forbade such accusations in the future.[14] We should note, however, that if he forbade the accusation of ritual cannibalism, he said nothing about the older myth of English origin that accused Jews of ritually crucifying a Christian child each year, even though that accusation had also been made at Valréas. Moreover, since Thomas of Cantimpré would assert some years later that the Jews took blood for medicinal purposes,[15] it should also be emphasized that the new German accusation that had moved the emperor and the pope to action had nothing to do with medicine. The original accusation was that Jews engaged in a form of ritual cannibalism, an accusation soon connected with their rites at Passover.

II

The events at Fulda had a wide impact. They engaged the attention of the highest authorities in Europe at the time, and the blood libel they initiated would pursue Jews to the twentieth century. Modern historians, however, have paid surprisingly little attention to them. The silence of non-Jewish historians is not surprising, since, in general, they have long and lamentably been little interested in examining accusations against Jews. What requires explanation is the lack of attention by Jewish historians. So far as I know, the only Jewish historian to give any specific explanation of why Jews were accused of ritual cannibalism in Germany in 1235 was that outstanding historian, Georg Caro. But Caro did not stress the novelty of the charge or try to explain its character. He only suggested that the struggle between Frederick II and his son Henry and the proclamation in Germany at that time of crusades against both Moslems and heretics must have inflamed people's emotions and excited them to accuse Jews of ritual murder.[16]

Most Jewish historians, because of their particular perspective, did not even see a problem. Most of the historiography on the blood libel was written in the nineteenth and early twentieth centuries by Jewish historians in central Europe who heavily influenced all later Jewish historians. Since those earlier historians were Ashkenazim, most familiar with the medieval history of Germany and of Jews in Germany, they tended to interpret what happened elsewhere in medieval Europe in the light of what they knew had happened in Germany.[17] And since the typical German accusation of ritual murder was that of ritual cannibalism, they thought of all accusations of ritual murder, including the crucifixion accusations in England and France which had preceded the Fulda accusation, as the *Blutbeschuldigung* or Blood Libel. They were doubtless strengthened in that conviction by their knowledge that Jews in the time of the Temple had been accused of ritual cannibalism; that Christians in the second century and Christian heretics in the twelfth century had also been accused of ritual cannibalism; and that such accusations still threatened Jews in their own time. The paradoxical result of that fixation on the blood libel, however, was that the accusation at Fulda did not seem that novel or important to them.

If you consult *The Universal Jewish Encyclopedia*, you will read under the rubric "Blood Accusation" that "in the twelfth cent. the blood accusation flared up in England, and spread from there all over Europe. The earliest case was that of William of Norwich." The only reference to Fulda is a passing one: "The notion of the healing or curing properties of blood, a basis of some of the medieval blood murder accusations (e.g. Fulda, 1235) is an old one."[18] Even Baron, perhaps because he was born and educated in Germany, erroneously assumed in 1967 that the accusation against the Jews of Inmestar about 416 was a blood libel and continued, "But after 416 . . . this libel went underground to reappear against the Jews of Norwich in 1144." He assumed, also without warrant, that the cases at Gloucester and Blois were blood libels. Fulda was important for him only because of Frederick II's investigation and condemnation of the blood libel.[19] Even Solomon Grayzel, who certainly should have known better, asserted that the charge that Jews used the blood of Christians for ritual purposes "made its first appearance in 1144 in Norwich" and "caused the destruction of the Jewish community in Blois, France, in 1171."[20]

In the recent *Encyclopaedia Judaica*, all ritual murder accusations are still discussed in the entry for "Blood Libel" — which takes up more space than the entry for "Blessings and Curses." And there Haim Ben-Sasson still informs us that "the first distinct case of blood libel against Jews in the Middle Ages [was] that of Norwich in 1144." Although Ben-Sasson could not avoid recognizing that crucifixion had played a central role in the accusations before Fulda, he nonetheless thought of those accusations as blood libels and confused the issue yet further by stating that "the crucifixion motif explains why the blood libels occurred at the time of Passover." As for Fulda, despite the imperial and papal assertion that Jews had been accused of cannibalism for ritual purposes, he only tells us that "in the blood libel of Fulda (1236) another motif comes to the fore: the Jews taking blood for medicinal remedies."[21] Thus, for him as for many others, what distinguished the events at Fulda from other cases was only the accusation — which was not in fact the original accusation at Fulda — that the Jews used the blood they took for medical purposes and the fact that the incident had inspired Frederick II to investigate and condemn the fantasy.

There is little excuse for such historiography. In a famous book that appeared first in 1891 and in final form in 1909 as *The Jew and Human Sacrifice*, Hermann Strack, the courageous Regius Professor of

Theology of Berlin University, emphasized with italics that "it should be carefully noted, that *even in the case of the twelfth century, the utilization of Christian blood* by the Jews *is not mentioned by any ancient writers.*" He repeated the point a hundred pages later: "We read nothing about a Jewish blood ritual for much longer than a thousand years, till right into the thirteenth century. It is mentioned for the first time in 1236 on the occasion of the Fulda case ... but then already as being generally believed in Germany."[22] The same point was made in 1943 by an American historian, Joshua Trachtenberg, who discussed the twelfth-century cases in England and France at some length and demonstrated unambiguously that they did not involve a blood libel, and that "the collecting of blood was first mentioned in a case at Fulda in 1235," although unfortunately he did not try to explain why the libel arose there and then.[23] In 1954, moreover, Cecil Roth, doubtless because he was thoroughly familiar with the earlier English cases and knew they did not involve the blood libel, noted in a passing comment in his general history that the blood accusation had only appeared after the earlier crucifixion accusations.[24]

Strack's, Trachtenberg's, and Roth's recognition of the novelty of the charge at Fulda had, however, little influence on Jewish historiography in general, perhaps because of a desire to make Jewish identity universal and to make the uniformity of Christian reactions bear witness to that unique and universal identity. As a result, in most general histories of the Jews, as in Jewish encyclopedias, what is thoroughly obscured is that, from the medieval creation of the ritual murder charge against Jews in 1150 right down to 1235, for nearly a century, Jews in England and northern France were accused of crucifying Christian children, but not of ritual cannibalism. Even more completely camouflaged is the fact that no accusations of ritual murder of any kind were made in Germany until 1235, and that when the accusation did appear its form was strikingly novel. It is true that between 1146 and 1235 Jews in Germany were several times accused of killing Christians of various ages, and were attacked on that ground, but there is no evidence of any accusation of ritual murder before 1235.[25] In 1235, however, Jews in Germany were indeed accused of ritual murder, but not a crucifixion. The accusation was the novel one of ritual cannibalism, and it was made at Christmas, not at Easter or Passover.

III

Once we recognize how novel the accusation of ritual cannibalism against medieval Jews was, and only then, an obvious and long neglected question arises: Why did that accusation first appear at that time and place? So long as the Fulda case was seen as but one example of an enduring fantasy about Jews, the question could not arise. All that seemed needed was a very general explanation about the significance of blood and Christian reactions to Jews. Even Strack, who emphasized that Fulda was the first medieval instance of the blood accusation, was content to explain the charge at Fulda—as elsewhere—by a long and fascinating disquisition on the religious, magical, and medicinal properties attributed to blood throughout the ages. He pointed out that such beliefs had often led people throughout the ages to believe that outgroups they mistrusted secretly killed members of the ingroup and used their blood, as the Romans had alleged about Christians in the second century and as Catholics had alleged about heretics in the twelfth century. Yet whatever the polemical value of Strack's argument to refute those who still believed in the fantasy at the end of the nineteenth century, his explanation—and Trachtenberg's explanation is little different—is thoroughly inadequate on several grounds.

A general history of beliefs about the powerful properties of blood through the centuries cannot explain why the first medieval accusation of ritual cannibalism against Jews was made then and there. While the widespread existence of such beliefs was a necessary condition for what happened, their existence is thoroughly inadequate to explain why medieval Jews were first accused of ritual cannibalism in Germany at Fulda in 1235 and not earlier or elsewhere. Nor, similarly, will it help to talk about Jewish customs at Passover and Christian perceptions of them, for those customs had been practiced for centuries before 1235, and the charge arose at Christmas.

We cannot examine the vast and diverse folklore about blood and suggest explanations for it here. I can only indicate my perspective. People in the Middle Ages knew little reliably about blood, save that it was necessary for life, and most of what they believed about it was false. Blood was therefore vital but mysterious, and when they used the term for more than the observable fluid itself, they used it primarily as a symbol or metaphor to emphasize the importance of other things which they desperately wanted—relations which they believed vital for the continuity of their life and identity—or to express what they felt as fundamental threats to their life and identity. So strong, indeed, was this symbolic sense that blood itself, like the bones of saints, was often used, not in conformity with its observable characteristics, but in conformity with its symbolic associations. Hence the many and diverse medieval beliefs about the medicinal and magic properties of blood.

Yet if a diversity of beliefs about the medicinal and magical properties of blood abounded in thirteenth-century Europe, one kind of belief about blood was common throughout Europe. This belief differed radically from the medical and magical lore in that the power the belief attributed to the blood was not corporeal or of this world; it was spiritual and eschatological. Almost all Christians believed that salvation could be obtained only by the blood of Christ; all were officially commanded so to believe; and the ritual that provided that necessary blood, the Eucharist, was the central and most frequently performed rite in medieval Europe. Not only that, but even before the thirteenth century, attention on the Eucharist had come to focus primarily on the moment at which the bread and wine were consecrated as the body and blood of Christ.

There were, nonetheless, many who did not believe that any real blood was present in the Eucharist. In the ninth century, Radbertus and Ratramnus had debated as to whether believers actually partook of the historical blood of Christ, but it was only in the eleventh century that the denials of heretics and the theses of Berengar of Tours provoked widespread discussion and debate about the reality of the blood. And only then were those considered heretics accused of engaging in a literal form of ritual cannibalism. The speed and unanimity with which Berengar's views were condemned by ecclesiastics and the immense intellectual effort devoted thereafter to developing the theories of consubstantiation and transubstantiation indicate how important belief in the ritual consumption of Christ's real blood was for the status of the sacramental priesthood. The vigor of the reaction also testifies to ecclesiastical awareness of the menace of the mounting pressure of doubt.[26]

Of course, most Christians, yearning for salvation, believed firmly that the wine really became the blood of Christ, or they earnestly sought to repress doubts with the help of host miracles. But others such as the Petrobrusians did not. And though such doubts were condemned as heretical and the doubters extirpated or driven under-

ground by the rapidly increasing strength of the institutional church
and by the declaration of transubstantiation as dogma in 1215, doubts
remained and their existence was known. If outwardly conforming but
doubting theologians, clerics, and lay people tried to keep their doubts
secret, one widely known group did not. From the middle of the
twelfth century, the Cathars emphatically denied the efficacy of the
Eucharist and the value of Christ's blood. By the end of the century,
their numbers had increased dramatically. And though they were dec-
imated by the Albigensian Crusade, the effort to eliminate them was
only partially successful by 1235. Moreover, the massive campaign
against them had made many more people, particularly the higher
clergy and new mendicant orders, acutely aware of the Cathars and
their beliefs. Nonetheless, despite all that concern with symbolic ritual
cannibalism and doubts about it, neither in Languedoc, where Jews
were numerous, nor elsewhere were Jews accused of ritual cannibalism
before 1235.

IV

Thus far and no further can we get with generalities about blood
lore and ritual cannibalism. They cannot explain the emergence of the
accusation at Fulda at that time. For that, as Caro suggested, we must
return to the troubled Germany of Frederick II. A central issue of the
first half of Frederick's reign was his crusading intentions. He had
taken the Cross in 1215, but his numerous postponements complicated
his uneasy relations with popes Honorius III and Gregory IX, and it
was as an excommunicate that he finally sailed for the Holy Land in
1228. While he was absent, Gregory IX organized an invasion of Sicily, and Frederick's crowned son Henry was preparing to rebel in Germany. Frederick returned in 1229, regained full control in Italy, was
absolved in 1230, but only returned to Germany to subdue his son in
1235.

If Germany was politically unsettled around 1235, the crusade
against the Moslems was also much on people's minds. Innocent III,
Honorius III, and Gregory IX had done all they could to ensure that
it would be. They had commissioned prominent ecclesiastics whose
loyalty they could trust and of whose abilities they were confident to
preach the crusade.[27] Increasingly prominent among these was the ascetic Conrad of Marburg in Thuringia, not far from Fulda. Conrad of
Marburg was either a secular cleric closely related to the Praemon-

stratensians or a Praemonstratensian.[28] He may have first attracted papal attention by his preaching against heresy just after 1200.[29] In any case, he was charged in 1216 with preaching the crusade in the dioceses of Bremen and Trier, and in the following years he preached the crusade ever more widely, while also acting as a papally appointed arbitrator.[30]

In 1224, crusading emotions became particularly strong in Thuringia and Hesse, when Ludwig IV, the powerful landgrave of Thuringia, decided to take the Cross and Conrad, the most influential preacher of crusade, became closely connected with Ludwig's court. Conrad's relations with the court became even closer in 1226 when Ludwig's wife and the mother of their three children, the eighteen or nineteen-year-old Elisabeth of Hungary, swore obedience to Conrad as her father confessor and promised eternal chastity should her husband die on the crusade.[31]

I cannot examine Conrad's relations with Elisabeth here, including his extremely harsh treatment of her after her husband's death in September of 1227, when Conrad acquired complete authority over her at the hospital founded at Marburg. That treatment has frequently been condemned, yet it should be remembered that even before she met him, Elisabeth had been highly attracted to the new piety of poverty and had a Franciscan confessor, and that it was she who chose Conrad as her confessor. That said, it remains true, as Elisabeth herself declared, that he enforced his will on her so completely and dealt with her so severely that the only person she feared more was God himself.[32] It is also true that after she died on 17 November 1231, worn out at age 24, and as miracles immediately occurred around her body, Conrad rapidly wrote to Gregory IX to obtain her canonization, which was proclaimed in May of 1235.[33]

Conrad's name is inextricably tied to Elisabeth's fame, but between 1226 and 1231, while she was still alive, he could not spend all his time with the saint he was molding, for he traveled widely preaching. In January of 1227, Honorius III had announced that the impending crusade would depart in August and had written directly to Conrad, among others, commanding him to preach the crusade.[34] On 12 June 1227, the new pope, Gregory IX, wrote to Conrad, praising his prior pursuit of heretics and urging him to increase his efforts with the help of others whom he could choose.[35] Gregory also commissioned him in June as a visitor and reformer of both the regular and secular clergy of Germany.[36] On 20 June 1231, Gregory IX commanded all German prelates to intensify their campaign against heresy, and on 11 October

1231 he wrote to Conrad praising his efforts, urging him on, and granting him the authority to judge heretics himself,[37] an authorization sometimes seen as the origin of the papal inquisition.

We shall never know what Elisabeth's death in November of 1231 meant to Conrad, but it ended what was probably the most intense personal relation he had known as an adult. In any case, nothing now distracted him from preaching against the alleged heretics, and every history of heresy or the Inquisition tells what happened. In March of 1232, Frederick II ordered the secular authorities in Germany to support the ecclesiastical campaign against heresy.[38] On 29 October 1232, Gregory IX declared a crusade against the Stedingers in the province of Bremen, whom he accused, amongst other horrible things, of mistreating the Eucharist and crucifying clerics.[39] Although the poor peasants were apparently not in fact heretics but rebels against the worldly ambitions of the archbishop of Bremen, the reports sent the pope must have been imaginatively frightening—albeit it took little to excite Gregory about heresy. Indeed, on the same day that he called for a crusade against the Stedingers, he also wrote to the archbishop of Mainz commanding him and those he commissioned to seek out the heretics in the province and deal with them according to what had recently been promulgated concerning heretics.[40]

The heretics that the archbishop of Mainz, the bishop of Hildesheim, and Conrad of Marburg were to pursue were completely separate from the Stedingers; and in March of 1233 the provincial council of Mainz deplored the heresy in their own province.[41] Unfortunately, we do not have the letters that reported what they had found to Gregory IX, but we can be sure that they were luridly alarming. On 10 June 1233, Gregory wrote to Conrad that he had been greatly shocked to hear that those whom the blood of Christ had redeemed were held captive by the Devil. He commanded a crusade with indulgences against the heretics, and he authorized Conrad to grant absolution to those excommunicated for acts of violence and arson while fighting for God—provided their excesses were not too enormous![42] Immediately thereafter, from 11 to 14 June, Gregory sent letters about this alarming heresy to Frederick II, his son King Henry, the archbishop of Mainz, the bishop of Hildesheim, Conrad of Marburg, and all the bishops of the province of Mainz.[43]

This is the famous bull, *Vox in Rama*, which figures prominently in Russell's study of medieval witchcraft and in Cohn's fascinating analysis of the transmission of fantasies of devil worship and witchcraft.[44] In that work, Cohn traced the origins of the witchcraft charge back to the obviously similar fantasies that had attributed promiscuous orgies and ritual cannibalism to Christians in the second century, to the Montanists in the fifth century, to the Paulicians in the eighth century, and to the Bogomils in the eleventh century. The path then switches to western Europe in the eleventh century, where similar orgies, cannibalism, and devil worship were attributed by Adhemar of Chabannes and Paul of Saint-Père of Chartres to those burnt as heretics at Orléans in 1022, fantasies which Walter Map happily retailed at the end of the twelfth century.

The high point of the literary transmission of these chimerical fantasies in the thirteenth century was their papal acceptance in *Vox in Rama*. Thanks to Conrad and his associates, and to his own predilections, the pope believed that in the province of Mainz and elsewhere, many people engaged in those nocturnal rituals involving toads, cats, an ice-cold thin man, the Devil, and incestuous orgies with which we are all—if only intellectually, I hope—familiar. *Vox in Rama* does not, however, describe horrific ritual cannibalism; it contents itself with the charge that each year, when these heretics received the consecrated hosts from the priest, they kept them in their mouths and then threw them in the latrine. The Continuator of Trier also reports that the alleged heretics did not believe in the body of Christ, or that they believed that bad priests could not confect it and that it could be confected by anyone, man or woman, ordained or not ordained.[45]

These, then, were the fantasies on the basis of which Conrad executed an unknown but large number of people as heretics between 1231 and 1234. And if official documents do not describe how Conrad conducted his search, the chronicles do. Conrad, soon aided by Conrad of Tors, a Dominican, and John, a layman without an eye and an arm, would go from place to place, followed by a crowd of unnamed, and probably primarily rustic, supporters. Inquiry would be made, accusations heard, and those accused would be given no chance to defend themselves. The only choice offered was that of confessing heresy, accusing others as associates, and repenting or being burnt. And the sole judge of the validity of the accusations he sought was Conrad himself.

As Patschovsky has recently argued, most of the charges against Conrad's victims were what churchmen had come to believe were the beliefs and practices of the Cathars. And it may be, as Patschowsky has also argued, that the procedures wherewith Conrad pursued his victims were not illegal in the light of the early development of inquisi-

torial practice. They did, however, violate all customary German procedures and were seen as shocking and frightening.[46] Most frightening
was the authority granted the inquisitor to evaluate the validity of
accusations by himself without any defense from the accused, an authority which Conrad used without restraint or insight.

From his predilection for preaching campaigns against evil, whether
external or domestic, from his treatment of St. Elisabeth, and from the
lack of restraint with which he pursued his inquisitorial activities, it
would seem that Conrad had what is known as an authoritarian personality, a personality that cannot tolerate ambiguity, sees things only
in black and white, and is incapable of compromise. In our day we
might think of him as one of those dictatorial and ambitious gurus
with whom we are all too familiar. And like them, Conrad did not
know when to stop. He began to accuse nobles, which finally led the
archbishops of Mainz, Cologne, and Trier to try to get him to conduct
himself more moderately and discreetly. He refused, and in 1234 King
Henry and the imperial princes wrote to Gregory IX, asking him to
restrain Conrad.[47]

Gregory, obsessed with heresy, would doubtless have refused, but
others restrained Conrad in the most decisive way possible. After Conrad had accused an important noble, the count of Seyn, the count
appealed to the archbishop of Mainz. The archbishop called a synod
at Mainz on 25 July 1234, which was attended not only by the clergy
of the province but also by King Henry and many secular magnates
because a royal Diet had also been called.[48] Conrad appeared to sus-
tain his accusation, but his witnesses either did not appear or declared
that they had testified falsely because of fear and coercion. The archbishop believed the count innocent and advised him to appeal to
Rome. Conrad then left the synod with only a few followers and was
murdered five days later, as were some other of his followers in the
following days. He was buried at Marburg beside the shrine of St.
Elisabeth, a striking complementarity of opposites.

If Gregory IX broke out in unrestrained anger when he heard of
Conrad's death, most Germans apparently breathed a sigh of relief, for
the reaction against Conrad's activities ensured that Germany would
be free of inquisitorial activity for a century. But all was still far from
calm after the tumultuous years from October of 1231 to July of 1234.
Not only were the heads of many Germans now full of fantasies about
fiendish religious conspiracies, but civil war between Frederick II and
King Henry threatened. Then, in September of 1234, came new ex-

citement as Gregory IX proclaimed another crusade for the Holy Land—and crusades always meant danger for Jews.

V

Ever since 1096, calls to crusade had brought massacres of Jews in Germany. Initially they had been attacked as Christ-killers, and to that, since the middle of the twelfth century, had been added the hostility against them as moneylenders. As the papacy and secular authorities, particularly the emperor, had become increasingly aware of that possibility, they had taken steps on the occasion of crusades that had sharply reduced such attacks. Nonetheless, when crusades were called, many people's attention was suddenly directed toward Jews. For those reasons, on 3 May 1235, Gregory IX reissued the famous papal bull of protection for Jews, *Sicut Judeis*, which included the now-usual demand that Jews be forced to remit interest on debts owed them by crusaders.[49]

Before that, however, between 1 and 3 January 1235, eight Jews were killed and burned at Lauda on the Tauber for killing a Christian.[50] Then, for nearly a year, we hear no more of massacres, but on 12 November Jews at Wolfshagen were accused of killing a Christian, and eighteen Jews were cruelly killed. As the annalist at Erfurt put it, "it was seen proper that those who thirsted for blood should shed their own blood in accordance with the prophecy that 'since you hate blood, blood will follow you.' "[51] Yet although Christ's blood came immediately to the Dominican annalist's mind, he did not accuse the Jews of Wolfshagen of ritual cannibalism.

On 13 December, a very different kind of injustice by the abbot and monastery of Fulda against a former Jew received papal attention. Many years before, Innnocent III had granted to the wife and sons of the deceased Master B. of Mainz, all converted Jews, the income of a prebend at Mainz, and in 1221 Honorius III had commanded the archbishop and chapter to obey Innocent's order on pain of punishment. Then, from a letter of Gregory IX of July 1234, we learn that Master B.'s son William, canon of St. John of Mainz, had been provided with a benefice worth ten marks of silver at Fulda, which the abbot and monastery were refusing to give him. Despite a papal warning, the abbot and monastery of Fulda remained contumacious and were excommunicated by the provost and deans of Mainz for over a year, until late in 1235. Fulda then got the sentence lifted by a promise it never fulfilled, and Canon John had to appeal once again to the pope to try and obtain his benefice. On 13 December 1235, Gregory responded and ordered that Fulda comply or again suffer punishment.[52] While it is most unlikely that news of the pope's action traveled from Viterbo by way of Mainz to Fulda in time to be a Christmas present for the abbot, he doubtless knew about Canon John's appeal and was aware of the likely outcome. He may well have felt particularly hostile toward Jews in 1235.

Then, between 25 and 28 December 1235, the Jews of Fulda were accused of ritual cannibalism and thirty-four of them slain. Since we can now recognize how novel that accusation was, a fascinating question for which the evidence provides no clear answer arises: Where did the idea that Jews had committed ritual cannibalism come from? We will never be able to say precisely who first suggested the accusation at Fulda, but one general explanation seems reasonably certain. Conrad of Marburg's fantasies about evil had mightily disturbed the minds of Germans at just that time. Fulda was but fifty miles from Marburg, from Elizabeth's shrine and the center of Conrad's activities. The monks and citizens of Fulda must have been highly excited—and some fascinated—by the horrible stories of repulsive secret rituals that Conrad had been ruthlessly propagating, and some of the monks and citizens may well have been jealous of the emergence of a new and nearby center of religious power.

We cannot, however, say that Conrad himself invented the fantasy of Jewish ritual cannibalism, for our most direct evidence of what he propagated, *Vox in Rama*, says nothing about ritual cannibalism by the heretics and nothing about Jews. Moreover, Conrad died before the events at Fulda. Yet one of his major charges against the allegedly orgiastic heretics was that they did not accept the church's position on the Eucharist. Thoughts about blood and illegal rituals must have been on many people's minds. And we should not forget that the previous versions of the fantasy that Conrad had exploited did involve ritual cannibalism. The simplest explanation, therefore, would seem to be that the accusation against Jews sprang from the heads of the crusaders or citizens of Fulda who had heard all the horrifying stories about the heretics' secret rituals and were stimulated by the summons to crusade to project something similar on the worst enemies of Christ, the Jews. The attractiveness of this new fantasy about Jews to wide sections of the population at large is obvious from its rapid spread, to which Frederick II's bull of 1236 and Gregory IX's bull of 1247 testify.

But one cannot help wondering what the monks at Fulda were doing in that exciting week at the end of December. As Cohn has shown,
Conrad's fantasy about the orgiastic rituals of the heretics owed much
to the literary transmission of the fantasy about orgiastic rituals by
educated if wildly imaginative ecclesiastics. And although *Vox in
Rama* said nothing about ritual cannibalism, that literary tradition did.
According to it, the participants in such orgies not only engaged in
devil worship, intercourse, and incest, but the babies resulting from
such activities were thrown on a fire and their ashes consumed by the
participants.

We can only speculate about the transmission of the fantasy. If the
rich library of Fulda contained one of the works that recounted that
fantasy of ritual cannibalism, some monk might have read about it and
mentioned it to others. The library might also have contained a copy
of Flavius Josephus's *Against Apion*, which recounted the accusation
that Jews in the second century before the Common Era had annually
practiced ritual cannibalism with the body of a Greek. If that were the
case, it would have been but a short step for someone who read the
work at Fulda to project ritual cannibalism on contemporary Jews.

Nor is it hard to imagine why the accusation when projected on
Jews would refer to blood rather than the ashes of babies. The association of Jews with the blood of Christ ensured as much. When the
Erfurt Dominican described the massacre at Wolfshagen in November,
before the events at Fulda, his scriptural idea of Jews led him immediately to say that Jews "thirsted for blood." The accusations that
spread immediately after Fulda used the same phrase, as we know
from Frederick II's imperial bull of 1236. Moreover, at a time when
the campaign against heretics had made people very aware of doubts
about Christ's real presence in the Eucharist, the idea that the literal-
minded Jews engaged in a ritual with real human blood might have
been particularly appealing to some clerics. Indeed, we know that another Dominican somewhat later linked the Jews' alleged belief that
they had to obtain blood with their failure to recognize that they could
only be saved by the blood of Christ.[53]

It may seem unfair to suggest that the abbot or monks of Fulda
played any role at all in the tragedy at Fulda, save perhaps a passive
one, for there is no direct evidence to support the charge. Yet middle-
level clerics had played a major role in creating and disseminating the
earlier form of the ritual murder accusation, the crucifixion fantasy,
and they would play a major role in later blood accusations. More

proximately, there is the hard evidence of the fantastic imaginings of Conrad of Marburg and Gregory IX. Moreover, it seems clear that it was Franciscans who introduced that fantasy into the tragedy at Valréas in 1247. The fantasy has a clerical ring that makes one wonder what the monks were thinking and saying that Christmas.

As for the abbot of Fulda, Conrad III, we will never know what role he played in the tragedy. The chronicles give no details about how the thirty-four Jews were killed. We do not know whether confessions were extorted by semiofficial torture, whether the Jews were killed after some semblance of an official trial, or whether they were lynched by a mob. Our most reliable account, the Erfurt Annals, makes crusaders responsible, while the Marbach annalist states that the Jews were killed by the citizens of Fulda. In either case, the simplest explanation is that someone started a rumor that incited an angry mob to torture and lynch Jews.

It should be noted, however, that three days elapsed between the death of the miller's sons on Christmas Day and the cruel killing of Jews on 28 December. One cannot help wondering what Conrad, princely abbot of the great imperial monastery of Fulda, was doing while his town seethed with talk about the horrible religious crime committed on Christmas Day. If there was some kind of trial, the abbot would have been very important, since he had high justice. And even if there was no trial, he or those to whom he had delegated his authority were responsible for maintaining peace. But no chronicle reports any resistance by the abbot or his officials to the massacre.

It is hard to escape the suspicion that the abbot must have been involved in some way. Surely he had—and expressed—an opinion about the news, which must have spread like wildfire, that a horrible religious crime had been committed in his town. Did he oppose the fantasy or support it? The answer one gives is important, for his attitude would have been a major influence on many.

One well-known fact whose significance has never struck anyone is highly significant. We know that the bodies of the boys were carried in early winter weather, presumably in a cart accompanied by a sizable number of people, at least 150 miles to the west across the Rhine to Hagenau and there laid before the emperor as evidence that, in Frederick's word, Jews thirsted for human blood. A moment's reflection will suggest how unusual that action was. It is very hard to imagine a small band of either crusaders or citizens of Fulda who had been involved in killing Jews doing it on their own. The action required unusually concerted and sustained organization and was unique in the annals of medieval ritual murder. It also involved danger, for the participants thereby acknowledged involvement in the killing of Jews, people peculiarly under imperial protection. Moreover, it seems most unlikely that any group of citizens or crusaders who had massacred Jews in a moment of excitement would have felt any responsibility to bring the matter before the emperor as an accusation against all the Jews of Germany. It therefore seems very plausible that the enterprise was encouraged and supported by someone with a wide perspective, strong—albeit perverted—religious concerns, and considerable prestige.

A further fact is worth remembering. As soon as Frederick II had first learned of the accusation, before he had summoned the converts from across Europe, he discussed the charge with a special assembly of his magnates. His words are worth quoting.

> As, in consequence of the murder of some boys at Fulda, a grievous accusation was brought against the Jews then living there, and hence a menacing public opinion arose generally against the rest of the Jews in Germany on account of the sad event, although the traffic in secret crime was not revealed, we, in order to clear up the truth in respect of the aforementioned accusation, resolved to summon before us from every quarter princes, magnates, and nobles of the empire, as well as abbots and ecclesiastics, and to question them. Now as these were of different opinions about the matter, and could not arrive at a satisfactory issue in relation to it . . . [we asked all the kings of the west to send converts].[54]

The first thing that should strike us is how quickly the rumor spread and, in consequence, how seriously the emperor took it. One explanation is obvious: the unusual cortege that brought the bodies across Germany had spread the fantasy all along the way and brought the bodies and the fantasy directly to Frederick's attention. The second striking feature is the seriousness of the first official discussion of the fantasy and the divided opinions within it. Unfortunately, we do not know how many magnates were present or which of them argued that the accusation was plausible. There is no direct evidence that Abbot Conrad was present. Yet, as one of the greatest imperial abbots, he would have been summoned; and as the most notable ecclesiastic with the most direct information about the alleged events—and the greatest interest in the outcome—it would be surprising if he had not attended. If he was there, it would be surprising if he had not defended the truth of the accusation. But whatever he may have hoped, after Frederick had consulted the converts and, by his bull of July 1236, prohibited clerics and lay people from making the accusation, Conrad could not have the miller's children venerated as saints.

The fantasy at Fulda was the creation of many minds and many bodies, including the bodies of Conrad of Marburg's victims, the miller's dead boys, and the thirty-four dead Jews of Fulda. Given the limits of our evidence, we can only surmise who did many of the things that must have happened to produce the events we do know happened. We can be reasonably sure that the ravings of Conrad of Marburg and clerical fantasies about ritual orgies played a major role, but we can only have grave suspicions about the role of the abbot and monks of Fulda. Of one thing, however, we can be certain. A new fantasy, the medieval libel of Jewish ritual cannibalism, was created by some people at Fulda in 1235. It caused the death of thirty-four Jews immediately; it attracted the attention of the highest authorities throughout Europe immediately after; it was soon responsible for the death of more Jews; and, directly or indirectly, it was responsible for the death of many more in the centuries to come.

12.
Historiographic Crucifixion

If history and historiography—human happenings and historians' assertions about what happened—are as different as a battle and a book, they are nonetheless inextricably linked. Not only is the writing of history one consequence of past events and memory of them; it is itself a historical event, sometimes of considerable consequence. This is peculiarly true in the case of accusations of ritual murder against Jews, for such accusations have been as much a phenomenon of historiography as of history. Indeed, it is highly probable that the first such accusations, whether in antiquity or the Middle Ages, were not made by people present at the time and place of the alleged incident but were created by people who wrote some time later or at some distance from the alleged event and attributed their own accusations to the people at the scene of the crime. Moreover, many literary figures, chroniclers, and historians who reported past accusations also asserted or implied that they were true. And later historians have indisputably played a major role in preserving, transmitting, and confirming such accusations. Since the historiography on ritual murder is too extensive to be examined here, we will have to restrict ourselves to an examination of the historiography about the first such accusation in the Middle Ages. Yet even that theme will take us from the middle of the twelfth century to the second half of the twentieth and will illustrate the peculiarity of the historiographic phenomenon.

The first medieval accusation of ritual murder against Jews emerged in connection with the death of young William at Norwich in 1144, and our best and most direct evidence for it is historiographic, the *The Life and Miracles of St. William of Norwich* by Thomas of Monmouth, a contemporary who was not present when the alleged crime was committed and only came to the priory of Norwich cathedral as a monk some five years after William's death.[1] Since the modern editors of the *Life* suggested that the Norwich accusation might have been partially inspired by historiographic transmission of the fifth-century accusation against the Jews of Inmestar, they recognized the possibility of distorting historiographic influence, but they did not recognize where it came from.[2] It seems as certain as such things can be, given the nature of the evidence, that the accusations in antiquity were unknown at Norwich, and that the Norwich accusation was a myth invented by Thomas of Monmouth about 1150. On the basis of biased testimony and his own imagination, Thomas wrote a compelling saint's life that combined fact and fiction and described the Jews' crucifixion of William almost as if Thomas had been an eyewitness. The series of accusations of ritual murder that Jews have had to face from the twelfth to the twentieth century began with a historiographic fantasy.

Thomas of Monmouth sought the earthly prestige and transcendental protection that peculiarly devoted service to a local patron saint might bring, and his wishful thinking created a potent symbol, the image of a protector who was a victim of Jews like unto Christ—a point emphasized in some of the miracle stories. If the fantasy did not cause the death of any Jews at Norwich at the time, partly because it was only fashioned some time after the alleged event, its ultimate consequences were deadly. The tragedy for Jews lay precisely in the powerful psychological appeal of his historiographic myth through the centuries to those Christians who felt as defenseless as a child against forces they could not understand.

Thomas of Monmouth's *Life* of William was not widely copied. Only one late-twelfth-century manuscript of it is extant, and the *Life* itself may have been unknown outside of East Anglia during the Middle Ages. But once Thomas had created the myth and inspired the second translation to the chapter house on 12 April 1150, William's local fame was assured, and the basic theme of the myth spread rapidly, as the sudden increase of miracles and the geographic dispersion of the recipients indicate. Other evidence is the final continuation of the *Anglo-Saxon Chronicle* at not-too-distant Peterborough. It was written in 1154 or 1155; and in a section in which, misleadingly, the

only year mentioned is 1137, the chronicler records that the Jews of
Norwich had crucified a child on Good Friday (not on the Wednesday,
as it was told at Norwich), and that many wonderful miracles had
occurred.[3] Obviously the chronicler had not seen the *Life* but had
learned of the basic idea of the myth by rumor.

The further diffusion of the accusation is difficult to trace because
it was paralleled by the spread of a similar but simpler accusation. The
Norwich case had started with an accusation, not of ritual murder, but
simply of cruel murder by Jews to explain a death by persons unknown. The same accusation of cruel murder by Jews with no mention
of a crucifixion was made at Würzburg in 1147, at Gloucester in 1168,
at Blois in 1171, at Bury St. Edmunds in 1181, and at Winchester in
1192. In none of these cases is a crucifixion mentioned in the earliest
accounts, including the detailed acccounts by contemporaries at or
near Gloucester and Blois.[4] Indeed, the Hebrew report of the Blois
incident implies that it was becoming common, when a body was
found in cities or the countryside, for Jews to be accused of the crime.
By the second half of the twelfth century, the Jews were increasingly
perceived as a strange and potentially dangerous people and a possible
explanation for otherwise inexplicable crimes. When the future Philip
II of France was growing up in the 1170s, he was told by boys in the
palace that the Jews of Paris annually killed or cut the throat (*jugu-
labant*) of a Christian in crypts under Paris as a kind of sacrifice to
dishonor Christianity.[5]

Jews were thus thought to kill defenseless Christians out of religious
hatred, just as Christians had killed Jews in 1096 and 1147, but as yet
there was no accusation of ritual murder. The first to make that accusation was Thomas of Monmouth. The next known crucifixion accusation appears in the annals written by Lambert of Waterloo, who
was born in 1108, became a canon at Cambrai, began writing his
annals in 1152, and apparently recorded events more or less as they
happened. He asserts that on Good Friday of 1163 the Jews of Paris
crucified Richard of Pontoise, in whose memory Christ worked many
miracles—a statement strikingly similar to that of the *Anglo-Saxon
Chronicle*.[6] But a slightly younger contemporary at Limoges whose
chronology is unreliable placed Richard's death in 1156. What is interesting is that although Geoffroi of Vigeois had heard of the death
and the many miracles, he said nothing about a crucifixion, only that
Jews had killed the boy.[7]

It is possible, therefore, that Jews had not initially been accused of crucifying Richard, and that that myth had been incorporated later to embellish Richard's halo, but we cannot be sure. Nor can we determine whether the idea of a crucifixion had developed independently at Paris or been brought by clerics or others from Norwich. A continuation of the chronicle of Sigebert of Gembloux was written at Ourscamp, less than a hundred kilometers from Paris. Since it stops at 1154, it may have been written before the death of Richard of Pontoise, which is interesting because it reports William's alleged crucifixion and, although it places the event in 1146, adds information that can only have come fairly directly from Norwich: that William's body was discovered because of a light from heaven.[8]

The Channel was, after all, as much a means of communication as a barrier, as the connections of Mont-Saint-Michel would remind us. In fact, its abbot, Robert of Torigny, was the first chronicler after Lambert of Waterloo to accuse the Jews of crucifying their alleged victims. More than that, he knew about William of Norwich shortly after the death of Richard of Pontoise and was the first to connect the incidents at Pontoise, Blois, Norwich, and Gloucester. He recorded that many Jews of Blois had been burned in 1171 because they had crucified some child during the Easter season. He immediately went on to note that they had done the same in Stephen's reign to St. William at Norwich, where many miracles had occurred, to some other person in Gloucester in Henry II's reign, and to St. Richard, at whose tomb in Paris many miracles had occurred. "And frequently, it is said, they do this in Easter season if they find the opportunity."[9] Since we know that no one had initially accused the Jews of a crucifixion at Blois or Gloucester, and since Torigny did not even know Harold of Gloucester's name, it is clear that Torigny, a historian of little critical judgment,[10] was engaging in unwarranted overgeneralization. The historiographic phenomenon was rapidly outrunning the events.

Since Torigny's chronicle was much copied, while Thomas of Monmouth's *Life* had only very restricted circulation, Torigny may be credited with being the first well-known medieval historian to make a generalized accusation of ritual murder against Jews. He thereby helped keep the memory of William of Norwich alive. If Ralph Diceto and Roger of Wendover, who borrowed from Torigny, said nothing about William and his fate, Nicholas Trivet obviously drew on Torigny in the early fourteenth century for his report of the Blois incident and probably also for his reference to William of Norwich.[11] Far more important, however, is the fact that, in the sixteenth century, Baronius read Torigny, with the result that William was enshrined in Baronius's great *Annales Ecclesiastici*, a work that also gave the Inmestar incident a place in church history.[12]

We would expect William of Norwich's story to have been much better known in England than on the Continent, yet most English chroniclers did not mention it or did so only briefly. Henry of Huntingdon, Ralph Niger, Ralph Diceto, William of Newburgh, Roger of Howden, Roger of Wendover, and Matthew Paris (in the *Chronica majora* and *Historia Anglorum*) do not mention the Norwich incident even though they report other accusations against Jews. Those who did report William's death did so very succinctly. Ralph of Coggeshall (about sixty miles from Norwich) noted that in 1144 "the boy William was crucified by Jews at Norwich"; the Waverley, Bermondsey, and Worcester annals have similar brief notices; the *Flores historiarum* presently attributed to Matthew Paris also has a brief notice, as does the chronicle once attributed to John Brompton; and as we have seen, Trivet mentioned the story briefly.[13] The scarcity and brevity of these notices may be partly explained by the fact that William's fame, such as it was, was eclipsed after 1255 by that of England's most famous alleged victim of ritual murder, young Hugh of Lincoln, whose fate was elaborately if most inaccurately described by Matthew Paris, transmuted in ballads, and remembered by Chaucer.[14] So limited was William's fame by the sixteenth century that the famous Protestant martyrologist John Foxe apparently knew no more than that "during the time of the said King Stephen, A.D. 1144, the miserable Jews crucified a child in the city of Norwich."[15] Even Tovey in the eighteenth century only knew of the brief report in the chronicles ascribed to Brompton and Matthew of Westminster, although he differed sharply from them and other previous historians in being highly skeptical about the ritual murder charge.[16] But help was about to come from Norwich.

The chroniclers mentioned thus far had not read the *Life* by Thomas of Monmouth, but it was still in existence at Norwich. With the great revival of historiography that began in the fifteenth century, it was all but inevitable that some industrious scholar would unearth it and use it. The first scholar to do so was the extremely learned English Augustinian of the fifteenth century, John Capgrave. More important perhaps for his attention to William than his scholarship was the fact that he was a Norfolk man who spent most of his life in the Augustinian house at Lynn and had easy access to the Norwich cathedral library.[17] He read Thomas of Monmouth's *Life* of William and included a long summary of book 1 in his *Nova Legenda Angliae*, which was published in an English translation in 1516. Thereby he gave William's death a new lease on life, for in 1668 the Bollandists used Capgrave's account to provide William's *acta*.[18] They recognized that this was the earliest medieval accusation of ritual murder, and prefaced the entry on William with a brief discussion of the alleged phenomenon. After listing the charges against Jews at Gloucester in 1168, at Bury St. Edmunds in 1181, and at Lincoln in 1255, they then generalized: "Whence we may suspect that they vented their rage in the blood of innocent Christians more frequently than it would please historians to report in chronicles or than God would permit to become known publicly." They then listed other accusations down to the seventeenth century.

Although sixteenth-century English scholars were aware of the existence of the *Life* at Norwich, and although a quite detailed account of William's alleged fate was now widely available to scholars through the *Acta Sanctorum*, only one English scholar seems to have used the manuscript between the fifteenth and the end of the nineteenth century, and almost predictably it was another famous hagiographer. Alban Butler was made chaplain and tutor to the nephew of the Catholic duke of Norfolk and first resided with his pupil in Norwich before going with him to Paris. There Butler completed *The Lives of the Fathers, Martyrs, and Other Principal Saints*, better known in its many later editions as *The Lives of the Saints*.[19] The first edition was published anonymously in London from 1756 to 1759, and in it, for the date of 24 March, Butler gave entries for the most famous of the alleged victims of Jewish ritual murder, Simon of Trent, and for William of Norwich, "another victim of the implacable rage of the Jews against our holy religion."[20] Butler devoted a long paragraph to William, citing as his authorities the short account in the *Anglo-Saxon Chronicle* and Thomas of Monmouth. He did not cite Capgrave or the *Acta Sanctorum* because he had gone back to the original source. Moreover, as his account indicates, Butler knew the topography of the drama. Strangely enough, however, misled by the *Anglo-Saxon Chronicle*, Butler put William's death in 1137 and then stated that William was translated in 1144 to the monks' cemetery, thereby leaving William buried in unconsecrated ground for seven years! Butler then mentioned Richard of Pontoise and Hugh of Lincoln but—with greater charity than the Bollandists—concluded: "Nevertheless it is a notorious slander of some authors, who from these singular and extraordinary instances infer this to have been at any time the custom or maxim of that people." That qualification was omitted from at least one of the later editions but is emphasized in the most recent edition of that so frequently reprinted work.[21]

Whether the manuscript Butler saw was the one now extant is uncertain, since the editors of the *Life* state that their manuscript was the only one extant and had been bequeathed by a Cambridge man to a parish in Suffolk about 1700, to be purchased in 1887 by the Bodleian Library and in 1889 by the Cambridge University Library.[22] Be that as it may, no one used the *Life* between Butler in the eighteenth century and Jessopp and James in 1889. In 1863, Milman relied on the *Anglo-Saxon Chronicle* for his knowledge of the Norwich incident, of which he was highly skeptical, seeing in it the fabrication of a saint for the benefit of Norwich cathedral.[23] Also in 1863, Hart used only Capgrave for the Norwich case in his lengthy discussion of ritual murder accusations in connection with the Gloucester incident of 1168. Hart states that "in the year 1144 the Jews at Norwich crucified a boy named William,"[24] but he concludes his discussion of the medieval accusations by noting that Depping had treated them all as fables, "and though it is not my province here to enter into such a discussion, yet I am bound to say that, in my judgment, the evidence in support of *many* of these supposed martyrdoms would not bear a strict scrutiny."[25] It is hard to say whether this grudging and partial exoneration was motivated by concern for accuracy about Jews or dislike of Catholic legends.

A very different spirit informs the lengthy discussion by Vacandard in 1912.[26] He noted that the definitive book on the accusation of ritual murder remained to be written, discussed the various accusations, dismissed them all as false and blindly transmitted "à la faveur des haines de races," and asked that belief in them be abandoned, if not because of Christian charity, at least because simple natural equity demanded it. As for the Norwich accusation, Vacandard knew of it only through Torigny and Capgrave in the *Acta Sanctorum* but remarked on the absurdity of the facts reported in the legend.[27]

Understandably, the father of modern Jewish historiography, Heinrich Graetz, knew even less than Christian historians, since he had never heard of little William of Norwich and thought that the Blois accusation of 1171 was the first "blood" accusation.[28] By the 1920s, thanks to Jacobs' *The Jews of Angevin England*, Simon Dubnow was aware of the Norwich case, even though he misdated it, placing William's death in 1146.[29] Since Graetz and Dubnow had so heavy an influence on subsequent Jewish historiography, one is hardly surprised to find that a book published in 1965 states that the Blois incident was the first accusation of ritual murder, or that another in 1966 states incorrectly that Apion's story of ritual cannibalism turns up in Tacitus, and that William was killed in 1146.[30]

Nonetheless, even though ignored by some writers, the appearance of the edition of Thomas of Monmouth's *Life* in 1896 marked a watershed in serious historiography about the Norwich case. Attitudes toward Jews, moreover, had changed, at least in more sophisticated non-Jewish circles, as can be seen from Charles Bémont's eminently sane review in 1897. Without giving his reasons, he recognized that Thomas of Monmouth had begun to write or collect testimony in 1150, and he described the result as a "tissue of incoherences and puerility" that would convince no impartial judge. He noted that the accusation itself was "the oldest known example of the alleged 'ritual murder' which some still feel authorizes them to deliver the Jews to the disdain and hatred of Christians."[31] But although he emphasized the economic value of the accusation that provided the cathedral with a new saint, he did not suggest how the accusation had originated.

Notably different was the reaction of one of the editors of the *Life*. M. R. James anticipated that most readers of his day would believe that William had been killed by an unknown person, and he graciously doubted that "the educated Jews of Norwich in *their corporate capacity* would perpetrate this crime as an act of Christian spite."[32] James knew that ritual murder charges had been falsely raised against Christians and heretics by uneducated people, and he recognized that the simplest hypothesis was that the whole story about Jews was a fabrication. James also dismissed as incredible the story of the Christian servant and felt that Aelward Ded's silence up to 1149 raised serious questions about his confession.[33] But James refused to leave it there. He described Theobald's fable and said: "If this is a lie—and we are assured that it is by those who have studied the subject—it is one of the most notable and disastrous lies of history; and we must look upon Theobald of Cambridge as *responsible* for the blood of thousands of his fellow-countrymen."[34] After that note of uncertainty, James speculated about a mad Jewish hatred of the dominant system and "a reversion to half-forgotten practices of a darker age," and he concluded by suggesting that a bad Jew of Norwich might have put the fantasy of ritual murder into practice, and that that Jew might have been Theobald.[35] James seems to have wanted to exonerate Christians by any loophole he could find, even one that defied the only evidence he had, since it said that Theobald had been at Cambridge when the crime was committed.

Wishful thinking, however, could work both ways. When Joseph Jacobs initially completed his documentary history, *The Jews of Angevin England*, he only knew of the accounts of William's fate in the *Anglo-Saxon Chronicle* and in Capgrave,[36] but as publication approached he discovered additional documents which he included in a supplement at the end of the book. Since James had just informed him of the discovery of the *Life* and provided him with some details and brief extracts, Jacobs presented the extracts and commented on what he had learned in the supplement.[37] With only the material James had provided to go on, Jacobs dismissed the story as a fable and attributed the whole theory of ritual murder to Theobald. But once he saw the whole *Life*, he no longer blamed everything on Theobald.

In his review of the *Life* in 1897, Jacobs noted the bias of Thomas of Monmouth and the testimonies he reported, and he emphasized the frail foundations of the myth of ritual murder, "this huge structure of malice and hatred" supported by many churchmen through the ages.[38] While still willing to blame Theobald as the founder of the myth, he suggested that Theobald might really have described the symbolic hanging of Haman at Purim, and that Thomas might have distorted that information to build his myth. But Jacobs wanted to exonerate Jews as James had tried to exonerate Christians, and he too was unwilling to leave well enough alone. To solve the problem of who had killed William and why, Jacobs took the hagiographical topos about the sweet smell and lack of decomposition of William's body at face value, combined it with Godwin Sturt's undatable assertion that, when he and his son and nephew had dug the body up, the earth had surged up as if pushed from below, and decided that William had been in a cataleptic fit when buried and had died only when his relatives dug him up. With the help of other tenuous arguments, Jacobs then advanced what he felt was the most probable solution. The Sturts were fanatical Christians who had used William to stage a reenactment of the Crucifixion on Good Friday, during which William had fallen into his cataleptic fit. Thinking he was dead and fearful of the consequences, his relatives had disposed of him in the wood, where he was first found and buried by the forester. "William was indeed a martyr, but a martyr to Christian, not to Jewish, bigotry."[39]

Once Jacobs had used this wild conjecture in his article in the *Universal Jewish Encyclopedia*,[40] it became the accepted explanation in Jewish historiography. It was taken over in 1933 by Cecil Roth, who stated that "recent theory maintains that the child had died in a cataleptic fit and was buried alive by his relatives, who endeavored to shield themselves by putting the blame on the Jews."[41] By 1935, Roth had multiplied Jacobs under anonymity: "Modern enquirers, after careful examination of the facts, have concluded that the child probably lost consciousness in consequence of a cataleptic fit, and was buried prematurely by his relatives,"[42] a position that Roth maintained to the end of his life.[43] It was also the position adopted more cautiously by Baron, who suggested that the story at Norwich was "perhaps first created as a diversion by the child's family which had overhastily buried him while he was suffering from a mere epileptic fit."[44] The same explanation appeared in *The Jewish Encyclopedia* in 1943,[45] but was finally abandoned by Ben-Sasson in his very brief reference, a quotation from the *Anglo-Saxon Chronicle*, in the *Encyclopaedia Judaica* in 1971.[46]

But Roth had done more in 1933 than explain William's death; he had developed a theory to explain the origin of the ritual murder accusation. He conjectured that Christians suspected that Jewish conduct at Purim, the hanging of an effigy of Haman, was a mockery of Christianity, that those suspicions were the basis of the ritual murder accusations, and that the Inmestar incident was the prototype of the whole series.[47] Unfortunately for his theory, he was able to come up with only a single case throughout the Middle Ages in which a killing connected with Jews was linked with Purim in the evidence. It involved alleged Jewish conduct at an execution commanded by the countess of Champagne in 1192. That alleged conduct was horrifyingly punished by Philip Augustus, but neither he nor any chronicler adduced it as an instance of ritual murder.[48] Roth's only other example of Christian reaction to Jewish conduct at Purim during the Middle Ages also had nothing to do with ritual murder; it was a reaction to the punishment of a Jew by the Jewish community of Manosque that did not even have a fatal outcome.[49] Indeed, so far as I know, Purim is mentioned only in connection with one very different kind of medieval accusation of ritual murder.[50] In any case, Roth could find no connection between

Purim and the first accusation at Norwich. His theory was very weak, but because it was for so long the only effort to explain the whole phenomenon, scholars kept referring to his article, ultimately with very peculiar results, as we shall see.

No new analysis of the events at Norwich appeared in the first half of the twentieth century, though the Nazis used the general accusation of ritual murder to increase support for their "Final Solution." But when Hitler's defeat made a resurgence of scholarship about medieval Jews possible, it was marked by greater objectivity about the relations between Jews and non-Jews, an outstanding example being the work of Bernhard Blumenkranz. A reexamination of the Norwich case from this altered perspective was therefore probable. What was not predictable was the nature of the book that appeared in 1964. M. D. Anderson had previously written about woodcarving and images in English churches and was inspired by a painting of William of Norwich in a parish church to reread the *Life* and play "amateur detective."[51] As was to be expected after Auschwitz, Anderson duly deplored interracial hatred and antisemitism, but the depth of her understanding of those phenomena is rapidly apparent: while describing the background and the position of the Jews at the time, she speaks of "all the subtlety that characterises their race."[52] After a description of the crime that follows Thomas of Monmouth's sequence, she seeks a verdict. The cataleptic theory is rapidly dismissed.[53] Anderson also raises the possibility of a sadistic lunatic but promptly dismisses it on incomprehensible grounds. She argues that wounds suggestive of a crucifixion would not have been inflicted by such a lunatic then (even though she does not believe the boy was crucified) because the crucifixion accusation had not yet been made against Jews.[54] She repressed the fact that crucifixion was integral to Christianity, not Judaism, and that Christians did not need the accusation against Jews to fantasize about crucifixion. Some in fact did reenact the Crucifixion.[55]

Even Anderson could not accept the Christian servant's story or Leviva's story about her little daughter. Instead she accepted Thomas's report of Wicheman's unbelievable story about Aelward Ded's confession, which indicted all Jews. She did not attempt to explain how the sheriff could have compelled Aelward to keep silent, and her only explanation of his continuing silence after the sheriff's death is her suggestion that perhaps Aelward was an honest man![56] So determined was Anderson to connect Jews collectively with crime that she suggested without a scrap of evidence that the murder occurred in

Theobald's house, thereby making him an eyewitness, even though Thomas had explicitly said that it was Eleazar's house. And as if to be impartial, she even suggested that the then prior and later bishop, William Turbe, promised Theobald immunity in return for a full confession that would ensure a new saint for the cathedral![57]

Why did the Jews kill William? To answer that question, Anderson drew on Roth's conjecture of 1933, which she found too useful to examine closely. For while it did not permit her to produce "an authoritative solution," it enabled her to proffer the following "credible framework."[58] The recent and small Jewish community of Norwich celebrated Purim on 21 February 1144 by hanging either a Christian who survived or a Jew who died, which would not have mattered since Jews would not have accused themselves and caused a trial. But rumors spread, arousing feelings against Jews among the citizens of Norwich. Fearing an attack, the Jews captured little William to discover what was planned. When he could not or would not tell them, they tortured him. No longer daring to release him, they decided to carry him far away. Two Jews smuggled the gagged and unconscious boy out of Norwich but were discovered by Aelward Ded. Because Aelward would probably return and incite an attack on all Jews, the Jews had to be warned immediately, but it was unsafe either to take William back to Norwich or to leave him alive so close. So the two knifed him without quite killing him, and he did not die until he was dug up by his relatives three days later.[59]

Anderson's need to think Jews guilty seems as great as Thomas of Monmouth's, and Bémont's remark about a tissue of incoherences comes irresistibly to mind. It did not, however, come to the mind of three reviewers of her book. One praised her for having constructively ventilated the issues afresh,[60] another for meticulous scholarship more enlightening than a mixture of fact and surmise,[61] and a third for making the whole episode much more comprehensible and giving an extremely credible explanation of how responsibility came to be pinned on the Jews.[62] None of them mentioned that her solution was a new kind of accusation that still made Jews collectively responsible for the crime and even for the crucifixion accusation. Apparently that solution had their tacit approval. Only one remarkably brief review stated flatly without comment that "the book offers no satisfactory explanation for the murder of the boy."[63]

The only serious appraisal of Anderson's book so far was made by V. D. Lipman in 1967.[64] Unlike the reviewers, Lipman had read the evidence carefully and recognized how suspect it was and how impossible it was to determine who killed little William. He dismissed Anderson's reconstruction of the crime as "dependent on too many assumptions, including the supposed horseplay at Purim." He felt that the self-styled cook was the most likely murderer, and was inclined to think that William had been killed by "a sexual criminal, indulging in sadistic impulses."[65] Yet, perhaps because he was more concerned to rebut Anderson's charge against Jews, he did not analyze responsibility for the appearance of the crucifixion accusation otherwise than by agreeing with Anderson and others that Thomas and other clerics had wanted a new saint for their cathedral.

It might be thought that Lipman's sane appraisal would have prevented Anderson's imaginative accusation from having any further influence, but something even wilder appeared in 1971. A pathologist, William D. Sharpe, M.D., read Anderson's book and was inspired to provide his own solution.[66] The result shocked Jews and is reported to have bemused Sharpe's colleagues.[67] For whatever his expertise as a pathologist, Sharpe was no historian. All his footnotes could have come from only two books, the *Life* and Anderson's work, and he never refers to Lipman's book.

Untrained in the analysis of medieval evidence, unfamiliar with the mentality of medieval monks, and apparently totally unaware of the extreme ignorance of pathology in the Middle Ages, Sharpe plunged ahead to establish the hypothesis that attracted him. He accepted almost all of Thomas of Monmouth's assertions about the events of 1144, including Leviva's story about her little daughter and Wicheman's report of Aelward Ded's confession, thus ensuring that Jews would be guilty of the crime.[68] But since his only authoritative contribution had to be that of a pathologist, he also accepted all of Thomas's assertions about the state of the body and the nature of the wounds. The problem here of course is that no one familiar with medieval evidence would trust those assertions even if Thomas's bias could be discounted. Not only was Thomas heaven-bent to make a saint, but the body had received very hard treatment before it was examined by the monks. It had been left to the attention of animals for three days, then been buried, dug up, reburied, left in the ground for a month, and dug up again. Given the miraculous ignorance of medicine of the period,[69] and given the fact that Thomas himself had never seen the body and was relying on the assertions of those who wished to promote William's fame, it is impossible to trust anything Thomas says about the state of the body—except perhaps that it was severely damaged.

Since Sharpe accepted Thomas's assertions about the body, and since he also accepted the stories that most clearly, if totally unbelievably, connected Jews with the crime, an accusation of ritual murder would seem to follow. But Sharpe reluctantly stopped just short. He asserted that "ritual murder is too easily dismissed" but was forced to recognize that in the Norwich case "ritual murder can neither be implicated nor excluded on the evidence."[70] "The simplest explanation, if ritual murder can be excluded," according to Sharpe, was that a sexual deviate, possibly with one or two companions, took William to a Jew's house, engaged in sexual acts, tortured him, possibly crucified him, and stabbed him. "When the more responsible members of the Jewish community learned of the murder, assuming they were not accomplices," they disposed of the body and bribed the sheriff to conceal the crime. Moreover, although Thomas of Monmouth had stated that William had been killed in a way that would conceal a crucifixion, Sharpe somehow detected "ritual components" in the murder. He therefore suggested that the sexual deviate was also a morbidly anti-Christian Jewish religious fanatic.[71] Despite his ignorance of the period and the relevant literature, Sharpe was as determined as Thomas to make Jews collectively responsible for the crime, and to implicate Judaism.

Anderson and Sharpe's conjectures might seem worthy of notice only as aberrations that demonstrate that irrational attempts to blame Jews still continue under the guise of scholarship. But that would be to forget the favorable reviews of Anderson's book and to fail to recognize the extent to which both Anderson and Sharpe's conjectures were not deviations from, but the consequence of, prior historiography. Already in the eighteenth century, Butler had emphatically denied that ritual murder was a Jewish custom, but he still believed that Jews had martyrized children at times and that William of Norwich was "another victim of the implacable rage of the Jews against our holy religion." In 1896, M. R. James had hypothesized, without any respectable evidence, that some bad Jew, possibly Theobald, might have reverted to "half-forgotten practices of a darker age." And about 1930, Father Thurston had praised Butler for denying the generalized accusation but still declared that "it is possible that such child-murders

may occasionally have been committed by Jewish maniacs."[72] That
insistence on the possibility is all the more noteworthy because Thurston had ringingly condemned the accusation of ritual murder against
Jews in 1898 and had taken up the cudgels again in 1913 in connection
with the Beilis case.[73] Yet even then he drew the distinction: "In isolated cases, it is possible that criminals of that race may really have
been guilty of the homicides attributed to them, but the only point of
real importance is the fact that there is nothing in the Hebrew religion
or practice which enjoins or approves this kind of human sacrifice."[74]

The possibility that William had been martyrized by Jews, at least
by some Jews, whether sane, mad, or bad, remained open, a loophole
that encouraged conjectures to that effect. More than that, it encouraged such conjectures in dealing with the richly documented case of
William of Norwich. For if Jews had killed William, then the first
crucifixion accusation was the result of an overgeneralized misinterpretation of what some Jews had actually done. And if that was the
case, then Jews, not Christians, were primarily responsible for the ritual murder accusation that would haunt them through the centuries.

The intellectual trick here is the argument from silence, or rather
ignorance: we do not know that Jews killed any of these alleged victims, but we cannot be absolutely certain that they did not, therefore
it is possible that some of the children were indeed killed by Jews, and
therefore the accusation of ritual murder so long supported by Christians may not be baseless. Thus in 1965, in a book that bitingly criticized Christian treatment of Jews and called the ritual murder cal-
umny a monstrous instrument of persecution, Father Flannery
nonetheless drew attention to the loophole. "Some students of the
question concede the possible existence of cases of ritual murder in the
wide sense, as might happen in cases of aberration. It is not impossible
that anti-Christian fanaticism and addiction to sorcery on the part of
a Jew by chance converged and resulted in the murder of a
Christian."[75] Flannery failed to emphasize that in every case for which
we have fair evidence it is far more likely that Jews did not do it and
that someone else did, and that that probability is even greater in the
case of accusations that attracted little attention and left little evidence.
It is empirically possible that one of the alleged victims of ritual murder was killed by a Jew but so improbable compared with other prob-
abilities as not to deserve mention. Yet it was this carefully preserved
loophole that enabled Anderson and Sharpe to engage in wishful think-

ing and conjecture what happened in one case—the case that initiated the long series of generalized accusations of ritual murder.

Joseph Jacobs, Cecil Roth, and Salo Baron contributed to the conjectures in their own way. Whether because they were insensitive to the power of irrationality, reluctant to attack Christian historiography too openly, or concerned to attribute an active role in history to Jews, they were predisposed to believe that something Jews had done—however misinterpreted by Christians—must have been a major cause of the charge. While Jacobs did not believe that Jews ever committed ritual murder and blamed Christians for killing William during a ritual, he nonetheless attributed principal responsibility for the generalized accusation to Theobald of Cambridge, and Roth made exuberant Jewish conduct at Purim the major explanation of the accusation. Yet whatever responsibility be attributed to Theobald, and it may be heavy, Theobald had said nothing about a crucifixion, and neither the *Anglo-Saxon Chronicle* nor almost any of the other reports of alleged crucifixions referred to his allegations.[76] Nor can Jewish conduct at Purim be used to explain the accusation at Norwich.

It may be that behind Jacobs and Roth's attribution of a direct causal role to Jews lay their awareness that the ultimate inspiration for the first medieval ritual murder accusation was the role of Jews in the crucifixion of Jesus. For it was the transmission of the Christian historiographical interpretation of that event that was ultimately responsible. Thomas of Monmouth knew nothing about the Inmestar incident or Purim, and Theobald had said nothing about crucifixion. But Thomas was continually reminded of the most famous crucifixion of all, and he arranged his conception of history and William's death around the interpretation placed on that pivotal event by his own culture. Because of his ethnocentric indoctrination and his personal needs, he created the myth that Jews crucified children; and ethnocentric loyalty has continued to exert a heavy influence on historiography about William of Norwich from 1150 to the present. Whether ignorance of people of a different culture, hostility toward them, or fear of them has played a larger role is hard to say, for they are closely related. What is obvious is the note of defensiveness on both sides of the historiographic tradition. Indeed, a defensive note can be found even in those historians whose relative freedom from ethnocentrism enabled them to see through the fables about William of Norwich. For they also had something of great value to defend that was threatened by most of the historiography about William of Norwich: the historian's obligation to consider the actions of any and all human beings with equal objectivity.

Part 5
Antisemitism

13

Medieval Antisemitism

The Mediterranean world of late antiquity bequeathed to the newly Germanized societies of sixth-century Europe a minority of Christians and a priesthood that sought to propagate Christianity with its corollary of anti-Judaism. Early medieval Europe also inherited dispersed Jews against whom that anti-Judaism could be directed. Both Christians and Jews were far more densely implanted in southern than in northern Europe where Germans ruled themselves or dominated a population little marked by Roman culture. Half a millennium later, however, in Rashi's lifetime at the end of the eleventh century, when Talmudic Judaism had been fully introduced into western Europe, a Christianity considerably different from that of late antiquity had become deep-rooted in both the north and south of a bellicose Europe that now thought of itself as Christendom. And the first major massacre of Jews in Europe, in the Rhineland in 1096, demonstrated that Christian anti-Judaism had, for the first time, gained merciless mass support.

The Jews who died in 1096 to sanctify the Holy Name at least had the satisfaction of dying significantly, dying for what they were proud to be: Jews who chose martyrdom rather than apostasy, not helpless victims of a collective delusion. Yet soon, long before the coining of the term "antisemitism" about 1873 or the catastrophic irrationality of the Nazi camps, Jews were being killed for what they were not.

If by "antisemitism" we mean not only its racist manifestation but all instances in which people, because they are labeled Jews, are feared as symbols of subhumanity and hated for threatening characteristics they do not in fact possess,[1] then antisemitism in all but name was widespread in northern Europe by 1350, when many believed that Jews were beings incapable of fully rational thought who conspired to overthrow Christendom, who committed ritual crucifixions, ritual cannibalism, and host profanation, and who caused the Black Death by poisoning wells—even though no one had observed Jews committing any of those crimes. Unknown to the ancient world, antisemitism emerged in the Middle Ages, along with so many other features of later Western culture. It is one contribution to which historians of the majority cannot point with pride, so most medievalists have avoided discussing it until very recently.[2]

That tragedy would not have occurred, nor would an intense and sophisticated Jewish culture have developed in Europe, had not the presence of Jews been tolerated. And when the Babylonian Talmud was being formed in the East, and the Roman Empire was drawing to an end in the West, that possibility was uncertain. After a Christian religion had been recognized as licit in the Roman Empire, gained political influence, become the official religion in 391, and secured the official suppression of paganism, the future of Judaism hung in the balance. Partly because most lay people got on only too well with Jews, many bishops and monks wanted to extirpate that contaminating influence and destroyed synagogues across the empire. St. Ambrose, bishop of Milan, threatened Theodosius I with excommunication if he punished the perpetrators of one of those incidents. Ambrose declared that it was right to destroy synagogues and that Christians had a duty to disobey any law that forbade their destruction.[3] But imperial reluctance to change Roman law, supported by Pauline theology about the providential role of Jews, preserved the synagogues, albeit with a lowered status.

That restricted toleration was finally made the official policy of the Western church about 600 by the man who has been described both as the last of the church fathers and the first of the medieval popes. Gregory I held that nonbelievers should be led to the faith by clear reasoning pleasantly presented, not by persecution, and that those who acted otherwise were pursuing their own ends, not those of God. It was Gregory the Great who formulated the statement that appears in the preamble of all the papal bulls of protection for Jews from 1120 to the end of the Middle Ages: "Just as license ought not to be allowed for Jews to do anything in their synagogues beyond what is permitted by law, so also they ought to suffer no injury in those things that have been granted to them." For better or worse, Gregory declared the right of Jews to live as Jews in Western Christian societies.[4]

Solomon Grayzel commented that "it is not difficult to imagine what the fate of Jews would have been had not the popes made it part of church policy to guarantee the Jews life and rights of religious observance."[5] But, fatally, that policy was never vigorously enough pursued by popes nor strongly enough enforced by local prelates to be decisive in time of need. Once Europe had fully accepted medieval Christianity, the expulsion of Jews began in earnest: from England and southern Italy in 1290, from France first in 1306 and finally in 1394, from many parts of Germany by 1350, and from Spain in 1492 and Portugal in 1497. While these expulsions were the work of secular authorities, impelled primarily by self-interested motives, no pope spoke out against them, and by 1500 much of Europe was *judenrein*. Although Jews were never expelled from Rome itself, the principle that Jews existed legitimately in Europe was never fully accepted in Christendom at large. The toleration extended by churchmen to those whom they considered both their forefathers in righteousness and Christ-killers was too ambivalent and half-hearted to provide reliable protection. The possibility of extirpation was always open.

I have thus far presented what may be considered the traditional picture of the Christian Middle Ages, in which the teaching of contempt of Jews by churchmen was carried to extremes by religious fanatics and lay people incapable of understanding the religious subtleties involved. But let us not be so naive as to reduce history to the conflict of religions or to think that every action of people labeled as Christians or Jews was dictated by their religions. Granted that the Roman Catholic church designated Jews within Christian society as an inferior religious outgroup, why did so many inhabitants of European Christendom treat Jews in ways that either were not prescribed by Christian doctrine or were explicitly prohibited by it? Why did people in northern Europe go far beyond the official anti-Judaism and create antisemitism?

Until about the year 1000, hostility toward Jews was purely anti-Judaic and generally insignificant. If some Mediterranean clerics did try to instill anti-Judaic attitudes in the minds of lay people, particularly rulers, they were rarely successful in a barbarized Europe whose Christian religiosity was so different from that of Christians in the Roman Empire.[6] Anti-Judaic laws were intermittently promulgated, and in some localities Jews were sometimes given the choice of baptism or exile. An excellent example of this kind of cleric is the Spaniard, Archbishop Agobard of Lyons, one of the most rational and conscientious Christians of the first half of the ninth century. He was shocked that, in the avowedly Christian society of the Carolingian Empire, the common people and nobles seemed to favor Jews as much as Christians, and he tried to persuade Charlemagne's successor, Louis the Pious, to enforce the anti-Judaic laws of the Catholic church—without success.[7] For there was no significant animus against the descendants of the prophets and the warriors of the Old Testament in that heavily Germanized and warlike society. During the next two centuries, however, the situation changed radically.

By 1000, the second great wave of invasions—by Saracens, Vikings, and Magyars—had been repulsed; the parish network had been completed; Benedictine monasteries were richly endowed across Europe; and Europeans had become self-consciously Christian in their own way. During the eleventh century, political stability and economic development progressed sufficiently for Europeans to go on the attack against their non-Christian neighbors in Spain, eastern Germany, and the Holy Land—and to do so under the sign of the Cross. Christian symbols had become accepted as the banner of European culture and of the European expansion that began with the First Crusade in 1096 and continued for centuries.

The first great massacre of Jews in Europe in 1096 marked the beginning of a new and tragic phase in Jewish history because of a radical change in the pattern of European hostility to Jews. Those massacres were not committed by the official crusading armies but by bands, consisting primarily of peasants, which set out from northern Europe before the official forces. The worst hostility was no longer Mediterranean, ecclesiastical, and official; it was northern, popular, and defied both ecclesiastical and secular prohibitions. The unofficial crusaders came from that area of Europe where Mediterranean influences were most directly confronted by Germanic culture: northeastern France and the Rhineland. Here illiterate people, whose Germanic religiosity emphasized warfare and drew little distinction between sacred and profane activities, had finally learned to define their cosmos in terms of salient Christian symbols and rituals. To them, it seemed ridiculous to go and kill distant Moslems before dealing first with God's worst enemies close at hand, the Jews who had killed their Christ. Yet although the Christianity of this ignorant and brutal rabble differed notably from that of Ambrose of Milan, the massacres were nonetheless still primarily anti-Judaic in motivation, an overflow of animus against disbelievers in an atmosphere of religious war.

The nature of the hostility was old; its pervasiveness and intensity, however, was new, and it forced Jews to adopt new forms of conduct that aroused new kinds of hostility; a self-fulfilling prophecy had been set in motion. The intense pressure of the majority increasingly circumscribed voluntary Jewish conduct and forced Jews to adapt to their more perilous situation. Before 1100, Jews had been considered fundamentally inferior because they could not recognize Christ's truth and had killed him, but most of the restrictions imposed by ecclesiastical law to separate Jews from Christians had been unenforceable. After 1100, however, in an ever more self-consciously Christian society, those old restrictions were more strictly enforced and new ones imposed, because now lay people as well as clerics had discovered that they could exploit the Jews.

In 1100, Jews were not concentrated in moneylending and were not stereotyped as usurers. But in the twelfth century, the commercial revolution brought to northern Europe the development of towns, monopolistic merchant and craft guilds, more financial transactions, and a demand for credit. Wealthier Jews, excluded from their former participation in long-distance trade and from local production, began to concentrate disproportionately in moneylending. By the second half of the twelfth century, ecclesiastical officials became seriously concerned with the new importance of borrowing and lending at interest. Their prohibitions fairly effectively stopped the monasteries, the first great suppliers of credit, from lending at interest, but only forced Christian merchants to camouflage their lending operations, and did not at first affect Jews at all. Yet if Jews were never the first, the only, or—except briefly in parts of northern Europe—the principal lenders, they nonetheless came to concentrate openly and very disproportionately in northern Europe in the unpopular but needed activity of pawnbroking and contract loans secured by gages of landed property. The needs and pressure of the majority had thus forced Jews to engage in new conduct.

Their increasing unpopularity as unbelieving Christ-killers and usurers in turn made Jews more dependent on the protection of secular authorities. In return for a large share of the profits, kings and princes were willing to protect Jews and their moneylending, despite ecclesiastical admonitions to the contrary; as a result, Jewish lenders in northern Europe reached their greatest prosperity around 1200.[8] Later on, as Italian lenders came to provide an alternative source of credit, rulers discovered that protecting unpopular Jews was a political liability of decreasing economic value. The period of expulsions was approaching.

As pressure mounted in the thirteenth century, Jews in northern Europe were increasingly identified as town-dwellers, constricted to certain quarters, marked by distinctive clothing, denied the right to bear arms, forbidden to leave their lords' jurisdiction, concentrated in moneylending, and forced to rely on money and bribery for self-protection. Not only were they now seen as Christ-killers; they were also stereotyped as usurers, bribers, and secret killers. And since thirteenth-century people did not realize that the new stereotyped conduct was a result of majority pressure, Jews now seemed even more inferior than they had in the fourth or the eleventh century. Jews were not inferior simply because they had disbelieved and killed Christ; rather, their disbelief and killing of Christ was only one, if the most important, manifestation of a much deeper essential inferiority that was evident also in such apparently unconnected conduct as usury, bribery, and military incapacity. It was now much easier to think of Jews as less than fully human and to treat them accordingly.

The anti-Jewish stereotypes mentioned thus far, which I shall call xenophobic stereotypes, all had a kernel of truth. (It should be remembered that, so long as it was safe, Jews always acknowledged that Jesus should have been killed as a heretic.) But now a new kind of stereotype appeared, which I shall call chimerical. These chimerical stereotypes had no kernel of truth; they depicted imaginary monsters, for they ascribed to Jews horrendous deeds imagined by Christians that Christians had never observed Jews committing. The "Jews" were used as a symbol to express repressed fantasies about crucifixion and cannibalism, repressed doubts about the real presence of Christ in the Eucharist, and unbearable doubts and fears about God's goodness and the bubonic bacillus that imperceptibly invaded people's bodies. By attacking "Jews," individuals who were poorly integrated in their societies and within themselves could express the tensions they felt as a conflict between good and bad people, between Christians and Jews. These psychologically troubled people discovered that they could even gain social approval for their struggle to support generally accepted values against hidden menaces by accusing and attacking Jews.

The first European accusation of Jewish ritual murder was created at Norwich about 1150 by the cumulative irrationality of a superstitious insignificant priest and his wife, a mendacious Jewish apostate, and an unimportant monk who sought to overcome his sense of inferiority. They transmuted the fact of a cruel murder of a boy by an unknown killer into a fantasy that Jews throughout Europe conspired to crucify a Christian child once a year as a sacrifice and to show contempt for Christianity. Despite much initial skepticism at Norwich, the fantasy gradually gained acceptance because people wanted a new local saint to work miraculous cures, and because local churchmen welcomed profitable new relics. As the rumor spread, other churchmen in England and northern France claimed that bodies discovered in their localities were also those of such martyrs and made shrines for them. Still other clerics chronicled these purported crucifixions as facts.

A century later, in 1235, Germany contributed its own variation: the fantasy that Jews killed Christians for ritual cannibalism. Such rumors, followed by massacres, became so frequent, particularly in Germany, that they provoked official investigations by the German emperor and then by the pope. But although both denied that ritual cannibalism was part of Judaism, no pope ever condemned the crucifixion fantasy, for it too conveniently supported Christian doctrine about the Jews as Christ-killers. Consequently, when Henry III, the weakly pious king of England, investigated the alleged crucifixion of young Hugh of Lincoln in 1255, nothing inhibited his credulity, and he became the first major authority to execute Jews for ritual murder. Although many members of the tiny educated class remained skeptical, it was becoming hard for peasants not to believe accusations supported by such authoritative confirmation.

By the end of the thirteenth century, when the fantasy of ritual murder had become firmly rooted in northern Europe, a new fantasy suddenly appeared. Christians had long debated whether and how Christ's body and blood were present in the consecrated bread and wine of the Eucharist. In 1215, the Fourth Lateran Council tried to settle the issue by promulgating the dogma of transubstantiation. Though doubts continued, the cult of the body of Christ, of the consecrated host, was massively developed. In 1264, the new feast of Corpus Christi was made official for the whole church; and during the troubled fourteenth century, the need for reassurance of Christ's real presence drove people to witness the Mass, some even rushing from church to church just to see the priest elevate the consecrated wafer. But was Christ really present?

The best indication that hidden doubts continued was the way Jews, who assuredly did not believe this dogma, were exploited to prove its truth. By a strange coincidence, only at the end of the thirteenth century, when so much had been staked on the reality of Christ's physical presence in the Mass, were Jews suddenly accused of torturing Christ by assaulting the consecrated host. By that time, Jews had been expelled from England and France, but the new fantasy spread like wildfire through Germany and Austria. Thousands of Jews were slaughtered, and new shrines were erected for the allegedly profaned hosts. Proof was supposedly provided by blood or cries emanating from the miraculous tortured host or, more naturally, by the discovery of a mutilated wafer in a Jew's house—evidence that, at least in one case, is known to have been planted by a priest. In fact, as one skeptical intellectual of the fifteenth century, Nicholas of Cusa, pointed out, the fantasy contradicted the dogma of transubstantiation, which declared that the visible characteristics of the bread and wine did not change, only their underlying substance. But that did not prevent waves of persecution which only stopped with the emergence of Protestantism.[9]

Thus, by the early fourteenth century, Jews were no longer slaughtered as a side-effect of crusades and out of anti-Judaic animus; instead they were killed by mobs organized to avenge ritual murders and profaned hosts. Many now saw Jews as inhuman beings who secretly conspired to commit the worst atrocities on defenseless hosts and children and to destroy Christendom. Antisemitism was firmly implanted. When the Black Death broke out in Europe between 1347 and 1350, it was all but inevitable that Jews would be accused of poisoning the wells in order to overthrow Christendom and be slaughtered in thousands despite papal prohibition.

It is significant that although xenophobic stereotypes were current throughout Europe, chimerical fantasies were largely restricted to northern Europe, especially to the least Romanized regions. Although militant friars and other clerics tried to implant these fantasies in Mediterranean Europe, they had little success—as the Nazis similarly failed to convert the Fascists to the Aryan myth.[10] In the Middle Ages, as in modern times, the heartland of antisemitism was northern Europe.

The chimerical fantasies had been developed in England, northern France, and Germany by a minority of anxious Christians who used the label "Jew," and the persons so identified, as a menacing symbol of their own weaknesses, their own guilt, doubts, and fears. Social confirmation through shrines and executions then convinced many more rational people (who had already been indoctrinated in the xenophobic stereotypes) that the chimerical accusations were true. But by the end of the Middle Ages, English and French people were denied this irrational way of dealing with weaknesses in their societies and in themselves because the Jews had been expelled from those kingdoms. Even though the label "Jew" retained its chimerical symbolism in French and English culture, other explanations for personal and social failure had to be found.

From Germany, however, where the Jews had first been massacred in large numbers in 1096, Jews had never been completely expelled. Here, perhaps partly because of the guilt and fear of reprisal aroused by those initial massacres of the defenseless, occurred most of the killing incited by chimerical fantasies during the Middle Ages. Here, from the later Middle Ages to Hitler, there was not only "the Jew" embedded in religion, literature, and art,[11] as a symbol of depravity and subhumanity; there were also real Jews whose isolation in the ghettos made it all the easier for people outside to perceive them, not as individual human beings, but as walking symbols of those social and personal threats that people could not confront in themselves but could attack directly when projected on Jews. And here it was that Protestantism had the least effect on attitudes toward Jews. Although Martin Luther broke the ecclesiastical unity of medieval Christendom and was briefly optimistic that his understanding of Christianity would convert the Jews, he soon returned to a virulent repetition of the medieval chimerical fantasies about them.

Much later, in 1935, when *Der Stürmer* was cautioning parents to keep their children away from Jews at Passover, a popular edition of Luther's pamphlet *The Jews and Their Lies* was reissued. One violent passage among many in that pamphlet stands out:

> We do not curse them but wish them well, physically and spiritually. We lodge them, we let them eat and drink with us. We do not kidnap their children and pierce them through; we do not poison their wells; we do not thirst for their blood. How, then, do we incur such terrible anger on the part of such great and holy children of God? There is no other explanation for this than . . . that God has struck them with "madness and blindness and confusion of mind." So we are even at fault in not avenging all this innocent blood of our Lord and of the Christians which they shed for three hundred years after the destruction of Jerusalem, and the blood of the

children they have shed since then (which still shines forth from their eyes and their skin). We are at fault in not slaying them.[12]

In contrast with the limited Calvinist tolerance in Holland and England, German Lutheranism only reinforced the medieval antisemitism that, together with its future victims, the Ashkenazim, was already so deeply rooted in German culture.

14.

Toward a Definition of Antisemitism

I

Whatever most who now use the term "antisemitism" mean by it, they
do not use it in its original and explicitly defined sense, and I will argue
that as presently used it impedes rather than aids understanding of
hostility against Jews.[1] "Antisemitism" was invented about 1873 by
Wilhelm Marr to describe the policy toward Jews based on "racism"
that he and others advocated. Although elements of the racist theory
can be traced back to the eighteenth century, if not earlier, the theory
itself was only fully elaborated in the latter half of the nineteenth. It
proclaimed that humans were divided into clearly distinguishable races
and that the intellectual, moral, and social conduct and potential of the
members of these races were biologically determined. As elaborated in
the Aryan myth, it maintained that Jews were a race and that, not only
were they, like other races, inferior to the Aryan race, but also that
Jews were the most dangerous of those inferior races.

If the meaning of "antisemitism" for its original proponents is clear,
their use of the term is empirically meaningless for us because the
Aryan myth on which it depended is now recognized as obviously
false. Contemporary biologists no longer believe there are distinct racial boundaries between humans, only differences in the relative com-
monness of certain hereditary traits, for every marriage circle is a potential race.[2] And since any man and woman who are not sterile can
breed, marriage circles or patterns of intercourse are decided, not by

biological processes, but by geographic or cultural proximity as determined by geographic and cultural barriers. Hence racial boundaries are no more distinct than cultural or geographic boundaries. Jews, who have lived in so many regions and cultures, certainly do not collectively constitute a race, even though some Jews may have some hereditary physiological traits that distinguish them from some other groups of the European population.

The greatest weakness of the Aryan myth, however, was not the belief that large human groups could be sharply differentiated according to hereditary biological traits, but the conviction that biological inheritance explained cultural differences, a conviction obvious in the confusion of language and biology involved in the concept of "Semitism." Since cultural and geographic proximity or barriers have affected patterns of intercourse, there have indeed been some obvious correlations between distinctive physiological and distinctive cultural traits, for example, in Chinese civilization. But where that has occurred, those traits have been connected contingently, not necessarily. Knowledge of such a historical correlation does not predict the mental or cultural potential of the offspring of such groups who are raised in a markedly different culture. And if a necessary correlation cannot be demonstrated by history, even less can it be demonstrated by biology.

Recent advances in genetic and behavioral biology have made it clear that our present knowledge of the relation between gross physiological characteristics and the functioning of the brain is minimal, that our understanding of the relation between the brain and mental processes is extremely limited, and that mental adaptation to environment is apparently constrained but not determined by our genetic inheritance. Hence it is impossible to infer the mental or cultural potential of large groups from biological data. Although some people still insist that it is possible to establish a statistical correlation between some gross physiological characteristics, such as pigmentation, of large groups and their mental and cultural potential, assertions of this kind have been so persuasively criticized as to seem worthless. Not only have the biological distinctions used been elementary or dubious, not only have the criteria used to measure mental and cultural performance and potential been recognized as crude and culturally biased to an unknown but vast degree, but it is now obvious that the strong biases of some of the most prominent proponents of such theories dictated their theories, controlled their empirical research, and led them into major fallacies and even fraud.[3]

Since the best present knowledge so obviously invalidates the Aryan theory, it follows that we cannot use "racism," the central and false concept of that myth, to explain the hostility toward Jews—or Blacks—displayed by the propagators of the myth. The Aryan myth was *their* (false) rationalization of their hostility, but since we do not believe that biological differences were the cause of their hostility, "racism" cannot be *our* explanation of the myth or of their hostility.

We may, of course, use "racism" to refer to those relatively recent historical beliefs, utterances, and actions which affirm, without empirical foundation, that racially different peoples necessarily have different mental or cultural potentials, and we may call those who hold such ideas racists. In that sense, the terms are convenient labels, like "Zoroastrian," to denote certain historical beliefs and those who have held them, and no confusion will arise if the terms are only used taxonomically to denote those historical beliefs. But only genuine racists, only people who believe that biological differences were the fundamental cause of such hostility, can use racism as an explanatory category. And to do so, they must argue, however illegitimately, from biological knowledge, not from social scientific knowledge.

Despite the biological propensities of early anthropologists,[4] "race" is not a term proper to the social sciences. Social scientists use the term either as it is defined by contemporary biologists or in their descriptions of the thoughts of the people they study. In the latter case, "race" refers not to a process of nature but to an artifact of human consciousness which, like phlogiston or centaurs, may have no existence outside the mind of the people studied. And if the best contemporary biological knowledge forces social scientists to accept that someone who rationalized his hostility by "race," for example, Alfred Rosenberg, was wrong in his beliefs about "race," then they must conclude that the biological fact of race (so far as it is a fact) did not cause Rosenberg's beliefs and hostility. They must then look to other features of human nature, such as irrational or wishful thinking, that fall within the purview of their own disciplines to explain why Rosenberg was so hostile to Jews and embraced that error about "race." And as they develop their explanation of such hostility, they should use terms that distinguish their own explanation clearly from the rationalizations they are trying to explain. To typify and explain the process that produced the erroneous thought of believers in the Aryan myth as "racism" is to confuse a symptom with a cause, a confusion that enables the Aryan myth to contaminate our scientific thinking.[5]

I have labored this point at some length because what has been said about "racism" applies equally to "antisemitism." In its original meaning, "antisemitism" is as erroneous an explanation of hostility toward Jews as the racism from which it emerged in 1873. And in its present use, "antisemitism," like "racism," has given hostages to the Aryan myth.

Of course, because of Hitler, the term has been transvalued. Not only are Jews good in their own eyes, but they are now seen as no worse than, or as good as, anyone else by many others in the West. Consequently, "antisemitism" is now understood as a highly pejorative term both by Jews and many non-Jews—which is what makes the charge of "antisemitism," loosely defined, so useful a weapon in political discourse. So long as memories of the "Final Solution" remain vivid, the use of that special term of dark origin implies that there is something unusually and uniquely evil about any serious hostility toward all Jews.

But the common use of "antisemitism" now to refer to any hostility against Jews collectively at any time has strange implications. Although it transvalues the original meaning of the term and rejects the categorization of Jews as a race, it nonetheless carries over from the Aryan myth the implication that hostility toward Jews is an enduring (if now bad) reaction of non-Jews to some unique and unchanging (if now good) real characteristics of Jews. It also implies, in agreement with that myth, that the hostility that made possible Hitler's "Final Solution" was no different in fundamental nature, only in intensity and the technology applied, from the riots in ancient Alexandria in the first century of the Common Era or from any other hostility Jews have ever had to face. The usage thus implies that there was nothing uniquely evil in quality about the Final Solution, only a quantitative difference.

In fact, there have been such obvious changes in some characteristics of hostility to Jews that scholars have felt the need to make some distinctions, typically by adding adjectives to "antisemitism." Thus Hannah Arendt and many other historically minded scholars have distinguished between religious and racial "antisemitism." But those adjectives only distinguish secondary characteristics of the hostility; they do not imply a fundamental difference in its nature. Although the adjectives distinguish different historical rationalizations for the hostility, the noun "antisemitism" still implies a constancy in the basic cause and quality of hostility against Jews at any time. That implication may be expressed negatively when looking at non-Jews or positively when the focus is on Jews. Thus one book traces "anti-Semitism" from the first century to the present and defines it as "actions and attitudes against Jews based on the belief that Jews are uniquely inferior, evil or deserving of condemnation by their very nature or by historical or supernatural dictates."[6] Jacob Katz puts it positively: "I regard the very presence of the unique Jewish community among the other nations as the stimulus to the animosity directed at them."[7]

Like the Aryan myth, this conception of "antisemitism" depends, I would argue, on the fallacy of misplaced concreteness or illicit reification, in this case on the unproven assumption that for centuries, and despite innumerable changes on both sides, there has been a distinctive kind of reaction of non-Jews directed only at Jews that corresponds to the concept presently evoked by the word "antisemitism." What makes that fallacy attractive to many people, I would suggest, is their prior assumption that, whether by divine choice or otherwise, there has always been something uniquely valuable in Jewishness, because Jews have always incorporated and preserved uniquely superior values. They then assume that the resolute and enduring expression of those unique values by Jews has aroused a correspondingly unique type of hostility against them as bearers of that unique quality throughout their existence.

Such a perspective might fairly be called ethnocentric; and, not surprisingly, those who accept it have not felt any need to examine non-Jews carefully to see whether the quality of their hostility to Jews has in fact been unique and unchanging. Yet the quality of hostility against Jews cannot be determined by premises about Jews, for it is a characteristic of the mentality of non-Jews, not of Jews, and it is determined, not by the objective reality of Jews, but by what the symbol "Jews" has signified to non-Jews. Moreover, the kind of hostility evoked has not been directed only against Jews.

II

There is, of course, another well-known definition of "antisemitism" that is not based on Jewish history yet implies that there has been something unusual about hostility toward Jews. Social psychologists and sociologists have defined antisemitism as an expression of ethnocentrism or "ethnic prejudice," or simply "prejudice." Since their disciplines, influenced by anthropology with its tendency to cultural relativity, involved a wider perspective on social conflict than historical study of a specific conflict, they were more prepared to see antisemitism as unique in historical detail but not in nature, to recognize that antisemitism was similar to the unusual hostility of whites against blacks in America and to the hostility faced by other groups that had never been categorized as races by the racists.[8] Yet although that broadening of perspective brought a major advance in the understanding of antisemitism, it also presents problems.

"Ethnic prejudice" has the advantage that it is a term of social science that receives its definition from the theories of the social sciences, not from the rationalizations of racists or the presuppositions of the victims of such hostility. And while the concept clearly includes in its purview those beliefs which have been termed "racism," it recognizes that false beliefs about race and about groups that have never been considered races may be identical in basic nature and etiology. It frees us to recognize that, despite differences in the concrete detail of their historical expression, unusual hostility toward a variety of groups may be manifestations of a single basic phenomenon or process.

Yet if "racism" is too misleading and restrictive in its connotations, the problem with "ethnic prejudice" as presently defined is that it is too inclusive. Some of the better-known definitions may indicate the problem.

> Ethnocentrism is based on a pervasive and rigid ingroup-outgroup distinction; it involves stereotyped negative imagery and hostile attitudes regarding outgroups, stereotyped positive imagery and submissive attitudes regarding ingroups, and a hierarchical, authoritarian view of group interaction in which ingroups are rightly dominant, outgroups subordinate.[9]
>
> Prejudice is a pattern of hostility in interpersonal relations which is directed against an entire group, or against its individual members; it fulfills a specific irrational function for its bearer.[10]
>
> We use the term prejudice to refer to a set of attitudes which causes, supports, or justifies discrimination.[11]
>
> Ethnic prejudice is an antipathy based upon a faulty and inflexible generalization. It may be felt or expressed. It may be directed toward a group as a whole, or toward an individual because he is a member of the group.[12]
>
> Our theory leads us to propose that what appears at first glance to be discriminations among men on the basis of race or ethnic group may turn out upon closer analysis to be discriminations on the basis of belief congruence over specific issues.[13]
>
> We shall define prejudice as an emotional, rigid attitude (a *predisposition* to respond to a certain stimulus in a certain way) toward a group of people.[14]

Prejudice is a negative attitude toward a socially defined group and toward any person perceived to be a member of that group.[15]

The fundamental weaknesses of all these definitions is most obvious in the last one: almost any form of intergroup hostility—including that all-too-normal component of history, war—involves prejudice. Hence any hostility to Jews collectively at any time can still be denoted as "antisemitism." Thus Glock and Stark have defined antisemitism as "the hatred and persecution of Jews as a group; not the hatred of persons who happen to be Jews, but rather the hatred of persons *because* they are Jews."[16] Yet I, for one, would be reluctant to assert that the hostility which, for example, many French people felt toward Germans between 1870 and 1945 differed only in intensity and overtness of expression from that directed against Jews and blacks in the same period. I do not wish to abandon the insight that the kind of hostility symbolized by Auschwitz differed in more than intensity from that symbolized by Sedan or Verdun or that evoked by the swastika on the Eiffel Tower.

The theories of "ethnic prejudice" were originally developed primarily to deal with the hostility to Jews and blacks that seemed the archetype of racism; they therefore suggested that this was an unusual kind of hostility. But "ethnic prejudice" rapidly came to refer to hostility against other groups, thereby diluting the unusual quality of "ethnic prejudice." A major reason for that extension was that the fundamental criterion underlying most definitions was cognitive performance about specific groups, the presence of a failure of learning as measured by some unstated standard, the maintenance of a "faulty and inflexible generalization" about a group, to use Allport's language. Indeed, that criterion is implicit in the term chosen from common usage, prejudice; to prejudge is to make a judgment without knowledge or without adequate knowledge. But by what standard is a generalization about groups to be considered faulty?

Thinking in terms of categories is inevitable and essential for human action, and no one has had perfect knowledge about something as intangible, complex, and ill-understood as "groups." The problem for the people who invented the term "ethnic prejudice" was, therefore, to find some standard by which they could assess generalizations about groups and distinguish between those which were so faulty as to be abnormal—as to indicate prejudice—and those which manifested only the normal, inevitable amount of prejudgment.

The standard the social scientists used was primarily their own standard of rationality or objectivity,[17] their own knowledge of social groups and their own judgment—frequently as liberals or members of the groups that were the objects of such hostility—as to which generalizations were most faulty and dangerous. That almost unconscious decision was ironic since social scientists spend much of their lives disagreeing with one another about the nature of groups and the effect of membership on an individual's conduct. A more serious problem, however, is that the presenticentric, ethnocentric, and egocentric quality of that standard makes it historically, culturally, and socially biased. People of different periods or contemporaries who had not had the same opportunity to acquire information about groups, to assess the reliability of that information, and to learn how to think analytically about abstractions would almost inevitably seem prejudiced in the eyes of these social scientists. Imagine applying the standard to medieval people!

To escape that dilemma, some scholars, such as Levinson, Allport, Jahoda, and Yinger, have emphasized that the generalizations must be not only faulty but also inflexible or rigid. The people who express faulty generalizations must also manifest an unwillingness to modify them when confronted with new information that implies that they are faulty. While the faults of the generalizations may simply reflect lack of social opportunity to know better, the inflexibility with which they are held suggests a refusal to learn, a psychological inhibition—as is implied in Ackerman and Jahoda's definition. It is this approach which underlies the whole conception of the prejudiced personality developed in *The Authoritarian Personality.*

The weakness of this solution is that either it necessitates an unacceptable psychological reductionism or else it has to face the very objections it was designed to overcome. Let it be assumed that one could examine some people psychologically, determine which psychological problems they had, and observe that some of their statements about groups were held inflexibly and were psychologically connected with their psychopathology. One might then infer that their generalizations about groups were faulty because the people were psychologically blocked and could not learn. It would also follow that the generalizations of other people with the same psychopathology could be assumed to be prejudiced. This approach, however, involves the assumption that a psychological assessment of people makes possible a decision about the *truth* of their assertions, an obvious reductionist fallacy.

That fallacy was so obvious that most social scientists who emphasized a psychological explanation of "prejudice" sought to avoid it. They argued instead that it was possible to show a clear correlation between the more extreme and apparently rigid faulty generalizations that were objectively invalid and some psychopathological conditions. Yet any such correlation still depends upon a prior judgment about the falsity of generalizations about groups and hence upon some standard of objectivity that is not culturally or socially biased, and that was just what was missing.

The reason this approach seemed plausible at all was that it was used within a society with a relatively uniform educational system and a highly developed system of mass communications. Researchers therefore tended to assume that any firmly maintained generalizations that deviated drastically from their own standard of rationality could not be explained by variations in cultural influence on cognitive performance and could, therefore, be considered to be inflexible rather than merely faulty. Yet that was only an assumption, and an assumption, moreover, that overlooked the difference between nonrational and irrational thought and encouraged the tendency to impute psychological weaknesses to those who disagreed notably with the social scientists' values and ideas about groups. Furthermore, it overlooked the problem that this approach could not be applied to study of earlier periods or of contemporary societies with markedly different cultures or subcultures.

A very different solution to the problem of distinguishing rigidity in beliefs from mere error was to disregard the specific content of people's beliefs about groups and examine the structure of their thinking in general. Regardless of the truth of their specific assertions, do people form their beliefs in different ways according to their personality? This was a major hypothesis of The Authoritarian Personality, and it was further developed by Milton Rokeach in The Open and Closed Mind. He designed a "Dogmatism" scale that measured, he believed, the difference in the extent to which people reacted to new information on the basis of its intrinsic merits or on the basis of such cognitively irrelevant factors as personal insecurity or fear of social authorities.

One problem with Rokeach's approach is that it is difficult to assess dogmatism in the abstract without reference to assertions on specific subjects. And since the items in his Dogmatism scale referred to universal problems and current issues, the assessment of the responses relied considerably on Rokeach's judgments about the correct or psychologically indicative answers, so that the problem of cultural bias may still be present. Were Rokeach's scale applied to earlier cultures, it would be discovered that most of them were highly dogmatic—even though we, using the criterion of Auschwitz, might judge them much less "prejudiced." There is also the problem of disagreement about nonrational values and the fact that peoples and cultures are selectively dogmatic, that Calvinists were highly dogmatic theologically while being highly flexible in economic matters. Rokeach's approach does not pay enough attention to the phenomena of historical change, social differentiation, and mental compartmentalization. For that reason, it is of little help in determining which people will make dogmatic negative assertions about which groups. There may, indeed, be a dogmatic refusal to make such assertions.

Confronted with these difficulties in finding any standard of objectivity that would distinguish between prejudiced and merely erroneous generalizations about groups, and that would be value-free, some scholars who did not favor a psychological explanation of "prejudice" solved the problem by cutting the Gordian knot. In order to eliminate sociocultural bias, they simply abandoned the effort to distinguish between faulty and valid generalizations about outgroups. Instead, they considered as "prejudice" any negative attitudes toward groups or toward individuals because they were members of groups, and also any discriminatory actions against groups and individuals as members. The definitions of Rose and Ashmore are examples of this approach, and its peculiar implications are apparent from Ashmore's definition of "prejudice reduction" as "any move toward perceiving, evaluating, and responding to members of the group in question as individuals."[18]

Not only negative but also positive evaluations of groups are, by implication, "prejudice." Absence of "prejudice" occurs only when all evaluations of groups are given up and individuals relate to other people simply as individuals. But from this extremely nominalistic and anarchic perspective, in this never-never land of individuals with personal but no social characteristics, according to a view of humanity that overlooks the importance of nonrational thought for values, any evaluation of people's conduct as members of social collectivities is impossible or illegitimate. The concept of prejudice is so broadened as to be useless for analyzing the social reality with which everyone, including social scientists, must deal.[19]

It might seem that "ethnic prejudice" is even more useless a concept than "racism" because, if it recognizes that the kind of hostility manifested against "races" has also been directed against people who constitute a cultural but not a racial group, and therefore avoids the trap of "racism," it fails to set limits to that widening of perspective and avoidance of the errors of racists. Yet that is not the case, for "ethnic prejudice" avoids the flagrantly erroneous implications of "racism," and, as I shall try to indicate, the work done by those who have defined it has been immensely valuable and indicates a way to avoid some of the dilemmas just discussed.

III

Serious study of intergroup hostility—as opposed to detailed descriptions of particular examples—began in the 1920s, perhaps partly in reaction to the carnage between 1914 and 1918. Anthropologists developed the concept of xenophobia, the idea of an instinctive hostility toward strange—little-known and differently constituted—outgroups; and the invention of the social distance scale by E. S. Bogardus in 1928 provided a way of measuring relative hostility toward different outgroups. In the same period, people began to speak of "race prejudice," but the theoretical basis for the recent conception of "ethnic prejudice" did not appear until 1938, when John Dollard linked the historical, anthropological, and sociological study of intergroup hostility with Freudian insights into irrationality and aggression;[20] and only after 1950 did the term "prejudice" become fairly standard, largely replacing its competitor, "ethnocentrism."

Bogardus and Dollard focused on hostility against blacks in the United States, but work on prejudice rapidly came to concentrate heavily on hostility toward Jews, because of the Nazi persecutions. Most of the early fundamental work, including *The Authoritarian Personality*, appeared in the *Studies in Prejudice* sponsored by the American Jewish Committee. The participation of European Jewish exiles familiar with Freud also strengthened the conjuncture between American social psychology and Freudian thought. By 1954, however, when Gordon Allport summed up the work of this early school in *The Nature of Prejudice*, the danger to Jews had diminished radically, and sociologists and psychologists in the United States concentrated again on the domestic scene and particularly on the flagrant problem of "prejudice" against blacks, although "prejudice" against Jews (or "antisemitism") remained a major topic, and increasing attention was paid to "prejudice" against other groups in America.

How did the analysts of "prejudice" up to 1954 understand the hostilities they examined? Many, often conflicting, definitions and theories of "prejudice" were formulated, but the hallmark of the original conception was its *cognitive definition* of prejudice as faulty and inflexible beliefs about outgroups and its *psychopathological* explanation of those cognitive errors. Since much of Nazi thought seemed patently irrational, and since those who rigidly held the most indisputably invalid ideas about Jews and blacks also contradicted themselves, manifested an obsession with Jews and blacks, and showed other symptoms of abnormality, psychological explanations seemed in order and were soon found, aided by the rising prestige of Freudian thought.

One of the more influential, if not the most valid, of these explanations was the oedipal theory about hostility against Jews. It is of interest here because it served to make the character of hostility against Jews unique. Implied in Freud's *Moses and Monotheism* (1939), developed by Rudolph M. Loewenstein in 1951, and accepted by Norman Cohn in 1969,[21] the oedipal theory—inevitably distorted in summary—proposes that Christians (believing or acculturated) identify with Christ the punished Son, associate Jews with the distant, punishing Father of the Old Testament, and hate Jews as father figures (disguised as sibling rivals) and ideal targets for the displacement of hostility resulting from personal failure to resolve the oedipal situation. If the oedipal theory had what some might consider the advantage of making hostility against Jews unique, it was not accepted by most psychologically oriented investigators because diagnosed oedipal conflicts also correlated with prejudice against blacks, and because no single psychological diagnosis correlated with all instances of prejudice.

All psychological explanations did, however, rely heavily on the Freudian concept of displaced aggression, the displacement of anger or the projection of guilt onto a socially provided target, a scapegoat; and that displacement was interpreted as a sign of some psychic weakness or mental ill-health. While this explanation was developed to explain the most manifestly hostile, it could also be applied in weakened form to explain the far greater numbers of people who were not patently neurotic or psychopathic and were only mildly hostile toward Jews and blacks. Because of some personal weakness, these people felt a need to conform closely to the values of their own group and to reject outgroups.

This early conception of "ethnic prejudice" presented it as something psychologically and socially abnormal, as the expression of psychopathological, authoritarian personalities, as a reflection of individual psychological problems. And just as Auschwitz could not be explained by any real threat Jews had posed to Germans, so this conception sharply distinguished ethnic prejudice from "normal" or "rational" hostility occasioned by real differences in values and real competition for scarce goods. The early school also insisted that prejudice might be directed against any culturally distinguishable outgroup, not just against those labeled as races.

Since 1954, work on "prejudice" has concentrated heavily on the most pervasive hostility in American society, that against blacks, in part because of black militancy. And it may be no accident that, when looking primarily at themselves rather than at Germans, American social scientists have focused primarily on the mass of the moderately hostile, have stressed the normality of "prejudice" under prevailing conditions, and have explained it, not as irrationality, but primarily as a failure of socially organized learning. While recognizing that general psychological factors such as anxiety can affect learning in general, this optimistic school has deemphasized the role of psychopathology—of displacement, projection, and scapegoating—in favor of an analysis of something that could be reorganized by social planning, the social conditioning of learning. While this school has continued to use a *cognitive definition* of prejudice, it has also given a *cognitive explanation* of how faulty generalizations are acquired.

Milton Rokeach, for example, argued that people were intolerant of Jews and blacks because the hostile persons "knew" that Jews or blacks had different values from their own. They believed so because, as a result of institutionalized discrimination or ghettoization, Jews and blacks were kept at a distance and socially presented as symbols of conflicting values. But if the hostile persons could only learn that individual Jews or blacks in fact shared some of their fundamental values, hostility would diminish sharply, and these outgroup members would seem preferable to members of their ingroup who disagreed about these values. If only they could meet, some of the best friends of these hostile persons would be Jews or blacks. Thus, although Rokeach asserts that general anxiety leads some people to be dogmatic, to use their belief systems as a defense mechanism, and to close their minds to alternative possibilities, what he analyzes primarily is cognitive behavior, social learning, leaving the whole question, for example, of why there was institutionalized discrimination against Jews and blacks out of consideration.

The tendency toward a purely cognitive explanation is marked in *The Tenacity of Prejudice* by Gertrude J. Selznick and Stephen Steinberg.[22] According to them, individual psychopathology plays no significant role in most people's acceptance of anti-Jewish and anti-black stereotypes. The single factor that correlates most clearly with routine "prejudice" in America—and with ignorance of democratic norms—is lack of a genuine education in the social sciences and humanities, in other words, a failure of social training of cognitive abilities. And in recent work on aggression in general,[23] not only is there almost no concern with "prejudice," but psychopathological explanations of aggression are almost completely neglected or rejected, and aggression is explained by social modeling, by observation of the rewards and punishments of imitating the conduct of others. Hence prejudice is but one aspect of learned behavior.

Thus, in contrast with earlier work, recent analyses of "prejudice" emphasize cognitive explanations of cognitive behavior over psychopathological explanations; they concentrate their attention on "normal" patterns of hostility; and they explain the "normality" of "prejudice." Yet part of the phenomenon escapes them. Rokeach admitted that, in different investigations, between 2 and 20 percent of his subjects responded primarily to racial or ethnic identifications, not to beliefs, and he wondered why these people responded so differently from the bulk of his subjects. Similarly, Selznick and Steinberg acknowledged that individual psychopathology, not educational deprivation, might explain the rabidly hostile who create and disseminate prejudiced stereotypes.

There have clearly been two broad conceptions of "prejudice" in the work of social scientists. The earlier school viewed prejudice in terms of the beliefs and conduct of a distinct minority of the population composed of markedly psychopathological people who actively created and sustained negative, faulty beliefs about outgroups, whereas later work has viewed prejudice as the beliefs and conduct of the much larger group of social conformists who readily learn and accept the socially provided negative stereotypes.

If both schools seem to be talking about the same phenomenon, "prejudice," that is because both have used similar questionnaires or other devices for self-reporting. The items in these instruments are designed to elicit reactions to assertions that liberal social scientists, Jews, and blacks have considered to be indicative of prejudice; and the items range from the most flagrant errors and the most vehement advocacy of discriminatory policies to assertions whose evaluation is much more a matter of judgment. Both the abnormally hostile and the mere conformists will assent to many or most of these items, so that the line drawn between the psychopathological and the conformists—and even those who view the outgroup objectively but disagree on values or goals—will be purely statistical. While these techniques make it possible to demonstrate that there is a continuum from highly hostile to highly favorable attitudes, they do not distinguish between different kinds of hostility, between psychopathological, conformist, and realistic hostility.

Both schools, therefore, face certain problems. In the first place, although they provide two different kinds of explanation for "prejudice," so that their findings taken together do suggest two—or three—different kinds of hostility, they cannot distinguish between the two because both schools use the same cognitive criterion to define assertions as prejudice or stereotypic. In the second place, if there is indeed a difference between psychopathologically prejudiced persons and mere conformists, these schools have not explained the dynamic relation between them; they have not shown how the assertions and the conduct of each have affected the other. In the third place, they have provided no such dynamic explanation because they have examined "prejudice" only horizontally or synchronically: they have only examined carefully people in contemporary societies in which the stereotypes are already deeply rooted in the culture. Lacking a strong historical foundation, they cannot explain, otherwise than by very superficial references to history, how the negative stereotypes became so culturally rooted or why particular groups became primary targets for prejudice.

Despite these problems, the work of both schools represents a huge advance in systematic analysis of a wide range of attitudes toward groups, and it has posed the problems that must be overcome if there is to be further advance. Intuitively, the distinction between the psychopathologically prejudiced and the social conformists seems highly valid. Moreover, Rokeach's effort to distinguish between the form of thought and the content of specific assertions seems very promising. If only one could find the right handle, one feels that most of the discrete findings would fall into place.

It is perhaps here that a historian's perspective can be helpful for, as we have suggested, a principal problem of the work on prejudice has been the presenticentric and ethnocentric character of the principal standard used to identify instances of "prejudice": the application of the standard of a modern, highly informed knowledge of group characteristics—often by a member of the outgroup in question—to decide which generalizations are so faulty and rigid as to satisfy the principal defining criterion of prejudice. Yet a knowledge of medieval history, for example, would suggest that many of the fourteenth-century European peasants who believed that Jews committed ritual murder were not psychopathological, that they would have been abnormal if they had not so believed, and that they were not peculiarly dogmatic or conformist given the standards and opportunities of their periods. For it was not they who had initiated the accusation; they merely accepted what the social authorities on whom they relied, who were much better educated, had told them; and they had no way to verify the accusation personally. That insight would suggest that there is a crucial distinction between the literal content of an assertion and the psychological state of the people who assert it, that an assertion that performs one function for some people may perform a different function for others. If this is so, we should perhaps pay less attention to the grammatical meaning of stereotypes and more to their contextual function.

IV

Directly or by implication, recent definitions of "prejudice" link verbal artifacts (grammatical assertions made about Jews which modern observers can judge to be true or false regardless of who has uttered them) with the emotional states and physical behavior of those who uttered them. More than that, study of prejudice has relied primarily on analysis of verbal behavior in an artificial situation: as has often been observed, research has relied heavily on the technique of self-reporting, on people's responses to the questionnaires and interviews of the researchers. And if only some definitions of prejudice are explicitly based on verbal behavior (faulty generalizations), almost all are so based implicitly because the phenomena referred to in the definitions (patterns of hostility, discrimination, sets of attitudes) have been established on the basis of verbal behavior because of the research techniques. Even greater has been the reliance on verbal behavior out of context in statements about historical prejudice, for example, the "antisemitism" of Tacitus. Yet it has long been observed with puzzlement or satisfaction that there often seems to be a great difference between what people may say about outgroups in an artificial context and what they actually say and do when confronted personally with clearly identifiable members of the outgroup in a normal context.[24]

The difference between what people say in an artificial and a normal context has often been explained by hypothesizing that social norms that oppose discrimination or violence have inhibited people from doing what they would like to have done.[25] Yet whatever the merit of that explanation, it leaves the obvious problem that verbal behavior as elicited and interpreted by the analysts of prejudice is not a reliable predictor of normal external—to say nothing of internal—behavior. That failure, I would suggest, is a result of the fact that analysts of "prejudice" have taken verbal behavior out of context, divided it into fragments, rearranged it, and placed their own interpretation on it.

Verbal communication, the technique humans have developed far beyond any other beings, is our best technique for understanding and empathizing with other people engaged in situations and conduct of any complexity. Yet a dictionary understanding of individual words and a syntactical understanding of phrases and sentences will not enable us to understand a speaker's intention unless we can also recognize the function the speaker wants those sounds to fulfill. And function can only be discovered by a recognition of the context or structure within which that verbal behavior occurs, as Freud, Wittgenstein, and the semioticists have emphatically insisted in very different ways. Moreover, as poetry and William Empson[26] would remind us, apparently declaratory statements may serve more than one function at a time.

If the primary function of verbal behavior is to communicate with and influence other humans, the primary questions to ask about assertions some of whose words refer to outgroups are: What is their function? What is the person who makes the assertion trying, consciously or subconsciously, to communicate? And is that intention realized by the recipient? As soon as we ask these questions, we become aware of a striking and hitherto unrecognized characteristic of many definitions of "prejudice": they say what prejudiced assertions are *not*, but they do not say what they *are*.[27] To say that assertions are faulty, rigid, inflexible, emotional, and pejorative does not tell us what kind of communication they themselves intrinsically are.

The definitions that follow are an effort to distinguish between assertions referring to outgroups on the basis of their intrinsic structure when viewed in context, and thereby to discover their intended function. The approach resembles that of Rokeach: I will try to distinguish the form of these assertions from their specific content. But I will not examine the form of people's whole belief systems about a variety of subjects; I will analyze only the form of assertions that contain verbal references to outgroups and imply a negative evaluation. And I will not try to define their form by some external criterion such as "dogmatism"; I will try to isolate formal characteristics intrinsic to the assertions—or vehicles of communication—themselves. I will then interpret the intention or function of assertions with these different formal characteristics.

> *Realistic assertions about outgroups are propositions that utilize the information available about an outgroup and are based on the same assumptions about the nature of groups and the effect of membership on individuals as those used to understand the ingroup and its reference groups and their members.*
>
> *Xenophobic assertions are propositions that grammatically attribute a socially menacing conduct to an outgroup and all its members but are empirically based only on the conduct of a historical minority of the members; they neglect other, unthreatening, characteristics of the outgroup; and they do not acknowledge that there are great differences between the individuals who compose the outgroup as there are between the individuals who compose the ingroup.*
>
> *Chimerical assertions are propositions that grammatically attribute with certitude to an outgroup and all its members characteristics that have never been empirically observed.*

All three of these kinds of assertions may obviously be used to justify hostility toward an outgroup and discriminatory treatment of it and its members; and when they are so used, we may speak of realistic hostility, xenophobia, and what I shall call chimeria. It is also obvious that these three kinds of hostility may be expressed by only a few individuals or by many people; and we would therefore say that realistic hostility, xenophobia, and chimeria become socially significant only when they are widespread and influence social policy. For reasons that I hope will become apparent, I would reserve use of the term "antisemitism," if it should be used at all, for socially significant chimerical hostility against Jews.

Let us look at each kind of assertion more carefully. By realistic assertions used to justify hostility I mean little more than that the person who makes them is trying to convey to others an understanding of the reality of the outgroup and its members and is using all readily available information and all the conceptual tools that he or she would use to analyze the ingroup, its subgroups, and their individual members. Since groups (including Jews) do have different values and do compete for scarce goods, these assertions may provide the basis for hostile attitudes and actions. But by realistic hostility I mean that an effort to analyze the outgroup and its members objectively without wishful or fearful thinking has preceded the negative evaluation or advocacy of discrimination.

The most obvious characteristic of xenophobic assertions (for example, "Jews are Christ-killers") is that they impute to all people labeled as members of an outgroup the actions of some members that have been considered a threat to the ingroup. All Jews are the same and do what those Jews did; individual Jews are no more than bearers of the outgroup's characteristics. In this way, the group is presented as the fundamental reality of which its members are no more than expressions. Yet a group of any size such as "the Jews" cannot be tangibly experienced: for centuries no one has been able to encounter "the Jews" as a whole or all individual Jews. The concept of "the Jews" or of any large outgroup is an abstraction. And what xenophobic assertions do is to make the abstraction more real than any individual components.

How then is the abstraction constituted? The characteristics ascribed to it are those ascribed by the ingroup to some members of the outgroup—for example, to some Jews whose real, observed conduct has been interpreted as a threat to the ingroup. Xenophobic assertions thus fit the "kernel of truth" theory of prejudice; and here it is well to remember that, so long as it was safe to do so, Jews readily asserted that they had killed Christ,[28] and Jews indeed engaged disproportionately in moneylending in the Middle Ages. Yet if we think of Jews as Christ-killers or moneylenders, it is obvious that these were not the only characteristics of the Jews who were involved in such threatening conduct, much less of Jews who were never involved in those threatening situations. Nor, in those threatening situations, were Jews the only element; very obviously, many more kinds of people and many more factors were involved in producing those situations than some Jews. A xenophobic assertion is neither a genuine effort to convey a realistic description of the outgroup nor a genuine attempt to provide a causal explanation of the threatening situations to which the assertion alludes.

Although, because of its grammatical meaning, an individual xenophobic assertion may appear to be intended as a description of the outgroup, examination of all xenophobic assertions about an outgroup such as "the Jews" indicates that they are far from including, or assuming knowledge of, all that was known about Jews or that might have been inferred about them with reasonable certainty. Xenophobic assertions have a different function that becomes obvious when we stop focusing obsessively on the outgroup and examine other obvious properties of these assertions.

An obvious formal feature of these assertions is that they link the abstraction of the outgroup label with another abstraction denoting a social menace, whether a threat from without or an internal weakness of the ingroup, which causes anxiety in the speaker, for example, "the Jews" with the persecution of Christians, indebtedness, lack of control of scarce goods, national disunity, international peril. A xenophobic assertion affirms the existence of a social peril that can be connected with the existence of the outgroup because some of its members have in fact been involved in the events considered threatening. Within a xenophobic assertion, the meaning of the outgroup label is supplied and delimited by grammatical connection with some threat, not by the empirical characteristics of the outgroup. The subject of a xenophobic assertion is not the outgroup; it is a felt social menace.

Less obvious but more striking is the fact that there is no mention or implicit recognition of the range of individual variation within the outgroup by a modifying adjective such as "some," even though the person who makes the assertion may be well aware that there are marked differences. Yet all members of the ingroup know from their most immediate experience that it is possible, even inevitable, to discriminate a wide range of individual variation within every group they have ever experienced: within the family and peer groups, at work, in the army—even among their animals, their cattle or dogs. They know that they have never been in or observed any group in which individual variation was not obvious, discussed, and important. Yet the people who make xenophobic assertions refuse or are unable to utilize that fundamental understanding of reality in their assertions. Why?

The reason for the absence of any reference to individual variation or to inoffensive characteristics of "the Jews" is that xenophobic assertions are not intended to function as empirical descriptions of Jews, and that the abstraction does not refer primarily to Jews. If we look at a set of xenophobic assertions that refer grammatically to an outgroup such as "the Jews," it becomes apparent that these assertions refer to a subset of a larger phenomenon; they draw attention to conditions that are believed to menace the ingroup, but only to those menaces in which some Jews have been noticeably involved. The abstraction "the Jews" does not function to signal descriptive statements about real Jews; it serves as a symbol for the kind of threat; and the outgroup label will not serve as an unambiguous symbol of the danger if individual variations and various positive qualities are attributed to "the Jews."

If we expand our horizon and look at all sets of xenophobic assertions made by an individual about various outgroups, we realize that they embrace most of the social conditions that the individual feels to be a serious menace to herself or himself and to any reference group with which he or she may unreservedly identify. It then becomes even more obvious that the outgroup labels are employed in these assertions not to signal a description of the outgroups but to identify felt threats. Xenophobes are not talking about real people but about something much more intangible, their sense of danger, of chaos.

Why is there this apparent contradiction between the manifest meaning of these xenophobic assertions when viewed in isolation and their intended function? At least two interpretations seem possible. The most obvious is that the assertions are made by people who feel threatened but know so little about social conditions, especially the more complicated, that they lack the concepts to deal with them. They try to communicate their alarm and call for help, but they understand so little that they can only point to some concrete actions and some salient real people and use them as symbols of the much broader menace.

In the assertions of such people, the name of the outgroup has a double function. On the one hand, by pointing to one salient example of humans engaged in the menacing conduct, the speaker avoids the necessity of describing the complex menacing condition; on the other hand, because the overgeneralization of the collective term implies that more people are engaged in this menacing conduct than anyone has concretely observed, the collective term serves to symbolize all the people who thus endanger the speaker's community, all the actions and conditions which he does not understand but believes to exist. And the more the symbolic sense of the outgroup label dominates, the more a xenophobic assertion becomes a tautological cry of alarm about a complex and ill-understood menace, for example, usurers ("the Jews") are undermining our society by their usury.

A further interpretation is suggested by the failure to employ the fundamental human awareness of individual variation. Xenophobic assertions may be not simply a reaction to an ill-understood menace but also a refusal to try to understand. Many people who are well aware of the complexities of social reality and have considerable information about an outgroup may nonetheless make xenophobic assertions, so that their assertions seem a willful refusal to try to understand. In some instances, of course, informed people make xenophobic assertions which they do not believe in order to inhibit understanding among the people they are addressing, whom they wish to manipulate. But when the assertions are not cynically hypocritical, their function would seem to be to short-circuit any genuine effort on the speaker's part to understand either the outgroup or the menace. Apparently the consciousness of menace is so great that the anxiety provoked makes objective thought impossible even for these relatively well-informed people. They seem to feel so immediately threatened that they are incapable of expending time and energy on indecisive examination of empirical complexities. Instead, they relieve their tension in one of two ways, or both: by inappropriate but immediate action and by repressing consciousness of some of the most deeply threatening causes of the menace.

Although the repression or destruction of members of the outgroup may have little effect on the basic menace, the action of attacking them is nonetheless one immediate way to reduce, at least temporarily, the tensions caused by the menace, both by expending the increased adrenaline, so to speak, in immediate action and by distracting attention from other deeper dimensions of the menace through concentration on immediate practical action. This kind of incitation and action is the weaker of the two forms of scapegoating. Some people, who are linked by their group label to people who have indeed been involved in the menace, are attacked as if their disappearance would end the menace.

But xenophobic assertions and action can also function to repress consciousness of those elements of the menacing condition that cannot be readily manipulated, such as the complexity of economic exchange. And, of much greater importance for the maintenance of social identity and cohesion, they can function to inhibit awareness of those elements of the menace whose recognition would weaken belief in the values and unity of the ingroup and undermine the self-esteem of its members, for example, recognition of a discrepancy between the stated values of some or all members of the ingroup and their actual behavior. Obsessive focusing on very partial, but manipulable and external, components of the menace distracts attention from more intimately threatening aspects, from weaknesses of ingroup organization and similarly menacing conduct of its own members.

According to this interpretation, the xenophobic assertion that "Jews are Christ-killers" reflects awareness that Jesus' death was a consequence of the refusal to believe of most of the people who should have been most able to understand his message, a refusal that undermined and threatened the convictions on which Christians relied for their eternal salvation and on which the Christian community was based. Significantly, that assertion only appeared about 90 C.E. in the fourth Gospel, when it had finally become clear that most Jews were not going to believe that Jesus was divine and had been resurrected. By asserting that "the Jews" had killed Christ because they were stubbornly blind to truth, Christians were able to avoid any effort to understand the real characteristics of Jews and hence any more penetrating explanation of why some people believed in Christ and others did not, which might have opened the jaws of chaos.[29] Thereby "the Jews" became the symbol of the fundamental and much more complex problem of unbelief in general. The various expressions of the concept of Jewish Christ-killers identified the fundamental menace—that Christ might be only a dead human and that Christian belief was lifeless. And through that xenophobic assertion or expression of alarm, not only was awareness of that most frightening menace repressed, but as accusation the charge enabled many Christians through many centuries to release their tensions or repress their own doubts by attacking Jews.

Viewed in this way, some familiar characteristics of xenophobic assertions become more comprehensible. The typical habit of referring to the outgroup in the singular, to "the Jew" instead of "the Jews," can be seen as a consequence of the fact that the abstraction functions primarily as a symbol of menace and refers only secondarily and syntactically to real humans; and the abstraction can so function only if the plurality of meanings with which "Jews" can be connected is blocked out so that one Jew is identical with all others. That need to repress awareness of individual variation also explains such familiar xenophobic expressions as "some of my best friends are Jews" or "he is a Jew but . . ." Since the abstraction "the Jews" has only the remotest connection with the diversity of real Jews, any close relations with individual Jews which do not confirm the sense of menace will force the xenophobe to redefine those individuals as exceptions who do not fit within the abstraction, as not being *real* Jews.

Another characteristic of xenophobes and their assertions is that they seem to contradict themselves. Yet that apparently illogical and psychopathological behavior becomes understandable when we realize that the abstraction is not used logically and empirically but is intended to symbolize ill-understood and unconnected menaces. If someone says both that the clannish Jews only look after their own and that the pushy Jews are taking over our welfare institutions, it may seem a contradiction, but it permits people to express both the fear that "we are not attractive or impressive enough for those people to want to join us" and the fear that "we are losing control of institutions vital to our well-being." There is contradiction only if we mistake xenophobic assertions for empirical or causal propositions.

We may deal with chimerical assertions much more briefly. I have introduced the neologism "chimeria" because "prejudice" has such a wide range of meanings in common usage, and because I wish to make a distinction that is not recognized in the social scientists' conception of "ethnic prejudice." The Greek root of "chimeria" makes it a fitting companion to "xenophobia," but, more important, the ancient use of "chimera" to refer to a fabulous monster emphasizes the central characteristic of the phenomenon I wish to distinguish from xenophobia. In contrast with xenophobic assertions, chimerical assertions present fantasies, figments of the imagination, monsters that, although dressed syntactically in the clothes of real humans, have never been seen and are projections of mental processes unconnected with the real people of the outgroup. Chimerical assertions have no "kernel of truth." This is the contrast which distinguishes the hostility that produced Auschwitz from that manifested against Jews in ancient Alexandria.

The clearest example is the assertion that Jews commit ritual murder. Had ritual murder occurred, that conduct would have been so corporeal that it could have been directly observed. But not only do we have no satisfactory evidence that Jews ever—to say nothing of a habit—committed ritual murder; a careful examination of the evidence makes it apparent that those who initiated the accusation had never observed that conduct themselves.[30] Moreover, not only are we skeptical of the assertion; many contemporaries were equally skeptical even though they did not have the benefit of Freudian insights into irrational processes.

A much less obvious example, because it is about an incorporeal quality not susceptible of direct observation and is still widely believed, is the chimerical assertion that blacks are innately inferior in mental potential to whites—an allegation strangely resembling assertions about the mental inferiority of females as compared with males.[31] When we assess this example, it would be well to bear in mind that, until the development of modern historical methods and knowledge, even those who did not believe that Jews habitually committed secret ritual murder could not decisively disprove it. And even now it is impossible to prove that no Jews ever committed a ritualized murder, for it is remarkably difficult to establish the negative proposition that physically possible conduct has never occurred.

In the case of the assertion about blacks, the difficulty of proving or disproving it is even greater because what is alleged is so intangible. We can observe particular acts or performances in a particular setting, but not "intelligence." Indeed, it seems probable that there is no such single entity or characteristic, but rather different types of mental activities each of which may be more or less developed in each individual. Nor can we observe what is "innate" in a group of individuals.

It has so far been impossible to estimate with any precision the extent to which an individual's mental performance is determined by genetic endowment and what by his or her environment. Even if environmental factors could be held constant in comparisons of individuals, which presently seems almost impossible, we have no knowledge of how genes are connected with the specific mental activities examined by "intelligence" tests. Specific purely biological information about an individual cannot yield anything but the grossest predictions about an individual's future mental activities, primarily negative assessments of the potential of biologically highly abnormal or physically damaged individuals. To determine an individual's biological potential for any particular mental activity with any precision is, therefore, impossible. And it is even more impossible to predict the mental potential of a group. Not only are the complexities to be considered vastly increased, but what is designated as a group is not stable. No one can predict with whom its present members and their descendants will breed, what conditions the progeny of those unions will face, or how they will react to them.

Since no one thus far has been able to devise any techniques of research based on sound theory that could decide objectively whether there is any difference in the innate mental potential of a group, and since the question itself may be meaningless because based on erroneous reifications of mental ability and of groups, ethnocentric assumptions, and ignorance of biology, any unhesitating assertion that blacks as a group are thus inferior has no kernel of truth and attributes to all blacks a characteristic they have never been observed to possess.[32]

In fact, of course, the accusation against blacks arose without the help of modern biological knowledge and sophisticated techniques of intelligence testing. It initially depended simply on the observation that blacks then could not—or did not want to—perform certain mental and physical acts that were highly valued in white culture. But that observed contrast provided no kernel of truth about innate abilities because it was susceptible of radically different interpretations, depending on the attitude of the interpreters. Many whites, especially Christians who believed that mankind descended from Adam and Eve, held that the differences were the result of different geographic and historic conditions and would disappear in a common environment; and those who held that view were encouraged by the ability with which blacks were adapting to the radically different and degrading conditions brutally imposed on them by whites, progress that seemed obvious evidence of the mental potential of blacks. Many others were uncertain. All too many whites, however, moved by self-interest, ethnocentrism, and fear, proclaimed that blacks were innately inferior in mental potential to whites. And although that was something they had never observed nor could observe, they asserted it with as much conviction as they did the indisputable fact of the existence of people with darker pigmentation.

Chimerical assertions thus attribute with certitude to outgroups characteristics that have never been empirically observed. Another characteristic of chimerical assertions that sharply distinguishes them from xenophobic assertions is that they apply to all real individuals who can somehow be identified as members of the outgroup. Here we may think of the Nuremberg laws and their consequences. Because the fantasy attributes a quality to the outgroup that is unobserved and unobservable—whether because of a conscious conspiracy of secrecy or an unconscious conspiracy of nature—no observable conduct of individual members can prove that they do not have that quality, that they are exceptions. To the contrary, they may be all the more dangerous because their alleged menace is so well camouflaged.

Chimerical assertions come in two types. The examples just given are of the stronger and more easily recognizable type in which the fantasy attributes qualities to the outgroup and all its members that they have never demonstrably possessed, and that few if any other people known to the ingroup have been believed to possess. Hence the attribution of these qualities makes the members of the outgroup seem inhuman or subhuman monsters who fall outside the norm of humanity of the ingroup.

The weaker type of chimerical assertions are difficult to detect because they seem similar to xenophobic assertions in that they seem to have some connection, however remote, with observable reality, some "kernel of truth." An example would be the situation in which a badly damaged body was found in a society in which many people committed brutal homicide, and although no evidence whatsoever connected Jews with the crime, they were nonetheless accused. Since there was no verifiable knowledge that any Jews had participated in any way in the menacing occurrence, the assertion would be chimerical. Yet, if it was known that Jews had in truth occasionally killed Christians, the assertion would have a surface plausibility—particularly since it would function to deny that any members of the ingroup were guilty. So long as one looks at single assertions of this kind about a specific event, they have an air of plausibility because some Jews could indeed have committed the crime. But the chimerical nature of the assertion becomes obvious when such individual assertions are stated as a generalization: if Jews are present in the area, all brutal murders for which the killers are unknown are committed by Jews.

One reason why such chimerical assertions seem more plausible than either the stronger form or xenophobic assertions is that when such an assertion is made about a specific event, it may be hard to distinguish between the statement as an assertion and the statement as a hypothesis. Since the crime could have been committed by Jews, that could be an acceptable hypothesis to investigate; yet if their guilt is asserted with complete conviction without any investigation, it is a chimerical assertion. It may be difficult to decide whether an assertion is a hypothesis or a chimerical assertion, but if it is immediately followed by incitation to action or by action against members of the outgroup, its chimerical nature can be recognized.

In contrast with xenophobic stereotypes, chimerical assertions use the abstraction of the group label primarily to point to all members of the outgroup. Since the attributed quality is unobservable, its attribution cannot be contradicted by any observation of differences between individual members. Moreover, since chimerical assertions allege conduct that can be committed by any living member, these assertions function to incite attacks against any and all members of the outgroup much more directly and forcibly than most xenophobic stereotypes, since the latter often refer to past conduct and permit exceptions of individuals as not real members of the outgroup. Chimerical assertions are thus the stronger of the two forms of scapegoating because of their greater potential for inciting immediate action against any and all members of the outgroup, and because the conduct attributed to the scapegoat has no empirical relation to it.

The initial or originating function of chimerical assertions would seem to be to express the awareness of individual members of the ingroup of a menace within themselves, their awareness at some psychic level that there are threatening cracks in their personality between their imagination or impulses and the social values they have internalized, their feeling that they are not comfortably integrated either with their society or within themselves. Chimerical assertions, I would suggest, function to relieve the resulting tension—the anger, fear, or guilt—by expressing its existence openly in a socially acceptable form, by presenting the interior conflict as a social problem, a struggle between the ingroup and its acknowledged enemies. Thereby, the microcosm of the individual psyche is harmonized with the macrocosm of socially acknowledged realities, the sense of separation from society with its values is diminished, and the individual may obtain social approval for his struggle to support those values against evil. And since, as with xenophobic assertions, the symbolization refers the menace syntactically to manipulable, concrete, external agents, it can serve to release tension temporarily by inciting immediate, if inappropriate, action, and it can distract attention from the real, internal, and more threatening causes and thereby reduce consciousness of their internality.[33]

Since no aspect of the study of prejudice has received more attention from the psychologically minded than the processes of displacement and projection in the individual psyche, there is no need to elaborate this last point. It is worth emphasizing, however, that xenophobic assertions seem to be reactions to ill-understood menaces to social organization, while chimerical assertions seem to be reactions to ill-understood menaces to individual psychic integration, which suggests that xenophobia may be explained largely in terms of social developments, whereas the origin of chimeria is to be sought primarily in individual development.

It may be noted that I have spoken thus far of the verbal or other behavior of members of the ingroup and said little about the characteristics of members of the outgroup. Yet for xenophobic and chimerical assertions to function, there must be an identifiable outgroup that is believed to be a threat. Although the verbal behavior we have been examining is not intended to function as an empirical description of outgroups, some awareness of the outgroup's existence is necessary for the outgroup label to serve as a symbol of social and personal menace. In the case of xenophobic assertions, it needs to be known that an outgroup exists and that some of its members have been involved in certain conduct that threatened the ingroup; and in the case of chimerical assertions, it is necessary to know that there is an outgroup with some social and cultural characteristics that distinguish it from the ingroup. Moreover, for either kind of assertion to incite to tension-relieving action, there must be human beings recognizable as members of the outgroup who can be discriminated against or destroyed.

All this can occur, however, without any of those physiological differences which are so important in racist theories. Despite the general tendency of humans to share scarce goods with as few people as possible and to use any discernible difference, however irrelevant or meaningless, as a line to defend against outsiders, an outgroup is not an aggregation of people with long noses, dark skins, or other physical characteristics. What identifies people originally as members of a group are the social and cultural characteristics that integrate them as a group and make them a social force or resource and a potential threat. And it is on the basis of those characteristics that the informed governing elite of the ingroup will identify and evaluate an external group in order to deal with it realistically. So long as members of the external group do not reside within the society of the ingroup, any physiological distinctiveness of the members is entirely secondary to the political, military, religious, and economic significance of the group.

Yet what may be true of external or international relations becomes less true when members of the outgroup move and live within the society of the ingroup, in other words, when the outgroup is a minority within the society of the ingroup. In this case, not only may social authorities want to be able to identify individual members for police or other purposes, but other members of the ingroup may wish to be able to recognize them in order to avoid them, and those predisposed to incite tension-relieving action by xenophobic or chimerical assertions will need to be able to point to the individuals to be attacked and to use them as symbols of social and personal menace.

Hence, when a subordinated group of socially and culturally distinguishable people within a society is the object of xenophobia and chimeria, there may be pressure to ensure that, in addition to any differences in religion, names, residential patterns, social conduct, and economic and legal status, the individual members shall also be physically distinguishable from members of the ingroup. If, as in the case of African Americans, a physical difference has always paralleled the social and cultural differences, the physiological difference will simply be increasingly emphasized as a symbol of the other differences. But if, as in the case of Jews, no perception of physiological difference accompanies the original consciousness of cultural and social differences, then the possibility of physical differentiation may be created by commanding the individual members of the outgroup to wear distinguishing clothes or to carry cards of identity or by developing a physiological stereotype based on characteristics that distinguish some members of the outgroup from many members of the ingroup.

In any case, whether individual members are distinguishable by cultural or by physiological differences, recognition of their empirical reality will be repressed by the symbolic significance of their label; that is, the sight of identifiable Jews will only bring the significance ascribed to "the Jews" to mind. Real Jews will be selectively perceived by some members of the ingroup simply as physical symbols of social and personal menace, thereby completing the confusion between syntax and experience, between symbol and reality.

V

The definitions proposed and their interpretation seek to distinguish rather than to relate three phenomena, and the phenomena are presented in a temporal vacuum. Yet realistic, xenophobic, and chimerical assertions are obviously related, and obvious questions remain. What relation, if any, is there between these three kinds of assertions? How are these assertions related to the people who utter them and the occasions on which they utter them? Can the same kind of assertion perform different functions for different people and at different times? Are some people merely initiators and some merely bearers?

Most psychological and sociological studies of "prejudice" have attempted to explain why some people in contemporary societies are more prejudiced than others; and they have examined societies in which stereotypes are already deeply embedded in the culture; yet lacking anything but the shortest temporal perspective, they have been unable to explain how the stereotypes got there. Can we now construct a dynamic model, however schematic, to describe how belief in chimerical assertions—in the inhumanity or subhumanity of some outgroups—developed in a society from which it was previously absent?

The moment we pose that question, we realize that there is no necessary relation between xenophobia and chimeria. If we think about European culture and its extensions outside of Europe from 500 to the present, it is obvious that many or most Europeans have made frequent xenophobic assertions about many groups within their society and about most external societies with which they have come in contact. There is, therefore, nothing at all unusual about xenophobic hostility against Jews.

Like every other major group, Jews have unique characteristics, a unique history, and their own particular goals. It is also true that Jews have maintained a very distinctive identity for millennia. And since they have maintained their identity for centuries as a minority within a larger society and refused, or not been allowed, to assimilate, it is not surprising that the xenophobia against them has been millennial and often intense. Yet the endurance and intensity of xenophobic hostility against Jews does not mean that it has been different in kind—in basic nature and causes—from xenophobia directed against other major groups, including Jewish xenophobia against other groups. Consequently, there seems no good reason to distinguish xenophobic hostility against Jews from that directed against other groups by giving it a special term, "antisemitism."

"Antisemitism" implies that there has been something peculiar about hostility against Jews, something more than a matter of duration and intensity. Of course, for Jews, any hostility against them is of particular importance just because it is directed against them and their values, but that is their value judgment, not an objective argument about humanity in general. Nonetheless, as the "Final Solution" indicated all too clearly, Jews do seem to have been the object of an unusual hostility; and provided that we refuse to regard xenophobia against Jews as peculiar, it can indeed be argued on objective grounds that Jews have also been the object of an unusual, if not unique, form of hostility for which a special term may seem in order. In addition to xenophobic hostility, Jews have been a primary target for socially significant chimerical hostility.

If we look for chimerical assertions of any frequency that have been general in European culture, we realize that they have been directed above all against Jews and blacks, save for those directed for a short period against the individuals labeled as witches. If xenophobia is so common a human reaction to outgroups that objectivity is the exception, socially significant chimeria has neither been continually present nor been directed against many outgroups and is obviously dependent on peculiar historical circumstances.

If we leave the case of witches aside, then chimeria seems to have been directed primarily against outgroups whose members, whatever their other characteristics, had certain cultural or physiological characteristics that the vast majority of them would not or could not change. These characteristics, however, became of fundamental significance to the ingroup only when it desired to exploit the outgroup and was able to do so decisively. Moreover, socially significant chimeria against Jews and blacks emerged only after the ingroup had made them almost completely powerless and heavily exploited minorities within the society of the ingroup. It is also important to notice that while control was initially imposed to permit one kind of exploitation, once it was firmly established and that kind of exploitation was well developed, other kinds of exploitation followed.

To deal with these historical characteristics of chimeria and to explain why only certain outgroups became objects of chimeria and scapegoats *par excellence* and why they came to be seen as inhuman or subhuman, we need to introduce the concept of the self-fulfilling prophecy. W. I. Thomas formulated the invaluable theorem that "if men define situations as real, they are real in their consequences"; and Robert K. Merton then formulated this definition: "The self-fulfilling prophecy is, in the beginning, a *false* definition of the situation evoking new behavior which makes the originally false conception come *true*."[34] I would like to modify Merton's definition for our purposes as follows: the self-fulfilling prophecy is, in the beginning, a motivated definition of an outgroup as inferior in one fundamental way that is accompanied by treatment that evokes new behavior in members of the outgroup that seems to corroborate and strengthen the original judgment of inferiority.

This definition assumes that the ingroup's control of the outgroup is sufficiently great that members of the outgroup are forced to conform in important ways to the expectations of the ingroup. The operation of the prophecy is directly dependent on the extent to which the ingroup can ensure that, in its transactions with the outgroup, the exchanges will be highly favorable to the ingroup—to paraphrase Michel Crozier's modification of Robert Dahl's definition of power.[35] The greater the ability of the ingroup to exploit members of the outgroup as a group, the more effective the self-fulfilling prophecy. And at its extreme, in the case of powerless and heavily exploited minorities within the ingroup's society, the operation of the prophecy can make it seem true that the drastically exploited outgroup falls outside the ingroup's normative definition of humanity and may be treated accordingly.

The self-fulfilling prophecy can operate decisively in intergroup relations whenever the exchanges are so favorable to one group that members of another are forced to modify basic forms of conduct in order to survive. Yet its effect will vary dramatically depending on the kind of exploitation, the original nature of the exploited group, the form of control that permits the original exploitation, and the relation between the original characteristics of the exploited group and the character of the initial exploitation.

There appear to be two main forms of exploitation, ideate or psychological and material or physical; and they may combine in different patterns. Thus the original, ideate, religious exploitation of Jews by Christians was followed by economic, political, and physical exploitation, whereas the original exploitation of blacks as physical labor was followed by sexual, psychological, and ideological exploitation. It would seem that even if one form of exploitation originally predominates, it leads to the other so that both are combined in the fully developed form. In other cases, however, the ideate and the material are combined in the initial exploitation, or the combination occurs so quickly that it is difficult to distinguish a single initial basis.

In Japan, people otherwise genetically and culturally indistinguishable from the majority of Japanese were concerned with the slaughter of animal products, activities that were related to the Shinto concept of religious pollution. The introduction of Buddhism and its fusion with Shintoism in the eighth and ninth centuries greatly strengthened the belief in the impurity of those activities and of the people who performed them. Those who engaged in those socially needed but religiously impure activities, the Eta, were exploited both physically and psychologically so that they became a rigidly segregated, endogamous, impoverished caste of untouchables with a subculture of its own. The belief developed among other Japanese that the Eta were foreigners of a different culture and race who had been introduced into Japan; and

Japanese people continued so to believe long after the abolition of the legal status in 1871, and long after the religious basis had been seriously undermined.[36]

In caste societies in which cultural norms of religious impurity brand groups of occupationally specialized people as pariah outcastes, it may be difficult or impossible to decide whether the original basis of exploitation was economic or religious. Indeed, all exploitation may necessarily have both a material and an ideate dimension, even though we do not have to treat the ideate as always or merely a rationalization of economic relationships. Yet in European culture and its extensions, no socially needed physical or occupational activity, except perhaps sexual intercourse, was considered religiously polluting—although fighting and supplying credit nearly came to be so viewed. And so far as there was an occupational caste sharply defined by the purity-impurity continuum, it was not the lowest classes but the superior caste of the priesthood (and to a much lesser extent the nobility). Religious deviation, however, was considered seriously polluting regardless of occupation. Thus physical exploitation was not directly linked with the concept of religious pollution, and psychological exploitation was not directly linked with occupation. Exploitation could therefore be predominantly psychological in origin without being initially physical (Jews), or predominantly physical in origin without being initially psychological (blacks), however much that might change thereafter.

Exploitation affected different kinds of outgroups within Western societies differently. Exploited groups can be divided into three broad categories. In the first, the people exploited, such as peasants, have belonged to the same society and had broadly the same culture, including religion, as their exploiters; in other words, they have been a class within the broadest reference group of the exploiters, and they have been distinguished only by the fact of their exploitation. Any individuals thus exploited who were able to escape the legal and economic constraints of their occupation ceased to be people who could be thus exploited. In this case, the self-fulfilling prophecy operates to maintain but not increase exploitation. It operates to retard exit from the exploited class because the deprivation of opportunities available to the exploiters makes the exploited seem inferior in other ways than the character of their occupations. We may think of the exploitation of agricultural or industrial workers which has evoked distinctive behavior other than occupational and produced a class subculture, which marked upwardly mobile members and retarded their access to higher occupations. Yet if an individual can escape that economic and legal status, although cultural lag may retard his or her ascent, it will not mark him or her as a person to be forcibly returned to that original status. Moreover, since downwardly mobile members of superior classes may slip into the exploited class, no sharp line distinguishes the exploiters occupationally and culturally from the exploited. In this case, although the self-fulfilling prophecy affects whole classes of people, it does not determine the fate of their individual members.

In the second category, the people exploited were outsiders who did not originate within the society of the exploiters and therefore differed markedly at the outset in cultural characteristics from the exploiters. Their exploitation was consequently associated with a difference in cultural characteristics which identified the exploited as members of an outgroup in relation to the whole society or the most extensive reference group of the exploiters. Thus both the legal and economic constraints of their exploitation and their marked cultural difference identified individual members as people to be exploited. Individuals who sought to escape that occupational exploitation were therefore culturally recognizable as strangers and as people to be exploited. Yet if their exploitation was not related to particular features of their cultural difference but only to the fact of difference, and if none of the differences was unchangeable, then here also, although the self-fulfilling prophecy operated to maintain the outgroup, to evoke new distinguishing behavior, and to retard the exit of individuals from the outgroup, it did not operate to increase control, exploitation, and enduring differentiation.

We may think of the slave societies of antiquity and the early Middle Ages, when captives in war of many different cultures were the main source of the most heavily exploited kind of labor. Exploitation and compelled changes in behavior were very severe at the outset and then diminished as the exploited abandoned their cultural distinctiveness and gradually merged with the less severely exploited and then the higher classes of the society. Since these societies made slaves out of diverse peoples, including some of their own, the outgroup of slaves had no distinctive common culture; no single cultural characteristic marked all members of the outgroup and indicated who should be exploited in this fashion. Moreover, no great significance was then attributed to cultural difference in general. Polytheistic tolerance of religious pluralism minimized the importance of religious difference;

and at least in Mediterranean Europe, long familiarity with a range of physiological differences that did not clearly parallel lines of exploitation diminished the significance even of physiological differences as independent indicators of who should be exploited.

If slaves were initially considered to be legally dead, as dead as their compatriots killed on the battlefield, to be things rather than humans, their humanity remained as self-evident as the humanity of the unconquered members with whom slave societies had diplomatic or commercial relations. And since slaves could abandon their original culture and assimilate that of their masters, they were increasingly treated as human beings: they acquired some legal protection, were freed, lost more of their cultural distinctiveness, and gradually became indistinguishable. Because none of their distinguishing characteristics was permanent, the exploited lost the signs that independently designated them as people to be thus exploited. In this case, the self-fulfilling prophecy, which had operated in full force at the beginning of the exploitation, only acted thereafter to retard the decrease in exploitation—which nonetheless continued to decrease until the only way to see who should be thus exploited was to see who was in fact being so exploited.

The fate of the third category has been very different. Here the people exploited did not originally belong to the same society as the exploited and hence differed in cultural characteristics. But, in contrast with the mere fact of difference, what identified them as people to be exploited were particular cultural or physiological characteristics peculiar to those particular outgroups; and those characteristics were ones that most members would not or could not change. Even though members of the outgroup assimilated many of the characteristics of the ingroup culture, their distinctiveness remained patent. The self-fulfilling prophecy could therefore operate in full force to produce an increase in distinctive behavior—and exploitation—for members of such outgroups remained clearly marked as people to be exploited regardless of where they were found or what they were doing.

In this case, the self-fulfilling prophecy operates through what I will label the institutionalization of an outgroup status of fundamental inferiority in contrast with the institutionalization of a contingent or conditional inferiority in the case of the first two categories. The prerequisite for the institutionalization of a status of fundamental inferiority is that the original exploitation of members of the outgroup and the judgment that they are inferior have been directly associated in the minds of members of the ingroup with the particular and unchanging characteristics that distinguished that outgroup from all other outgroups.

Thus early Christians judged that Jews were fundamentally inferior because of their uniquely informed disbelief in Christ and were therefore to be exploited to demonstrate the Christian monopoly of saving truth. And although other peoples had disbelieved and persecuted Christians, the judgment that Jews were inferior was inextricably associated with their enduring adherence to Judaism (despite long knowledge of Christianity), which distinguished Jews—save for those who abandoned Judaism and association with Jews—from all other populations and all members of the ingroup. In the case of blacks, the judgment that they were so fundamentally inferior in culture that they could be exploited as physical labor was inextricably associated with enduring physiological characteristics that distinguished them—save for some of the offspring of sexual unions with members of the ingroup—from all other populations and all members of the ingroup. Hence, so long as the judgment of inferiority and the exploitation continued, individual members of the outgroup could not escape designation as people who were unchangingly or fundamentally inferior and should therefore be exploited whenever possible.

For that reason, both exploitation and control of these outgroups could be maintained and increased to a degree impossible in the case of classes or slaves from diverse cultures; and the self-fulfilling prophecy could therefore operate with maximum efficiency. Members of such outgroups could be efficiently excluded from most social roles of prestige or of significant authority over members of the ingroup. Consequently, powerless as they were, they were also denied the opportunity to demonstrate their potentials and forced to adapt their conduct in basic ways to comply with the demands of the ingroup. Typically excluded from military service, the right to carry arms, or the exercise of political authority, and barred from education, trades, and professions, members of the outgroups had to develop different techniques of self-preservation such as marginal occupations, postures of submissiveness, bribery, flattery, and other forms of ingratiating behavior, as well as avoidance of responding to violence with violence for fear of merciless reprisals (the *Judenrat* being an extreme example). That adaptation produced not only new genuine characteristics of the outgroups but also new judgments by the ingroup that the outgroups were indeed fundamentally inferior.

Political exclusion, moreover, was accompanied immediately or gradually by economic specialization. When political control of the outgroup was firmly established, members of the outgroup were restricted to one or a few occupations which the ingroup considered inferior or degrading. And since the changing needs of the exploiters, not the original characteristics of the exploited, determined to which inferior but necessary activities the outgroup was assigned, the enforced occupational specialization of the outgroup bore no necessary relation either to the original characteristics of the outgroup or to the original way in which it was exploited.

When the self-fulfilling prophecy had operated to that extent, the institutionalization of a status of fundamental inferiority changed to the institutionalization of a status of essential inferiority, a status considered appropriate to people who were inferior, not in some particular characteristics, but in essence, by nature. The transition occurs when the conduct of an outgroup that had been the basis for the original judgment of inferiority ceases to be the sole or principal justification for exploitation and is seen as merely one major symptom of a much deeper, essential inferiority that can be recognized through its several specific manifestations but is itself too intangible to be observed directly.

As a result of the self-fulfilling prophecy, the outgroups had acquired several new cultural and social characteristics which the ingroup interpreted as further evidence of inferiority. Yet there was no necessary relation between those different forms of conduct save that the ingroup's self-fulfilling prophecy had imposed them on the outgroup. Consequently, the additional "inferior" characteristics of the outgroup could not be understood as an obvious consequence of the original fundamental inferiority; nor, conversely, could the original conduct be seen as the cause of the later inferior conduct—at least not without a damaging evaluation of the ingroup's conduct. Hence, both the original voluntary conduct and the later imposed conduct were understood as expressions of, as caused by, a deeper essential inferiority that infected all conduct; and any subsequent indications of inferiority could easily be attributed to that intangible essence. Jews were not inferior because they did not believe and killed Christ; they disbelieved and killed Christ because of their essentially inferior nature that was also manifest in their clannishness, avarice, and cowardice. Blacks were not inferior because of their ignorance of Western technology and culture but because of a natural inferiority that was also manifest in their laziness, cowardice, and sexual promiscuity. With the institutionalization of a status of essential inferiority, xenophobic hostility against an outgroup reaches a peak of intensity and opens the way for a new kind of hostility.

The outgroup and its individual members have now become identified and labeled by their enduring, original, distinctive characteristics, by their new adaptive characteristics, by their concentration in demeaning occupations, and by physical segregation. They have also become so powerless that not only can they not demonstrate their potentials, but they cannot even act so as to disprove totally false ideas about their conduct. Harshly exploited and controlled, surrounded by xenophobic stereotypes that use the outgroup label as a symbol of social menaces, and assigned a status as essentially but intangibly inferior beings, the outgroup and its individual members become ideal targets on which to project chimerical assertions, ideal scapegoats in the strongest sense.

If some individuals in the ingroup now make chimerical assertions, particularly of the weaker form that can be confused with hypotheses about specific events, the grammatical meaning of their assertions will receive a hearing from many xenophobes who are predisposed to believe additional evil about the outgroup that confirms their own feeling that the outgroup is a social menace. But worse, some social authorities with the same outlook may trust those who make chimerical assertions as fellow members of the ingroup and, on the basis of the assumed reliability of their testimony, take official action against members of the outgroup. Some judges may condemn members of the outgroup for specific crimes; and other social authorities, more skeptical but also more cynical, may find it advantageous to support accusations they themselves do not believe or turn a blind eye to unofficial actions such as lynchings. Thereby the chimerical accusations gain social confirmation and spread more rapidly through rumor. The stage is now set for chimerical assertions of the stronger form about inhuman conduct, about a general conscious conspiracy or an unconscious conspiracy of nature or biology.

Finally, in addition to the already socially significant xenophobia and the chimerical rumors, both kinds of chimerical accusations come to be used in literature, art, and other cultural media, where their function of symbolizing social and psychic menaces makes them peculiarly valuable. Thereby, they become deeply rooted in the culture, an almost unavoidable element in social indoctrination, and an influence on social policy. The essential inferiority produced by the self-fulfilling prophecy has acquired monstrous lineaments. The monster may in fact be a combination of the chinks in the social armor protecting the members of the ingroup and of the psychic cleavages within individual members, but for many in the ingroup those threatening fissures leading from cosmos to chaos will have been reassuringly located, localized, externalized, and concretized so that they may be attacked directly, immediately, and brutally.

Chimeria has become socially significant. However personal and individual in origin, chimerical assertions are now widely accepted and affect social policy. Yet it is crucial to recognize that the existence of socially significant chimeria does not mean either that all members of the ingroup believe the chimerical assertions or that all those who do believe them use them to perform the same function that they perform for those who initiated them or for those who accept and propagate them as originally intended. Precisely because of the discrepancy between what a chimerical assertion means manifestly according to common language and what those who originate them are trying to communicate, chimerical assertions can function differently and have different psychological implications for different people.

Once the self-fulfilling prophecy about outgroups with enduring characteristics has produced the institutionalization of a status of essential inferiority, with its inevitable accompaniment of widespread xenophobia, xenophobes can listen to the assertions invented by people prone to chimeria and reinterpret them to serve their own needs. Unable themselves to verify whether some members of the outgroup have indeed been observed to display the chimerically asserted conduct, many xenophobes will take in the manifest grammatical meaning of chimerical assertions, accept them on social authority as empirically true, and repeat and use them as xenophobic assertions, so that they now function to express what xenophobes feel as social, not personal psychic, menaces. That duality of function of chimerical assertions is the reason why modern questionnaires that rely on the artificial technique of self-reporting are poor indicators of psychological differences. Poor, but not completely inefficacious, because the xenophobes most likely to believe chimerical associations readily will be those whose individual psychology makes them resonate unconsciously to the latent, primary function of chimerical assertions.

VI

The need to define antisemitism and the definition toward which I have been moving should now be clear. Taken literally, "antisemitism" is most misleading and thoroughly contaminated with the erroneous presuppositions of the racists. I have sought to demonstrate that neither the theories of "racism" nor those of "ethnic prejudice" enable us to distinguish what has been unusual about some hostility toward Jews. Yet "antisemitism" is still used, as it was by racists, to refer to any hostility at any time against Jews collectively, and to imply that there has always been something special about that hostility. That usage depends on a value judgment about Jews but is no longer based on any empirical theory that would distinguish the quality of hostility against Jews from that directed against all other major groups— including hostility expressed by Jews against others. Objectively, it is therefore meaningless or platitudinous. If it is to have any importance for objective thought, not merely for feeling and political rhetoric, it must be demonstrated that Jews have in fact been the object of a kind of hostility different from that which all major groups have confronted.

The theory I have advanced does identify an unusual quality of hostility toward Jews: there has been socially significant chimerical hostility. Jews have been widely hated because large numbers of relatively normal people accepted beliefs that attributed to Jews characteristics and conduct that have never in fact been observed or empirically verified. If "antisemitism" is meant to refer to an unusual hostility against Jews, then that hostility can be termed "antisemitism." It might be argued that since socially significant chimeria has not been directed only against Jews, there is no reason to give it a special name when directed against Jews. Nonetheless, socially significant chimeria is an aberration that has seriously affected very few groups but has afflicted them terribly. The use of a special name to designate the peculiarly horrifying example that marked European culture for seven centuries and killed millions of victims during the "Final Solution" therefore seems justifiable.

Yet if we continue to use that literally most misleading term, we, as social scientists, should free "antisemitism" from its racist, ethnocentric, or religious implications and use it only for what can be distinguished empirically as an unusual kind of human hostility directed at

Jews. If we do so, we may then be able to distinguish more accurately between two very different kinds of threats to Jews. On the one hand, there are situations in which Jews, like any other major group, are confronted with realistic hostility, or with that well-nigh universal xenophobic hostility which uses the real conduct of some members of an outgroup to symbolize a social menace. On the other hand, there may still be situations in which Jewish existence is much more seriously endangered because real Jews have been irrationally converted in the minds of many into a symbol, "the Jews," a symbol whose meaning does not depend on the empirical characteristics of Jews yet justifies their total elimination from the earth.

Abbreviations

Baron, *SRH*	Salo W. Baron, *A Social and Religious History of the Jews*, 2d ed., 18 vols. (New York, 1952-1983)
Blumenkranz, *JC*	Bernhard Blumenkranz, *Juifs et chrétiens dans le monde occidental, 430-1096* (Paris, 1960)
Caro, *SWG*	Georg Caro, *Sozial-und Wirtschaftsgeschichte der Juden*, 2 vols. (Frankfurt, 1920-1924)
Grayzel, *Church*	Solomon Grayzel, *The Church and the Jews in the Thirteenth Century*, 2d ed. (New York, 1966)
HF	*Recueil des historiens des Gaules et de la France*, ed. M. Bouquet et al., 24 vols. (Paris, 1738-1904)
Layettes	*Layettes du Trésor des chartes*, ed. A. Teulet et al., 5 vols. (Paris, 1863-1909)
MGH SS	*Monumenta Germaniae Historica, Scriptores*, 32 vols. (Hanover, 1826-1934)
MGH EP	*Monumenta Germaniae Historica, Epistolae Saeculi XIII e Regestis Pontificum Romanorum*, vol. 1, ed. Carl Rodenberg (Berlin, 1883)
Ordonnances	*Ordonnances des rois de France de la troisième race*, ed. E.-J. Laurière, 21 vols. (Paris, 1723-1849)

Parkes, *CCS*   James Parkes, *The Conflict of the Church and the Synagogue* (Philadelphia, 1961)

Poliakov, *HA*   Léon Poliakov, *Histoire de l'antisémitisme*, 4 vols. (Paris, 1955-1977); vol. 1, *Du Christ aux Juifs de cour*; vol. 2, *De Mahomet aux marrannes*; vol. 3, *De Voltaire à Wagner*; vol. 4, *L'Europe suicidaire*

PL   *Patrologiae Cursus Completus, Series Latina*, ed. J.-P. Migne (Paris, 1844-1864)

Recueil   *Recueil des actes de Philippe Auguste*, 4 vols., ed. H.-F. Delaborde et al. (Paris, 1916-1979)

RS   *Chronicles and Memorials of Great Britain and Ireland*, published under the authority of the Master of the Rolls (London, 1858-1897)

Notes

Introduction

1. "The Jews and the Archives of Angevin England: Reflections on Medieval Anti-Semitism," *Traditio* 19 (1963): 183-244.

2. (Boston, 1954).

3. *History, Religion, and Antisemitism* (Berkeley, Los Angeles, Oxford, 1990).

4. That stereotype is discussed only in passing in the following chapters. For a recent discussion, see Joseph Shatzmiller, *Shylock Reconsidered: Jews, Moneylending, and Medieval Society* (Berkeley, Los Angeles, Oxford, 1990).

5. See *Histoire des Juifs en France*, ed. Bernhard Blumenkranz (Toulouse, 1972); Robert Chazan, *Medieval Jewry in Northern France* (Baltimore, 1973); and the meticulous analysis of William Chester Jordan, *The French Monarchy and the Jews* (Philadelphia, 1989).

6. An argument I have developed further in *History, Religion, and Antisemitism*.

1: Majority History and Postbiblical Jews

1. G. P. Gooch, *History and Historians in the Nineteenth Century*, 2d ed. (London, 1952), pp. xxix, 478-490.

2. Ibid., p. xxiii.

3. James Westfall Thompson and Bernard J. Holm, *A History of Historical Writing*, 2 vols. (New York, 1942), references in the index under "Jews."

4. Ibid. 2:587.

5. Max L. Margolis and Alexander Marx, *A History of the Jewish People* (Cleveland, 1962), p. 680.

6. *History of Historical Writing* 2:318. Freeman was forthright. W. R. W.

Stephens, *The Life and Letters of Edward A. Freeman* (London, 1895), 2:428: "If I were to say that every nation has a right to wallop anybody, I might be misunderstood, for I don't want to wallop anybody, even jews [*sic*]. The best thing is to kick them out altogether like King Edward Longshanks of famous memory." But cf. Edward A. Freeman, *The Reign of William Rufus* (Oxford, 1882), 1:160-161.

7. Cecil Roth, "The Jews in the Middle Ages," in *Cambridge Medieval History*, vol. 7 (Cambridge, 1932), pp. 937-947; Guido Kisch, *The Jews in Medieval Germany* (Chicago, 1949), 567-605. For Jews in England, see Cecil Roth, *Magna Bibliotheca Anglo-Judaica: A Bibliographical Guide to Anglo-Jewish History* (London, 1937), and Ruth P. Lehmann, *Nova Bibliotheca Anglo-Judaica: A Bibliographical Guide to Anglo-Jewish History 1937-1960* (London, 1961). I should now add two bibliographies that appeared after this article was published: Bernhard Blumenkranz, *Bibliographie des Juifs en France* (Toulouse, 1974), and *Bibliographic Essays in Medieval Jewish Studies*, ed. Yosef H. Yerushalmi (New York, 1976).

8. Eduard Fueter, *Geschichte der neueren Historiographie*, 1st ed. (Munich, 1911), 3d ed. (Munich, 1936); *Histoire et historiens depuis cinquante ans*, Bibliothèque de la Revue historique (Paris, 1927-1928), 2:679-697.

9. Harry Elmer Barnes, *A History of Historical Writing* (Norman, Okla., 1937), pp. 226-228.

10. Allan Nevins, *The Gateway to History* (Boston, 1938), p. 399.

11. Heinrich Ritter von Srbik, *Geist und Geschichte vom deutschen Humanismus bis zur Gegenwart* (Munich, 1950-1951), 2:349-362.

12. See under "Jews" in indexes of Auguste Molinier, *Les sources de l'histoire de France des origines aux guerres d'Italie* (Paris, 1901-1906); Charles Gross, *The Sources and Literature of English History from the Earliest Times to about 1485*, 2d ed. (London, 1915); Dahlmann-Waitz, *Quellenkunde der deutschen Geschichte*, 9th ed. (Leipzig, 1931-1932); L. J. Paetow, *A Guide to the Study of Medieval History*, 2d ed. (New York, 1931), and above, n. 7.

13. Joseph Calmette, *Le monde féodal*, 2d ed. (Paris, 1951), pp. 184, 199-295, 405; Yitzhak (Fritz) Baer, *Die Juden im christlichen Spanien*, Part 1, *Urkunden und Regesten* (Berlin, 1929-1936); *A History of the Jews in Christian Spain*, vol. 1, *From the Age of the Reconquest to the Fourteenth Century*, trans. Louis Schoffman from the Hebrew edition of 1945 (Philadelphia, 1961).

14. Parkes, CCS; Marcel Simon, *Verus Israël: Etudes sur les relations entre chrétiens et juifs dans l'Empire romain, 135-426*, 2d ed. (Paris 1964); Blumenkranz, JC; Bernhard Blumenkranz, *Les auteurs latins du moyen âge sur les Juifs et le judaïsme* (The Hague, 1964).

15. *Corpus Reformatorum* (Halle, 1834-1935), 12:928; W. K. Jordan, *The Development of Religious Toleration in England, 1558-1660* (Cambridge, Mass., 1932-1940), 3:208-209.

16. Jacob Katz, *Tradition and Crisis* (New York, 1961).

17. David Hume, *The History of England*, new ed. (New York, 1879), 1:607-608.

18. Ibid. 1:632; 2:14.

19. Ibid. 1:437.

20. Edward Gibbon, *The History of the Decline and Fall of the Roman Empire*, 9th ed. (London, 1925), 2:3.

21. Ibid. 2:73.

22. Jules Michelet, *Histoire de France*, new ed. (Paris, 1879), 1:201.

23. *The Complete Works of William Hickling Prescott*, ed. John Foster Kirk (London, 1896-1897), 1:272-273.

24. John Lingard, *The History of England to 1688*, new ed. (Boston, 1883), 2:246-249.

25. Ibid. 2:246, italics mine; see also 2:586.

26. Henry Hart Milman, *The History of the Jews from the Earliest Period Down to Modern Times*, new ed. (New York, n.d.), 3:431, 456, 461.

27. Ibid. 2:168-169.

28. Ibid. 2:178.

29. It is nonetheless a tremendous improvement over G. P. Depping, *Les Juifs au moyen âge* (Brussels, 1844), first written in 1823 and published in expanded form in 1834.

30. Leopold von Ranke, *A History of England Principally in the Seventeenth Century* (Oxford, 1875), 3:152-153 is an excellent example of neutrality and scanty information.

31. Wilhelm von Giesebrecht, *Geschichte der deutschen Kaiserzeit*, vols. 1-3, 5th ed. (Leipzig, 1881-1890); vol. 4, 2d ed. (1877); vol. 5 (1880); vol. 6, ed. B. von Simson (1890); 2:541-542, 546; 3:678-679, 688-689; 4:250; 5:882-883.

32. George Waitz, *Deutsche Verfassungsgeschichte*, vol. 5, 2d ed. (Berlin, 1893), pp. 423-424.

33. Thompson, *History of Historical Writing* 2:506-507; Gooch, *History and Historians*, p. 466.

34. Theodor Mommsen, *The History of Rome*, trans. William P. Dickson (New York, 1889-1894), 3:641-642.

35. John Richard Green, *A Short History of the English People*, new ed. (London, 1898), p. 205.

36. Ibid., p. 87.

37. George M. Trevelyan, *History of England* (London, 1929), p. 187.

38. W. E. Lunt, *History of England*, 4th ed. (New York, 1957), p. 157.

39. Walter Phelps Hall, Robert Greenlagh Albion, and Jennie Barnes Pope, *A History of England and the Empire-Commonwealth*, 4th ed. (Boston, 1961), pp. 58-59, 104, 414, 610-611, 701-703.

40. William Stubbs, *The Constitutional History of England*, vol. 2, 4th ed. (Oxford, 1906), p. 559, italics mine.

41. Sir Frederick Pollock and Frederick William Maitland, *The History of English Law before the Time of Edward I*, 2d ed. (Cambridge, 1898), 1:469.

42. Ibid. 1:470-471.

43. Austin Lane Poole, *From Domesday Book to Magna Carta*, 2d ed. (Oxford, 1955), p. 353; H. G. Richardson, *The English Jewry under Angevin Kings* (London, 1960), pp. vii-viii.

44. Sir Maurice Powicke, *The Thirteenth Century* (Oxford, 1953), references in index under "Jews."

45. G. O. Sayles, *The Medieval Foundations of England*, rev. ed. (Philadelphia, 1950), p. 396.

46. Doris M. Stenton, *England in the Early Middle Ages*, 2d ed. (Harmondsworth, 1952), pp. 190-198; G. G. Coulton, *Medieval Panorama* (Cambridge, 1947), pp. 346-365.

47. Henri Pirenne, *A History of Europe from the Invasions to the Sixteenth Century*, trans. Bernard Miall from the 8th French edition (New York, 1956), pp. 95-96, 195, 297, 483.

48. *Economic and Social History of Medieval Europe*, trans. I. E. Clegg (New York, n.d.), p. 134; see also pp. 11-12, 23-24, 133-135.

49. Louis Halphen, *L'essor de l'Europe (XIe-XIIIe siècles)*, 3d ed. (Paris, 1948), pp. 338, 382, 557.

50. Christopher Dawson, *Religion and the Rise of Western Culture* (New York, 1950).

51. *The First Hundred Years*, ed. M. W. Baldwin, vol. 1 of *A History of the Crusades*, ed. K. M. Setton (Philadelphia, 1955), p. 263: "Moneylending at usurious rates of interest made them prosper [in 1096], and riches gained by such unchristian practices, as well as their ostentation and exclusiveness, made these strangers (*exsules*) unpopular and even hated, and crusaders going forth to fight the enemies of their faith were easily persuaded to persecute and rob Jewish unbelievers."

52. *Propyläen Weltgeschichte*, ed. Golo Mann and Alfred Heuss (Berlin, 1960-1963), 5:504, 554; Joshua Trachtenberg, *The Devil and the Jews* (New Haven, 1943); Norman Cohn, *The Pursuit of the Millennium* (London, 1957).

53. *Propyläen Weltgeschichte* 5:423.

54. Ibid. 5:594, 615. For a typical treatment of Jews in German medieval history, see Bruno Gebhardt, *Handbuch der deutschen Geschichte*, 8th ed. (Stuttgart, 1958-1959), 1:252, 268, 295-296, 374, 457, 463, 511-512, 514, 651, 679; cf. 662-675.

55. Christopher Brooke, *Europe in the Central Middle Ages (962-1154)* (New York, 1964), p. 113.

56. Carl Stephenson and Bryce Lyon, *Medieval History*, 4th ed. (New York, 1962), p. 531, and see index under "Jews."

57. Joseph R. Strayer and Dana C. Munro, *The Middle Ages*, 4th ed. (New York, 1959), pp. 399-400, and see index under "Jews."

58. James W. Thompson and Edgar N. Johnson, *An Introduction to Medieval Europe 300-1500*, 2d ed. (New York, 1937), pp. 571-572, and (since the index is highly unreliable on this topic) see pp. 15, 26-28, 34, 46, 158-159, 176, 456, 509, 523-524, 552, 562, 651-652, 709, 718, 855, 868, 905. In an earlier work specifically concerned with economic history, Thompson had maintained the same position, even though he had to involve himself in a flagrant contradiction with his description of monastic lending to do so (*An Economic and Social History of the Middle Ages* [New York, 1928], pp. 394, 639). One is lost in admiration of his naive statement on p. 191 that the Jews in Spain were able to deceive the invading Moslems and acquire for trifling sums "the sacred utensils of the altar" and the jewels of beauties of the Visigothic court, and that from the enormous wealth so gained "dates the prom-

inence subsequently attained by the Jews in the political and financial affairs of Europe."

59. Sidney Painter, *A History of the Middle Ages 284-1500* (New York, 1953), p. 237, see also pp. 12-13, 202, 221, 320, 419.

60. Joseph H. Dahmus, *A History of Medieval Civilization* (New York, 1964), p. 398. Dahmus makes Jews in the twelfth century victims of "racial" prejudice!

61. John L. La Monte, *The World of the Middle Ages* (New York, 1949), p. 366, see also pp. 10, 22-23, 107, 120, 280, 286, 337, 403, 470, 488, 703-704; C. W. Previté-Orton, *The Shorter Cambridge Medieval History* (Cambridge, 1952), 1:549; 2:717, 818; cf. 2:1072, and see index under "Jews"; R. H. C. Davis, *A History of Medieval Europe from Constantine to Saint Louis* (London, 1957), pp. 179, 184, see also pp. 4, 11, 96, 178, 237, 269; Martin Scott, *Medieval Europe* (New York, 1964), pp. 135, 185, and see index under "Jews."

62. Robert S. Hoyt, *Europe in the Middle Ages* (New York, 1957). The eleven references to Jews and Judaism in the index are misleading, for several refer to half a sentence or less.

63. Hoyt, Lyon, Scott, and Dahmus do not mention them.

64. Robert S. Lopez, *Naissance de l'Europe* (Paris, 1962), see under "Jews" in the index.

65. Friedrich Heer, *The Medieval World*, trans. Janet Sonderheim (New York, 1963), pp. 309-317, and see references under "Jews" in the index.

66. Norman F. Cantor, *Medieval History* (New York, 1963), references under "Jews" and "Judaism" in the index.

67. A comparison of Carleton J. H. Hayes, *A Political and Cultural History of Modern Europe*, 2d ed. (New York, 1944) or R. R. Palmer, *A History of the Modern World*, 2d ed. (New York, 1956) with any of the ten medieval surveys examined above will illustrate the point.

68. Charles G. Starr, Charles E. Nowell, Bryce Lyon, Raymond P. Stearns, and Theodore S. Hamerow, *A History of the World* (Chicago, 1960), 1:458.

69. Some non-Jews have made important contributions to Jewish historiography; for the Middle Ages, one could cite Peter Browe, James Parkes, H. G. Richardson, Gustave Saige, J. E. Scherer, Otto Stobbe, and Hermann L. Strack. But their work, like that of Jewish historians, has had little influence on historians of the majority.

70. Poliakov, *HA* 1:191-228; cf. Bernard Gebanier, *The Truth about Shylock* (New York, 1962), pp. 17-75, and passim.

2: Tradition, History, and Prejudice

1. See above, chap. 1.

2. "The Significance of 'Wissenschaft des Judentums' for the Development of Judaism," *Historia Judaica* 16 (1954): 263.

3. "What Do the Jews Owe to Graetz?" *Historia Judaica* 3 (1941): 2.

4. *A History of the Jews* (Philadelphia, 1952), pp. 589-599.

5. "Nor is this all; every text-book written during the past fifty years has

openly, or silently though quite as obviously, based itself on Graetz" (Solomon Grayzel, "Graetz's *History* in America," *Historia Judaica* 3 [1941]: 62).

6. "Jewish History for Our Own Needs," *Menorah Journal* 14 (1928): 426-427.

7. "Ghetto and Emancipation," *Menorah Journal* 14 (1928): 515-526.

8. Baron, *History and Jewish Historians* (Philadelphia, 1964), p. 89.

9. "New Horizons in Jewish History," in *Freedom and Reason: Studies in Philosophy and Jewish Culture in Memory of Morris Raphael Cohen,* ed. Salo W. Baron, Ernest Nagel, and Koppel S. Pinson (Glencoe, Ill., 1951), p. 342.

10. *SRH* 1:4, 293 n. 1.

11. "Preconceptions and Stereotypes in Jewish Historiography," *Jewish Quarterly Review,* n.s., 51 (1960-1965): 242-253.

12. *History and Jewish Historians,* p. 102.

13. In 1955, Joshua Trachtenberg declared that "in general it must be said that Jewish historiography in the United States is just emerging into its own. The apologetic note remains strong, as is probably inevitable in view of the continuing instability of Jewish life, though there is evidence of a more objective trend" ("American Jewish Scholarship," in *The Jewish People Past and Present* [New York, 1964-1955], 4:439).

14. Yitzhak (Fritz) Baer, *A History of the Jews in Christian Spain* (Philadelphia, 1961-1966), 1:1.

15. *A History of the Jews,* p. vii.

16. *SRH* 1:31.

17. *A History of the Jews* (New York, 1961), pp. 423-424.

18. (London, 1963), 1:10.

19. Ibid. 2:483-484.

20. *The Course of Modern Jewish History* (Cleveland, 1958), p. 28.

21. Grayzel, *Church,* p. 81.

22. *The Meaning of Jewish History* 2:253; also 249.

23. Ibid. 2:232.

24. For further examples, see Abram L. Sachar, *A History of the Jews,* 5th ed. (New York, 1965), pp. 183-187, 191-197.

3: Anti-Judaism as the Necessary Preparation for Antisemitism

1. Jean Juster, *Les Juifs dans l'Empire romain,* 2 vols. (Paris, 1914); Bernhard Blumenkranz, "Tacite, antisémite ou xenophobe?" *Revue des études juives,* n.s., 11 (1951/1952): 187-191; A. N. Sherwin White, *Racial Prejudice in Imperial Rome* (Cambridge, 1967); Victor Tcherikover, *Hellenistic Civilization and the Jews* (Philadelphia, 1959); Simon, *Verus Israël,* p. 273.

2. Simon, *Verus Israël,* passim; Blumenkranz, *Les auteurs latins du moyen âge sur les Juifs et le judaïsme.*

3. Parkes, *CCS;* Jules Isaac, *Genèse de l'antisémitisme* (Paris, 1956); John Chrysostom, "Homilies against the Jews," in *Patrologiae Cursus Completus, Series Graeca,* ed. J.-P. Migne (Paris, 1857-1889), 48:875: "Or is it but a small

distance that separates us from the Jews? Or is controversy between us about light and everyday things, so that you believe that our practices and theirs are one and the same? Why do you confuse that which is not to be confused? They crucified the Christ whom you adore. Do you see how great the separation? How then does it happen that you, professing to adore the crucified, run to those who crucified Christ?"

4. Parkes, *CCS*, pp. 166-168, 174-182, 187-189, 199-206; Blumenkranz, *JC*, pp. 291-371.

5. Kisch, *The Jews in Medieval Germany*, pp. 32, 318.

6. Blumenkranz, *Les auteurs latins*, pp. 152-168, 195-200.

7. See Jeffrey B. Russell, *Dissent and Reform in the Early Middle Ages* (Berkeley and Los Angeles, 1965). I would argue that the appearance in the north only of peasant heresy of the type Russell styles extravagant, including the popular crusade of 1096, demonstrates that the bulk of the population in the north had finally identified firmly with Christianity—however they interpreted it.

8. E. L. Dietrich, "Das Judentum im Zeitalter der Kreuzzüge," *Saeculum* 3 (1952): 94-129; Baron, *SRH* 4:97-102; Hans Liebeschütz, "The Crusading Movement in Its Bearing on the Christian Attitude toward Jewry," *Journal of Jewish Social Studies* 10 (1959): 97-111. Norman Golb, "New Light on the Persecution of French Jews at the Time of the First Crusade," *Proceedings of the American Academy of Jewish Research* 34 (1966): 1-63, while interesting, does not significantly alter the accepted views of the geography of the massacres.

9. Solomon Grayzel, "The Papal Bull *Sicut Judeis*," in *Studies and Essays in Honor of A. A. Neuman* (Leiden, 1952), pp. 242-280; Kisch, *Jews in Medieval Germany*, pp. 107-153; my "The Jews and the Archives of Angevin England," *Traditio* 19 (1963): 196-202, 208-209; and chap. 6 below.

10. Robert K. Merton, *Social Theory and Social Structure*, 2d ed. (Glencoe, Ill., 1957), pp. 421-436.

11. Caro, *SWG* 1:220-223.

12. R. Génestal, *Rôle des monastères comme établissements de crédit* (Paris, 1901); H. van Wervecke, "Le mort-gage et son rôle économique en Flandre et en Lotharingie," *Revue belge de philologie et d'histoire* 8 (1929): 53-91; Jean Lestocquoy, "Les usuriers au début du moyen âge," in *Studi in onore di Gino Luzzatto*, 2 vols. (Milan, 1949-1950), 1:67-77; H. G. Richardson, *The English Jewry under Angevin Kings* (London, 1960).

13. Poliakov, *HA* 1:115-139.

14. Gordon W. Allport, *The Nature of Prejudice* (Cambridge, Mass., 1954), pp. 343-392.

15. Cf. Cecil Roth, "The Medieval Conception of the Jew," in *Essays and Studies in Memory of Linda R. Miller* (New York, 1938), pp. 171-190; and Isaac, *Genèse de l'antisémitisme*, pp. 319-320.

16. See, for example, Edward H. Flannery, *The Anguish of the Jews* (New York, 1965), 2d ed. (New York, 1985).

4: The Transformation of Anti-Judaism

1. Steven Runciman, *A History of the Crusades* (New York, 1964), 1:135.

2. Frederick Duncalf in *A History of the Crusades*, ed. Kenneth Setton, vol. 1, *The First Hundred Years*, ed. M. W. Baldwin, 2d ed. (Madison, 1969), p. 263.

3. R. Grousset, *Histoire des croisades* (Paris, 1964), 1:10 f.; see also Adolf Waas, "Volk Gottes und Militia Christi—Juden und Kreuzfahrer,"in *Judentum und Mittelalter*, Miscellanea Mediaevalia, 4 (Berlin, 1966), pp. 382-434.

4. H. E. Meyer, *The Crusades* (New York, 1972), p. 44.

5. Paul Alphandery, *La chrétienté et l'idée de croisade* (Paris, 1954), 1:75 f.; Norman Cohn, *The Pursuit of the Millennium* (London, 1957), pp. 32-74; Joshua Prawer, *Histoire du royaume latin de Jerusalem* (Paris, 1969), 1:180-184; cf. Bernard McGinn, "Iter Sancti Sepulchri: The Piety of the First Crusaders," in *Essays on Medieval Civilization*, ed. B. K. Lackner and K. R. Philp (Arlington, Tex., 1978), pp. 47 f. Since this paper was given, Jonathan Riley-Smith has emphasized the motive of vengeance for the death of Christ: "The First Crusade and the Persecution of the Jews," in *Persecution and Toleration*, ed. W. J. Sheils, Studies in Church History, vol. 21 (Oxford, 1984), pp. 51-72.

6. James Parkes, *The Jew in the Medieval Community* (London, 1938), p. 81; Joshua Trachtenberg, *The Devil and the Jews* (New York, 1961), p. 167; Baron, *SRH* 4:89; Cecil Roth, *History of the Jews* (New York, 1961), p. 180; Blumenkranz, *JC*, p. 388; Poliakov, *HA* 1:62. But cf. now Robert Chazan, *European Jewry and the First Crusade* (Berkeley, Los Angeles, London, 1987), where it is argued that 1096 was not a turning point in Jewish life. I would still maintain, however, that 1096 was a decisive turning point in the attitudes of many Christians toward Jews.

7. Caro, *SWG* 1:213. After 1933, historians of the majority should have known that economic factors were not important in 1096, since Henri Pirenne had recognized that Jews were not prominent as moneylenders in 1096 nor the major source of credit thereafter: *Histoire économique et sociale du moyen âge*, ed. H. V. Werveke (Paris, 1963), pp. 99-111.

8. Baron, *SRH* 4:102.

9. Since I have now modified my terminology for discussing religion and explained it at much greater length in *History, Religion, and Antisemitism*, this section is a shortened and modified version of the section originally presented at Spoleto.

10. Peter Brown, *The World of Late Antiquity* (London, 1971), pp. 82-94.

11. Roland Robertson, *The Sociological Interpretation of Religion* (New York, 1970), pp. 55 f.; Louis Schneider, *Sociological Approach to Religion* (New York, 1970), pp. 123-134.

12. Peter Brown, "The Rise and Function of the Holy Man in Late Antiquity," *Journal of Roman Studies* 61 (1971): 80-101.

13. Marcel Simon, *Verus Israël*, 2d ed. (Paris, 1964), pp. 264 f.

14. Ibid., p. 265.

15. "Mais compte tenu de tous les renseignements et indices dont nous

disposons, on peut affirmer que l'anti-judaïsme officiel était contrebalancé dans le peuple, et parfois chez certains éléments du clergé, par un philo-judaïsme également caractérisé. Ou plutôt, c'est dans ce philo-judaïsme populaire que réside l'explication véritable de l'antisémitisme chrétien. Celui-ci apparait en définitive comme la réaction de défense de la hiérarchie orthodox contre le danger juif, le mal juif" (ibid., p. 273).

16. "When Ambrose dispatched this singular effusion—which shows how religious prejudice could so warp the judgement of a good and wise man as to cause him to condone the crimes of robbery and arson, and actually plead the unpunished outrages of brutal mobs and heathen persecutors as precedents for pardoning fanatical Christian criminals . . ." (F. H. Dudden, *The Life and Times of St. Ambrose* [Oxford, 1925], 2:376).

17. J. Matthews, *Western Aristocracies and Imperial Court, A.D. 364-425* (Oxford, 1975), p. 186; see also G. B. Ladner, *The Idea of Reform* (Cambridge, Mass., 1959), p. 147 f.; Suzanne Lewis, "The Latin Iconography of the Single-Naved Cruciform Basilica Apostolorum in Milan," *Art Bulletin* 51 (1969): 205-219; Lewis, "San Lorenzo Revisited: A Theodosian Palace Church at Milan," *Journal of the Society of Architectural Historians* 32 (1973): 197-222.

18. Dudden, *The Life of St. Ambrose* 1:105-129; 2:557; G. Madec, "L'homme intérieur selon Saint Ambroise," in *Ambroise de Milan: XVIe Centenaire de son élection épiscopale*, ed. Y.-M. Duval (Paris, 1974), pp. 283-308.

19. Peter Brown, *Augustine of Hippo* (Berkeley and Los Angeles, 1969), pp. 82-85.

20. Ambrose, *Epistola* 40 in *PL* 16:1101-1113.

21. *Epistola* 41 in *PL* 16:1113-1121.

22. T. Ring, *Auctoritas bei Tertullian, Cyprian, und Ambrosius* (Würzburg, 1975), pp. 198 f.

23. C. Morino, *Church and State in the Teaching of St. Ambrose*, trans. J. Costello (Washington, 1969), pp. 25, 72 f.

24. Ring, *Auctoritas*, p. 204.

25. Morino, *Church and State*, p. 73.

26. Ring, *Auctoritas*, pp. 202-204.

27. Morino, *Church and State*, pp. 48-61, 80 f.; F. Heim, "Le thème de la victoire sans combat chez Ambroise," in *Ambroise de Milan: XVIe Centenaire*, pp. 267-281.

28. Morino, *Church and State*, p. 20.

29. Ibid., pp. 81-87, 92, 95 f.

30. Simon, *Verus Israël*, p. 268.

31. Ibid., pp. 268 f.

32. C. N. Cochrane, *Christianity and Classical Culture* (London, 1944), pp. 399-455.

33. Colin Morris, *The Discovery of the Individual, 1050-1200* (New York, 1972), pp. 20-36.

34. Jacques Fontaine, "Conversion et culture chez les Wisigoths d'Espagne," in *La conversione al cristianesimo nell'Europa dell'alto medioevo*,

Settimane di studio del Centro italiano di studi sull'alto medioevo, vol. 16 (Spoleto, 1967), p. 135.

35. *Lex Salica, 100 Titel-Text*, ed. K. A. Eckhardt, Germanenrechte, N.F. (Weimar, 1953), p. 88.

36. Alcuin, *Epistolae* in *MGH Epistolae* 4:51.

37. E. Delaruelle, "La pietà populare nel secolo XI," in *Storia del medioevo: Relazione del X Congresso internationale di scienze storiche*, vol. 3 (Florence, 1955), p. 318.

38. J. A. Jungmann, *Liturgische Erbe und Pastorale Gegenwart* (Innsbruck, 1960), pp. 30-44, describes but disregards the efforts of German Arians to subordinate the Son so that the Father emerges as the one eternal and supreme God and accepts the view that the German Arians in effect believed in two or three gods and were halfway between paganism and Christianity. He fully acknowledges, however, that the German Catholics made Christ the supreme figure but explains that as a reaction of Christian clerics to defend monotheism against polytheism. He does not envisage the possibility that the conflict in the German West was between two competing efforts to make Christianity more obviously monotheistic, both rejecting trinitarian equality and both fascinated by supreme power.

39. Fontaine, "Conversion et culture," p. 105.

40. Heinrich Fichtenau, *The Carolingian Empire*, trans. P. Munz (Oxford, 1957), p. 49.

41. Blumenkranz, *JC*.

42. A. Thompson, *The Goths in Spain* (Oxford, 1969), p. 74.

43. Blumenkranz, *JC*, pp. 182 f.

44. Thompson, *Goths in Spain*, p. 165.

45. Ibid., pp. 173 f., 181; Fontaine, "Conversion et culture," pp. 118, 139; J. DuQ. Adams, "Ideology and the Requirements of 'Citizenship' in Visigothic Spain," *Societas* 2 (1972): 317-332.

46. Parkes, *CCS*, pp. 347 f., 369 f.

47. B. S. Bachrach, *Early Medieval Jewish Policy in Western Europe* (Minneapolis, 1977), pp. 3-26.

48. Parkes, *CCS*, p. 370.

49. Fontaine, "Conversion et culture," pp. 106-123; Thompson, *Goths in Spain*, pp. 38, 58 f., 76 ff.

50. Thompson, *Goths in Spain*, pp. 57-91.

51. Ibid., pp. 181, 192; Fontaine, "Conversion et culture," pp. 140 f.

52. Marc Bloch, *Les rois thaumaturges* (Strasbourg, 1924), pp. 462 f.

53. Thompson, *Goths in Spain*, p. 216.

54. Ibid., pp. 198 f., 206 ff., 237.

55. Pectaric, Catholic king of the Lombards, may have commanded about 672 that Jews choose between baptism and death (Blumenkranz, *JC*, p. 134). If he did, it may have been for the same reasons as Sisebut, but the failure to pursue the policy suggests how impossible it must have seemed in a very weak kingdom amidst the cultural pluralism of Italy.

56. Blumenkranz, *JC*, pp. 99, 105.

57. Ibid., pp. 100, 105.

58. Ibid., pp. 135, 171-197, 316 f., 334 f., 342.

59. Fichtenau, *The Carolingian Empire*, p. 119.

60. Jean Leclercq, *The Love of Learning and the Desire for God*, trans. C. Mishari (New York, 1974), pp. 99-109.

61. E. Boshof, *Erzbischof Agobard von Lyon* (Cologne, 1969), p. 42.

62. Ibid., pp. 102-135.

63. Grayzel, *Church*, pp. 76-82.

64. Georges Duby, *Guerriers et paysans* (Paris, 1973).

65. Gerd Tellenbach, *Church, State and Christian Society*, trans. R. F. Bennett (Oxford, 1948), p. 164.

66. R. W. Southern, *Western Society and the Church in the Middle Ages* (Harmondsworth, 1970), p. 37.

67. M.-D. Chenu, *La théologie au douzième siècle* (Paris, 1957), p. 252.

68. Ibid., pp. 237, 245, 266.

69. See Victor Turner, *Dramas, Fields, and Metaphors* (Ithaca, N.Y., 1975), pp. 231-271.

70. The relevant bibliography can be found conveniently in Raoul Manselli, *La religion populaire au moyen âge: Conférences Albert le Grand 1973* (Paris and Montreal, 1975). And now see also R. I. Moore, *The Origins of European Dissent* (New York, 1977).

71. Raoul Manselli, *Studi sulle eresie de secolo XII*, 2d ed. (Rome, 1975), pp. 19-38.

72. J. B. Russell, *Dissent and Reform in the Early Middle Ages* (Berkeley and Los Angeles, 1965), pp. 101-124.

73. See above, nn. 1-6.

74. Robert Chazan, "Initial Crisis for Northern European Jewry 1007-1012," *Proceedings of the American Academy for Jewish Research* 38-39 (1970-1971): 101-117.

75. Blumenkranz, *JC*, pp. 384 f.

76. Turner, *Dramas, Fields, and Metaphors*, pp. 272-299.

5: Doubt in Christendom

1. After I had written this chapter, Susan Reynolds told me that she had written an article about disbelief in the Middle Ages, "Social Mentalities and the Case of Medieval Scepticism," which will appear in the *Transactions of the Royal Historical Society* in 1991. She kindly lent me a copy, and I was delighted to discover that she also maintains that there was significant variation in belief and considerable disbelief in the Middle Ages. Fortunately, our approaches differ sufficiently so that our analyses of the phenomenon do not directly overlap.

2. *Summa theologica* I.1.1.

3. See *History, Religion, and Antisemitism*, esp. chaps. 8-9 and 12-13.

4. Beryl Smalley, *The Study of the Bible in the Middle Ages*, 2d ed. (Oxford, 1952), p. 5.

5. Gerard E. Caspary, *Politics and Exegesis: Origen and the Two Swords* (Berkeley, Los Angeles, London, 1979).

6. 1 Corinthians 15:3-9, 12-18.

7. Mark 4:10-13.

8. Romans 11:7-8.

9. 2 Corinthians 3:14-16; 4:3-4.

10. John 8:43-44.

11. Henry Chadwick, *The Early Church* (Harmondsworth, 1967), p. 70.

12. Ibid.

13. Jaroslav Pelikan, *The Emergence of the Catholic Tradition*, vol. 1 of *The Christian Tradition* (Chicago, 1971), p. 15.

14. *Writings of Saint Justin Martyr*, trans. Thomas B. Falls (New York, 1948), p. 191.

15. To which I shall return in chap. 8.

16. *Writings of Saint Justin Martyr*, pp. 198-199.

17. Henri Irenée Marrou, *Saint Augustin et la fin de la culture antique*, 4th ed. (Paris, 1958), pp. 171, 231; see also Marrou, *Histoire de l'éducation dans l'antiquité*, 6th ed. (Paris, 1964), 1:313-315; 2:44-45, 83-84.

18. Marrou, *Saint Augustin et la fin de la culture antique*, pp. 277-283.

19. Maïeul Cappuyns, *Jean Scot Erigène* (Brussels, 1964), pp. 280-290, 302-315.

20. Achille Luchaire, *Social France at the Time of Philip Augustus*, trans. Edward B. Krehbiel (New York, 1912), p. 28.

21. See, for example, the argument of Barbara H. Rosenwein, *Rhinoceros Bound* (Philadelphia, 1982), pp. 101-110.

22. As Alexander Murray has emphasized: *Reason and Society in the Middle Ages* (Oxford, 1978).

23. Which Walter Ullmann sedulously assembled in *The Growth of Papal Government in the Middle Ages*, 2d ed. (London, 1962).

24. M.-D. Chenu, *Nature, Man, and Society in the Twelfth Century*, ed. and trans. Jerome Taylor and Lester K. Little (Chicago, 1968), pp. 162-269 and passim; R. W. Southern, *The Making of the Middle Ages* (New Haven, 1953), pp. 219-257.

25. *The Making of the Middle Ages*, p. 228.

26. See above, chap. 4, n. 70.

27. *Petri Venerabilis Contra Petrobrusianos hereticos*, ed. James Fearns, Corpus Christianorum, Continuatio Mediaevalis, vol. 10 (Turnhout, 1968); Raoui Manselli, "Il monaco Enrico e la sua eresia," *Bullettino dell'Istituto storico italiano per il medioevo e archivio muratoriano* 65 (1953): 1-63; and see Moore, *Origins of European Dissent*, chap. 4.

28. The spread of Manichean beliefs in western Europe after 1150 is too complicated a phenomenon to discuss here, but that development is certainly testimony to people's susceptibility to doubts about Catholic beliefs.

29. Brian Stock, *The Implications of Literacy* (Princeton, 1983), p. 523; see also p. 150.

30. Ibid., p. 525.

31. *Nature, Man, and Society in the Twelfth Century*, p. 5.

32. Ibid., p. 14.

33. An attitude most evident in Hugh of St. Victor.

34. Jaroslav Pelikan, *The Growth of Medieval Theology (600-1300)*, vol. 3 of *The Christian Tradition* (Chicago, 1978), pp. 73-74.

35. M. L. W. Laistner, *Thought and Letters in Western Europe, A.D. 500 to 900*, 2d ed. (London, 1957), p. 293.

36. Pelikan, *The Growth of Medieval Theology*, pp. 74-77.

37. Southern, *The Making of the Middle Ages*, p. 228.

38. I disagree here with Jean de Montclos, *Lanfranc et Bérenger: La controverse eucharistique du XIe siècle* (Louvain, 1971), pp. 34, 49-50, who thinks that Berengar only began to have doubts about the Real Presence around 1048, when he started to study the writings of the church fathers and encountered the treatise ascribed to John the Scot. I would agree more with A. J. Macdonald, *Berengar and the Reform of Sacramental Doctrine* (London, 1930; reprint, New York, 1977), pp. 48-54, who thinks Berengar was teaching his ideas as early as 1037. De Montclos does not ask why Berengar was predisposed to agree with Ratramnus. Since Berengar was noted for his medical knowledge, his attention to observable reality had probably made him dubious about the conversion of the bread and wine into flesh and blood well before he wrote his first treatise on the subject.

39. Pelikan, *The Growth of Medieval Theology*, pp. 186-199.

40. Ibid., p. 188. See also John H. Van Engen, *Rupert of Deutz* (Berkeley, Los Angeles, London, 1983), pp. 135-176, 241-248.

41. See Brian Tierney, *The Crisis of Church and State, 1050-1300* (Englewood Cliffs, N.J., 1964), p. 34.

42. See the preface to his *Proslogion*.

43. Ibid., chap. 1.

44. R. W. Southern, *Saint Anselm and His Biographer* (Cambridge, 1966), pp. 79-81, 88-91.

45. *The Letters of St. Bernard of Clairvaux*, trans. Bruno Scott James (London, 1953), p. 321, no. 241.

46. Peter Abelard, *A Dialogue of a Philosopher with a Jew and a Christian*, trans. Pierre J. Payer (Toronto, 1979), pp. 26-27.

47. See below, chap. 8.

48. See below, chap. 11.

49. See above, chap. 4.

50. Blumenkranz, *Les auteurs chrétiens latins du moyen âge sur les Juifs et le judaïsme*, pp. 222-225.

51. Ibid., pp. 184-191, 247-250.

52. R. W. Southern, *Medieval Humanism* (New York, 1970), p. 11: "The causes of these riots are difficult to determine but they are all associated with the fears and uncertainties of western Christian society. The recognition of the existence of the Jewish community as a distinct and alien society which positively rejected the Christian faith gave the West a shock of alarm. Their point of view seemed to require an answer, and the eleventh century saw the beginning of attempts to provide one."

53. For an encyclopedic survey of Christian writings against Jews in this period, with an admirable bibliography, see Heinz Schreckenberg, *Die christlichen Adversus-Judaeos-Texte (11.-13. Jh.)*, European University Studies, se-

ries 23, vol. 335 (Frankfurt am Main, 1988). See also David Berger, *The Jewish-Christian Debate in the High Middle Ages* (Philadelphia, 1979).

54. *Antilogus contra Iudaeos*, in PL 145:41-68.

55. Ibid., p. 41.

56. *Disputatio Judei et Christiani*, ed. Bernhard Blumenkranz (Utrecht, 1956).

57. See also Odo of Cambrai, *Disputatio contra Judaeum Leonem nomine de adventu Christi filii dei* (c. 1106), in PL 160:1112: "I gave these proofs about the advent of Christ, Brother Acardus, being forced to dispute some of them more acutely by some Catholics who were present and took the side of the Jews."

58. See below, chap. 8.

59. It is worth remembering that there was no official ecclesiastical concern with Jewish moneylending until 1198, and that there were many Christian lenders. Although there is no doubt that Jewish moneylending began to arouse hostility in northern Europe by the middle of the twelfth century, it was their Jewishness rather than their "usury" that made their lending seem particularly bad.

60. See below, Part 3.

61. See below, Part 4.

6: "Judei Nostri" and the Beginning of Capetian Legislation

1. A. Esmein, *Cours élémentaire du droit français*, 5th ed. (Paris 1903), p. 477; P. Viollet, *Histoire des institutions politiques et adminstratives de la France* (Paris, 1890-1903), 2:193; J. Declareuil, *Histoire générale du droit français* (Paris, 1925), pp. 795-796; E. Chénon, *Histoire générale du droit français* (Paris, 1926-1929), 1:522-523; E. Perrot, *Les institutions publiques et privées de l'ancienne France* (Paris, 1935), p. 365; R. Fawtier, *Les Capétiens et la France* (Paris, 1942), pp. 185-186; F. Olivier-Martin, *Histoire du droit français* (Paris, 1948), pp. 119-120; F. Lot and R. Fawtier, *Histoire des institutions françaises au moyen âge* (Paris, 1957-1958), 2:175-176, 291; J. Flammermont, *De Concessu Legis et Auxilii Tertio Decimo Saeculo* (Paris, 1883), pp. 13-17; A. Luchaire, *Histoire des institutions monarchiques*, 2d ed. (Paris, 1891), 1:243, 272; *Manuel des institutions françaises* (Paris, 1892), pp. 487-491, 508.

2. Brussel, *Nouvel examen de l'usage général des fiefs en France* (Paris, 1750), 1:39-40, 320-321, 583-590; R. Petiet, *Du pouvoir législatif en France* (Paris, 1891), pp. 41-50; E. Glasson, *Histoire du droit et des institutions de la France* (Paris, 1887-1903), 5:338-339; C. Petit-Dutaillis, *La monarchie féodale en France et en Angleterre* (Paris, 1933), pp. 343-344.

3. E.g., Flammermont, *De Concessu Legis*, p. 13; Petit-Dutaillis, *La monarchie féodale*, p. 343. Many of the documents to be discussed here have been published and examined in a different context by Solomon Grayzel, *Church*. When this article was written, there was no satisfactory general study of the Jews in medieval France, as was pointed out by Lot and Fawtier, *Histoire des institutions* 2:175 n. 1. Most of the regional studies then available were cited

in Richard W. Emery, *The Jews of Perpignan in the Thirteenth Century* (New York, 1959). The brilliant work of Caro, *SWG*, was the best account of royal policy toward the Jews in France. Since this article was written, there have been major studies of French royal policy toward Jews. See Robert Chazan, *Medieval Jewry in Northern France* and William Chester Jordan, *The French Monarchy and the Jews*.

4. "Possessory rights over Jews" should be stated more accurately as possession and exercise of numerous and extensive rights over *particular* Jews. The possessory language used throughout this article—possession, possessors, possessory rights, etc.—has been employed to refer briefly to the legal relationship expressed in the documents by phrases such as *Judeus meus*, and to avoid the tedious repetition of a number of more accurate circumlocutions. It also emphasizes that conflict arose not over the nature of the rights exercised by lords over Jews but over the claim of particular lords to exercise these rights over particular Jews whom they described as "their Jews." I do not, however, wish to imply by this language that I equate the status of Jews in medieval law either with that of things in medieval law or with that of slaves in classical Roman law, although the right to capture Jews for purposes of extortion approaches a concept of physical possession (see below, n. 105).

5. Fawtier, *Capétiens*, p. 185: "Très tot, d'ailleurs, le roi laissa entendre que sa requête devait être accueillie et qu'il prendrait en mauvaise part tout refus. Dès 1223, dans une ordonnance sur les Juifs, le roi déclare que cet établissement est valable, non seulement pour ceux qui l'ont 'juré,' c'est-à-dire accepté, mais aussi pour ceux qui ne l'ont point 'juré.' "

6. Robert Latouche, *Les origines de l'économie occidentale* (Paris, 1956), pp. 179-181, 188-190, 193, 195; Parkes, *The Jew in the Medieval Community*, pp. 27-29, 44-52; Kisch, *Jews in Medieval Germany*, pp. 136-137, 318.

7. Georges Duby, *La société aux XIe et XIIe siècles dans la région mâconnaise* (Paris, 1953), pp. 29-30, 119-121.

8. Parkes, *The Jew in the Medieval Community*, pp. 37-44, 62-89; but cf. Kisch, *Jews in Medieval Germany*, pp. 323-327.

9. Gratian, *Decretum* D. 54, cc. 13, 14; C. 17, q. 4 c. 31; *Decretals of Gregory IX* 5.6.1-3, 5; Kisch, *Jews in Medieval Germany*, pp. 58-64; Joshua Trachtenberg, *The Devil and the Jews* (New Haven, 1943), pp. 11-35; Norman Cohn, *The Pursuit of the Millennium* (London, 1957), pp. 58-63.

10. G. Balladore-Pallieri and G. Vismara, *Acta Pontificia Juris Gentium* (Milan, 1946), pp. 209-217, nos. 231, 236, 237, 239, 253, 271; Grayzel, *Church*, pp. 76-78.

11. *PL* 189:368; *The Letters of St. Bernard of Clairvaux*, nos. 391 and 393.

12. Kisch, *Jews in Medieval Germany*, pp. 107-145.

13. Cecil Roth, *A History of the Jews in England*, 3d ed. (Oxford, 1978), p. 6.

14. Kisch, *Jews in Medieval Germany*, p. 318; Duby, *La société aux XIIe et XIIe siècles*, pp. 35, 352-354; R. Génestal, *Rôle des monastères comme établissements de crédit, étudié en Normandie du XIe à la fin du XIIIe siècle* (Paris, 1901), passim.

15. Parkes, *The Jew in the Medieval Community*, p. 83.

16. Génestal, *Rôle des monastères*, pp. 79-84; Benjamin N. Nelson, *The Idea of Usury* (Princeton, 1949), pp. 6-16; John T. Noonan, *The Scholastic Analysis of Usury* (Cambridge, Mass., 1957), pp. 15-20.

17. See *Decretals of Gregory IX* 5.6.4, 5, 7, 8.

18. August Potthast, *Regesta Pontificum Romanorum* (Rome, 1874-1875), no. 327; *Decretals of Gregory IX* 5.19.12.

19. Potthast, *Regesta*, nos. 2373, 3274.

20. C. J. Hefele, *Histoire des conciles*, ed. H. Leclercq, vol. 5.2 (Paris, 1913), p. 1385; *Decretals of Gregory IX* 5.19.18.

21. Raymond of Pennaforte, *Summa de Casibus* 2.10 (p. 241 ed. Rome, 1503, p. 241 ed. Verona, 1744), p. 216; cf. Nelson, *Idea of Usury*, pp. 16-18.

22. Roth, *History of the Jews in England*, p. 16.

23. E.g., *Recueil*, vol. 2, no. 900.

24. Ludwig Buisson, *König Ludwig IX., der Heilige und das Recht* (Freiburg, 1954), particularly chap. 3.

25. Luchaire, *Histoire des institutions* 1:272; Lot and Fawtier, *Histoire des institutions* 2:290. The banishment of baptized Jews who had reverted to Judaism in 1144, the promulgation of a peace for ten years for certain classes of people and property in 1155, and the prohibition of the use of Brabançons in 1164 were clearly connected with the protection of the faith, the church, and the religious movement of the Peace of God (*HF* 16:8; 14:387; 16:697). The same is true of the crusading ordinances of 1188, 1201, and 1215, even though they affected secular rights of great importance. The obvious religious inspiration of these ordinances, the special circumstances of their appearance, and their close relationship with the development of canon law on the subject place them in a class apart (*Recueil*, vol. 1, no. 228; vol. 2, no. 681; *Ordonnances* 1:32; E. Bridrey, *La condition juridique des croisés et le privilège de croix* [Paris, 1900], p. 202).

26. Rigord, in *Œuvres de Rigord et Guillaume le Breton*, ed. H. F. Delaborde, Société de l'histoire de France (Paris, 1882-1885), 1:14-16, 24-29. Alexander Cartillieri, *Philipp II. August, König von Frankreich* (Leipzig, 1899-1922), 1:58, makes the surprising statement that in 1180 the Jews throughout the whole kingdom were captured by royal command. A. Vuitry, *Etudes sur le régime financier de la France* (Paris, 1878), 1:317, speaks of the Jews being chased from the kingdom in 1182. Both measures applied only to the royal domain, or *Francia*, not to the kingdom as Rigord misleadingly states (Caro, *SWG* 1:360-362). That Philip's actions affected only the domain is clear from the events of 1198.

27. Rigord, ed. cit., 1:25; Robert of Auxerre, *MGH SS* 26:243; Guillaume le Breton, ed. cit., 2:22.

28. Villehardouin, *La conquête de Constantinople*, ed. E. Faral (Paris, 1938-1939), 1:2.

29. Robert of Auxerre, *MGH SS* 26:258.

30. Rigord, ed. cit., 1:141.

31. *Recueil*, vol. 2, no. 582; *Layettes*, vol. 1, no. 479.

32. *Recueil*, vol. 2, no. 583, incorrectly dated September 1218 in Grayzel, *Church*, p. 352.

33. *Recueil*, vol. 2, no. 678; Brussel, *Nouvel examen* 2:xxii.

34. *Recueil*, vol. 2, no. 776.

35. Léopold Delisle, *Catalogue des actes de Philippe Auguste* (Paris, 1856), nos. 890, 890A; *Layettes*, vol. 1, nos. 723, 724.

36. *Recueil*, vol. 2, no. 955; Caro, *SWG* 1:364-365.

37. Rising ecclesiastical concern over Jews and Jewish usury found expression in the synodal canons of the bishop of Paris about 1200 (Joannes Mansi, *Sacrorum Conciliorum Nova et Amplissima Collectio* [Paris and Venice, 1759-1798], 22:685), in Innocent III's letter to Philip Augustus of 16 January 1205 (Potthast, *Regesta*, no. 2373), and in his letter to the archbishop of Sens and the bishop of Paris of 15 July 1205 (ibid., no. 2565).

38. An undated order to the bailiffs of *Francia* and Normandy, apparently falling between 1206 and 1219, further defined procedure for Jewish loans and ordered bailiffs to enforce legitimate debts to Jews without delay. Parkes, *The Jew in the Medieval Community*, p. 396, gives the date of 1190; in *Ordonnances* 11:315 n. a, it is related to the ordinance of 1206; Delisle, *Catalogue*, no. 1874, relates it to the ordinance of 1219 and tentatively dates it February 1219.

39. *Layettes*, vol. 1, no. 873. The ordinance of 1164 prohibiting the use of Brabançons (*HF* 16:697), although concerned with the peace and backed by the sanction of excommunication, directly affected secular prerogatives; the adhesion of all lords within the area concerned was claimed by Louis VII.

40. *Layettes*, vol. 1, nos. 922, 923; Brussel, *Nouvel examen* 1:579 n. a. R. De Lespinasse, *Le Nivernais et les comtes de Nevers* (Paris, 1909-1914), 2:44, states that Hervé "signa avec d'autres barons la promesse de ne pas retenir sur ses terres les juifs du roi ou de la comtesse de Champagne." Neither in Teulet's abstract (*Layettes*, vol. 1, no. 923) nor that of Delisle (*Catalogue*, no. 1215) is there any suggestion of anything more than a reciprocal promise between Hervé and the king. There was no single covenant subscribed by several barons, only a series of charters between individuals.

41. Brussel, *Nouvel examen* 1:580 n. a.

42. H. Arbois de Jubainville, *Histoire des ducs et des comtes de Champagne* (Paris, 1859-1869), vol. 5, no. 743; printed in Grayzel, *Church*, pp. 352-353.

43. Brussel, *Nouvel examen* 1:581.

44. Jubainville, *Histoire des comtes de Champagne*, vol. 5, nos. 953, 1163; Grayzel, *Church*, pp. 352-353.

45. *Le traité 'de usura' de Robert de Courçon*, ed. and trans. G. Lefèvre, Travaux et mémoires de l'Université de Lille, 10.30 (Lille, 1902), pp. 5, 23, 51-55, denies Jews the right to take usury from Christians. Nelson, *Idea of Usury*, pp. 10-13, discusses the development of arguments against usury around Paris. For royal-baronial reactions to Robert's activities, see Innocent III's letter to Philip Augustus of 14 May 1214 (Potthast, *Regesta*, no. 4922).

46. Hefele-Leclercq, *Histoire des conciles* 5.2:1385-1388.

47. *Ordonnances* 1:36.

48. Caro, *SWG* 1:367-368.

49. Jubainville, *Histoire des comtes de Champagne*, vol. 5, no. 1209; printed in Grayzel, *Church*, p. 353.

50. Jubainville, *Histoire des comtes de Champagne*, vol. 5, no. 1277.

51. Maximilien Quantin, *Cartulaire générale de l'Yonne* (Auxerre, 1854-1872), vol. 3, no. 254.

52. It would be interesting to know how far this change should be attributed to Blanche of Castile. Certainly she must have been largely responsible for the ordinances of 1227 and 1230, as well as for policy toward the Jews thereafter up to her death in 1252. It is more difficult to estimate the extent of her influence, as Louis VIII's wife, on the ordinance of 1223, or the extent to which Louis VIII himself initiated the new policy toward Jews. C. Petit-Dutaillis, *Etude sur la vie et le règne de Louis VIII* (Paris, 1894), pp. 14-15, mentions Louis VIII's saintly reputation, but see below, n. 55.

53. *Layettes*, vol. 2, no. 1610.

54. "Nullum debitum Judeorum curret ad usuram ab hac die octabarum Omnium Sanctorum in antea. Nec nos nec barones nostri faciemus de cetero reddi Judei usuras que current ab hac die . . . in antea." Caro, *SWG* 1:369, interprets this clause as a prohibition of any usury in the future. J. R. Strayer, *The Administration of Normandy under Saint Louis* (Cambridge, Mass., 1932), p. 49, says that usury was forbidden only during the term provided for the payment of outstanding debts and that "in 1235 the king took the final step of forbidding the Jews to live by usury." Auguste Dumas, *Dictionnaire de droit canonique* (Paris, 1939–), 5:1489, seems also to hold that the prohibition of usury applied only to debts contracted as of 8 November. Both interpretations are possible, but that of Caro seems more likely. Apparently both the 1223 ordinance and the domain ordinance of 1228 (below, n. 76) expressed a policy of undermining Jewish moneylending by prohibition of usury and its enforcement. By 1230 the king went as far as to prohibit enforcement of debts to Jews, a considerable step beyond the prohibition of usury. By 1234 there seems to have been a new royal policy of trying to force Jews out of moneylending and into other occupations, which can first be seen in a charter of Archambaud of Bourbon of May 1234 (*Layettes*, vol. 2, no. 2284): "ego, de voluntate et assensu . . . regis Francie illustris, pro salute mea et predecessorum meorum, volo et concedo quod omnes Judei, qui in terra mea voluerint de cetero morari, propriis vivant laboribus et negociantibus licitis ab usuaria exactione penitus abstinentes." It is this new policy which appears in the domain ordinance of 1235 cited by Strayer.

55. Vuitry, *Régime financière*, p. 324, attributes the ordinance to Louis's desire to enforce the condemnation of usury. Petit-Dutaillis, *Louis VIII*, p. 417, says that "in sum, it was an ordinance of purely fiscal inspiration," and points out that in August 1225 Louis granted privileges to citizens of Asti whereby they made much money by usury. Caro, *SWG* 1:369-370, sees both religious and fiscal motives.

56. Petit-Dutaillis, *Louis VIII*, p. 417.

57. Ralph of Coggeshall, *Chronicon Anglicanum*, ed. J. Stevenson, *RS* (London, 1875), p. 197.

58. See above, n. 1.

59. Vuitry, *Régime financière*, pp. 323-324; Caro, *SWG* 1:369.

60. *Louis VIII*, p. 426; *Monarchie féodale*, pp. 343-344.

61. Petiet, *Du pouvoir législatif*, p. 49. According to the preamble, those who had been present, but had not sworn, had consented to the making of the ordinance.

62. See above, n. 60.

63. Louis VIII, Alix duchess of Burgundy, Peter count of Brittany, Robert III count of Dreux, Mathilde countess of Nevers, Archambaud of Bourbon, William of Dampierre, and Guy count of Saint-Pol, who swore the ordinance, are indicated as possessors of Jews: nn. 40, 41, 44, 108.

64. *Layettes*, vol. 2, no. 1615: "Excellentie vestre notum facimus quod nos stabilimentum quod factum est de Judeis juravimus, sicut alii barones, bona fide observandum, prout nobis per vestras litteras mandavistis; et super hoc litteras nostras patentes per clericum vestrum vobis transmittimus." The letter suggests both the possibility of royal pressure on some of the jurors and the possibility that not all the jurors had been present. But it testifies even more strongly to the king's consciousness of the necessity of individual consent, however obtained, to validate the ordinance in the lands of a magnate.

65. Ibid., no. 1612.

66. "Ego Theobaldus comes Campanie et Brie palatinus, notum facio universis me creatisse karissimo domino meo Ludovico regi Francie illustri quod non retinebo aliquem de Judeis suis nec baronum nec hominum suorum qui stabilimentum de Judeis a domino rege factum juraverunt tenendum. Nec dominus rex, nec barones nec homines sui, qui dictum juraverunt stabilimentum, possint retinere Judeos meos nec aliquam de Judeis meis" (ibid., no. 1620).

67. Above, n. 39.

68. Above, n. 38.

69. Petit-Dutaillis, *Louis VIII*, p. 456, no. 55; p. 459, no. 79; Strayer, *Administration of Normandy*, pp. 49-50; Caro, *SWG* 1:370.

70. Jubainville, *Histoire des comtes de Champagne*, vol. 5, no. 1646.

71. *Layettes*, vol. 2, nos. 1619, 1648.

72. Max Fazy, *Catalogue des actes concernant l'histoire du Bourbonnais* (Moulins, 1924), no. 674; *Layettes*, vol. 2, no. 1996; Brussel, *Nouvel examen* 1:586.

73. *Layettes*, vol. 2, no. 2049.

74. E. Martène and U. Durand, *Veterum Scriptorum . . . Amplissima Collectio* (Paris, 1724-1733), 1:1294. Martène includes this order among documents of 1245, but Caro, *SWG* 1:507, places it between the death of Louis VIII and 24 June 1227, doubtless because, although it mentions the ordinance of 1223 of Louis VIII, then dead, it does not mention the ordinance of 1227, whereas the domain ordinance of 1228 mentions both the ordinances of 1223 and 1227.

75. Caro, *SWG* 1:370. But see now Jordan, *The French Monarchy and the Jews*, pp. 129-130.

76. Martène, *Amplissima Collectio* 1:1222: ". . . nos volumus et statuimus quod stabilimentum factum de Judeis a clarae memoriae genitore nostro anno primo regni sui super debitis contractis ante illud stabilimentum firmiter observetur. De novo autem statuimus et volumus de debitis post illud stablimentum contractis usque ad festum S. Johannis praeteritum, de quibus litterae inde confectae testificantur quod sint catallum, adterminentur ad tres annos et novem terminos, sicut fuit stabilitum in stabilimento anni praecedentis . . ."

77. Above, n. 53.

78. Above, nn. 36, 47.

79. Grayzel, *Church*, no. 70.

80. Below, n. 83.

81. Whereas the final payment ordered by the 1227 ordinance was due on 16 May 1230, the final payment under the 1230 ordinance was due on 1 November 1233, more than six months after the date of the bull. Yet the bull clearly states that the assigned term of four (in fact three) years had already been completed some time previously. At the end of those four years, according to the bull, the Jews were captured and their debts totaled, which could refer to the enrollment of debts by 1 November 1231 ordered by the ordinance of 1230. The bull also mentions that at this time there was a demand for money from the Jews in connection with the enforcement, or nonenforcement, of their debts. This may be associated with the conclusion of Strayer, *Administration of Normandy*, p. 50, that in 1231 royal Jews probably had to pay for the privilege of collecting their debts after the royal intervention of 1230.

82. Grayzel, *Church*, nos. 70, 117. The fact that in 1233 and in 1247 both Gregory IX and Innocent IV regarded the ordinances on the Jews as conventions or oaths between certain magnates is interesting evidence of the way informed contemporaries viewed such embryonic general legislation.

83. "Noverint universi, presentes pariter et futuri, quod nos pro salute anime nostre et inclite recordationis regis Ludovici genitoris nostri et antecessorum nostrorum, pensata etiam ad hoc utilitate totius regni nostri, de sincere voluntate nostra et de communi consilio baronum nostrorum statuimus . . ." (*Layettes*, vol. 2, no. 2083).

84. Caro, *SWG* 1:371.

85. ". . . nos et barones nostri Judeis nulla debita de cetero contrahenda faciemus haberi. . . ." G. P. Depping, *Les Juifs dans le moyen âge* (Paris, 1834), p. 190, interprets this phrase to mean that the king and the barons would no longer force Jews to lend them money. Jean Richard, *Les ducs de Bourgogne et la formation du duché* (Dijon, 1954), p. 361, says that the ordinance prohibited barons "de retenir les juifs d'autrui et de faire contracter à leur profit de nouvelles dettes." Comparison of this phrase with the phrase in the bull of 1233, "servari non facient ipsis pactiones initas vel ineundas inter Christianos et illos," and with Hugh of Lusignan's promise in 1232, "et tenemur eis facere haberi debita que legitima probare potuerunt" (below, n. 102), confirms that the provision meant that those authorities would not use their power to enforce loan contracts contracted with the Jews in the future.

86. The canonical origin of the definition needs no comment: see Noonan, *Scholastic Analysis of Usury*, pp. 18-20.

87. See Gregory IX's bull of 1233 (above, n. 79) and Innocent IV's bull of 6 July 1247 (Grayzel, *Church*, no. 117): ". . . mutuatam ab eis pecuniam non obstantibus talibus iuramentis a Christianis sicut quislibet tuis subditis facias sibi reddi et conservari eos in bonis consuetudinibus predecessorum tuorum temporibus observatis."

88. By the Capetians. There had been Carolingian prohibitions of usury (Latouche, *Origines de l'économie occidentale*, pp. 180-182).

89. Kisch, *Jews in Medieval Germany*, pp. 147-148.

90. Grayzel, *Church*, no. 18; *Compilatio III* 5.3.1; *Decretals of Gregory IX* 5.6.13.

91. *Philippide*, ed. cit. (above, n. 26), 2:22: "Et poterat totum sibi tollere si voluisset, / Nec prejudicium super hoc fecisset eisdem, / Tamquam servorum res et catella suorum." For the probable date that this was written, see ibid. 1:lxx-lxxi.

92. Kisch, *Jews in Medieval Germany*, pp. 148-152, argues that the concept was transmitted from theology to canon law by the inclusion of Innocent's decretal of 1205 in the *Decretals of Gregory IX* in 1234, when the decretal "for the first time found admission into papal legislation," and that regulation of the status of Jews was postponed by Frederick II from 1235 to 1236 when the concept, "canonized by incorporation in the papal code," could influence the formulation of the *servitus camerae* in 1236. But the decretal was included in *Compilatio III*, "die erste offizielle Dekretalensammlung" (Stephan Kuttner, *Repertorium der Kanonistik 1140-1234* [Vatican City, 1937], p. 355). It is worth noting that the phrase *tanquam servi*, which appears both in Guillaume le Breton and in the ordinance of 1230, was used in the bull of 1205 directed to French ecclesiastics, which strongly suggests that the concept in French secular law came from the bull and was current around the royal court by 1217.

93. See above, nn. 1 and 2. The only clear exceptions among those cited there are Luchaire and Petiet. Luchaire, *Manuel des institutions*, pp. 490-491, discusses thirteenth-century legislation only in general terms, suggesting that some were applicable to the whole kingdom. Petiet, *Du pouvoir législatif*, pp. 49-51, thinks that the ordinance bound only those present and, because of the enforcement clause, their vassals. Lot and Fawtier are ambiguous on the point (see below, n. 109).

94. *Histoire du droit*, p. 120. Philip Augustus's ordinance *pro communi utilitate* on champions of 1215, which he ordered Blanche of Champagne to observe in her lands, although her consent is not recorded, apparently applied only to her lands and the royal domain despite the reference to common utility. Further, its imposition on Blanche was the result of special circumstances (*Ordonnances* 1:35; Williston Walker, *On the Increase of Royal Power under Philip Augustus* [Leipzig, 1888], p. 109; Flammermont, *De Concessu Legis*, p. 12; Viollet, *Histoire des institutions* 2:193; Petit-Dutaillis, *Monarchie féodale*, p. 343). Reference to common utility probably did not make an ordinance universally binding but expressed a royal attitude. It is difficult to conceive that

mention of this consideration in the preamble of the 1230 ordinance would make the magnates realize that the ordinance was therefore meant to be universally binding; a clear statement that the provisions were to be observed throughout the kingdom would have had a more obvious legal significance.

95. "Hec vero statuta servabimus et faciemus servari in terra nostra, et barones nostri in terris suis; et si aliqui barones noluerint hec servare, ipsos ad hoc compellemus; ad quod alii barones, cum posse suo, bona fide nos juvare tenebuntur. Et si aliqui in terris baronum invenirentur rebelles, nos et alii barones nostri juvabimus ad compellendum rebelles predicta statuta servare. Hec autem in perpetuum volumus illibata servari a nobis et baronibus nostris, et barones nostri similiter concesserunt se et heredes suos hec perpetuo servaturos. Ego Ph. comes Bolonie ea que premissa sunt volui, consului, et juravi." Lot and Fawtier, *Histoire des institutions* 2:291, state that this provision says that only those who had sworn would be constrained: the provision does not say so explicitly, although that is its meaning according to my interpretation.

96. The ordinance was sealed by only fifteen of the seventeen magnates whose statements of consent appear in the text; there are four seals of persons not named in the text. Lot and Fawtier say that twenty barons subscribed the ordinance. There are twenty seals, but one is the royal seal. Twenty-one persons, other than the king, are indicated by the text or by seals. There are statements of adhesion by Louis IX, Thibaut IV of Champagne, Hugh X of Lusignan, Hugh IV of Burgundy, Hugh V of Saint-Pol, Henry II of Bar-le-Duc, Archambaud of Bourbon, William of Dampierre, and Guy of Dampierre, who are indicated as possessors of Jews by other evidence (see nn. 40-42, 44, 50, 105).

97. Above, nn. 63 and 64.

98. "De Christianis vero statuimus quod nullas usuras de debitis contrahendis eos faciemus habere, nos seu barones nostri. Usuras autem intelligimus quicquid est ultra sortem."

99. Above, n. 79.

100. Sidney Painter, *The Scourge of the Clergy: Peter of Dreux, Duke of Brittany* (Baltimore, 1937), pp. 54 ff.

101. Cf. Viollet, *Histoire des institutions* 2:193: "En 1230, il proclame une seconde fois ce même droit souverain . . ."; Petit-Dutaillis, *Monarchie féodale*, p. 343: "Louis VIII, en 1223, va bien plus loin. . . . Le comte de Champagne n'ayant pas assisté à l'assemblée de 1223, le roi Louis VIII exigea de lui la promesse de respecter la clause susdite; s'il y était refusé, les vingt-quatres signataires de l'ordonannce eussent aidé le roi à l'y contraindre"; Olivier-Martin, *Histoire du droit*, p. 120: "Les établissements royaux les plus importants sont ceux qui sont faits pour l'utilité du royaume and qui sont applicables, *par la même, per totum regnum*" (italics mine). Lot and Fawtier, *Histoire des institutions* 2:291, take a more moderate if ambiguous position (see below, n. 109).

102. *Correspondance administrative d'Alfonse de Poitiers*, ed. A. Molinier, Collection de documents inédits sur l'histoire de France (Paris, 1894-1900), vol. 1, nos. 667-670. The prohibition of enforcement of debts to Jews became

known within the royal domain, as can be seen from a complaint of 1247. "Querimoniae Turonum, Pictavorum, et Santonum, anno 1247," *HF*, vol. 24, no. 745: "Petit Guillermus . . . XI libras, quas compulit solvere cuidam Judeo Paganus de Sancto Venancio, tunc praepositus, a XX annis citra, cum jam facta esset prohibicio a rege, ut dicitur, quod non compellerentur christiani per baillivos ad solvendum. Juratum est, et credit Mattheus quod a XX annis fuit facta prohibicio praedicta, et tempore eciam regis Philippi." See also ibid., nos. 72, 553, 1086, 1097, 1103, 1104, 1260, 1343, 1456, 1459, 1461, 1530, 1535, 1883, and 1884. In the complaint quoted the reference may be to the prohibition of 1226/27 rather than to that of 1230, although the memories of the witnesses seem vague and inaccurate. It is clear from other complaints that some royal officials continued to enforce debts and usury after 1230.

103. The impact of the change from profitable enforcement of debts to Jews to denial of the validity of Jewish debts and usury seems to have been very gradual. The *Coutume de Touraine-Anjou*, probably composed about 1246, stressed possessory rights over Jews and the profits from them. *Les établissements de Saint Louis*, ed. P. Viollet (Société de l'histoire de France; Paris, 1881-1886), 2:249-251: "Se aucuns hom estoit qui deüst deniers au juif lou roi, et lit juis s'an fust clamez à la joutise le roi et li bers en qui chastelrie li hom seroit en demandast la cort à avoir, se il bien le trovoit defendant, si n'en avroit il point, car li meuble au juif sunt au roi. . . . Et einsinc se li bers avoit juif qui se plainsist des homes au vavasor . . . car tuit li meuble au juif sunt au baron." Beaumanoir, about 1280, does not discuss these profitable rights but stresses the illegality of usurious contracts whether by Christians or by Jews. Philippe de Beaumanoir, *Coutumes de Beauvaisie*, ed. A. Salmon, Collection de textes pour servir à l'étude et à l'enseignement de l'histoire (Paris, 1889-1900), 2:474: "Il est defendu as crestiens, pour ce n'est il pas abandonné a juis, car en toutes manières et à toutes gens usure doit estre defendue ne, puis qu'ele soit prouvée, nule justice ne la doit fere paier."

104. Richard, *Ducs de Bourgogne*, p. 361.

105. In 1246 the abbot of Saint-Remi of Reims issued a *vidimus* of the royal letters of 1228/29 containing mutual nonretention promises of the king and Thibaut of Champagne (Grayzel, *Church*, no. 15). In 1247 the abbot of Saint-Loup of Troyes and the abbot of Pruillé separately conducted inquests to prove that Jews had lived in the lands and been under the *dominium* of Thibaut for over nineteen years (ibid., no. 18; *Layettes*, vol. 3, no. 3591). In all three instances, the right seems to be based on the nonretention charter of 1228/29 (above, n. 72), not on the ordinance of 1230. Thibaut was probably protecting his possessions against a royal capture of Jews of 1246, for Louis IX ordered his officials to return the Jews of others who had been captured with royal Jews (Claude De Vic and Joseph Vaissete, *Histoire générale de Languedoc*, new ed. [Toulouse, 1864-1889], 8:1191). A similar problem arose between Thibaut and the king from the capture of Jews of 1268 (*Layettes*, vol. 4, no. 5488). The officials of Alfonse de Poitiers in 1257 and 1268/69 captured the Jews of other magnates, who complained, and the officials were ordered to return their Jews (Antoine Thomas, "Les plaintes de la comtesse de la Marche contre Thibaud de Neuvi, sénéchal de Poitou (vers 1257)," *Bib-*

liothèque de l'Ecole des Chartes 68 [1907]: 509-524; *Correspondance administrative d'Alfonse de Poitiers*, vol. 1, nos. 646-650, 658, 761, 888, 1047, 1459; vol. 2, nos. 1747, 1817). See also the cases in *Les Olim ou régistres des arrêts rendus par la cour du roi*, ed. A. A. Beugnot, Collection de documents inédits sur l'histoire de France (Paris, 1839), 1:122, no. 13; 791, no. 4; 793, no. 7; 811, no. 32; 821, no. 16, etc. In none of these documents is there any reference to the ordinance of 1230, or to its reaffirmation in St. Louis's reforming ordinances of 1254 (*Ordonnances* 1:75).

106. It should be clear that the rule, that no one could take the Jew of another, neither inaugurated rights over Jews nor laid down a criterion for rightful exercise of such rights over particular Jews. Proof of rights over a particular Jew consisted in proof of seisin of such rights, proof that a Jew had lived in the lands and been under the *dominium* of a lord for a length of time. The ordinance of 1230 may have tended to make 1230 the date from which seisin had to be proved, but it did not define which rights exercised for what length of time would substantiate a claim that a Jew was *Judeus meus*. All the rule demanded was that possession of rights over particular Jews, already a recognized concept when Philip Augustus spoke of *Judei nostri* in 1198, should be respected by all.

107. Painter, *Scourge of the Clergy*, p. 88.

108. Brussel, *Nouvel examen* 1:590 n. a.

109. Lot and Fawtier, *Histoire des institutions* 2:175, say that the ordinance of 1223 was intended to apply to the whole kingdom, but later (ibid., 291) they say that the texts of the ordinances of 1223 and 1230 do not absolutely prove that absent barons were bound to observe the ordinances. They suggest that absent barons were morally bound to observe them. This distinction between the legal and moral obligations of the absent barons confuses the legal issue of whether barons were legally bound to observe ordinances intended to bind them, but made in their absence and without their consent. Although Thibaut had consented to the ordinance, the nonretention provision was intended to be legally binding throughout the kingdom, and there is little reason to think that Louis would have made any distinction between those who had been present and those who had been absent if they failed to observe this provision. Any difference in treatment would probably have depended purely on the importance of the case and the practical possibility of enforcement. Any other supposition makes the careful wording of the nonretention provision meaningless. It is difficult to believe that a baron in 1230 would feel a moral obligation to observe a secular law not legally applicable to him. He might feel a moral obligation if the law was intended to accomplish a recognized religious purpose, but then it would be the authority of the church, not of the king, that would make it morally binding.

110. The ordinance of 1230 might be said, with some exaggeration, to be the limit of legislative memory in thirteenth-century France inasmuch as St. Louis's reforming orders of 1254 (*Ordonnances* 1:74-75) rehearsed only two previous ordinances: an ordinance commanding, *inter alia*, the burning of Jewish books and therefore promulgated after the campaign to burn the Talmud which began in 1239 (Caro, *SWG* 1:376); and the ordinance of 1230.

The ordinance of 1223 is not mentioned. Beaumanoir, ed. cit., 1:212, does, however, refer to an ordinance on dowry of 1214/15 which, according to Beaumanoir, Philip Augustus commanded to be held throughout the kingdom with certain exceptions. Beaumanoir is probably wrong; Lot and Fawtier, *Histoire des institutions* 2:291, believe that it was only a domain ordinance. There were also memories within the domain of the prohibition of usury and enforcement of debts to Jews, which did not apply to the whole kingdom either (above, n. 103).

111. C. V. Langlois, *Le règne de Philippe III le Hardi* (Paris, 1887), p. 285.

112. *Histoire des institutions* 2:243.

113. Although the sworn associations of the peace should not be forgotten as an indication of the instinctive tendency to common regulation when strong secular authority was lacking.

114. Grayzel, *Church*, no. 1.

7: "Tanquam Servi": The Change in Jewish Status in French Law about 1200

1. Baron, *SRH* 9:4; see also Baron, *Ancient and Medieval Jewish History* (New Brunswick, N.J., 1972), p. xxi: "As a variant of the papal theory there appeared the doctrine of royal supremacy, which insisted that the Jews were 'serfs' of any monarch under whose reign they lived."

2. (New York, 1971-1972), 14:1188.

3. *Layettes*, vol. 1, no. 2083.

4. The reference is to the article reprinted in the previous chapter.

5. Baron, *SRH* 10:59.

6. Simon Schwartzfuchs, "De la condition des Juifs en France aux XIIe et XIIIe siècles," *Revue des études juives* 125 (1966): 224, 230-232.

7. *Histoire des Juifs en France*, pp. 45-47.

8. Chazan, *Medieval Jewry in Northern France*, p. 139.

9. Karl Friederich Eichhorn, *Deutsche Staats-und Rechtsgeschichte*, 3d ed. (Göttingen, 1821-1822), vol. 1, no. 350; Selig Cassel, "Juden (Geschichte)," in Ersch and Gruber, *Allgemeine Encyklopädie*, 2d sec., vol. 27 (Leipzig, 1850), p. 84; Arthur Beugnot, *Les Juifs d'Occident* (Paris, 1824), p. 82; J. E. Scherer, *Die Rechtsverhältnisse der Juden* (Leipzig, 1901), pp. 4-8 and passim.

10. Isak M. Jost, *Allgemeine Geschichte des Israelitischen Volkes* (Leipzig, 1850), 2:308-309, 315; G. B. Depping, *Les Juifs d'Occident* (Paris, 1844), p. 114; Heinrich Graetz, *Geschichte der Juden*, 2d ed. (Leipzig, 1866-1874), 5:192-196, 218-235; Otto Stobbe, *Die Juden in Deutschland* (Braunschweig, 1866), pp. 3-4, 8; Simon Dubnow, *History of the Jews*, translated from the 4th Russian ed. (New York, 1967-1973), 2:507, 547, 558, 556.

11. Caro, *SWG* 1:166; Kisch, *The Jews in Medieval Germany*, pp. 135-139, 307; Blumenkranz, *JC*, pp. 299-301, 352, 386. Baron, however disagrees: see below, n. 23.

12. Jost and Depping equated the status of Jews with that of serfs; Eichhorn, Beugnot, Cassel, Stobbe, and Dubnow emphasized the difference; and

Graetz asserted that the status of the Jewish *servi camere* was initially above that of serfs but then fell below it.

13. Eichhorn, *Reschtsgeschichte*, vol. 1, no. 297; Cassel, "Juden," pp. 83-85; Graetz, *Geschichte* 6:248-249; Stobbe, *Juden in Deutschland*, p. 12; Dubnow, *History* 3:135.

14. Cassel, "Juden," pp. 83-85; Kisch, *Jews in Germany*, pp. 153-157; Baron, *Ancient and Medieval Jewish History*, p. 306; *SRH* 9:147.

15. Cassel, "Juden," pp. 63-64, 66-70.

16. Ibid., p. 85.

17. Ibid., pp. 83, 85.

18. For the historiography on chamber serfdom in Germany between the early scholars discussed here and the most recent scholarship, see Kisch, *Jews in Germany*, p. 129 n. 1; and Lea Dasberg, *Untersuchungen über die Entwertung des Judenstatus im 11. Jahrhundert* (Paris, 1965), pp. 50-87.

19. Kisch, *Jews in Medieval Germany*, pp. 145-146, 151-153.

20. Baron, " 'Plenitude of Apostolic Powers' and Medieval 'Jewish Serfdom,' " in *Ancient and Medieval Jewish History*, pp. 284-307.

21. "Medieval Nationalism and Jewish Serfdom," in *Ancient and Medieval Jewish History*, pp. 308-322; *SRH* 10:52-53; 11:4. The most extreme argument for the impact of the papal drive for hegemony on Jewish status is that of Dasberg, *Untersuchungen*, pp. 115-142.

22. Kisch, *Jews in Medieval Germany*, pp. 137, 142-143, 144-145, 307.

23. Baron, *SRH* 4:50; 9:139.

24. Ibid. 4:70-71.

25. Ibid. 9:136-147.

26. Baron, *Ancient and Medieval Jewish History*, p. 302.

27. Ibid., p. 307.

28. Ibid., p. 322.

29. Graetz, *Geschichte* 6:249.

30. Dubnow, *History* 3:134-135.

31. Baer, *The Jews in Christian Spain*, 1:85.

32. Cecil Roth, *A History of the Jews in England*, 3d ed. (Oxford, 1964), p. 96.

33. Above, nn. 4, 8.

34. *SRH* 11:3-4.

35. Ibid. 10:52-53.

36. Ibid. 10:54.

37. Ibid. 10:55, 105, italics Baron's.

38. Baron, *Ancient and Medieval Jewish History*, pp. 316-317; *SRH* 10:54-55.

39. *SRH* 11:7.

40. Ibid. 11:9.

41. Above, n. 2.

42. See above, n. 8.

43. See generally Roth, *History of the Jews in England*; Richardson, *The English Jewry under Angevin Kings*; my "The Jews and the Archives of Angevin England," *Traditio* 19 (1963): 183-244; Paul Hyams, "The Jewish Mi-

nority in Medieval England," *Journal of Jewish Studies* 25 (1974): 270-293.

44. *Die Gesetze der Angelsachsen*, ed. Fritz Liebermann (Halle a.S., 1903-1916), 1:650.

45. *Rotuli Chartarum*, ed. T. Duffus Hardy, vol. 1, Record Commission (London, 1837), p. 93.

46. William Stubbs, *Select Charters*, 9th ed. (Oxford, 1942), p. 196.

47. Langmuir, "The Jews and the Archives of Angevin England," pp. 199-200.

48. Richardson, *English Jewry*, p. 294.

49. Henry de Bracton, *De legibus et consuetudinibus Angliae*, RS (London, 1878-1883), 6:50; but see Bracton, *De legibus*, ed. George E. Woodbine (New Haven, 1915-1942), 1:417.

50. Quoted in Roth, *History of the Jews in England*, p. 33.

51. *Ordonnances* 1:74.

52. See Charles Verlinden, *L'esclavage dans l'Europe médiévale* (Bruges, 1955).

53. Olivier-Martin, *Histoire du droit français*, pp. 246-256; Georges Duby, *L'économie rurale et la vie des campagnes dans l'Occident médiéval* (Paris, 1962), 2:401-414, 449-452; Guy Fourquin, *Les campagnes de la région parisienne* (Paris, 1964), pp. 160-167; Robert Fossier, *Histoire sociale de l'Occident médiéval* (Paris, 1970), pp. 158-167.

54. Marc Bloch, *Rois et serfs* (Paris, 1920), p. 22.

55. Fossier, *Histoire sociale*, p. 162; Georges Duby, *Hommes et structures du moyen âge* (Paris, 1973), pp. 83-86.

56. Duby, *Economie rurale* 1:153-161; Duby, *Guerriers et paysans*, pp. 231-236; Robert Fossier, *Les hommes et la terre en Picardie* (Paris, 1968), 1:318-320; 2:554-555, 589, 645-646, 698.

57. E.g., *Recueil*, vol. 3, no. 1095, and most of the documents cited hereafter.

58. Ibid., vol. 1, nos. 156, 208; vol. 2, no. 114.

59. Ibid., vol. 1, no. 114; vol. 3, no. 1210.

60. Ibid., vol. 3, no. 1312.

61. Ibid., vol. 1, no. 156; Duby, *Economie rurale* 1:204.

62. *Receuil*, vol. 1, no. 196; vol. 2, nos. 503, 660, 917.

63. Ibid., vol. 2, no. 527.

64. Ibid., vol. 2, no. 531.

65. *Ordonnances* 8:34-35; *Recueil*, vol. 1, nos. 156, 208, 234, 280; vol. 2, nos. 487, 491, 642, 893.

66. *Receuil*, vol. 1, no. 177; vol. 2, no. 487; vol. 3, no. 1389.

67. Ibid., vol. 3, no. 1177; see also vol. 1, nos. 71, 217.

68. Luchaire, *Histoire des institutions monarchiques* 2:326.

69. *Layettes*, vol. 1, no. 1012; *Recueil*, vol. 3, no. 1250; see also no. 967.

70. William Mendel Newman, *Les seigneurs de Nesle en Picardie* (Philadelphia, 1971), vol. 2, no. 48.

71. *Recueil*, vol. 1, no. 80; see also vol. 3, no. 1175.

72. Above, n. 69; Duby, *Economie rurale* 2:747.

73. *Ordonnances* 8:34-35.

74. *Recueil*, vol. 3, no 1094.

75. Ibid., vol. 3, no. 1138; *Layettes*, vol. 1, no. 939.

76. Blumenkranz, *JC*, pp. 291-371; note especially p. 352, where Blumenkranz argues from taxation that Jews ceased to be equal in law to others and became only tolerated in the second half of the twelfth century; cf. Chazan, *Medieval Jewry*, pp. 38-40.

77. Grayzel, *Church*, no. 5.

78. As discussed in the previous chapter; see also Blumenkranz, *Histoire des Juifs en France*, pp. 44-50; and Chazan, *Medieval Jewry*, pp. 63-124.

79. *Œuvres de Rigord et Guillaume le Breton*, ed. H. F. Delaborde, 2:22.

80. *Recueil*, vol. 2, no. 582; *Layettes*, vol. 1, no. 479.

81. *Recueil*, vol. 3, no. 1127.

82. *Layettes*, vol. 1, no. 922.

83. Above, nn. 4, 6, 8.

84. *Recueil*, vol. 2, no. 780.

85. Grayzel, *Church*, nos. 69, 70.

86. *Summa theologica* IIa-IIae, 10.12. We should remember that the theologians and popes were familiar with the meaning of *servus* in Roman law, and that no Christians in Europe belonged in that status.

87. *HF* 20:34. The biographer also makes the point, which is at least formally correct, that Louis did not wish to convert the goods of the Jews to his own use, which was hardly a typical attitude toward serfs.

88. Kisch has objected to the translation for other reasons: *Jews in Medieval Germany*, p. 428 n. 48.

8: Peter the Venerable: Defense against Doubts

1. *The Letters of Peter the Venerable*, ed. Giles Constable (Cambridge, Mass., 1967), 1:118, no. 37.

2. Ibid. 1:135, no. 40.

3. *Petrus Venerabilis Contra Petrobrusianos hereticos*, p. 12.

4. *Epistola ad Petrum de Johanne contra eos qui dicunt Christum numquam se in Evangeliis aperte Deum dixisse*, in *PL* 189:489.

5. *Adversus Judeorum inveteratam duritiem*, ed. Yvonne Friedman, Corpus Christianorum, Continuatio Mediaevalis, vol. 58 (Turnhout, 1985), p. 109.

6. Virginia Berry, "Peter the Venerable and the Crusades," in *Petrus Venerabilis 1156-1956*, ed. Giles Constable and James Kritzeck, Studia Anselmiana, vol. 40 (Rome, 1956), p. 152.

7. "De laude dominici sepulchri," in "Petri Venerabilis Sermones Tres," ed. Giles Constable, *Revue Bénédictine* 64 (1954): 246-247.

8. *Letters* 1:395, no. 162.

9. Duby, *Hommes et structures du moyen âge*, p. 71.

10. Ibid., p. 76.

11. *Letters* 1:177-178, no. 56.

12. Duby, *Hommes et structures*, pp. 76-77; *La société aux XIe et XIIe siècles dans la région mâconnaise* (Paris, 1953), pp. 347, 351-352.

13. *Letters* 1:328-330, no. 130.

14. Jean Leclercq, *Pierre le Vénérable* (Abbaye S. Wandrille, 1946), pp. 235-236.

15. "Peter the Venerable and the Crusades," pp. 149-150.

16. *Peter the Venerable and Islam* (Princeton, 1964), p. 26.

17. *Letters* 2:185.

18. *The Letters of St. Bernard of Clairvaux*, p. 463, no. 391.

19. *Histoire des Juifs en France*, ed. Blumenkranz, p. 17; *The Letters of St. Bernard*, p. 427, no. 349.

20. *Pierre Abélard—Pierre le Vénérable*, Colloques internationaux du Centre national de la recherche scientifique, no. 546 (Paris, 1975), p. 139.

21. Since this paper was presented at the meeting of the Medieval Academy of America in 1977, other scholars have come independently to recognize the depth of Peter's hatred of Jews: Manfred Kniewasser, "Die antijüdische Polemik des Petrus Alfonsi (getauft 1106) und des Abtes Petrus Venerabilis von Cluny (d. 1156)," *Kairos* 22 (1980): 34-76; *Adversus Judeorum duritiem*, ed. Yvonne Friedman, pp. vii-viii, xx-xxii; Jean-Pierre Torell, "Les Juifs dans l'œuvre de Pierre le Vénérable," *Cahiers de civilisation médiévale* 30 (1987): 331-346. Torell (p. 346) sees in Peter a symptom of the formidable wave of antisemitism that was developing at the time.

22. *Adversus Judaeorum duritiem*, p. 70.

23. These fill some 360 columns in vol. 189 of *PL*, while *De miraculis* takes some 100 columns. The remainder of Peter's writings in Migne are comprised of some 425 columns of correspondence, 52 of sermons, 18 of poetry, 23 of statutes, and 8 of the *Dispositio*.

24. J. P. Valery Patin and Jacques Le Goff, "A propos de la typologie des miracles dans le *De miraculis* de Pierre le Vénérable," in *Pierre Abélard—Pierre le Vénérable*, p. 182; Jean-Pierre Torrell and Denise Bouthillier, *Pierre le Vénérable et sa vision du monde*, Spicilegium Sacrum Lovaniense, Etudes et documents, vol. 42 (Louvain, 1986).

25. *Letters*, vol. 1, nos. 28, 111.

26. Kritzeck, *Peter the Venerable and Islam*, p. 37.

27. Leclercq, *Pierre le Vénérable*, pp. 53-54, 57, 290-291; cf. Lester Little, "Intellectual Training and Attitudes toward Reform, 1075-1150," in *Pierre Abélard—Pierre le Vénérable*, p. 237.

28. Leclercq, *Pierre le Vénérable*, pp. 234-241; Constable, *Letters* 2:185; Kritzeck, *Peter the Venerable and Islam*, pp. 25-27, 47.

29. 'Pierre le Vénérable et les Petrobrusiens," in *Pierre Abélard—Pierre le Vénérable*, pp. 174, 177.

30. Kritzeck, *Peter the Venerable and Islam*, pp. 44-45, 158.

31. Baron, *SRH* 4:122-123; Chazan, *Medieval Jewry in Northern France*, p. 46.

32. Giles Constable, "Manuscripts of Works by Peter the Venerable," in *Petrus Venerabilis*, pp. 236-237. Only five manuscripts of the treatise against the Jews are known, a testimony to "the book's limited circulation" (*Adversus Judeorum duritiem*, p. xxviii).

33. *De miraculis*, in *PL* 189:939-940.

34. Leclercq, *Pierre le Vénérable*, pp. 293-295.

35. *Adversus Judaeorum duritiem*, pp. 106-114. See "De laude dominici sepulchri," in Constable, "Petri Venerabilis Sermones Tres," p. 250: "Ita omnipotens dispensator, qui unicuique tempori congrua prouidet et dispensat, rarescentibus prioribus miraculis, istud eis iam ex longo tempore succedere uoluit, tantumque esse decreuit, ut et uicem praecentium signorum compleret, et se mundo atque Christianae fidei non solum per gratium, sed nec etiam per miranda opera, ubi necessaria sunt, posse deesse monstraret." On the novelty of this approach, see Leclercq, *Pierre le Vénérable*, p. 239. Cf. Patin, "A propos de la typologie des miracles," p. 182, who thinks that Peter is only expressing a common medieval view and is affirming the superiority of faith over reason.

36. *Adversus Judaeorum duritiem*, pp. 122-124.

37. G. Klameth, *Das Karsamstagsfeuer-Wunder der heiligen Grabeskirche*, Studien und Mitteilungen aus dem kirchengeschichtlichen Seminar der Universität Wien, vol. 13 (Vienna, 1913); Fulcher of Chartres, *Historia Hierosolymitana*, ed. Heinrich Hagenmeyer (Heidelberg, 1913), pp. 395-396, 831-837; A. S. Triton, "The Easter Fire at Jerusalem," *Journal of the Royal Asiatic Society*, 1963:249-250.

38. It is also heavily emphasized in his "De laude dominici sepulchri" (Constable, "Petri Venerabilis Sermones Tres," pp. 248-252).

39. Ibid., p. 249.

40. *Adversus Judaeorum duritiem*, p. 125.

41. P. Séjourné, "Pierre le Vénérable," *Dictionnaire de théologie catholique*, vol. 12 (Paris, 1935), col. 2075; Kritzeck, *Peter the Venerable and Islam*, p. 26.

42. *Adversus Judaeorum duritiem*, p. 187.

43. In terms of the categories developed in chap. 14 below, Peter was an extreme xenophobe who manifested distinct traces of chimerical thinking and would probably have supported chimerical charges initiated by others.

9: Thomas of Monmouth: Detector of Ritual Murder

1. *The Life and Miracles of St. William of Norwich*, trans. and ed., with an introduction, Augustus Jessopp and M. R. James (Cambridge, 1896), cited hereafter as *Life*. When I quote from the *Life*, I will sometimes follow the editors' translation and sometimes use my own. The title in the text is the only one indicated in the manuscript.

2. The dating of the writing of the *Life* is discussed below.

3. *The Anglo-Saxon Chronicle*, trans. Dorothy Whitelock (London, 1961), p. 200; and for the date see p. xvi.

4. For the historiography on the Norwich incident, see below, chap. 12. For a brief overview of the medieval accusations of ritual murder, see my "L'absence d'accusation de meurtre rituel à l'ouest du Rhône," in *Juifs et judaïsme de Languedoc*, ed. M.-H. Vicaire and Bernhard Blumenkranz, Cahiers de Fanjeaux, vol. 12 (Toulouse, 1977), pp. 235-249. And for a general overview, see *Encyclopaedia Judaica* (New York, 1971), 4:1120-1131. For an

interpretation of the fundamental importance of such mythic charges in the formation of antisemitism, see below, chaps. 13 and 14.

5. *Life*, pp. lxii-lxiv.

6. *Greek and Latin Authors on Jews and Judaism*, ed. Menahem Stern, 2 vols. (Jerusalem, 1974-1980), 1:141.

7. Victor Tcherikover, *Hellenistic Civilization and the Jews* (Philadelphia, 1959), pp. 366-367. Tcherikover considers the charge a literary phenomenon, as do Mary E. Smallwood, *The Jews under Roman Rule* (Leiden, 1976), p. 224, and J. N. Sevenster, *The Roots of Pagan Anti-Semitism in the Ancient World* (Leiden, 1975), pp. 140-142.

8. *Greek and Latin Authors*, ed. Stern, 1:152-155, 530-531.

9. Ibid. 1:410-412.

10. Heinz Schreckenberg, *Rezeptionsgeschichtliche und textkritische Untersuchungen zu Flavius Josephus* (Leiden, 1977), p. 157.

11. Heinz Schreckenberg, *Die Flavius-Josephus-Tradition in Antike und Mittelalter* (Leiden, 1972), pp. 79-88, 201-203.

12. Schreckenberg, *Rezeptionsgeschichtliche Untersuchungen*, p. 157.

13. Franz Blatt, *The Latin Josephus*, vol. 1 (Copenhagen, 1958), pp. 26-94, nos. 3, 4, 6, 7, 16-18, 23, 31, 32, 96, 108, 109, 111, 128, 135, 143.

14. Carolus Boysen, *Flavii Iosephi Opera ex Versione Latina Antiqua*, part 6, book 2, Corpus Scriptorum Ecclesiasticorum Latinorum, 37 (Vienna, 1898; reprint, New York, 1964), pp. ii-x, nos. 8, 12, 15, 23, 26.

15. Schreckenberg, *Josephus-Tradition*, pp. 147-149.

16. Ibid., pp. 201-203.

17. Blatt, *The Latin Josephus*, p. 90, no. 161.

18. Ibid., pp. 87-94.

19. Boysen, *Flavii Iosephi Opera*, p. vii, no. 20; Blatt, *The Latin Josephus*, p. 28, no. 4.

20. Boysen, *Flavii Iosephi Opera*, pp. viii-viiii, no. 24; Blatt, *The Latin Josephus*, p. 29, no. 6.

21. Norman Cohn, *Europe's Inner Demons* (New York, 1975), pp. 19-31.

22. Simon, *Verus Israël*, p. 160.

23. Parkes, *CCS*, p. 234.

24. Ibid.; Simon, *Verus Israël*, p. 160.

25. Jean Juster, *Les Juifs dans l'Empire romain*, 2 vols. (Paris, 1914), 2:204.

26. Cecil Roth, "The Feast of Purim and the Origins of the Blood Accusation," *Speculum* 8 (1933): 522; Blumenkranz, *Les auteurs chrétiens latins du moyen âge*, p. 58.

27. *Historia ecclesiastica tripartita*, ed. Walter Jacob and Rudolph Hanslik, Corpus Scriptorum Ecclesiasticorum Latinorum, 81 (Vienna, 1952), pp. 644-645; Walter Jacob, *Die handschriftliche Überlieferung der sogenannten Historia tripartita des Epiphanius-Cassiodor* (Berlin, 1954), pp. 8-54, esp. nos. 104, 124.

28. *Chronica Sigeberti Gemblacensis*, in *MGH SS* 4:304, 305.

29. *Historia tripartita*, pp. 645-656.

30. *Chronica Sigeberti*, p. 306; *Annales Monastici*, ed. H. R. Luard, *RS* (London, 1864-1869), 2:144.

31. Blumenkranz, *Les auteurs chrétiens*.

32. For background, see *Life*, pp. xix-xxv; M. D. Anderson, *A Saint at Stake: The Strange Death of William of Norwich* (London, 1964), pp. 25-53; V. D. Lipman, *The Jews of Medieval Norwich* (London, 1967), pp. 3-18.

33. H. A. Cronne, *The Reign of King Stephen 1135-1154* (London, 1970), pp. 149-150.

34. H. G. Richardson, *The English Jewry under Angevin Kings* (London, 1960), pp. 8-9.

35. The evidence for the accusation at Valréas in 1247 is also exceptionally rich: Auguste Molinier, "Enquête sur un meurtre imputé aux Juifs de Valréas (1247)," *Le cabinet historique*, n.s., 2 (1883): 121-133.

36. *Life*, pp. 14-16.

37. *Life*, pp. 16-19.

38. *Life*, pp. 31-39. Thomas gives a very unlikely explanation of why Henry of Sprowston did not have the body buried in consecrated ground, but does not even attempt to explain why Godwin did not do it, reporting instead that Godwin, Robert, and Alexander "celebrated the obsequies" on the spot. Godwin later complained to the synod that William had not yet received a Christian burial, but Godwin himself did nothing about it until he decided to accuse Jews formally in public.

39. *Life*, pp. 40-42.

40. *Life*, pp. 43-45.

41. *Life*, p. 46.

42. *Life*, pp. 45-49. Although Thomas alleges (pp. 36-37) that people already suspected the Jews on the Easter weekend and were so angry that they would have attacked the Jews had they not feared the sheriff, the fact that the body was left unburied in the wood throughout the weekend and then buried there makes the assertion completely implausible.

43. *Life*, pp. 49-55.

44. *Life*, pp. 51-53.

45. *Life*, pp. 66-85.

46. *Life*, p. 84.

47. *Life*, pp. 79-85.

48. *Life*, pp. 27-30.

49. *Life*, p. 77.

50. *Life*, pp. 19, 89.

51. *Life*, pp. 89-91.

52. *Life*, p. 94.

53. *Life*, pp. 93-94.

54. "St. William of Norwich," *Jewish Quarterly Review*, o.s., 9 (1897): 752.

55. The fascination of some disturbed Christians with a reenactment of the Crucifixion is evident in the case of the youth condemned at the council of Oxford in 1222 for piercing his own hands, feet, and side and giving himself out to be Christ: Ralph of Coggeshall, *Chronicon Anglicanum*, ed. W. Stubbs,

RS (London, 1875), p. 190; see also *Die Exempla aus dem Sermones feriales des Jakub von Vitry*, ed. Joseph Greven (Heidelberg, 1914), no. 44.

56. *Life*, p. 15.

57. *Life*, pp. 23-26.

58. *Life*, pp. 125-126.

59. *Life*, p. 127.

60. *Life*, pp. 128-132.

61. *Life*, p. 131.

62. *Life*, pp. 132-145.

63. *Life*, pp. 165-166.

64. *Life*, pp. 172-174.

65. Ronald C. Finucane, *Miracles and Pilgrims: Popular Beliefs in Medieval England* (Totowa, N.J., 1977), p. 161.

66. *Life*, pp. 185-186.

67. Finucane, *Miracles and Pilgrims*, p. 162.

68. *Life*, pp. 220-222.

69. *Life*, p. liii.

70. *Life*, p. 262.

71. *Life*, pp. 92, 95.

72. *Life*, p. 65.

73. *Life*, p. 57.

74. *Life*, p. 85.

75. *Life*, pp. 46, 48, 49.

76. *Life*, pp. 20-22, 34, 90, 192.

77. Finucane, *Miracles and Pilgrims*, pp. 59-82.

78. *Life*, p. 107.

79. *Life*, pp. 22, 91.

80. *Life*, pp. 85-86.

81. *Life*, pp. 57-65, 85-112.

82. *Life*, p. 95.

83. *Life*, p. 16.

84. Finucane, *Miracles and Pilgrims*, pp. 161-162.

85. Lambert of Waterloo, *Annales Cameracenses*, in *MGH SS* 16:536.

86. *The Chronicle of Robert de Torigny*, in *Chronicles of the Reigns of Stephen, Henry II, and Richard I*, ed. R. Howlett, *RS* (London, 1889), 4:150-151.

87. See below, chap. 10.

88. *Life*, p. 77.

89. See below, chap. 12.

10: The Knight's Tale of Young Hugh of Lincoln

1. Abbreviations used in this chapter for publications of the Public Record Office: *C. Ch. R.* for *Calendar of the Charter Rolls*; *Pat. R.* for *Patent Rolls*; *C. Pat. R.* for *Calendar of Patent Rolls*; *Cl. R.* for *Close Rolls*; *C. Lib. R.* for *Calendar of Liberate Rolls*; *C. Inq. P. M.* for *Calendar of Inquisitions Post Mortem*; *C. Inq. Misc.* for *Calendar of Inquisitions Miscellaneous*; *C. Papal R.*

for *Calendar of Entries in the Papal Registers Relating to Great Britain and Ireland; Book of Fees* for *Liber Feodorum, The Book of Fees Commonly Called Testa de Nevill.* Other abbreviations: *R. Litt. Pat.* for *Rotuli Litterarum Patentium,* ed. T. D. Hardy (Record Commission, 1835); *R. Litt. Cl.* for *Rotuli Litterarum Clausarum,* ed. T. D. Hardy (Record Commission, 1833-1834); *Ex. Rot. Fin.* for *Excerpta e Rotulis Finium,* ed. C. Roberts (Record Commission, 1835-1836); *Chron. maj.* for Matthew Paris, *Chronica majora,* ed. H. R. Luard, *RS* (1872-1883); *Ann. Mon.* for *Annales Monastici,* ed. H. R. Luard, *RS.*

2. Carleton Brown, *Study of the Miracles of Our Lady Told by Chaucer's Prioress,* Chaucer Society Publications, 2d ser., no. 45 (London, 1910); "The Prioress's Tale," in *Sources and Analogues of Chaucer's Canterbury Tales,* ed. W. F. Bryan and G. Demster (Chicago, 1941), pp. 447-485; see also Margaret H. Statler, "The Analogues of Chaucer's Prioress' Tale: The Relation of Group C to Group A," *Proceedings of the Modern Language Association* 65 (1950): 896-910; J. C. Wenk, "On the Sources of the Prioress's Tale," *Mediaeval Studies* 24 (1955): 214-219.

3. *Sources and Analogues,* pp. 451-454.

4. *Chron. maj.* 5:516-519, 546, 552; *Ann. Mon.* 1:340-346, 348 (Burton annals); 2:346-348 (Waverley annals); Francisque Michel, *Hughes de Lincoln* (Paris, 1834), pp. 1-16. Since these are brief accounts, I will refer to them hereafter in the text without footnotes.

5. Act 3, scene 6.

6. *Acta Sanctorum,* new ed. (Paris, 1863-1931), 33:494-495. The old edition of this volume was published in 1729.

7. "Imperfect Sympathies," in *Essays of Elia,* ed. M. Elwin (London, 1952), pp. 96-105; first published in the *London Magazine* in August 1821 as "Jews, Quakers, Scotchmen and Other Imperfect Sympathies."

8. J. W. F. Hill, *Mediaeval Lincoln* (Cambridge, 1965), p. 231.

9. Francis James Child, *The English and Scottish Popular Ballads,* 5 vols. in 3 (New York, 1956), 3:233-254; 4:497; 5:241.

10. *Reliques of Ancient English Poetry,* 2d ed. (London, 1767), 1:35-38.

11. An example of the neglect discussed above, chap. 1.

12. *Mediaeval Lincoln,* pp. 224-232.

13. "Little St. Hugh of Lincoln," in *Jewish Ideals and Other Essays* (New York, 1896), pp. 192-224.

14. *History of the Jews in England,* pp. 56-57.

15. As discussed above, chap. 9.

16. *Historia et Cartularium Monasterii Sancti Petri Gloucestriae,* ed. W. H. Hart, *RS* (London, 1863-1865), 1:20-22. The nine-year-old Henry III was crowned at Gloucester in 1216.

17. *Lamberti Waterlos Annales Camaracenses, MGH SS* 16:536; *Œuvres de Rigord et Guillaume le Breton,* ed. Delaborde, 1:15; and see below, chap. 12.

18. Robert Chazan, "The Blois Incident of 1171," *Proceedings of the American Academy for Jewish Research* 36 (1968): 13-31.

19. Roth, *History of the Jews in England*, pp. 13, 21-22.

20. Rigord (above, n. 17).

21. Grayzel, *Church*, no. 14.

22. Roth, *History of the Jews in England*, pp. 22, 42, 273 n. b.

23. *Chron. maj.* 4:377-378.

24. Ibid. 5:114-115; *Cl. R., 1247-51*, pp. 235, 263, 284, 299, 320, 339, 360, 375.

25. Richard Vaughan, *Matthew Paris* (Cambridge, 1958), pp. 131-136, 142-143, 150.

26. Hill, *Mediaeval Lincoln*, p. 228.

27. Below, n. 92.

28. *Sources and Analogues*, p. 467.

29. *Cl. R., 1254-56*, p. 227.

30. Ibid., pp. 142-143, 145.

31. T. F. Tout, *Chapters in Mediaeval Administrative History* (Manchester, 1920-1933), 1:288; see also ibid. 1:250, 284-287; 6:116; L. B. Dibben, "Chancellor and Keeper of the Seal under Henry III," *English Historical Review* 27 (1912): 39-51; Bertie Wilkinson, *The Chancery under Edward III* (Manchester, 1929), p. 195.

32. F. M. Powicke, *King Henry and the Lord Edward* (Oxford, 1947), 1:294.

33. Vol. 33 (London, 1893), pp. 202-204.

34. I. J. Sanders, *English Baronies* (Oxford, 1960), pp. 76-77; *The Registrum Antiquissimum of the Cathedral Church of Lincoln*, ed. C. W. Foster and K. Major, Lincoln Record Society (1931-1968), 7:209-217; J. C. Holt, *The Northerners* (Oxford, 1961), pp. 30, 160-161, 221-222; *C. Inq. P. M.* 2: no. 638.

35. *R. Litt. Cl.* 1:7, 21, 65, 83, 90b; *Pipe Roll 6 John*, pp. 161, 172; *Pipe Roll 7 John*, pp. 221, 226; *Pipe Roll 8 John*, pp. 79, 81; *Pipe Roll 9 John*, pp. 118, 124-127; *Pipe Roll 11 John*, pp. 112, 116-117; *Pipe Roll 12 John*, p. 127.

36. When I wrote this article, I was unaware that Christopher Holdsworth had been working out aspects of the family histories of the Lexington and Sutton families for a different purpose: *Rufford Charters*, ed. C. J. Holdsworth, Thoroton Society, Record Series, vols. 29, 30, 32 (Nottingham, 1972-1980), l:xcii-xcix, cvii-cxvi. I have now corrected a few items in my account in the light of his findings. Holdsworth does not mention the connection of the Lexingtons with the Hugh of Lincoln affair.

37. *Pipe Roll 8 John*, p. 79; *Pipe Roll 9 John*, p. 118; *Pipe Roll 12 John*, p. 156.

38. *Pipe Roll 14 John*, p. 2; *Pipe Roll 16 John*, p. 67; *Pipe Roll 17 John*, p. 11.

39. *R. Litt. Cl.* 1:208, 209b, 210b.

40. W. W. Shirley, *Royal and Other Historical Letters Illustrative of the Reign of Henry III*, RS (London, 1862-1866), 1:171-172; *R. Litt. Cl.* 1:439, 446.

41. *Pat. R., 1216-25*, pp. 209, 393, 418, 485, 558, 560-561, 576; *Pat. R., 1225-32*, pp. 69-70, 79, 83, 166, 276, etc.; *C. Ch. R., 1226-57*, pp. 92, 114, 204, etc.

42. *Pat. R., 1225-32*, p. 511; *Roberti Grosseteste Epistolae*, ed. H. R. Luard, RS (London, 1861), pp. 266-268.

43. *R. Litt. Pat.*, p. 115b; *C. Papal R.* 1:168; *Ann. Mon.* 3:149; *Visitations and Memorials of Southwell Minster*, ed. A. F. Leach, Camden Society (1891), pp. lxii, 178.

44. *Chron. maj.* 5:138.

45. *Ex Rot. Fin.* 1:116-117; *C. Ch. R. 1226-57*, pp. 141, 149-150, 176, 215; *Curia Regis Rolls 1230-32*, no. 1198; *Curia Regis Rolls 1227-30*, no. 2119; *Book of Fees* 1:448, 531; 2:823; *C. Inq. Misc.*, vol. 1, no. 1017.

46. *Curia Regis Rolls 1230-32*, nos. 103, 1534.

47. *R. Litt. Pat.*, pp. 59b, 129b; *The Register or Rolls of Walter Gray*, ed. J. Raine, Surtees Society (1870-1872), pp. 34, 104.

48. David Knowles, *The Religious Orders in England* (Cambridge, 1948-1961), 1:6.

49. *Registrum Epistolarum Stephani de Lexinton*, ed. P. Bruno Griesser, Analecta Sacri Ordinis Cisterciensis, vol. 2 (1946), pp. 1-118; vol. 8 (1952), pp. 181-378; A. Emden, *A Biographical Register of the University of Oxford to A.D. 1500* (Oxford, 1957-1959), 2:1140-1141; *R. Litt. Pat.*, p. 138; *Ann. Mon.* 3:67.

50. *Register of Walter Gray*, pp. 196, 249; *Ann. Mon.* 3:190; *Chron. maj.* 4:416, 422, 431, 442, 508, 618; *C. Pat. R. 1247-58*, p. 366; *Cl. R. 1254-56*, p. 207.

51. *C. Papal R.*, vol. 1, no. 1110; *C. Pat. R. 1247-58*, p. 556; *Cartulary of Osney Abbey*, ed. H. E. Salter, Oxford Historical Society (1928-1936), 4:47; *Registrum Antiquissimum of Lincoln*, vol. 3, no. 949.

52. *C. Inq. P. M.*, vol. 1, no. 402; *Rotuli Ricardi Gravesend*, ed. F. N. Davis, C. W. Foster, and A. H. Thompson, Canterbury and York Society (1925), p. vi.

53. *Rotuli Hugonis de Welles*, ed. W. P. W. Phillimore, Canterbury and York Society (1907-1909), 3:200; *C. Papal R.* 1:211; *Rotuli Gravesend*, p. xxxvii; *Ann. Mon.* 4:31; *Registrum Antiquissimum*, vol. 3, nos. 758, 2551; *The Register of Walter Giffard*, ed. W. Brown, Surtees Society (1904), pp. 4-5, 84, 221-224; *C. Pat. R. 1266-72*, pp. 255, 266.

54. See John de Schalby, "Lives of the Bishops of Lincoln," in *Giraldi Cambrensis Opera*, ed. J. S. Brewer et al., RS (London, 1861-1891), vol. 7, app. E; *The Rolls and Register of Bishop Oliver de Sutton*, ed. R. M. T. Hill, Lincoln Record Society (1948-1969), 3:xiii-xviii; R. M. T. Hill, "Oliver Sutton, Bishop of Lincoln, and the University of Oxford," *Transactions of the Royal Historical Society*, 4th ser., 31 (1949): 1-16.

55. *R. Litt. Cl.* 1:249b, 326b; 2:151; *Pat. R. 1225-32*, pp. 296, 353; *The Cartulary of Dale Abbey*, ed. Avrom Saltman, Historical Manuscripts Commission, JP 11 (London, 1957), nos. 546, 548; *C. Ch. R. 1226-57*, p. 215; *Cl. R. 1288-96*, p. 223.

56. *C. Inq. P. M.*, vol. 1, nos. 402, 682, 870, 1017; vol. 2, no. 61; *Ex. Rot. Fin.* 2:250, 257, 287.

57. *C. Pat. R. 1232-47*, p. 296; ibid. *1266-72*, p. 110; *The Register of John le Romeyn*, ed. W. Brown, Surtees Society (1913-1917), 1:257.

58. *C. Pat. R. 1232-47*, p. 21; *C. Papal R.* 1:326; *Register Gifford*, p. 88.

59. *Register Gifford*, pp. 69, 83, 88; *C. Pat. R. 1272-81*, p. 97.

60. *Register of William Wickwane*, ed. W. Brown, Surtees Society (1907), pp. 75, 264; *Register Romeyn* 1:257.

61. *C. Pat. R. 1281-92*, pp. 58, 275; ibid., *1292-1301*, pp. 109, 118; *Register Romeyn* 2:71.

62. *Rolls Sutton* 3:85.

63. *Monumenta Franciscana*, ed. J. S. Brewer, RS (1858), p. 97; *C. Papal R.* 1:211; *Rotuli Roberti Grosseteste necnon Henrici de Lexinton*, ed. F. N. Davis, Lincoln Record Society (1914), p. 46; above, nn. 50, 53.

64. *C. Pat. R. 1281-92*, p. 92; *Rolls Sutton* 3:xvii; *Visitations of Southwell*, p. 179.

65. *Visitations of Southwell*, pp. lxi-lxii.

66. *Register Gifford*, p. 84; *C. Papal R.* 1:210; *Register Gray*, p. 95.

67. *C. Papal R.* 1:326; *C. Pat. R. 1247-58*, p. 556.

68. January 1257: *Ex Rot. Fin.* 2:246; *C. Inq. P. M.*, vol. 1, no. 378.

69. *C. Pat. R. 1232-47*, p. 119; *Cl. R. 1234-37*, pp. 282, 415; *C. Lib. R. 1226-40*, p. 252.

70. *C. Ch. R. 1226-57*, pp. 228, 231, 241.

71. *C. Pat. R. 1232-47*, pp. 139, 142, 176; *C. Lib. R. 1226-40*, pp. 116, 256-257, 302.

72. *C. Pat. R. 1232-47*, p. 228; *Cl. R. 1237-42*, pp. 106, 129, 143; *Chron. maj.* 3:495; *Ann. Mon.* 1:110.

73. *Chapters* 1:205.

74. *Chartularium Universitatis Parisiensis*, ed. H. Denifle and E. Chatelain (Paris, 1889-1897), vol. 1, nos. 232, 233, 274.

75. *C. Lib. R. 1226-40*, pp. 360, 363; *C. Ch. R. 1226-57*, pp. 241, 242, 247.

76. *Cl. R. 1237-42*, pp. 173, 188, 200, 210, 215, 222, 252, 271-272; *C. Pat. R. 1232-47*, p. 240.

77. *C. Pat. R. 1232-47*, pp. 244, 245; *C. Lib. R. 1240-45*, p. 36; *Chron. maj.* 4:124-130, 150; *Cl. R. 1237-42*, p. 328.

78. *Registrum Stephani de Lexinton* 7:376-377; *Cl. R. 1242-47*, p. 114; *C. Ch. R. 1226-57*, p. 363; *C. Inq. P. M.*, vol. 2, no. 722; vol. 3, no. 11.

79. *C. Pat. R. 1232-47*, pp. 296, 306.

80. Ibid., p. 359; *Cl. R. 1242-47*, pp. 18, 114.

81. *Cl. R. 1242-47*, pp. 502, 517; *C. Pat. R. 1232-47*, pp. 348, 390.

82. *C. Pat. R. 1232-47*, p. 462; *Calendar of Documents relating to Ireland, 1172-1251*, nos. 2771, 2780.

83. *C. Pat. R. 1232-47*, p. 490; *C. Lib. R. 1245-51*, p. 31; *Chron. maj.* 4:581.

84. *C. Lib. R. 1245-51*, p. 140; *Cl. R. 1242-47*, p. 536; *Cl. R. 1247-51*, p. 47.

85. *Cl. R. 1247-51*, pp. 209, 266, 267, 276, 285; *C. Lib. R. 1245-51*, pp. 255, 288.

86. *C. Pat. R. 1247-58*, pp. 3-6, 8, 9, 14, 24, 59; *Cl. R. 1247-51*, pp. 14, 91.

87. He was with the king until October 1251 (*Cl. R. 1247-51*, pp. 355, 436, 442, 449-451, 462, 517, 535, 542, 545).

88. *C. Pat. R. 1247-58*, pp. 165, 173, 193, 204, 217, 234, 413, 416, 449; *Chron. maj.* 5:379.

89. *C. Pat. R. 1247-58*, pp. 60, 110, 160, 361, 362, 372, 438; *Cl. R. 1247-51*, pp. 555, 557; *Ex Rot. Fin.* 2:119, 141, 153, 178, 198, 216.

90. *C. Pat. R. 1247-58*, p. 373; *C. Lib. R. 1251-60*, p. 189.

91. *C. Lib. R. 1251-60*, p. 238; *Cl. R. 1254-56*, pp. 129, 130, 218, 220, 221; *C. Pat. R. 1247-58*, p. 423.

92. *Cl. R. 1254-56*, p. 231; *C. Lib. R. 1251-60*, p. 237.

93. *C. Lib. R. 1251-60*, p. 242; *Cl. R. 1254-56*, pp. 131-136, 138, 221-223, 137, 139-142, 227; *C. Pat. R. 1247-58*, p. 428.

94. *C. Pat. R. 1247-58*, p. 453.

95. *Cl. R. 1254-56*, pp. 142-143, 145, 241, 451, 493, 510; *Liber de Antiquis Legibus*, ed. T. Stapleton, Camden Society (London, 1846), p. 23. On the question of the necessity of submission to a jury and the inclusion of Jews on a jury, see Henry de Bracton, *On the Laws and Customs of England*, ed. S. E. Thorne (Cambridge, Mass., 1968), 2:402-405; Frederick Pollock and F. W. Maitland, *The History of English Law*, 2d ed. (Cambridge, 1898), 2:650-651; *Cl. R. 1237-42*, pp. 168, 175, 247.

96. *C. Pat. R. 1247-58*, pp. 453, 457, 555, 630; *Cl. R. 1254-56*, pp. 34, 383; Jacobs, *Jewish Ideals*, pp. 208-209; Roth, *History*, p. 56.

97. Shirley, *Royal Letters* 2:110.

98. N. Denholm-Young, *Richard of Cornwall* (New York, 1947), pp. 69, 80-81, 159-160.

99. Shirley, *Royal Letters* 2:8; and see below, chap. 11.

100. Molinier, "Enquête sur un meurtre imputé aux Juifs de Valréas (1247)" (above, chap. 9, n. 35).

101. Grayzel, *Church*, nos. 113, 114, 116.

102. Ibid., no 118.

103. While numerous authors have given the papacy credit for attempting to check accusations of ritual murder, none has noticed or stressed that only the blood libel, not the crucifixion libel, was prohibited: e.g., Grayzel, *Church*, pp. 79-80; *A History of the Jews*, 2d ed. (New York, 1968), p. 315; Baron, *SRH* 11:147; Edward H. Flannery, *The Anguish of the Jews*, 2d ed. (New York, 1985), p. 100; Edward A. Synan, *The Popes and the Jews in the Middle Ages* (New York, 1965), p. 114; Fred G. Bratton, *The Crime of Christendom* (Boston, 1969), p. 117.

104. F. M. Powicke, *The Thirteenth Century*, Oxford History of England (Oxford, 1953), p. 59.

105. Ibid., p. 19; *King Henry III* 1:70-72, 156-157, 335-336, 342; 2:688.

106. *Chron. maj.* 5:383-384.

107. Cf. Richard J. Schoeck, "Chaucer's Prioress: Mercy and Tender Heart," in *Chaucer Criticism*, ed. Richard J. Schoeck and Jerome Taylor (Notre Dame, Ind., 1960-1961), 1:245-258.

11: Ritual Cannibalism

1. Pierre Riché, *Daily Life in the World of Charlemagne* (Philadelphia, 1978), p. 67.

2. Friedrich Lütge, *Deutsche Sozial-und Wirtschaftgeschichte*, 3d ed. (Berlin, 1966), p. 66.

3. M. L. W. Laistner, *Thought and Letters in Western Europe A.D. 500 to 900*, 2d ed. (London, 1957), p. 232.

4. Konrad Lübeck, *Die Fuldaer Abte und Furstäbte des Mittelalters* (Fulda, 1952), p. 165; Anneliese Hofemann, *Studien zur Entwicklung des Territoriums der Reichsabtei Fulda und seiner Amter*, Schriften des Hessischen Landesamt für geschichtliche Landeskunde, vol. 25 (Marburg, 1958), pp. 1-8.

5. *Annales Ephordenses*, in *MGH SS* 16:31.

6. *Annales Marbacenses*, in *MGH SS* 17:178.

7. *Gesta Senoniensis ecclesiae*, in *MGH SS* 25:324.

8. "Privilegium et sententia in favorem Iudeorum," in *MGH, Constitutiones* 2:274-276.

9. W. W. Shirley, *Royal and Other Historical Letters Illustrative of the Reign of Henry III*, RS (London, 1862-1866), 2:8.

10. Above, n. 8.

11. Molinier, "Enquête sur un meurtre imputé aux Juifs de Valréas (1247)" (above, chap. 9, n. 35).

12. Grayzel, *Church*, nos. 113, 114.

13. Ibid., no. 116.

14. Ibid., no. 118.

15. *Bonum universale de apibus* (Douai, 1627), 3.29.23. See also his *Liber de natura rerum*, ed. H. Boese (Berlin, 1973), pp. 32, 49-53, for his interest in blood as a natural phenomenon.

16. *SWG* 1:410.

17. See above, chap. 7.

18. (New York, 1940), 2:407-408.

19. *SRH* 11:146-147.

20. *A History of the Jews* (New York, 1968), p. 314.

21. (New York, 1971), 4:1121-1123.

22. (New York, 1909), pp. 178, 277.

23. *The Devil and the Jews*, pp. 130-132.

24. *A History of the Jews* (New York, 1963), p. 184.

25. *Annales Herbipolenses*, in *MGH SS* 16:3-4; *Hebräische Berichte über die Judenverfolgungen während der Kreuzzüüge*, ed. A. Neubauer and M. Stern (Berlin, 1892), 192, 203-204, 209-210, 211-212.

26. See above, chap. 5.

27. Paul B. Pixton, "Die Anwerbung des Heeres Christi: Prediger des Fünften Kreuzzuges in Deutschland," *Deutches Archiv* 34 (1978): 166-191.

28. Wilhelm Maurer, *Kirche und Geschichte* (Göttingen, 1970), pp. 249-255; Matthias Werner, "Die heilige Elisabeth und Konrad von Marburg," in *Sankt Elisabeth*, ed. Carl Graepler, Fred Schwind, and Matthias Werner (Sigmaringen, 1981), p. 46.

29. Pixton, "Die Anwerbung des Heeres Christi," p. 175.

30. Werner, "Die heilige Elisabeth und Konrad von Marburg," p. 46.

31. Ibid., p. 49.

32. Ibid., p. 59

33. Ibid., p. 61.

34. *MGH Epist.*, pp. 252-253, no. 334.

35. Ibid., p. 277, no. 362.

36. Werner, "Die heilige Elisabeth und Konrad von Marburg," p. 56.

37. Alexander Patschovsky, "Zur Ketzerverfolgung Konrads von Marburg," *Deutsches Archiv* 37 (1981): 643 and n. 4.

38. *MGH Constitutiones* 2:195-197, no. 158.

39. *MGH Epist.*, pp. 393-394, no. 489.

40. Ibid., pp. 394-396, no. 490.

41. Ludwig Förg, *Die Ketzerverfolgung in Deutschland unter Gregor IX.*, Historische Studien, vol. 218 (Berlin, 1932; reprint, Vaduz, 1965), pp. 79-80.

42. *MGH Epist.*, pp. 429-430, no. 533.

43. Ibid., pp. 432-435, no. 537.

44. Jeffrey B. Russell, *Witchcraft in the Middle Ages* (Ithaca, N.Y., 1972), pp. 159-163; Cohn, *Europe's Inner Demons*, pp. 29-30, 34.

45. *MGH SS* 24:401; see also the *Annals of Worms*, in *MGH SS* 17:38-40, and the Chronicle of Albert of Troisfontaines, in *MGH SS* 23:931-932.

46. "Zur Ketzerverfolgung Konrads von Marburg," pp. 641-693.

47. Ibid., pp. 686-687.

48. Förg, *Die Ketzerverfolgung in Deutschland unter Gregor IX.*, p. 81.

49. Grayzel, *Church*, no. 81.

50. Siegmund Salfeld, *Das Martyrologium des Nürnberger Memorbuches* (Berlin, 1898), pp. 124-125.

51. *MGH SS* 16:31.

52. Grayzel, *Church*, nos. 48, 75, 76, 83, 84, 94.

53. Above, n. 15.

54. Above, n. 8.

12: Historiographic Crucifixion

1. Ed. Augustus Jessopp and M. R. James, cited hereafter as *Life*. See above, chap. 9.

2. Hermann L. Strack, *The Jew and Human Sacrifice* (London, 1909), p. 177, also suggested that the Norwich accusation was an imitation of what was reported to have happened at Inmestar.

3. *The Anglo-Saxon Chronicle*, ed. Dorothy Whitelock (London, 1961), pp. xvi, 200.

4. *Annales Herbipolenses*, in *MGH SS* 16:3-4; *Hebraische Berichte über die Judenverfolgungen wahrend der Kreuzzuge*, ed. Neubauer and Stern, pp. 149-152, 191-194; *Historia et Cartularium Monasterii Sancti Petri Gloucestriae*, ed. W. H. Hart, RS 33 (London, 1863-1867), 1:20-21; *The Chronicle of Jocelyn of Brakelond*, ed. H. E. Butler (New York, 1949), p. 16; *Chronicles of the Reigns of Stephen, Henry II, and Richard I*, ed. Richard Howlett, RS 82; (London, 1884-1889), 3:439-440.

5. *Œuvres de Rigord et Guillaume le Breton*, ed. H.-F. Delaborde (Paris, 1882-1885), 1:15.

6. *Annales Cameracenses*, in *MGH SS* 16:536.

7. *HF* 12:421.

8. *Auctorium Ursicampinum*, in *MGH SS* 6:472.

9. *Chronicles of the Reigns of Stephen, Henry II, and Richard I* 4:250-251.

10. Antonia Gransden, *Historical Writing in England c. 550 to c. 1307* (Ithaca, N.Y., 1974), p. 263.

11. *Annales sex regum Angliae*, ed. Thomas Hog, English Historical Society (London, 1845), pp. 18, 68.

12. Cesare Baronio, *Annales Ecclesiastici*, ed. A. Theiner (Bar-le-Duc, 1864-1883), 7:56-57; 18:647-648.

13. Ralph of Coggeshall, *Chronicon Anglicanum*, ed. J. Stevenson, RS 66 (London, 1875), p. 20; *Annales Monastici*, ed. H. R. Luard, RS 36 (London, 1864-1869), 2:230; 3:437; 4:379; *Flores historiarum*, ed. H. R. Luard, RS 95 (London, 1890), 1:65; Roger Twysden, *Historiae Anglicanae Scriptores X* (London, 1652), p. 1043.

14. See above, chap. 10.

15. *Actes and Monuments*, ed. George Townsend (London, 1841; reprint, New York, 1965), 2:188.

16. D'Blossiers Tovey, *Anglia Judaica* (Oxford, 1738; reprint, New York, 1967), p. 11.

17. *Dictionary of National Biography*, vol. 9 (London, 1887), pp. 20-22.

18. *Acta Sanctorum* 9:586-588.

19. *Dictionary of National Biography*, vol. 8 (London, 1886), pp. 43-44.

20. *The Lives of the Fathers, Martyrs, and Other Principal Saints* (London, 1756-1759), 1:524-525.

21. *Lives of the Saints* (Dublin: J. Cumming, n.d.), 1:344-345; *Butler's Lives of the Saints*, ed. Herbert Thurston and Donald Attwater (New York, 1956), 1:672.

22. *Life*, p. l.

23. Henry Hart Milman, *The History of the Jews*, new ed. (New York, n.d.), 3:238. Of William of Norwich, G.-B. Depping said only that "under King Stephen in 1135, they [the Jews] were accused, at Norwich as elsewhere, of having crucified a child" (*Les Juifs dans le moyen âge* [Brussels, 1844], p. 98).

24. W. H. Hart (above, n. 4), 1:xli.

25. Ibid., li. Italics mine.

26. Elphège Vacandard, "La question du meurtre ritual chez les Juifs," in *Etudes de critique et d'histoire religieuse*, 3d ser. (Paris, 1912), pp. 311-377.

27. Ibid., p. 329.

28. *Geschichte der Juden*, 2d ed. (Leipzig, 1866-1874), 6:201. Isak M. Jost knew even fewer details of the charge (*Allgemeine Geschichte des Israelitischen Volkes* [Berlin, 1832; Leipzig, 1850], 2:360).

29. *History of the Jews*, trans. from the 4th Russian ed. (New York, 1967-1973), 2:692-693.

30. *Judentum: Schicksal, Wesen, und Gegenwart*, ed. Franz Bohn and Walter Dirks (Wiesbaden, 1965), 1:142; Werner Keller, *Und worden zerstreut unter aller Völker* (Munich, 1966), pp. 58, 230.

31. "Bulletin historique," *Revue historique* 64 (1897): 116-119.

32. *Life*, p. lxxvii. Italics James's.

33. Ibid., pp. lxviii, lxxxi.

34. Ibid., pp. lxxi-lxxii. Italics mine.

35. Ibid., pp. lxxviii-lxxxix.

36. (London, 1893), pp. 19-21.

37. Ibid., pp. 256-258.

38. "St. William, of Norwich," *Jewish Quarterly Review*, o.s., 9 (1897): 749.

39. Ibid., p. 754.

40. Vol. 3 (London, 1903), p. 230.

41. "The Feast of Purim and the Origins of the Blood Accusation," *Speculum* 8 (1933): 523.

42. *The Ritual Murder Libel and the Jew: The Report of Cardinal Lorenzo Ganganelli*, ed. Cecil Roth (London, 1935), p. 15.

43. Cecil Roth, *A History of the Jews in England*, 1st-3d eds. (Oxford, 1941, 1949, 1978), p. 9.

44. *SRH* 4:135-136.

45. Vol. 10 (New York, 1943), pp. 522-523.

46. Vol. 4 (New York, 1971), p. 1121.

47. "The Feast of Purim and the Origins of the Blood Accusation," p. 526.

48. Robert Chazan, "The Bray Incident of 1192: Realpolitik and Folk Slander," *Proceedings of the American Academy for Jewish Research* 37 (1969): 1-18.

49. Joseph Schatzmiller, *Recherches sur la communauté juive de Manosque au moyen âge, 1241-1329* (Paris, 1973), pp. 127-129; see also pp. 129-131.

50. Above, chap. 11, n. 7.

51. M. D. Anderson, *A Saint at Stake: The Strange Death of William of Norwich, 1144* (London, 1964), p. 15.

52. Ibid., p. 59.

53. Ibid., p. 97.

54. Ibid., p. 100.

55. See above, chap. 9, n. 55.

56. *A Saint at Stake*, pp. 87-88.

57. Ibid., p. 108.

58. Ibid., p. 101.

59. Ibid., pp. 107-108.

60. Anonymous, *Times Literary Supplement*, 21 January 1965, p. 50.

61. Anonymous, *The Economist*, 14 November 1964, p. 719.

62. C. J. Holdsworth, *History* 51 (1966): 206.

63. M. Deanesly, *Church Quarterly Review*, April-June 1965, pp. 241-242.

64. *The Jews of Medieval Norwich* (London, 1967), pp. 54-57.

65. Ibid., p. 55.

66. "The Strange Murder of William of Norwich, 1144," *New York State Journal of Medicine*, 1 November 1971, pp. 2569-2574.

67. Saul S. Friedman, *The Incident at Massena* (New York, 1978), p. 184.

68. Sharpe, "Strange Murder," pp. 2570-2571.

69. Finucane, *Miracles and Pilgrims*, pp. 59-82.

70. Sharpe, "Strange Murder," pp. 2572, 2573.

71. Ibid., p. 2574.

72. Above, n. 24.

73. "Anti-Semitism and the Charge of Ritual Murder," *The Month* 90 (June 1898): 561-574; "The Ritual Murder Trial at Kiev," *The Month* 122 (November 1913): 502-513.

74. "The Ritual Murder Trial at Kiev," p. 507. For a fascinating affirmation of the probability of isolated crucifixions, see S. Baring-Gould, *The Lives of the Saints*, 3d ed. (Edinburgh, 1914), 4:463-464.

75. Edward H. Flannery, *The Anguish of the Jews* (New York, 1965), p. 100. *The Catholic Encyclopedia*, vol. 15 (New York, 1912), p. 636 preserves the loophole, but the *New Catholic Encyclopedia*, vol. 14 (New York, 1967), p. 931, does not. Both are extremely suspicious of Thomas of Monmouth's account.

76. The most distinctive item of Theobald's fable, the annual lottery, is not mentioned in the chronicle reports of accusations but does appear in the confessions extracted by torture at Valréas in 1247 and is mentioned by Thomas of Cantimpré (Molinier, "Enquête sur un meurtre imputé aux Juifs de Valréas," p. 130; Thomas of Cantimpré, *Bonum universale de apibus* [Douai, 1627], 3.29.23). Apparently this item was being circulated among the Mendicants by the middle of the thirteenth century.

13: Medieval Antisemitism

1. The theoretical argument for this definition is presented in the next chapter.

2. See above, chap. 1.

3. See above, chap. 4.

4. Blumenkranz, *JC*, pp. 98-99, 105, 311-312.

5. *Church*, p. 81.

6. See Fichtenau, *The Carolingian Empire*, pp. 47-65; Pierre Riché, *Daily Life in the World of Charlemagne*, trans. Jo Ann McNamara (Philadelphia, 1978), pp. 181-202.

7. Blumenkranz, *Les auteurs chrétiens latins du moyen âge sur les Juifs et le judaïsme*, pp. 152-168.

8. See Richardson, *The English Jewry under Angevin Kings*; Chazan, *Me-*

dieval Jewry in Northern France. In Germany, however, Jewish moneylending prospered up to the early fourteenth century (Baron, *SRH* 12:150).

9. For an excellent brief survey, see Sister Marie Despina, "Les accusations de profanation d'hosties portées contre les Juifs," *Rencontre* 22 and 23 (1971): 150-173, 180-196; and see now Friedrich Lotter, "Die Judenverfolgung des 'König Rintfleisch' in Franken um 1298," *Zeitschrift für historische Forschung* 15 (1988): 385-422.

10. See my "L'absence d'accusation de meurtre rituel à l'ouest du Rhône" (above, chap. 9, n. 4).

11. See, for example, Isaiah Schachar, *The Judensau: A Medieval Anti-Jewish Motif and Its History* (London, 1974).

12. Martin Luther, *Works*, ed. Jaroslav Pelikan and Helmut T. Lehman (St. Louis, Mo., 1955-1975), 47:267.

14: Toward a Definition of Antisemitism

1. This is a revised version of my "Prolegomena to Any Present Discussion of Hostility against Jews," *Social Science Information* (Paris) 15, no. 4/5 (1976): 689-727; Italian translation in *Communità* 181 (1979): 212-257. It is dedicated, with great affection, to the pioneering scholar and sensitive human being who first commissioned it, Léon Poliakov.

2. L. C. Dunn, "Race and Biology," in *Race, Science and Society* (New York: UNESCO, 1975), pp. 41, 53. See also Michael Banton, *Racial and Ethnic Competition* (Cambridge, 1983).

3. The vigor of the debate indicates the subjectivity of any dogmatic assertions on the issue. See for example: Arthur R. Jensen et al., *Environment, Heredity, and Intelligence*, Harvard Educational Reprint Series, no. 2 (Cambridge, Mass., 1969); Hans J. Eysenck, *The IQ Argument* (New York, 1971); Luca L. Cavalli-Sforza and Walter F. Bodner, *The Genetics of Human Evolution* (San Francisco, 1971); R. H. Herrnstein, "I.Q.," *Atlantic Monthly* 228, no. 3 (1971): 44-64; S. Scarr-Salapatek, "Unknowns in the IQ Equation," *Science* 174 (1971): 1223-1238; Leon J. Kamin, "Heritability Analysis of IQ Scores: Science or Numerology?" *Science* 183 (1974): 1259-1266; Stephen J. Gould, *The Mismeasure of Man* (New York, 1981); Melvin Konner, *The Tangled Web: Biological Constraints on the Human Spirit* (New York, 1982); Howard Gardner, *Frames of Mind* (New York, 1983); R. C. Lewontin, Steven Rose, and Leon J. Kamin, *Not in Our Genes* (New York, 1984); Daniel J. Kevles, *In the Name of Eugenics* (New York, 1985).

4. See Léon Poliakov, *Le mythe aryen* (Paris, 1971), pp. 150-189, 263-282.

5. Despite the careful distinctions which P. L. Berghe makes to avoid that pitfall in his valuable book, *Race and Racism* (New York, 1967), it seems to me that he comes very close to falling in because he, as a social scientist, decided to use "race" with the meaning given it by the racists he was studying and to treat "racism" as a unitary phenomenon sufficiently distinct to be susceptible of a separate, general, socioanthropological explanation. Conversely, Christian Delacampagne uses so broad a conception of "racisme" to develop his fascinating argument that he can locate its emergence among the

Greeks in antiquity (*L'invention du racisme* [Paris, 1983]; rev. ed., *Racismo y occidente* [Barcelona, 1983]).

6. Paul E. Grosser and Edwin G. Halperin, *Anti-Semitism: The Causes and Effects of a Prejudice* (Secaucus, N.J., 1979), p. 5.

7. Jacob Katz, *From Prejudice to Destruction* (Cambridge, Mass., 1980), p. 322.

8. Gordon W. Allport's classic *The Nature of Prejudice* (Boston, 1954) indicates the extent of that broadening of perspective.

9. Daniel J. Levinson, "The Study of Ethnocentric Ideology," in Theodor W. Adorno et al., *The Authoritarian Personality* (New York, 1950), p. 150.

10. Nathan W. Ackerman and Marie Jahoda, *Anti-Semitism and Emotional Disorder* (New York, 1951), pp. 3-4.

11. Arnold M. Rose, "The Roots of Prejudice," in *Race and Science* (New York: UNESCO, 1961), p. 393.

12. Allport, *The Nature of Prejudice*, p. 9.

13. Milton Rokeach, *The Open and Closed Mind* (New York, 1960), p. 135.

14. George E. Simpson and J. Milton Yinger, *Racial and Cultural Minorities*, 4th ed. (New York, 1972), p. 24.

15. Richard D. Ashmore, "Prejudice: Causes and Cures," in Barry E. Collins, *Social Psychology* (Reading, Mass., 1970), p. 253.

16. Charles Y. Glock and Rodney Stark, *Christian Beliefs and Anti-Semitism* (New York, 1966), p. 102.

17. Howard Shuman and John Harding, "Prejudice and the Norm of Rationality," *Sociometry* 27 (1964): 353-371; the article accepts the validity of the norm of rationality.

18. Collins, *Social Psychology*, p. 255.

19. Robert A. Levine and Donald T. Campbell, *Ethnocentrism* (New York, 1972), provides an exhaustive survey of theories relevant to "ethnocentrism" which illustrates how diversely and broadly that term has also been used.

20. John Dollard, *Caste and Class in a Southern Town* (New Haven, 1937); "Hostility and Fear in Social Life," *Social Forces* 17 (1938): 15-26.

21. Rudolph M. Loewenstein, *Christians and Jews* (New York, 1951); Norman Cohn, *Warrant for Genocide* (New York, 1969). In the revised edition of his book (Chico, Calif., 1981), Cohn has abandoned this explanation.

22. (New York, 1969).

23. E.g., Albert Bandura, *Aggression* (Englewood Cliffs, N.J., 1973).

24. Richard T. Lapierre, "Attitudes vs. Actions," *Social Forces* 13 (1934): 230-237.

25. E.g., Gunnar Myrdal, *An American Dilemma* (New York, 1944); Bruno Bettelheim and Morris Janowitz, *Social Change and Prejudice* (New York, 1964).

26. *Seven Types of Ambiguity*, 3d ed. (New York, 1955), p. 3: "I propose to use the word in an extended sense, and shall think relevant to my subject any verbal nuance, however slight, which gives room for alternative reactions to the same piece of language."

27. John Harding, Harold Proshansky, Bernard Kutner, and Isidor Chein,

"Prejudice and Ethnic Relations," in *The Handbook of Social Psychology*, ed. Gardner Lindzey and E. Aronson, 2d ed. (Reading, Mass., 1968-1969), 2:6: "Consequently, it seems most useful to us to define prejudice as a failure of rationality *or* a failure of justice *or* a failure of human-heartedness in an individual's attitude toward members of another ethnic group."

28. Parkes, *CCS*, pp. 46, 80; Blumenkranz, *JC*, pp. 45, 169-171, 269-270.

29. Peter L. Berger, *The Sacred Canopy* (New York, 1969), p. 51: "Every human society is, in the last resort, men banded together in the face of death."

30. See above, chaps. 9-11.

31. The same might be said of assertions about female sexual appetite, emotionality, or lack of courage. Since women are not by any biological definition a race and participate in the same culture as males, perhaps nothing is more indicative of the human propensity, even in the most intimate relations, to exploit others who are enduringly different than male xenophobic and chimerical assertions about females. An analysis of male attitudes to women according to the hypotheses presented here would be most interesting.

32. Above, n. 3.

33. This formulation seems compatible both with psychoanalytic interpretations and with social learning theories.

34. Robert K. Merton, *Social Theory and Social Structure*, 2d ed. (Glencoe, Ill., 1957), p. 423.

35. *La société bloquée* (Paris, 1970), p. 34.

36. George A. De Vos and Hiroshi Wagatsuma, *Japan's Invisible Race* (Berkeley and Los Angeles, 1967).

Acknowledgments

The following chapters were originally published in somewhat different form as noted below:

1. Reprinted by permission from the *Journal of the History of Ideas* 27 (1966): 343-364.

2. Reprinted by permission from *Jewish Social Studies* 30 (1968): 157-168.

3. Reprinted by permission from *Viator* 2 (1971): 383-389. Copyright © 1971 by the Regents of the University of California.

4. Originally titled "From Ambrose of Milan to Emicho of Leiningen: The Transformation of Hostility against Jews in Northern Christendom." Reprinted by permission from *Gli ebrei nell'alto medioevo*, Settimane del Centro italiano di studi sull'alto medioevo, vol. 26 (Spoleto, 1980), pp. 313-368.

6. Reprinted by permission of the publisher from *Traditio* 16 (1960): 203-239. Copyright © 1960 by Fordham University Press, New York.

7. Reprinted by permission from *Les Juifs dans l'histoire de France*, ed. Myriam Yardeni (Leiden, 1980), pp. 25- 54. Copyright © 1980 by E. J. Brill, Leiden.

9. Reprinted by permission from *Speculum 59* (1984): 822-846.

10. Reprinted by permission from *Speculum* 47 (1972): 459-482.

12. Reprinted with the authorization of the Editions A. et J. Picard from *Les Juifs au regard de l'histoire: Mélanges en l'honneur de Bern-*

hard Blumenkranz, ed. Gilbert Dahan (Paris: Picard, 1985), pp. 109-127.

13. This article originally appeared in *The Holocaust: Ideology, Bureaucracy, and Genocide*, ed. Henry Friedlander and Sybil Milton (Millwood, N.Y.: Kraus International Publications, 1982), pp. 27-36. Reproduced with permission of The Kraus Organization Limited.

14. Reprinted from *The Persisting Question: Sociological Perspectives and Social Contexts of Modern Antisemitism*, ed. Helen Fein, vol. 1 of *Current Research on Antisemitism*, ed. Herbert A. Strauss and Werner Bergmann (Berlin: Walter de Gruyter, 1987), pp. 86-127.

General Index

Aaron of Lincoln, 140
Abelard, Peter, 125–126
Abraham of Berkhamsted, 242, 247
Ackerman, Nathan W., 318
Adhemar of Chabannes, 274
Aggression, displaced, 322
Agobard, archbishop of Lyons, 59, 84, 85–86, 304
Albigensian Crusade, 90, 271
Alexander III, king of Scotland, 257
Alexandrian riots, 6
Altercatio Aecclesie contra Synagogam, 128
Ambrose, bishop of Milan, 70–75, 86, 90, 108, 113, 115, 302; attitude of, toward Jews, 74, 75; religiosity of, 70–73
Amulo, 59, 86
Anglo-Saxon Chronicle, 210, 283, 284, 287, 288
Anselm of Aosta, 116, 124–125, 130, 131
Anthropologists, 321
Anti-Judaism, 4–6, 132, 303–304; versus antisemitism, 4–6, 7–8; character of, 57; Christian, 7, 57–62; and Christian beliefs and attitudes, 8, 62; and Christian identity, 7; Christian versus non-Christian, 7; coexistence with antisemitism, 62; defined, 57; doctrinal aspects of, 58, 61; establishment of, 7; forms of, 57; legal aspects of, 58–59, 61; pagan,

57; of Peter the Venerable, 132, 201–202, 204, 205–206, 207–208; popular, 59, 61. *See also* Antisemitism *headings*; Hostility, toward Jews
Antiochus IV (Epiphanes), 212
Antisemitism: versus anti-Judaism, 4–6, 8; and chimerical assertions, 14–15, 351–352; coexistence with anti-Judaism, 62, 317; emergence of, 11; endurance of, 45–46; from ethnocentric perspective, 315; historian's view of, 45; medieval, 25, 133, 301–310; perpetuation of, through historiography, 39–40, 45; and racism, 314; reasons for creation of, in northern Europe, 303–306; from social scientists' perspective, 315–326; spread of, 61. *See also* Anti-Judaism; "Antisemitism" (term); Hostility, toward Jews
"Antisemitism" (term): implications of, 314–315; lack of reason for use of, 341; need for more precise definition, 2–3, 16–17, 311–352; original meaning, 311, 314; popular use of term, 5, 16, 311, 314, 351
Apion, 289
Apollonius Molon, 212
Aquinas, Thomas, 101, 123, 126–127, 190, 208
Arians/Arianism, 69, 70, 77, 78–79, 80, 103

Index of Secondary Authors

Designer:	U. C. Press Staff
Compositor:	Auto Graphics, Inc.
Printer:	Bookcrafters
Binder:	Bookcrafters
Text:	10/13 Sabon
Display:	Sabon